JMX in Action

BEN G. SULLINS

MARK B. WHIPPLE

MANNING

Greenwich
(74° w. long.)

For electronic information and ordering of this and other Manning books,
go to www.manning.com. The publisher offers discounts on this book
when ordered in quantity. For more information, please contact:

 Special Sales Department
 Manning Publications Co.
 209 Bruce Park Avenue   Fax: (203) 661-9018
 Greenwich, CT 06830   email: orders@manning.com

Manning Publications Co.   Copyeditor: Tiffany Taylor
32 Lafayette Place   Typesetter: Denis Dalinnik
Greenwich, CT 06830   Cover designer: Leslie Haimes

ISBN 1-930110-56-1

Printed in the United States of America
1 2 3 4 5 6 7 8 9 10 – VHG – 05 04 03 02

brief contents

contents

preface

The increasing demand for faster development cycles combined with the desire for more functionality has left less time for building adequate application configuration and management into Java applications. Without allowing for reconfiguration, management, and monitoring, applications fail to deliver to customers their full potential of usefulness and flexibility.

A Java programmer can provide a certain amount of configuration for an application by using property files. Developers typically use property files to configure a Java program with an initial set of parameters at startup. Imagine an application that commits certain data to a log file at a given interval. Both the path to the file and the interval could be configured in a property file. However, unless the program continues to refresh these properties, it is left with that single configuration.

Realistically, property files cannot provide complete and thorough application configuration management. With more and more configurable attributes, you will quickly find yourself stuck in a mire of property files. You could develop a management console for the application, but do you really want to have to maintain two applications and possibly construct a new console for each new application? In addition, what are you to do with your non-Java and hardware resources? These resources may have their own management consoles, but now you are looking at an array of different consoles and management tools.

Ideally, you would like to configure your Java applications once during initialization and as often as needed during runtime. The same is true for non-Java and hardware resources. The ability to change the configuration at runtime relieves you of possibly having to shut down or restart an application or resource. You could provide runtime configuration management yourself programmatically, but maintaining a proprietary configuration system can be overwhelming when included with the normal range of requirements for developing useful software—especially if you consider that you might want to do this for each product being developed. Given time-to-market considerations, most development projects do not have the resources for this type of work.

However, this was the situation before the creation of Java Management Extensions (JMX). Using JMX, you can expose your application components, attributes, and configuration to management tools in a process called *instrumentation*. JMX uses Java classes called *managed beans* (MBeans for short) to expose predefined portions of your application. Management tools access these MBeans by interacting with JMX agents that make the MBeans available to any number of protocols and technologies such as SNMP, Java RMI, and HTTP.

In addition to software, MBeans can wrap native libraries that interface to hardware such as printers. JMX is independent of purpose: it can expose software components or hardware interfaces. Management applications will see all managed resources (MBeans) using the same interfaces and metadata through a JMX agent. By creating a JMX-compliant application, you expose it to remote, in-house, or third-party application management tools using a variety of protocols. Consequently, you have given your program a longer period of usefulness by creating a framework for componentization. Because JMX is written in Java, all Java applications and technologies can use it.

JMX exists because of the need for cross-platform, consistent application and resource management. This book covers all aspects of JMX today, including MBean development, protocol adapters and connectors, and all agent services. In addition, the book discusses using JMX with J2EE technologies such as Enterprise JavaBeans and the Java Message Service.

acknowledgments

Many people helped get this book into your hands. Without the help we received from many sources, we could not have created a book of the quality we envisioned. We would especially like to thank the people at Manning: Marjan Bace, Lianna Wlasiuk, and Ted Kennedy. Thanks to Marjan for responding to the first email inquiry about JMX as a topic for a book and for having enough patience to let some first-time writers learn on the job. Special thanks to Lianna, whose incredible editing skills helped deliver this book to the shelves. In addition, we would like to thank our reviewers: Cyrus Dadgar, Robert Treese, Lydia Davis, Jason Dornback, Chris Kraus, John Jacobs, Andrew Jenkins, Shyam Lingegowda, Alex Vekselman, and Michael Yuan. Special thanks to Cyrus Dadgar for a final technical review of the book, just before it went to press.

Mark and I would also like to thank the production team for completing our book. Each person did a fantastic job to get our book to market. They are: project editor Mary Piergies, copyeditor Tiffany Taylor, design editor Syd Brown, typesetter Denis Dalinnik, and publicist Helen Trimes. Also, we would like to thank Liz Welch for doing the final proofread. She was great at catching those small and hidden mistakes.

In addition, Ben would like to thank his parents for fostering an environment of love and learning that set him on his way through life, enabling him to acquire the skills to be successful. Thanks to Mark Whipple for being a great co-author and a great foosball mentor. Ben would especially like to thank his wife Jenny and new baby Elijah. Without Jenny, this book never would have been begun or completed. She has incredible patience and faith—she always finds the right words to help during hard times (did you *ever* think I would finish?). Finally, thanks go to the Lord above for providing this opportunity.

Also, Mark would like to thank his family for putting up with the late nights. Mark's contribution to this book would not be possible without his wife Margie's perfect timing with the arrival of much-needed coffee supplies and his four-year-old son Alexander's patience when more important things such as playing transformer robots had to be put off for a while. Thanks go to Mark's parents, whose support throughout his life has enabled him to build the skills necessary to succeed. Mark would also like to thank Ben Sullins, whose ability to play foosball almost rivals his skill as a developer. Mark would especially like to thank Ben for putting in the extra effort required to organize this work.

about this book

This book is a detailed guide to the 1.01 specification of the Java Management Extensions from Sun Microsystems. In fact, this book uses the Sun reference implementation for all the program examples.

At the time we're writing this book, the JMX specification still has some optional sections: the Open MBean and the connector/adapter architecture for distributing JMX agents. However, this book includes lengthy examples of connectors and adapters, as well as an appendix covering Open MBeans, which you will find useful in your JMX development.

Chapter roadmap

In case you are the type of person who likes to pick and choose where to begin reading a book, the following sections summarize the contents of each chapter. However, we think it would be great if you read this book from start to finish.

Chapter 1: Resource management and JMX

Chapter 1 gets you started by discussing the average monitoring and application management environment in today's enterprise. This chapter introduces what we consider the essential areas of application monitoring and management, and how JMX applies well to each. Concluding this chapter is a discussion of the JMX architecture.

Chapter 2: "Hello World," the JMX way

Chapter 2 serves as this book's Hello World example. The only purpose of this chapter is to acquaint you with all the major components in the JMX framework. In this chapter, you will create a simple MBean, a simple agent, and a notification. In addition, this chapter sets up your working environment for the remaining examples in other chapters. This chapter also introduces you to the HTML adapter from Sun Microsystems.

Chapter 3: Building a foundation

With Chapter 3, we lay the groundwork for most of the examples in the remainder of the book. Most of our examples center around writing different types of MBeans in different situations. To run all these examples, we thought it would be convenient to use a single JMX agent. In chapter 3 you'll write this agent, and we'll introduce you to the Java Remote Method Invocation (RMI) connector for use in contacting the agent.

Chapter 4: MBeans for stable resources

Starting with chapter 4, we get into the real meat of the book. In this chapter, we introduce the first of the MBean types we'll present: the Standard MBean. Chapter 4 covers the common construction rules for all MBeans, as well as the rules specifically for Standard MBeans. The examples in this chapter use MBeans for application configuration and componentization.

Chapter 5: MBeans for changing resources

Chapter 5 advances the discussion to the Dynamic MBean. This chapter covers the `DynamicMBean` interface and the best time to use Dynamic MBeans. You'll construct a super class for your Dynamic MBeans that will provide some utility methods for creating the management interface at runtime. This chapter includes a great example about managing Jini services with Dynamic MBeans.

Chapter 6: Communication with MBeans using notifications

Using this chapter as a break between MBean types, we present material about MBean notifications. Chapter 6 covers the JMX notification model and provides some examples concerning the `AttributeChangeNotification` class, persisting notifications, and creating an application heartbeat.

Chapter 7: MBeans on-the-fly

Chapter 7 is the last chapter focusing on an MBean type; it covers the Model MBean. (We discuss one more MBean type in the book, but only in an appendix.) Because Model MBeans are related to the Dynamic MBean, this chapter contains a utility class similar to the super class created in chapter 5. Of course, this chapter also covers the advantages and features of the Model MBean.

Chapter 8: Working with an MBean server

At this point in the book, we are done presenting the instrumentation layer of JMX and move into the agent layer. Chapter 8 discusses the MBean server API and how to use the query methods of the MBeanServer class. This chapter provides some great examples of using queries.

Chapter 9: Communicating with JMX agents

Chapter 9 is one of the most informative chapters of this book. This chapter discusses creating and using different protocol adapters and connectors with JMX agents. It presents the RMI connector, a Jini connector, and a Transmission Control Protocol (TCP) adapter. There is also some discussion about using Simple Network Management Protocol (SNMP) and JMX.

Chapter 10: Advanced MBean loading

Chapter 10 begins our coverage of the four agent services available in JMX by discussing the M-let service used for dynamic class loading. This chapter not only presents using the M-let service to load MBean classes from remote locations, but also has you create an M-let wrapper MBean to provide notifications when new MBeans are loaded.

Chapter 11: Working with the relation service

The relation agent service is covered in chapter 11. We describe it by developing a phone and fax management system. After you complete this example, you will understand how to use MBean relationships and the relation service to easily manage large groups of MBeans.

Chapter 12: More agent services: monitors and timers

Chapter 12 concludes the part of the book focusing on the JMX agent layer by discussing the remaining two agent services: the JMX monitoring service and timer service.

Chapter 13: Using JMX with the Java Message Service

Chapter 13 begins the final part of the book. It covers JMX and Java 2 Enterprise Edition (J2EE) technologies by introducing using JMX with the Java Message Service (JMS). This chapter uses a home theater system to demonstrate how MBeans can be combined with the Publish-Subscribe mode of JMS applications.

Chapter 14: Using JMX with Enterprise JavaBeans

The final chapter of this book discusses using JMX with Enterprise Java Beans (EJBs). This chapter introduces some potential uses for MBeans in an EJB application by showing you how to manage an EJB that controls a user login process. The second example in the chapter deals with EJBs that create their own MBean at deployment time.

How to use this book

Like most technical books, this book can be read in two ways.

You can read the book from start to finish, in which case you will probably gain a better understanding of JMX. By reading the chapters in order, you will have a better foundation for the material presented in each successive chapter.

However, some of you will want to jump around to specific areas of the book—most of the chapters can stand alone, with some containing only a single reference back to chapter 3. (Chapter 3 contains the basic JMX agent that many of the other MBean examples use.) If you do choose to skip around, we suggest you at least read chapters 2 and 3; these chapters lay the groundwork for the book and for the examples in the remaining chapters.

Source code

Source code for all examples presented in *JMX in Action* is available for download from the publisher's web site, www.manning.com/sullins.

Conventions

Courier typeface is used for code examples. **Bold Courier** typeface is used in some code examples to highlight code that has been changed from previous examples. Certain references to code in text, such as functions, properties, and methods, also appear in Courier typeface.

Code annotations accompany many segments of code. Certain annotations are marked with numbered bullets ❶. These annotations have further explanations that follow the code.

For clarity, specific query examples have been set in *italics*. Text or code to be entered in various dialog boxes is set in **bold** type.

Author Online

Purchase of *JMX in Action* includes free access to a private web forum run by Manning Publications where you can make comments about the book, ask technical questions, and receive help from the authors and from other users. To access the forum and subscribe to it, point your browser to www.manning.com/sullins. This page provides information on how to get on the forum once you are registered, what kind of help is available, and the rules of conduct on the forum.

Manning's commitment to our readers is to provide a venue where a meaningful dialogue between individual readers and between readers and the authors can take place. It is not a commitment to any specific amount of participation on the part of the authors, whose contribution to the AO remains voluntary (and unpaid). We suggest you try asking them some challenging questions, lest their interest stray!

The Author Online forum and the archives of previous discussions will remain accessible from the publisher's web site for as long as the book is in print.

about the cover illustration

The figure on the cover of *JMX in Action* is a "Chingala de Ceylon," a Sinhalese inhabitant of Sri Lanka, formerly known as Ceylon. The Sinhalese people have lived in Sri Lanka for over 2,000 years and are the largest ethnic group on the island, representing 75 percent of the population.

Those who know how quickly programming languages evolve might be pleased to reflect on the changes that natural human languages constantly undergo; the descriptions that come with this source material are only about two hundred years old, but they are not all easily translated by speakers of modern Spanish. Some captions that accompany the illustrations contain words that are archaic but can be found in dictionaries; others have now disappeared, not only from the oral language but also from common written sources.

The title page of the Spanish compendium states:

Coleccion general de los Trages que usan actualmente todas las Nacionas del Mundo desubierto, dibujados y grabados con la mayor exactitud por R.M.V.A.R.. Obra muy util y en special para los que tienen la del viajero universal

which we translate, as literally as possible, thus:

General collection of costumes currently used in the nations of the known world, designed and printed with great exactitude by R.M.V.A.R. This work is very useful especially for those who hold themselves to be universal travelers

Although nothing is known of the designers, engravers, and workers who colored this illustration by hand, the "exactitude" of their execution is evident in this drawing. The "Chingala de Ceylon" is just one of many figures in this colorful collection. Their diversity speaks vividly of the uniqueness and individuality of the world's towns and regions just 200 years ago. This was a time when the dress codes of two regions separated by a few dozen miles identified people uniquely as belonging to one or the other. The collection brings to life a sense of isolation and distance of that period and of every other historic period except our own hyperkinetic present.

Dress codes have changed since then and the diversity by region, so rich at the time, has faded away. It is now often hard to tell the inhabitant of one continent from another. Perhaps, trying to view it optimistically, we have traded a cultural and visual diversity for a more varied personal life. Or a more varied and interesting intellectual and technical life.

We at Manning celebrate the inventiveness, the initiative, and the fun of the computer business with book covers based on the rich diversity of regional life of two centuries ago brought back to life by the pictures from this collection.

Part 1

Getting started

This part of the book will get you started with JMX quickly and effectively. In this part of the book, you will learn about the following:

- Why does JMX exist today?
- How can it help you with your Java development?

You will also get your first JMX application up and running, as we lay the groundwork for the remaining examples in the book.

Chapter 1 introduces you to JMX by walking you through today's application management and monitoring environment. In this chapter, you will see how a typical web application could be enhanced through the use of JMX. In addition, chapter 1 defines basic JMX terms used throughout the book and closes by explaining the JMX architecture.

The main objective of chapter 2 is to acquaint you with JMX code and the runtime environment. In this chapter, you will perform the JMX version of the Hello World program. As you read chapter 2, you will begin to understand many of the basic concepts of JMX, such as MBeans, notifications, and agents.

The last chapter of this part of the book begins the construction of a JMX agent that will be used in many of the following chapters. As the book progresses, you will add functionality to this agent and use it for many of the examples.

Resource management and JMX

- Exploring the benefits of JMX
- Defining common JMX terms
- Understanding the JMX architecture

Distributed applications, devices, and services appear in many different arrangements in an enterprise. At your company, you probably access data from your intranet services, from computers distributed throughout the company network, and from services across the firewall out on the Web. For example, you might access a calendar-sharing application or a financial application to fill out expense sheets. Someone must maintain all these applications. Not only the applications, but also the hardware that supports them must be maintained. Resource management encompasses both applications and hardware. In fact, both application and hardware management can be supported through the development of Java Management Extensions (JMX) resource management software. This book will show how you can use JMX to manage and monitor all your resources across an enterprise—both software and hardware.

Whether you're familiar with JMX already or have purchased this book to find out what JMX is all about, you need to understand why JMX exists today. In this chapter, you will learn the basis for JMX, the definitions of some common JMX terms, and the essentials of JMX architecture. Throughout our discussion, we'll use as an example a bicycle shop web application on the Internet: people come to this site to purchase bicycles and gear, and to access articles and content related to bicycling.

1.1 Resource management

Resource management is a management concept that provides a plan and tools for the management of enterprise applications and resources. For typical enterprises, resource management means having tools that report the health of enterprise applications and hardware. Based on the health of resources, IT employees can react to system failures and critical events.

Improved resource monitoring and management capabilities across an enterprise provide the IT employee with insight into the health of enterprise applications, as well as a way to resolve problems when they occur; the IT employee thus moves from a purely reactionary mode to a more active role. For instance, if you're made aware of the fact that resources are performing below par, you can help avoid a catastrophic failure. In addition, you'll be able to tune the applications or devices remotely from a single management console.

The current management environment in many enterprises lacks the quick responsiveness needed for today's enterprise applications. In addition, many application-monitoring and -management solutions are costly and difficult to implement. In this section, we'll compare the typical environments in place today with our vision of the perfect environment. (The disparity between the two may surprise you.) Then, we'll look at what you can achieve in terms of typical development resources, effort, and support.

1.1.1 Today's management environment

Today's management solutions can be divided into two categories: network and application. The most common tool used for networking (hardware) management is Simple Network Management Protocol (SNMP). For applications like web sites, most enterprise developers must either use the management tools that come built-in with the application (and the web servers that drive the application) or write their own tools. As mentioned earlier, resource management includes both application and hardware aspects.

Hardware and network management

Most network monitoring and management systems today use an SNMP solution to provide monitoring and management capabilities for hardware. SNMP is a monitoring standard that has been in wide use for several years. For the example Internet bike shop, you would use SNMP to monitor the health and activity of the servers running your web site and back-end applications.

Information about managed devices is stored in a Management Information Base (MIB). The MIB is a hierarchical representation of information about devices. A managed device can be located on an MIB tree using an object name or object identifier. An example name might be iso.identified-organization.dod.internet.private.enterprise.myenterprise.myvariables.myProduct or something similar. An object identifier is set of numbers that represents the textual name. (For more information about MIBs, read the SNMP specifications at http://www.ietf.org.)

Fortunately, many hardware vendors provide MIB definitions and SNMP hooks into their devices. However, due to the difficulty of SNMP development, few applications have hooks into SNMP.

SNMP development is not an easy task, and most developers are not trained to tackle it. Unfortunately, SNMP does not easily provide monitoring and management for applications like your bicycle store. For everyday Java developers, working with SNMP is not a suitable option.

Application management

When they're creating applications, software companies often do not think about runtime configuration and management; so, at deployment time, there is usually a scramble to figure out how to maintain the system and be informed of critical events. Some companies develop their own tools for management or build management consoles directly into their products. For many companies, application management comes from the platform that hosts their application: the web or application server.

When the bicycle shop web site and application were developed, you had to consider the health of not only your application, but also the application server, web server, and database (as well as any other software systems). Without a standard and consistent management platform, you might have to write specific code in order to expose application properties, health, and statistics. In fact, the manner in which you manage your application will likely change if you purchase a different monitoring solution.

In today's typical management environment, IT personnel will always be in a reactionary mode when maintaining applications. Hardware and application management solutions are often developed *ad hoc* at deployment time. In fact, currently it is difficult to develop a generic, reusable management and monitoring solution for applications.

1.1.2 *The ideal management environment*

An ideal management environment would have a proactive capability for dealing with problems. A management system would constantly monitor the health of both devices and applications. If a device was down, the management system could discover an alternative device, reroute services to the alternate, and notify the administrator of the problem. For instance, if the bicycle shop's web site was down or started to experience too much load, the management system could change some of the services the application provides, notify participating services to find an alternate service provider, and notify the administrator that problems exist. The management system could even start secondary web sites and services to take the load off the initial application.

Ideal management systems not only would be aware of the health of the applications, but also would have knowledge of application internals. For example, the management solution could quickly produce reports comparing successful and failed bicycle shop transactions. On the system management level, the number of threads executing could be changed at runtime. The management system would make informed decisions and take action based on information it gathered from applications and devices.

Unfortunately, an ideal management system would take too much time and development resources to achieve. In addition to writing the management tools, you might need to write custom interfaces for your applications and network resources. Such an environment also would require many resources and constant configuration to ensure that systems were maximized in availability and performance. Therefore, rather than build a perfect management environment, you must create something that's better than what exists today but that is feasible to construct and maintain.

1.1.3 Management for the real world

A feasible solution would blend the current management capabilities and the ideal environment. By gathering and combining information about the health of network devices and applications, better decisions can be made and proactive management can occur either automatically or by IT personnel. Let's walk through the example bicycle shop web application, which has been built with management in mind.

A proposed management solution

Suppose you are running the online bicycle shop we've mentioned previously: customers can purchase bicycles and bike gear from your web site. In order to ensure that the customer's shopping experience is not interrupted, you have installed a secondary server to take queries if the first server fails. In this environment, web servers, application servers, a database, and networking hardware provide your web site services. The following items represent the major monitoring and management needs for such an application and its environment:

- *Monitoring the system health of platforms and hardware*—You need to know the health of your web and application servers, as well as the hardware that hosts them. The networking hardware exposes SNMP interfaces that report its health and any faults that occur. Likewise, the web server is instrumented to report errors and has a mechanism that allows you to query its health. The database is instrumented so that its performance can be queried, along with its health and possible faults.

- *Configuring resources at the application level*—You probably want to be able to make direct contact with your bicycle shop services for configuration and management. When you wrote your bicycle shop application, you had the foresight to instrument it to give you the information you need to actively manage the system with a management tool built specifically for your environment. For instance, you can connect to your bicycle shop server process and change the number of items displayed on one page of the catalog. Your management application can also query the environment services. If you query the database and determine that the load on the database is too great, you can reduce the number of active connections available in a connection pool. You can also reduce the number of threads that are available to service requests from the outside world. Upon further queries, these resources can be readjusted as the load decreases on database resources.

- *Collecting application statistics*—In addition to configuring your bicycle shop applications, you will also want to gather important statistics on transactions, inquiries, and so forth over time. For instance, you would like to see a comparison of the number of visits to the catalog verses the number of purchases made from the site. You would also like to collect the number of attempts to break into the system by hostile attackers. In fact, you properly instrumented the application to push this information into the management system.

- *Debugging options*—Don't overlook the amount of information being stored for analysis. Fortunately, you had the foresight to realize that you will want to be able to turn logging verbosity up or down when you debug possible problems with the bicycle shop application. By exposing management APIs, you allow yourself to turn on debugging and change the logging output to the console so that you can observe the functions of the application without having to shut it down to make changes.

- *Monitoring server performance*—Your web application needs to be monitored for health and overall load. If the load is too great on the first server, you want to be able to shift some load to the backup server. To avoid cases of failure, you need to be notified about critical events via a pager or email.

Providing this solution

The monitoring and management framework described in this section covers the major areas of many of today's application management needs. However, achieving such a framework can be costly and difficult. In the end, application administrators could be left with many different management consoles and interfaces to all the different services and hardware.

1.2 Providing a Java solution: Java Management Extensions

In the previous section, we described a monitoring and management environment that covers the needs of enterprise applications. However, we also noted that building such an environment is difficult and can leave administrators with many different tools in which to manage the system. As this book will show, using Java Management Extensions, you can build a management environment that's less expensive and more flexible, in a shorter amount of time. JMX is a new framework added to the Java language; it can provide a management solution that covers the standards described in the previous section. JMX allows you to encapsulate all your resources (hardware or software) with Java objects and expose them in a distributed environment. In addition, JMX provides a mechanism for easily mapping existing management protocols such as SNMP into its own management structures.

Let's look at the management areas identified in the previous section and how JMX can address them:

- *Platform health*—As previously mentioned, using JMX, you can wrap non-Java resources and hardware interfaces with Java objects in order to fit them into a JMX management system. Using Java wrappers, you can interface to your web and application servers and communicate with the hardware driving your system.

- *Configuring resources and collecting application statistics*—Using JMX, you can directly expose the API of applications and services. In addition, you can dynamically choose what parts of the API to expose. With a JMX management tool, you can then invoke and query the API at any time. In fact, if you know you will be using JMX ahead of time, you can build into your application the simple JMX component that will expose it to the JMX management environment. However, you can use JMX to very quickly instrument an application even if development is already completed.

- *Debug options*—Debug options are configurable like any other application or resource attribute. Once an interface is exposed through JMX, it can be invoked.

- *Application performance*—With JMX, you can easily monitor the system for critical events. When an event is noticed, JMX can emit notifications to a predefined listener process. Listeners can be configured to send pages, write email messages, and so forth; the process is entirely customizable.

1.2.1 *Benefits of using JMX*

Using a Java-based solution such as JMX offers several benefits, some of which are probably evident to you as a Java programmer. For example, Java is a portable language (write once run anywhere), so you can develop your application without regard to platform dependency. In addition to the benefits of the Java language, JMX has some persuasive advantages.

Ease of use

JMX has a significant advantage over technologies like SNMP because a programmer with Java experience can quickly pick up the concepts of JMX and become productive. The knowledge level required to master SNMP is significant: the developer must know the development language used and master the concepts of SNMP, which are not easily understood. The study of SNMP and the encoding and compilers is a lengthy process.

On the other hand, managing an application with JMX is simple and straightforward (especially if your applications are written in Java). A developer can instrument an application for management with just a few lines of code.

Leveraging existing technologies

When you're building a JMX management environment, you do not have to throw out your existing management structure: existing management tools can plug into the JMX technology. As mentioned earlier, JMX provides the capability for building communication with any protocol (such as SNMP or HTTP) and connectivity with any other transport (such as Java RMI). In addition, if no management capabilities are natively built into the existing enterprise devices and applications, you can build JMX agents that act on their behalf and present management capabilities to the operations center.

Componentization

JMX allows you to build your management solution in a componentized fashion. You can choose to expose entire devices or applications, or just a subset of their configurable features. In addition, if you send your applications to a customer, you can include management components that will plug directly into their management solution suite.

Alerts, events, and statistics

With JMX, you can instrument your application to push information about its current state of health as well as useful statistics you want to maintain. Using JMX, you can gather information from other managed resources such as the web server or databases.

JMX provides a notification system that takes advantage of Java as an object-oriented language. Notifications provide a rich capability to distribute Java objects as opposed to just data elements. A management system can send notifications that encapsulate both data and behavior; this is a powerful concept that's familiar to object-oriented programmers but that has not been present in previous monitoring systems.

With JMX, you can emit data elements (alerts and system events) and also send along a mechanism for interpreting the data. For example, you might send out a notification with the status of the processor load. This information by itself might not be useful to a management system (so what if the CPU load is 50%?); but it would be useful to send an object that contained the data, along with a mechanism that could provide the application's view of the load's importance. For example, the notification could contain a method isLoadCritical() that would return the application's concept of load criticality. The management system could make decisions based not only on the load, but also on whether the application was in a stressful state.

Rapid monitoring solutions

You may have experienced a development environment in which many development teams had to coordinate efforts to provide application monitoring and management APIs. With JMX, each development team is only responsible for developing managed beans (MBeans) for their application.

As applications are executed, they can deploy their MBeans into a waiting JMX agent. With all the MBeans in a central but distributed host, a single management tool can manage and configure all the applications. Using JMX to provide your management solution provides the benefits of other management technologies with less implementation difficulty and richer capabilities, due to the object-oriented behavior and portability afforded with Java.

1.2.2 Essential JMX terms

The following terms are the building blocks for the entire JMX discussion in this book. We define them here, but you will learn more about them in the next section. In addition, as other chapters cover these terms, you will acquire a more robust understanding of them. We're presenting the terms now in order to help explain the JMX architecture in the next section.

Manageable resource

A manageable resource is any application, device, or existing entity that can be accessed or wrapped by Java. It is the entity that will be exposed for management by using JMX. Applications can expose components, APIs, or additional resources for a JMX environment to manage. Manageable resources can even be network devices such as printers. The manageable resource is the entity managed by a JMX MBean.

MBean

An MBean (managed bean) is a Java class that meets certain naming and inheritance standards dictated by the JMX specification. Instantiated MBeans are Java objects that expose management interfaces for the manipulation and access of manageable resources. An MBean's management interface is made up of the MBean's attributes and operations that are exposed for management.

Management applications access MBeans to access attributes and invoke operations. This book covers three types of MBeans: Standard, Dynamic, and Model MBeans. Each type of MBean has specific advantages for specific resources. MBeans reside in another JMX component called the MBean server.

MBean server

An MBean server is a Java class that manages a group of MBeans. It is the heart of the JMX management environment—it acts as a registry for looking up MBeans. The MBean server exposes the management interface of any registered MBean, but it never exposes the object reference. In addition, the MBean server is implemented to present users with an identical interface regardless of the type of MBean being accessed: it treats all MBeans equally. The MBean server also provides methods for performing queries to find MBeans and for other objects to register as notification listeners (like event listeners) with MBeans.

JMX agent

A JMX agent is a Java process that provides a set of services for managing a set of MBeans—it is the container for an MBean server. JMX agents provide services for creating MBean relationships, dynamically loading classes, simple monitoring services, and timers.

Agents can expect to have a set of protocol adapters and connectors that enable remote and different clients to make use of the agent. Protocol adapters and connectors are Java classes, usually MBeans, which can internally map an outside protocol (like HTTP or SNMP) or expose the agent to remote connectivity (like RMI or Jini). This means JMX agents can be used by a variety of different management protocols and tools.

Protocol adapters and connectors

Protocol adapters and connectors are objects residing within a JMX agent that expose the agent to management application and protocols. For example, SNMP could be mapped into a JMX agent using an SNMP adapter object of the agent. In addition, an agent could have an RMI connector that opens it up for management applications that use RMI clients. Protocol adapters consist of a single object within an agent, whereas connectors have both an object in the agent and an object used by a client.

An agent can have any number of adapters and connectors, essentially giving you the ability to reach the agent using new tools or existing management protocols and applications. Not only does your agent have the flexibility to be managed by many applications, but you also have a mechanism for distributing agents across a network.

Management application

A management application is any user application that is used to interface to any number of JMX agents. JMX agents can work with management applications designed to work with JMX technology or those that are not. A compatible JMX management application will be able to take advantage of JMX's advanced features. You can provide a JMX agent with the ability to interact with existing (non-JMX) managers by writing custom adapters and connectors. For instance, an SNMP manager can be used to work with JMX agents by creating an SNMP adapter. Later in this book, we will work with connectors and adapters covering RMI, Jini, and TCP.

Notification

Notifications are Java objects emitted by MBeans and the MBean server to encapsulate events, alerts, or general information. Other MBeans or Java objects can register as listeners to receive notifications. In fact, the JMX notification model is similar to the Java event model, as you will see in chapter 6.

Instrumentation

Instrumentation is the process of exposing a manageable resource using an MBean (or set of MBeans). Instrumentation of an application can take place alongside development, or developers can work to create MBeans that use existing APIs of currently active systems. You will discover that with several types of MBeans from which to choose, you will be able to find an easy way to expose parts of your applications and resources to JMX.

1.3 The JMX architecture

The JMX architecture is a component architecture designed to build flexibility and usefulness into a management environment. It does so by providing a mechanism for agents (and ultimately MBeans) to be reached by many different protocols and by many different mechanisms. This section breaks the architecture into its three main layers—instrumentation, agent, and distributed—and discusses each by following a simple use case as it applies to each layer. Table 1.1 lists the three layers with brief descriptions.

Table 1.1   The three JMX architectural layers

Layer	Description
Distributed layer	Contains components that enable management applications to communicate with JMX agents
Agent layer	Consists of agents and their MBean servers
Instrumentation layer	Contains MBeans representing their manageable resources

Each layer contains some of the various components we have already discussed, but you need to understand how everything works together.

1.3.1 Example: managing the bicycle shop server

In order to help you better understand the purpose of each layer, and to tie them together at the same time, we will walk through a simple use case. Let's say the bicycle shop web site has a server application that manages inventory and suppliers. This application is used to keep track of sales, inventory, and orders to suppliers on a scheduled basis. Suppose this application can be configured to use different order formats, logging levels, and schedules. Because this application is critical to the business, it needs to be configurable (or manageable) without causing a shutdown of operations.

In many situations like this, you would expect the application to have a console to which you could connect in order to change the logging level, validation process, or storage location. However, a business may have many such applications, each with its own configuration or management tools; in this case, you would have to go to each application and use the individual tool to change the logging level. Managing such an environment as a unit would be very difficult. Figure 1.1 shows this type of situation.

In contrast, let's consider this situation from a JMX point of view. How can JMX make this heterogeneous management environment work better? You can

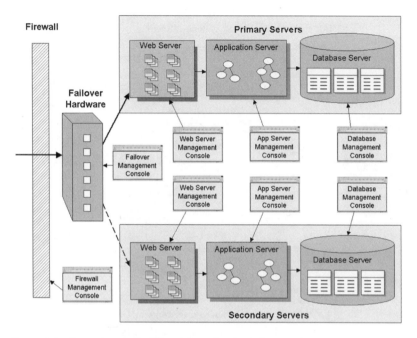

**Figure 1.1 An environment with many applications that need management.
Each has its own set of configuration and management tools.**

model the management interface of each application with an MBean. Next, you can expose the MBeans for management in a JMX agent, which is available for any of your existing protocols. Doing so would allow a single point to control all the applications. From the users' perspective, a single application is presented, as opposed to a collection of disparate software components. This environment provides a more uniform and robust solution to the management of the application suite. Figure 1.2 illustrates your new environment.

Let's walk through a typical configuration use case for the data storage application. Assume a user needs to change the logging level of the application. The following steps define this use case:

1 The user opens his favorite management tool and connects to the JMX agent.

2 The user finds the particular MBean that represents the application and makes the appropriate log level change.

3 The MBean interacts with the bicycle shop application to configure its log level.

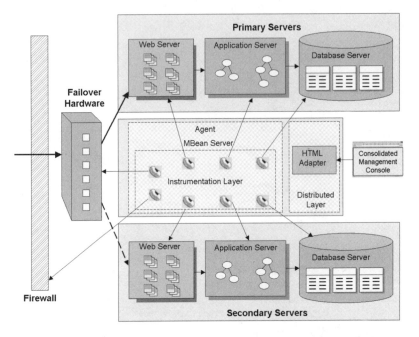

Figure 1.2 An environment with many applications that need management. Each is represented by its own MBean and managed through a single management tool using any number of protocols or transports. The three JMX layers are delimited by dotted lines.

The following sections highlight the layers of the JMX architecture by discussing what takes place at each step in this use case. The first layer used in the use case is the distributed layer.

1.3.2 *The distributed layer*

The distributed layer is the outermost layer of the JMX architecture. This layer is responsible for making JMX agents available to the outside world. There are two kinds of distributed interaction. The first type is achieved by using objects called *adapters*, which provide visibility to MBeans via different protocols such as HTTP and SNMP. Second, JMX agents have components called *connectors* that expose the agent API to other distributed technologies such as Java RMI. In fact, as figure 1.3 shows, an agent can work with many different technologies. Adapters and connectors provide the same functionality in a JMX environment. They are broken into two groups (adapters and connectors) at the time we're writing this book, but plans call for them to be labeled as JMX adapters in the next release of JMX.

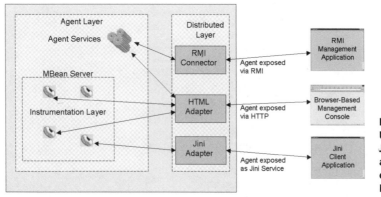

Figure 1.3
Up-close view of a JMX agent showing adapters and connectors for HTTP, RMI, and Jini

Our use case moves through this layer with step 1 from the previous list: a user uses a management tool to connect with the JMX agent. The JMX agent contains an MBean that can manage the bicycle shop application. However, in its distributed layer, it contains a component that allows clients to make a connection to the agent. This component can connect the user to the agent via a web browser, Java RMI, or SNMP. As shown in figure 1.3, the user's management tool can be a JMX-knowledgeable management tool or a tool using another technology or protocol.

Once the connection to the agent has been made, the user can use a management tool to interact with MBeans registered in the agent. At this point, the use case moves into the agent layer of the architecture.

1.3.3 *The agent layer*

The main component of the agent layer is the MBean server. An MBean server is a Java object that acts as a registry for MBeans; it's the heart of a JMX agent. In addition, the agent layer provides four agent services that make managing MBeans easier: timer, monitoring, dynamic MBean loading, and relationship services. Figure 1.4 shows a JMX agent's MBean server and agent services.

The agent layer provides access to managed resources from the management application. A JMX agent can run in a JVM embedded in the machine that hosts the resources, or it can be remotely located. The agent does not require knowledge of the resources that it exposes or the manager application that uses the exposed MBeans. It acts as a service for handling MBeans and allows manipulation of MBeans through a collection of protocols exposed via connectors or adapters.

Moving to step 2, the user finds the MBean that manages the configuration for the bicycle shop application. After finding the MBean, the user invokes an

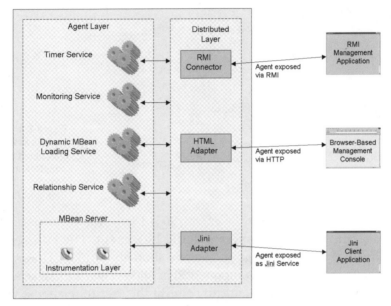

Figure 1.4 Up-close view of an MBean server with registered MBeans and agent services

exposed operation that configures the logging level of the application. At this point, the MBean takes over, and we move into the instrumentation layer.

1.3.4 *The instrumentation layer*

The instrumentation layer is the closest layer to the managed resources. It comprises the MBeans registered in an agent. The MBean allows the resource to be managed through the use of the JMX agent. Each MBean exposes a piece of the configuration or functionality of an underlying resource; the MBean exposes the management capabilities of the resource in a Java object. If the resource does not natively speak Java, the MBean acts as a translator from the agent to the resource.

For example, if you have a legacy application that exposes a management capability through a lookup of data in a database table, you can build an MBean that makes a JDBC call to the database tables to read or change data. The management application will not have to worry how the underlying technology is built because the MBean abstracts it away.

An MBean is a lightweight class that knows how to use, acquire, and manipulate its resource in order to provide access or functionality to the agent and user. Figure 1.5 shows an MBean directly interfacing with its resource.

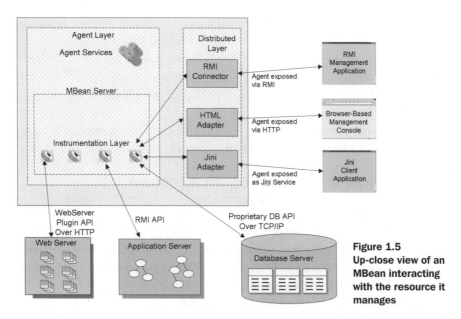

**Figure 1.5
Up-close view of an
MBean interacting
with the resource it
manages**

If you desire, you can even create an MBean that presents a collection of applications as one unit and lets you set the logging level on all the applications through one call. For example, if you want to change the database and the application logging level to debug mode, you can have an MBean make calls to the separate applications to set the debug levels. Even the underlying technologies to communicate with the different applications can be different; the MBean will abstract that knowledge from the manager of the system, and the different technologies will appear as a cohesive unit.

We have reached the last step of our use case. With this step, the user has invoked an MBean operation, and the MBean works with its resource in order to change its logging level.

1.3.5 *Notifications*

In addition to the three layers presented in the architecture, JMX provides a notification model that closely resembles the Java event model. Notifications provide the final necessary component for a complete management system. The three architectural layers allow the agent to perform configuration and control operations on the resource, but a large portion of the management requirements rely on reacting to interesting events that occur to the resources. By using notifications, JMX agents and MBeans can send alerts or report information to management applications or other MBeans. Users can receive notifications as a way of being informed of critical events or requests for attention.

For instance, the bicycle shop application might have the ability to notice when transactions are in an error state. For these transactions, the application could be able to push an event to its MBean, which can emit notifications to interested clients (such as a pager or email address).

As this book will make evident, JMX is the ideal environment for applications to expose their management and configuration APIs.

1.4 *Using JMX as an application architecture*

The JMX agent layer is ideal for building applications. The MBean server can be used as a backbone for an application component such as a data layer, a logging component, or a transaction manager. By defining application components with MBeans, you can insulate other parts of your application from the implementation details of each component. Figure 1.6 illustrates this concept.

By using JMX in this manner and by defining stable interfaces to your component MBeans, you can create an application that can easily swap out component

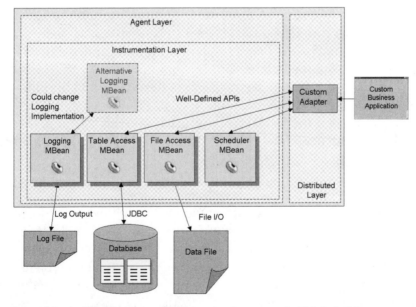

Figure 1.6   An MBean server acting as a structure around which to build an application. The MBean server contains the various application components as MBeans, shielding the application from component implementation changes.

implementations. In addition, it is easy to add components by registering a new MBean on the MBean server internal to your application.

If this type of architecture seems unlikely, consider the fact that JMX is already being used in this manner. For example, the JBoss application server is constructed in a component architecture using a JMX MBean server as its backbone. This way, JBoss developers can easily add, change, and remove application services and components from the server.

1.5 *JMX in use today*

If you are worried about investing in a new management framework without knowing if it will be adopted by software providers, this section is for you. JMX is a new technology, but is already being widely adopted as a means of configuring and instrumenting application servers and building management tools. Table 1.2 lists some products that incorporate JMX.

Table 1.2 Products using JMX

Product	Company	Description
WebLogic Application Server	BEA Systems	JMX is used to monitor J2EE services running in the server.
JBoss Application Server	JBoss	JMX is used for the application server architecture and to monitor services running in the server.
Bluestone Application Server	Hewlett-Packard	JMX is used to configure the application server.
OpenView	Hewlett-Packard	The OpenView monitoring suite can interface to JMX MBeans.
Adventnet Manager	Adventnet	This is a JMX-based monitoring solution.
JDMK (Java Dynamic Management Kit)	Sun Microsystems	This development kit is used to build JMX products.
Tivoli JMX	IBM	Tivoli is IBM's reference Implementation of JMX.
JOnAS Application Server	Bull	JMX is used to monitor J2EE services running in the server.

This table lists only a fraction of the products beginning to use JMX. As the J2EE platform becomes more widely adopted, JMX will become the standard for instrumentation and management solutions.

1.6 Developing with JMX

The Java Management Extensions API is currently an extension to the J2SE platform. However, with JSR (Java Specification Request) 000174, JMX is being evaluated for inclusion in the next release of J2SE. Having chosen to develop applications with JMX, you will find ample support in the Java community. Not only does Sun provide a JMX implementation, but you can also download one from IBM.

In addition, many makers of application servers have built JMX support directly into their products. By using servers like JBoss or WebLogic, you can expect a certain level of JMX to be available to your applications at runtime. However, even without support for JMX in an application server, you can quickly and easily include a JMX agent in your Java applications. You will see examples throughout this book.

1.7 Summary

At this point, you should have a good understanding of the resource management concept. We compared the current resource management environment with an ideal one and proposed a combined environment that could be implemented in the real world.

JMX provides the required services to enable the proposed managed environment. It does so with an architecture consisting of three layers: the instrumentation layer, the agent layer, and the distributed layer. The three layers help JMX provide a scalable and flexible management system for any environment.

Chapter 2 gets you started with JMX using a typical Hello World example. You will create a simple JMX agent and your first MBean.

"Hello World,"
the JMX way

2

- Writing your first MBean
- Writing a simple JMX agent
- Introducing object names
- Using the HTML adapter from Sun

Imagine that you decide to buy a new stereo. You go to the store, pick one out, and bring it home. Are you the type of person who carefully unwraps everything, checks the parts list, and follows the setup instructions step by step? Or do you open everything and start figuring out all the connections on your own? This chapter is written for those of you in the second group. If you fall into the first group, please be sure to read chapter 1; it presents the need for the JMX framework, as well as JMX's overall architecture (which is only recapped here in chapter 2).

This purpose of this chapter is to familiarize you with the JMX Reference Implementation (RI) provided by Sun Microsystems. After completing this chapter, you will have managed your first resource, created a simple JMX agent, and communicated with the agent from a web browser. In other words, you will create an MBean, use the MBean server, and manage your MBean using the HTML adapter provided by Sun in the JMX RI.

NOTE   The remainder of the book assumes that you already have the JDK 1.3 (at minimum) installed on your machine and that you have it included in your PATH. If necessary, you can download it from http://www.javasoft.com.

2.1 *Getting started*

Before we get too far along, let's have a quick architectural review and create a development environment.

2.1.1 *A JMX architecture refresher*

Chapter 1 detailed the JMX architecture and discussed how it provides a management solution. However, to ensure you get the most of this chapter, let's have a brief refresher. The JMX architecture lays out a Java framework consisting of three main parts, or layers, that work together to provide a Java management solution. Table 2.1 lists the three layers of the JMX architecture.

Table 2.1   The three JMX component layers

Layer	Description
Instrumentation layer	Contains MBeans and their manageable resources
Agent layer	Contains the JMX agents used to expose the MBeans
Distributed layer	Contains components that enable management applications to communicate with JMX agents

Figure 2.1 illustrates how the layers work together.

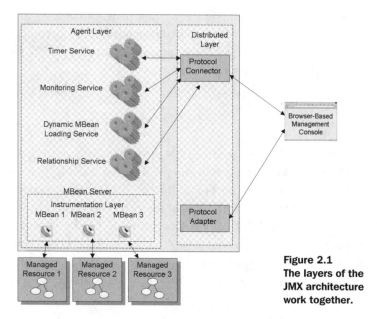

Figure 2.1
The layers of the
JMX architecture
work together.

In this chapter, you will interact with components from each layer. From the instrumentation layer, you will be using an MBean. MBeans are Java objects that encapsulate a resource and expose it for management. From the agent layer, you will use a JMX agent. Actually, you will write your own agent to contain your MBean. And finally, from the distributed layer, you will use the HTML adapter, which is a Java object that allows management applications to communicate with your agent over HTML as a communication protocol. Management applications are any applications that are interested in accessing, configuring, or manipulating manageable resources.

2.1.2 *Setting up the development environment*

If you don't already have the JMX RI from Sun Microsystems, download it from http://www.java.sun.com. Download the 1.0 version of JMX. Once you have downloaded the zip file, extract it to your hard drive. The extracted zip file produces a JMX parent directory containing the following directories:

- *contrib*—Contains unsupported contributions from Sun Microsystems. For example, Sun provides a Java RMI connector, which, like the adapters, allows management applications to communicate with JMX agents.

- *jmx*—Contains the JMX RI, examples, and documentation.

For the remainder of this book, you will keep your Java source files in a folder called JMXBook. In addition, you will use a setup batch file to set your PATH and CLASSPATH for compiling and running the examples from the JMXBook directory. The batch file contains the following lines:

```
set CLASSPATH=c:\JMXBook;C:\jmx-1_0_1-ribin\jmx\lib\jmxri.jar;
C:\jmx-1_0_1-ribin\jmx\lib\jmxtools.jar;
C:\jmx-1_0_1-ri-bin\contrib\remoting\jar\jmx_remoting.jar;
set PATH=c:\jdk1.3\bin
```

The setup batch file is used to set up the JMX environment for compiling and running the examples in a Windows environment. If you are using Unix, you will need to modify the script accordingly. As you can see from the PATH environment variable, we are using the JDK version 1.3, but every example should work with any Java 2 Platform Standard Edition. When working from the command line, you will invoke this file (setup.bat in our case) before doing anything else. After running the setup script, you can test your CLASSPATH by typing **java javax.management.ObjectName**. You should get an error indicating that the class does not contain a main() method.

NOTE   Using Ant: For those of you familiar with Ant (or willing to find out more), we included an Ant build system setup in appendix B. In the appendix you will find the Ant XML build doc and information for setting up your environment.

2.2 *Managing your first resource*

So far we have refreshed what you already know about the major JMX components, and ensured that you have a good working environment. Now you are ready to create your first MBean. Keep in mind that this chapter is intended only as an introduction to MBeans; more complex examples are presented in later chapters.

For the first example, you'll create a simple HelloWorld MBean. The HelloWorld MBean exposes a Java String object, its only member variable, as a manageable resource. We will use this example as a tool to introduce you to working with the entirety of JMX, including the MBean server and the HTML adapter. Remember, a manageable resource is any resource that can be accessed and configured via an MBean. (For this chapter, don't worry about the coding standards of MBeans. However, remember from chapter 1 that this book covers three types of MBeans: Standard, Dynamic, and Model. You will create only a Standard MBean in this chapter; the exact rules for developing MBeans are presented in detail in later chapters.) Figure 2.2 shows the UML diagram for the HelloWorld MBean.

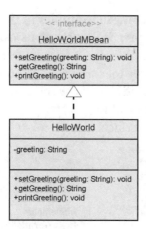

Figure 2.2
The HelloWorld class

The next section discusses writing both the interface and implementing class shown in the figure.

2.2.1 *Writing the HelloWorld MBean*

The first step in developing the HelloWorld MBean is to write its Java interface. The interface declares three methods: one *getter*, one *setter*, and an additional method for printing the HelloWorld MBean's greeting. Normally, you might not write an interface for a simple HelloWorld example class like this one. However, as you will learn in chapters 4 and 5, JMX uses interfaces to describe the exposed attributes and operations of an MBean.

Recall that a getter method is a class method with a name in the form of get-Member(), and a setter method is a class method with a name in the form of set-Member(). Think of the methods in a Standard MBean interface as the description of the implementation class. Put simply, you should be able to understand the purpose of the methods by their names. In addition, the getter and setter methods define the member variable access granted to objects that use the MBean. By creating a getter method for a member variable, you grant *read* access to it. A setter method grants *write* access. As you can see from the following interface, this MBean is quite simple:

```
package jmxbook.ch2;
public interface HelloWorldMBean
{
  public void setGreeting( String greeting );

  public String getGreeting();

  public void printGreeting();
}
```

An important item to notice is the `package` statement. All examples in this chapter are in the package `jmxbook.ch2`, and each chapter will package its examples accordingly (for example, `jmxbook.ch3` for chapter 3).

The `HelloWorldMBean` interface declares a getter (`getGreeting()`) and setter (`setGreeting()`), as well as a `printGreeting()` method. You'll use the `printGreeting()` method later to display the MBean's greeting value.

Listing 2.1 shows the implementation of the interface.

Listing 2.1   HelloWorld.java

```
package jmxbook.ch2;

public class HelloWorld implements HelloWorldMBean        ◁── Implements
{                                                             HelloWorldMBean
                                                              interface
    private String greeting = null;

    public HelloWorld()
    {
      this.greeting = "Hello World! I am a Standard MBean";
    }

    public HelloWorld( String greeting )
    {
      this.greeting = greeting;
    }

    public void setGreeting( String greeting )
    {
      this.greeting = greeting;
    }

    public String getGreeting()
    {
      return greeting;
    }

    public void printGreeting()
    {
      System.out.println( greeting );
    }

}
```

And with that, you have created your first MBean. Now, in order to test the MBean, you need to create a JMX agent to contain it. The next section discusses the creation of the `HelloAgent` class. After creating your agent, you can begin using the MBean.

2.3 *Creating a JMX agent*

Now that you have your first MBean, you need to make it available for use. To do so, you must register it in a JMX agent. Therefore, you need to create the Hello-Agent class, which is a simple JMX agent.

As described in chapter 1, JMX agents are JMX components in the agent layer of JMX and are the containers for MBeans. Part 3 of the book covers JMX agents in detail.

The HelloAgent class performs three important tasks:

- It creates an MBeanServer instance to contain MBeans.
- It creates an HTML adapter to handle connections from HTML clients.
- It registers a new instance of the HelloWorld MBean.

As you are about to see, the HelloAgent class is probably the simplest agent you will ever write, but it is still quite powerful. This fact again highlights one of the benefits of using JMX: it is simple and yet useful. In a matter of moments, you have developed the HelloWorld MBean. You can now easily manage this MBean by writing a simple agent that uses the HTML adapter provided by Sun Microsystems.

Using any web browser, the adapter allows you to interact with the agent to view all registered MBeans and their attributes. Figure 2.3 depicts this interaction.

Specifically, the adapter lets you:

- View the *readable* MBean attributes
- Update the *writable* attributes
- Invoke the other remaining methods

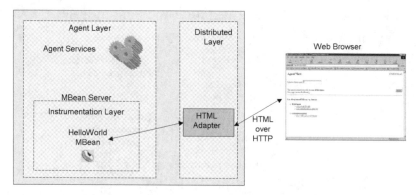

Figure 2.3   Using a Web browser to contact the HTML adapter present in the MBean server

Not only that, the adapter gives you a quick method of dynamically creating and registering additional MBeans. Essentially, the HTML adapter provides you a simple management tool for working with MBeans. The HTML adapter returns a protocol (HTML) that your web browser renders as a useable application. But let's not get ahead of ourselves; first you need to create the simple JMX agent.

2.3.1 *Writing the HelloAgent class*

Listing 2.2 presents the `HelloAgent` class. Don't worry if you don't understand or recognize what is going on in the listing; you will learn more about agents as the book progresses (part 3). For now, you need only a basic understanding of the agent code. Boiled down to the simplest steps, listing 2.2 does the following:

1   Creates the MBean server and HTML adapter

2   Registers (and thus enables you to manage) the MBean

3   Uniquely identifies the MBean

4   Registers and starts the HTML adapter

Listing 2.2   HelloAgent.java

```
package jmxbook.ch2;

import javax.management.*;
import com.sun.jdmk.comm.*;

public class HelloAgent
{
  private MBeanServer mbs = null;

    public HelloAgent()
  {
    mbs = MBeanServerFactory.createMBeanServer( "HelloAgent" );    ❶ Creates
                                                                      HTML
    HtmlAdaptorServer adapter = new HtmlAdaptorServer();           ❷ adapter

    HelloWorld hw = new HelloWorld();    ←── Creates HelloWorld
                                              MBean instance
    ObjectName adapterName = null;
    ObjectName helloWorldName = null;

    try                                      Creates ObjectName  ❸
    {                                        instance; registers
                                             HelloWorld MBean
      helloWorldName =
          new ObjectName( "HelloAgent:name=helloWorld1" );

      mbs.registerMBean( hw, helloWorldName );

      adapterName =
    new ObjectName( "HelloAgent:name=htmladapter,port=9092" );    ❹
```

```
        adapter.setPort( 9092 );
            mbs.registerMBean( adapter, adapterName );
        adapter.start();

        }
    catch( Exception e )
    {
        e.printStackTrace();
    }

  }

  public static void main( String args[] )
  {
    System.out.println( "HelloAgent is running" );
    HelloAgent agent = new HelloAgent();
  }
}//class
```

**Registers and
starts HTML
adapter MBean** 4

Note the import statements in the listing. All classes in the JMX framework are in the package javax.management. An additional package, com.sun.jdmk.comm, is provided by the RI provider, Sun Microsystems. This package is considered an unsupported contribution, meaning that the code is useful for JMX development but is not part of the JMX specification. In particular, this package contains the classes you need to instantiate the HTML adapter.

Creating the MBean server and HTML adapter

❶❷ The HelloAgent class implements a main method that allows it to be started as a standalone process. All it does is call the HelloAgent constructor, so let's start our code examination there. The first step performed by the agent constructor is the creation of the MBeanServer object.

Remember from chapter 1 that the MBean server is a Java object used to contain and manipulate JMX MBeans. The MBean server is a standard JMX class and is the heart of JMX agents. Agents acquire an instance of the MBeanServer class by using the javax.management.MBeanServerFactory class. This MBeanServerFactory class is a JMX class that implements the factory pattern to provide instances of the MBeanServer class. When you need an instance of an MBeanServer, use the factory object to create or acquire a new instance. The factory can manage many instances of the MBeanServer class, returning a specific instance or creating a new one (as in the case of the HelloAgent class).

Notice that the parameter HelloAgent was passed to the factory's createMBeanServer() method. This parameter is a String value indicating the name for this agent's domain. A domain name is a unique identifier used to indicate a group of MBeans; the domain uniquely differentiates this MBeanServer from any other. Each MBeanServer contains a supplied domain name, allowing you to group MBeans in a meaningful way. If you invoke the factory create() method again with an identical domain name parameter, it will simply return the previously created HelloAgent MBeanServer instance. (You will learn more about the MBeanServer class later in chapter 8. For now, keep in mind that an MBeanServer object acts as a registry, enabling storage, lookup, and manipulation of MBeans.)

❸ The next step is to create some way for management applications to contact the HelloAgent. Recall that agents open themselves up to management applications by constructing protocol adapters and connectors. Adapters and connectors are a major reason why JMX is so powerful and versatile. These components are Java objects that allow management applications to use a specific protocol to contact JMX agents. (You will learn more about them, and create more complex examples, as the book continues.) This chapter only makes use of the HTML adapter; to create the adapter, you just need to invoke its default constructor, as seen in the HelloAgent class.

Registering and managing the MBean

❹ Once the adapter has been created, you need to register it on the MBeanServer. This brings up an interesting point about adapters (and connectors): they are also MBeans. Thus the Java classes that make up the adapters and connectors are written to conform to one of the MBean types defined by the JMX specification. Because they are MBeans, they can be managed during runtime like other MBeans. However, before you can register an MBean, you need to make sure you can identify and find it again; this is where the javax.management.ObjectName class comes into play.

Uniquely identifying MBeans

So far, the agent has created the MBeanServer and registered an HTML adapter with it. Now it is time to examine how the MBeanServer keeps track of objects registered with it. Look back at the code that registers the HelloWorld MBean instance on the MBeanServer ❸. When registering an MBean, you need to be able to distinguish it from every other MBean that might be registered.

To do this, you must create an instance of the javax.management.ObjectName class. The ObjectName class is a JMX class that provides a naming system for MBeans, allowing unique identification of MBeans registered in the MBean server. Each ObjectName consists of two parts:

- *A domain name*—The domain name usually coincides with the domain name of the MBeanServer in which the MBean wants to register. When it does not, it is usually meant to segregate one MBean from the others.

- *A key=value property list*—Property name/value pairs are used to uniquely identify MBeans, and also to provide information about the MBean. The object name may be the first representation a user will see of your MBean. You can supply information such as names, port values, locations, and purposes with a few property values.

In this case, the ObjectName for the HelloWorld MBean looks like this:

```
"HelloAgent:name=helloWorld1"
```

Now that you have an ObjectName instance, you will be able to identify and find the MBean once it is registered.

Registering and starting the HTML adapter

❹ As previously mentioned, the agent creates an ObjectName for the adapter and registers the adapter in the MBeanServer object. Because they are MBeans, each adapter can choose to expose as many attributes as necessary for configuration by a management application.

Even though at this point in the code the adapter has been created and registered, management applications still cannot contact it. For clients to make use of the HTML adapter, it must be started. To start the adapter, you call its start() method. The start() method tells the adapter MBean to begin listening for HTTP clients on the default port of 9092. The HelloAgent is now ready to receive client calls.

2.3.2 *More about object names*

We briefly described an ObjectName value in the previous section. Having completed the code examination, let's return our focus to the ObjectName class. As you noticed, object names have a specific structure that must be followed when constructing a value.

Figure 2.4 shows the structure of an ObjectName value.

Domain names

Domain names provides context for the agent in relation to other agents. For example, an agent might be created to contain MBeans managing resources on a particular computer. In this case, the domain could be the computer's hostname. A domain name does not have to be a meaningful value like a computer's hostname, but as a rule of thumb, you should try to provide some meaning in the name. That way, you will be able to look at an `ObjectName` value and possibly understand something about its MBean.

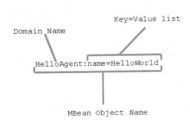

Figure 2.4   The structure of an ObjectName value

As you can tell from figure 2.4, the domain name does not even have to be specified. If it's left blank, the MBean server provides a default domain name. The same is true for the `MBeanServerFactory` class. If you use `createMBeanServer()` without a domain name parameter, the factory will provide you with an `MBeanServer` with a default domain.

Right about now, you may have noticed that both `MBeanServer` objects and MBeans (through the `ObjectName`) are associated with a domain. In fact, MBeans of a certain domain can be registered on an `MBeanServer` containing a different domain name. This situation is acceptable because domain names do not impose any rules or constraints on which MBeans can be registered on an `MBeanServer` object.

Key/value property list

The key/value list portion of the object name is a set of comma-separated property values that provide the mechanism for uniquely identifying MBeans within an MBean server. The properties do not have to be actual MBean attributes; the only requirement is that they are unique when compared to other instances of `ObjectName`. In each `ObjectName`, you must specify at least one property value that makes it distinct from all other `ObjectName` instances in an MBean server.

The `ObjectName` class provides three constructors that build the name `String` with various parameters. In the `HelloAgent` class, you create an `Object-Name` as follows:

```
helloWorldName = new ObjectName( "HelloAgent:name=helloWorld1" );
```

This `ObjectName` uniquely identifies the `HelloWorld` instance by giving it an attribute of `name` and value `helloWorld1`. If you register any other MBeans, you cannot use this property value on its own again; instead, you'll need an additional property combined with it.

Registering object name conflicts

You can think of the registry function like a more complex `Hashtable`. You put objects into the table and associated them with a key. The key in this case is the `ObjectName` object. To register the MBean, the `HelloAgent` class invokes the registerMBean() method of the MBeanServer object. If the ObjectName is not unique, the MBeanServer will throw a javax.management.InstanceAlreadyExist-sException exception, indicating that an MBean was already registered with an identical ObjectName. The MBean server does not compare actual MBean object values for equality—only their associated object names.

2.4 Running the agent

Let's review what you have accomplished so far. First, you created your first MBean, contained in the HelloWorld class. It exposes a single attribute—its greeting—as a manageable resource. (Recall that a manageable resource is any resource that can be encapsulated by an MBean to provide access and/or configuration.)

Next, you created the HelloAgent class, which is a simple JMX agent. The agent will contain your MBean and provide you with a mechanism for managing it. That leaves you with one more task to do: compile, run, and contact this agent.

2.4.1 Compiling the agent

To get the agent started, you need to compile your Java source code and execute the HelloAgent class. To compile your classes, execute the following command after ensuring your environment is set up correctly (CLASSPATH and so forth):

```
javac jmxbook\ch2\*.java
```

2.4.2 Running the agent

The following command will run the HelloAgent:

```
java jmxbook.ch2.HelloAgent
```

After executing these commands, your agent should be running. The command prompt will not return, because the HelloAgent process does not exit. However, you should see the output "HelloAgent is running", indicating that the agent has started.

2.4.3 Contacting the agent

To contact the running HelloAgent, you need to use an HTML client. Any web browser will do the trick. For this example, the HTML adapter of the HelloAgent defaults to listening on port 9092. If you do not have that port available, go back to the HelloAgent code, add the following line after the adapter's constructor is called, and add your own port value:

```
adapter.setPort( [port value] );
```

Make the port a value that is available for use. For the remainder of this book, we will use the HTML adapter on port 9092.

Once you have a valid port value, open your browser and point it to http://localhost:9092. (If you have specified a different port, be sure to use that one instead of 9092.)

The HTML adapter running in your agent is now listening on the specified port for HTTP requests. When you open your browser to that address, the adapter responds by sending back HTML. You can now manage your agent by interacting with the adapter via this HTML.

Before continuing, you should congratulate yourself: you have successfully created your first MBean and agent. The next section will walk you through communicating with your agent using the HTML adapter.

2.5   *Working with the HTML adapter*

Now that you have the HTML adapter up and running on an agent that contains an MBean, it is time to connect and see what it provides for you. The HTML adapter provides access to a JMX agent through an HTML client (any web browser will do). It contains three main pages:

- *Agent View*—The Agent View is the first page you will see; it provides a summary of the MBeans contained within the agent. From this page you can filter the MBean list to provide more refined views.

- *MBean View*—This page provides details about a specific MBean. From this page you can set and get MBean attributes and invoke MBean operations.

- *Admin View*—This page enables you to register new MBeans on the agent.

2.5.1   *Agent View*

After contacting the agent with your web browser, the Agent View page appears (figure 2.5). Agent View is an HTML page received from the agent's HTML adapter; it shows you all the registered MBeans in this agent, representing them by presenting their `ObjectName` values. From this page, you can get to the MBean View or Admin View HTML page. Before checking out the other views, notice the Filter by Object Name field at the top of the page. Right now it displays *:*, which tells the agent to return a list of all the MBeans it contains. The MBean count on this page displays the total MBeans returned by each search.

This filter form allows you to filter the MBean list by partial or whole object names. For instance, if you type **HelloAgent:name=helloWorld1** into the field,

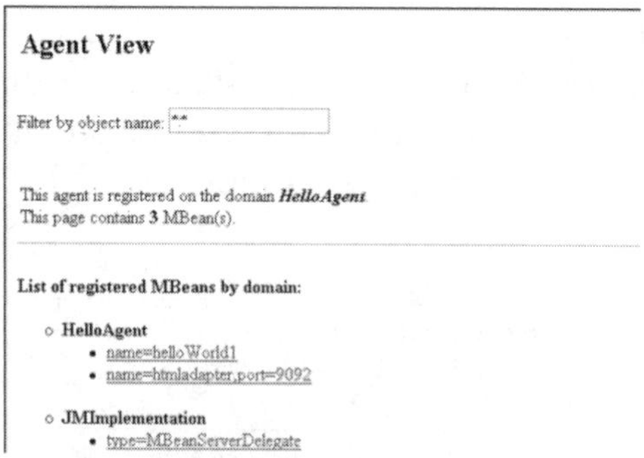

Agent View

Filter by object name: `*:*`

This agent is registered on the domain *HelloAgent*.
This page contains **3** MBean(s).

List of registered MBeans by domain:

o **HelloAgent**
  - name=helloWorld1
  - name=htmladapter,port=9092
o **JMImplementation**
  - type=MBeanServerDelegate

**Figure 2.5
The Agent View page
presented by the
HTML adapter**

the list will only show your `HelloWorld` MBean. You can enter partial object names by following the rules listed in table 2.2.

Table 2.2   Agent View filtering rules

MBean filter rule	Example
Use the * character as an alphanumeric wildcard for multiple characters, and as a wildcard for key/value pairs.	*:name=helloWorld1,*
Use the ? character as a wildcard for one character.	??Agent:name=helloWorld1
If you do not specify a domain name, the filter assumes you mean the default domain. You must specify at least one key/value pair (or use *).	*:*
Partial domain names are valid, but you cannot specify partial key/value pairs (for the key or the value).	??Agent:name=helloWorld1
All keys must be matched exactly or use a wildcard.	??Agent:*
Key/value pairs can be specified in any order.	

Try filtering the MBean list on your own; doing so will help you get the hang of the `ObjectName` format. When you are done, return the filter to *:* so you can view all MBeans.

Note that the list includes an MBean you did not register in section 2.4: the `MBeanServerDelegate` MBean. The `MBeanServerDelegate` is an MBean created by the `MBeanServer` to handle certain tasks—specifically, sending out notifications for the MBean server. The `MBeanServer` registers this MBean with a different domain in order to keep it separated from any others that will be registered.

Now that all the MBeans are visible, click the `MBeanServerDelegate` MBean link; it will take you to the MBean View presented by the HTML adapter.

2.5.2 *MBean View*

MBean View is another HTML page received from the HTML adapter that shows information about the MBean you clicked. MBean View presents you with all the details of the selected MBean, including the information shown in table 2.3.

Table 2.3 The elements of MBean View

MBean detail	Description or example
Class name	Main class of the MBean, such as `HelloWorld`.
Object name	Object name of the MBean, such as `HelloAgent:name=helloWorld1`.
Description	Description of the MBean. For Standard MBeans, the `MBeanServer` creates the description.
Attributes table	Lists the exposed attributes of the selected MBean, including the type, access, and value if possible. The attributes table also allows you to change writable attributes.
Exposed operations	List of operations exposed by the MBean. From here you can invoke an operation.
Reload Period	Tells the `MBeanServer` if it needs to reinstantiate this MBean, and if so, how often.
Unregister button	Tells the `MBeanServer` to unregister this MBean.

Figure 2.6 depicts the MBean view of the `MBeanServerDelegate` MBean.

Look at the table of MBean attributes in figure 2.6, and notice the values in the Access column. Currently, all rows contain the value RO, which stands for Read Only. Other possible values are WO (Write Only) and RW (Read/Write) access. As you might suspect, RO implies that the MBean's Java interface has provided only a getter method for an attribute. WO access implies that there is only a setter method, and RW implies that both a setter and a getter exist for this attribute.

The HTML adapter is using the reflection API to examine the method names from the interface. It removes the `get` or `set` of each method name and creates the attribute name from the remaining method name portion. Remaining methods (those without `get` or `set` at the start of their names) go into the Operations section of the MBean View.

By looking back at figure 2.6, you see that the `MBeanServerDelegate` exposes only read-only attributes. These attributes describe the reference implementation being used and which version of the JMX specification it implements.

Let's go back to the Agent View by clicking the Back to Agent View link. This time, select your `HelloWorld` MBean. Figure 2.7 shows what you should see.

The view of the `HelloWorld` MBean is displayed exactly like that of the `MBeanServerDelegate` MBean, except for two important differences. Remember that

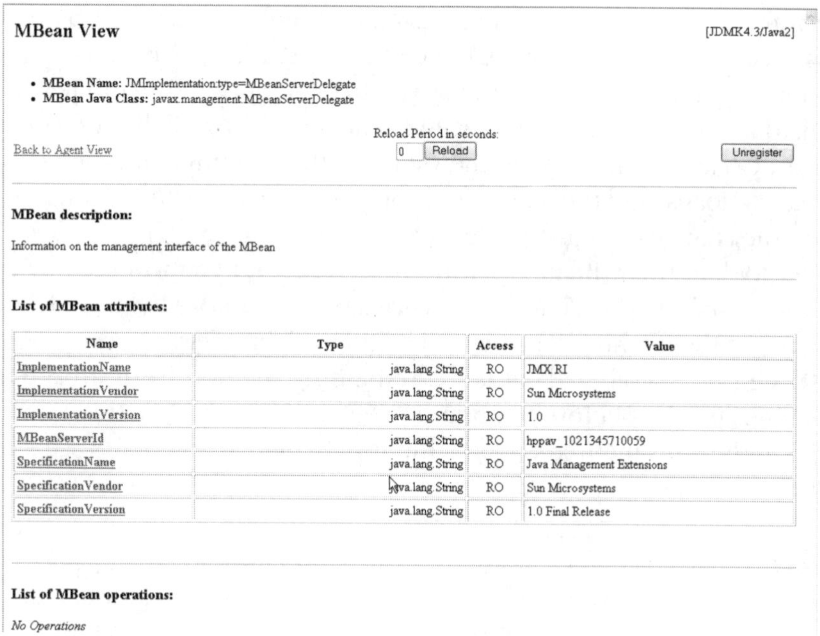

Figure 2.6   MBean View presented by the HTML adapter

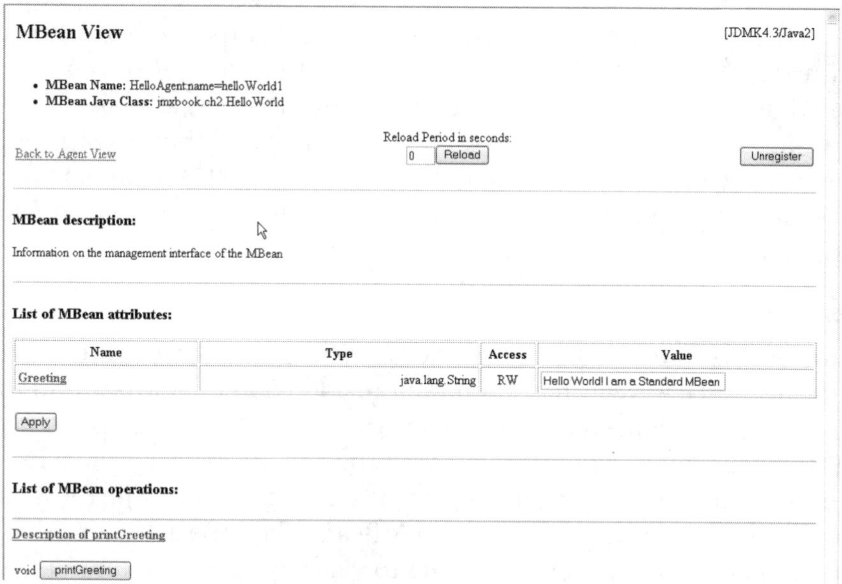

Figure 2.7   The HelloWorld MBean View

you wrote the `HelloWorld` MBean to contain a single exposed attribute: its greeting. That means the greeting attribute of the `HelloWorld` MBean is accessible for both reading and writing, and the attribute table of the MBean View includes a text field allowing you to enter a value. Clicking the Apply button commits any changes. Go ahead and change the value for the greeting, and then click Apply. The page reloads, and the text field displays the current value of `Greeting`, which reflects the changes you just made.

Now look at the MBean Operations section, and you will see one available operation. The MBean View constructs each operation as a button labeled with the name of the method. For the `HelloWorld` MBean View, you see a button with printGreeting as a label. That is the remaining method from the `HelloWorld-MBean` interface. Just before the button, you see *void*, which is the return type of the method. If this method had any input parameters, you would see a text field for each input value.

NOTE   The HTML adapter can provide input only for certain types of parameters. It supports only `Strings`, primitive types, and the standard classes related to the primitive types, such as `java.lang.Integer`.

When you click the printGreeting button, you will see two things happen. First, the web browser navigates to a page indicating that the method succeeded and did not return a value. Second, if you look at the output of your agent, you should see the update value you entered for the `Greeting` attribute.

Congratulations—you have successfully managed the `HelloWorld` MBean. There is only one more page to examine from the HTML adapter: the Admin View. Go back to the Agent View and click the Admin button to go to the Admin View of the `HelloAgent`.

2.5.3 Admin View

Using the first two HTML pages, you can configure and query MBeans registered in the agent. However, what if you want to add additional MBeans to the agent without writing more code? The Admin View is an HTML page presented by the HTML adapter that gives you access to the agent's MBean server in order to remove or add MBeans. From this page, you can specify an `ObjectName` value and associate it with a Java class that is an MBean. The MBean server will construct and register an MBean corresponding to your input. The Admin View presents four text fields (see figure 2.8):

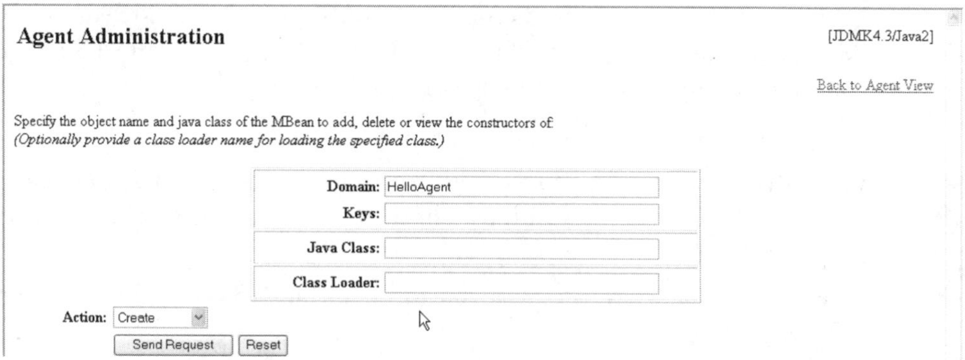

Agent Administration   [JDMK4.3/Java2]

Back to Agent View

Specify the object name and java class of the MBean to add, delete or view the constructors of.
(Optionally provide a class loader name for loading the specified class.)

Domain: HelloAgent

Keys:

Java Class:

Class Loader:

Action: Create

Send Request   Reset

Figure 2.8   The Admin View presented by the HTML adapter

- *Domain*—The HTML adapter defaults the Domain field to the domain of the agent. Currently, it shows `HelloAgent`, which is your domain. This is the first part of the object name.

- *Keys*—The Keys field requires input in the form *[name=value],* * . This field represents the key/value portion of an object name.

- *Java Class*—This field requires a full Java class name of the class of the MBean you want to create.

- *Class Loader*—The Class Loader field is the only field that is optional. You can specify a class loader for the MBean server to use when attempting to load the Java class specified in the previous field.

To get a good understanding of this page, let's use it to create some more MBeans. As you will see in the next section, you can have many MBeans of the same type in one `MBeanServer`, as long as their object names are unique.

2.5.4 *Registering/unregistering MBeans on the HelloAgent*

Let's load another instance of the `HelloWorld` MBean into the agent by using the Admin View. Leave the domain value as `HelloAgent`. Type in **name=helloWorld2** for the Keys field. For the Java Class field, type **jmxbook.ch2.HelloWorld**, the implementation of the `HelloWorldMBean` interface.

NOTE   Any class you specify in the Java Class field must be accessible to the `MBeanServer` of the agent. For the `HelloAgent`, this requirement means the input Java Class value must be in its local `CLASSPATH`.

Leave the Class Loader field empty, to tell the `HelloAgent` MBean server to use the default class loader to find the Java Class value. The agent will use the values you have entered to create an object name like

```
HelloAgent:name=helloWorld2
```

With all the values in place, you are ready to create this new `HelloWorld` instance. At this point, you have three Action options to choose from in the drop-down list:

- *Create*—Tells the `MBeanServer` to create an MBean using a no-argument constructor
- *Unregister*—Works only if you have specified an `ObjectName` of an existing MBean registered in the agent
- *Constructors*—Loads the specified MBean class and presents you with a list of constructors to use in creation of the MBean

These options are similar to the Operations section of the MBean View. For now, choose the Create option.

Click the Send Request button, and you will see a success message telling you the agent created and registered the new MBean. Go back to the Agent View and verify this using the list of MBeans.

Using constructors with arguments

Remember that your `HelloWorldMBean` implementation class, `HelloWorld`, has two constructors: the default constructor and a constructor that takes an initial value for the `Greeting` attribute. Let's register a final instance of the `HelloWorld` MBean by using this second constructor. To do so, perform the following steps:

1 Go back to the Admin View and enter appropriate values to create a new `HelloWorld` MBean. Be sure to enter a unique Key value (such as **name=helloWorld3**).

2 This time, select Constructors from the Action list and click the Send Request button. You will see a list of constructors (in this case, two), one of which displays a text field for its single input parameter.

3 Type a value for the `Greeting` attribute, and then click the Create button associated with the constructor. If you entered valid data for the object name and class fields, you will see the "creation successful" message again.

4 Go back to the Agent View to verify that the MBean list now contains three instances of the `HelloWorld` MBean.

2.6 Using MBean notifications

After creating and registering your own MBean in the previous section, you already have enough knowledge to start working with JMX. You have learned how to create a Standard MBean, how to add it to a simple JMX agent, and how to manage that agent by using the HTML adapter. However, you are still missing a key ingredient: notifications.

JMX notifications are Java objects used to send information from MBeans and agents to other objects that have registered to receive them (see figure 2.9). Objects interested in receiving events are notification listeners—they implement the `javax.management.NotificationListener` interface.

Notifications are an important piece of JMX because they allow for the transmission of events. JMX events can be anything from the changing of an MBean attribute to the registration of a new MBean on an MBean server.

To give you a quick introduction to notifications, you'll add them to the `HelloWorld` MBean in this section. In chapter 6, we'll cover the notification model in depth.

2.6.1 Adding notification code to the HelloWorld MBean

For the `HelloWorld` MBean to send notifications, it needs to allow objects interested in receiving notifications to register for them. JMX supports two mechanisms for MBeans to provide listeners to register for notifications:

- Implement the `javax.management.NotificationBroadcaster` interface
- Extend the `javax.management.NotificationBroadcasterSupport` class (which in turn implements the `NotificationBroadcaster` interface)

The advantage of implementing the interface is that it frees your class from being tied to a particular super class. The advantage of extending the broadcaster

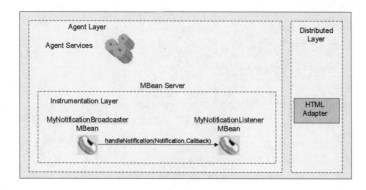

Figure 2.9
Notification being sent to a registered listener from an MBean

support class is that you do not have to write code for the broadcaster interface. If your MBean does not need to extend a class, then have it extend the NotificationBroadcasterSupport class and reuse that implementation. The HelloWorld class does not need any special super class, so you are free to extend the broadcaster support class, NotificationBroadcasterSupport, as shown in listing 2.3.

Listing 2.3   HelloWorld.java

```
package jmxbook.ch2;

import javax.management.*;

public class HelloWorld extends NotificationBroadcasterSupport
implements HelloWorldMBean        ❶ Extend NotificationBroadcasterSupport class
{
    public HelloWorld()     ❷ Define two public
    {                          constructors
      this.greeting = "Hello World! I am a Standard MBean";
    }

      public HelloWorld( String greeting )     ❷ Define two public
    {                                             constructors
      this.greeting = greeting;
    }

    public void setGreeting( String greeting )
    {
      this.greeting = greeting;

      Notification notification = new Notification(
        "jmxbook.ch2.helloWorld.test", this, -1,
        System.currentTimeMillis(), greeting );     ❸ Create
      sendNotification( notification );   ←─┐          javax.management.Notification
    }                                        │          object
                                             │
    public String getGreeting()             Send notification
    {
      return greeting;
    }

    public void printGreeting()
    {
      System.out.println( greeting );
    }

    private String greeting;

}//class
```

❶ You change the declaration of the `HelloWorld` class by extending the `Notifica-tionBroadcasterSupport` class. This super class provides the MBean with methods that allow other objects to register as notification listeners and allow the MBean to send notifications. The super class implements the `javax.management.NotificationBroadcaster` interface examined after this code discussion.

❷ For this example, you are sending only basic notifications. At this step in the code, you create a `Notification` object with the constructor

```
public Notification(java.lang.String type, java.lang.Object source,
           long sequenceNumber,long timeStamp,
           java.lang.String message)
```

The parameters of this constructor are listed in table 2.4.

Table 2.4 The `Notification` constructor parameters

Parameter	Description
`java.lang.String` type	Dot-separated `String` value used to identify the notification. Used as a short description of the purpose and meaning for the notification.
`java.lang.Object` source	The MBean that generated this notification. This will be either the object reference or the `ObjectName` of an MBean.
`long` sequenceNumber	A number that identifies this notification in a possible sequence of notifications.
`long` timestamp	A timestamp of the creation of the notification.
`java.lang.String` message	A `String` value containing a message from the notification source.

❸ By extending the `NotificationBroadcasterSupport` class, you not only gain the implementation of the `NotificationBroadcaster` interface, but also inherit the `sendNotification()` method. Your `HelloWorld` MBean can use this convenience method when it needs to send a notification, and the super class will send it to all appropriate listeners. Appropriate listeners are those that have registered with the MBean and whose filter object accepts the particular type of notification.

Examination of the NotificationBroadcaster interface

The previous example used the `NotificationBroadcasterSupport` class. This class provides subclasses with an implementation of the `NotificationBroad-caster` interface. The super class implements the `NotificationBroadcaster` interface shown next:

```
public interface NotificationBroadcaster
{
  public void addNotificationListener(
              NotificationListener listener,
```

```
                         NotificationFilter filter,
                         Object handback )
                         throws IllegalArgumentException;
      public MBeanNotificationInfo[] getNotificationInfo();

      public void removeNotificationListener(
                    NotificationListener listener )
                    throws ListenerNotFoundException;

}
```

MBeans implementing this interface provide other objects with a mechanism to register for notifications by using the `addNotificationListener()` method. This method accepts a `NotificationListener` object, a `NotificationFilter` object, and a handback object as parameters.

The `NotificationListener` parameter is an object that implements the `NotificationListener` interface, which specifies a `handleNotification()` method. This method will be invoked as a callback when a notification needs to be delivered to a listener.

The `NotificationFilter` parameter is an optional argument that will allow the MBean to filter which notifications to send to the listener based on the listener's preferences created in the filter. The handback argument is sent back to the client each time a notification is delivered.

Notice the similarity between this notification registration and delivery mechanism and the Java event model of listener registration.

2.6.2 *Changes to the HelloAgent class*

In order to send notifications, you need to have something to receive them. For this small notification example, you'll make your `HelloAgent` class act as a notification listener. You need to modify your code in a few ways. First, the `HelloAgent` class needs to implement the `NotificationListener` interface. The `HelloAgent` will still create and register both the HTML adapter and the `HelloWorld` MBean. After it has created the MBeans, it can now register with the `HelloWorld` MBean as a notification listener interested in receiving notifications. The code changes for the `HelloAgent` class appear in listing 2.4 in bold.

Listing 2.4   HelloAgent.java

```
package jmxbook.ch2;                                       Implement  ❶
                                                     NotificationListener
import javax.management.*;                                      interface
import com.sun.jdmk.comm.HtmlAdaptorServer;

public class HelloAgent implements NotificationListener
```

```
{
    private MBeanServer mbs = null;
  public HelloAgent ( )
    {
       mbs = MBeanServerFactory.createMBeanServer( "HelloAgent" );
       HtmlAdaptorServer adapter = new HtmlAdaptorServer();
       HelloWorld hw = new HelloWorld();
     ObjectName adapterName = null;
     ObjectName helloWorldName = null;
     try
       {
        adapterName = new ObjectName(
                          "HelloAgent:name=htmladapter,port=9092" );
        mbs.registerMBean( adapter, adapterName );
          adapter.setPort( 9092 )
          adapter.start();
          helloWorldName = new ObjectName(
            "HelloAgent:name=helloWorld1" );
          mbs.registerMBean( hw, helloWorldName );
          hw.addNotificationListener( this, null, null );
      }
        catch( Exception e )
        {
          e.printStackTrace();
      }
    }//constructor
    public void handleNotification(
          Notification notif, Object handback )
      {
       System.out.println( "Receiving notification..." );
       System.out.println( notif.getType() );
       System.out.println( notif.getMessage() );
      }
    public static void main( String args[] )
      {
       HelloAgent agent = new HelloAgent();
      }
  }//class
```

❷ Register to receive notifications

❸ Implemented from listener interface

❶ The first addition to the agent is the inclusion of the NotificationListener interface. Recall that this interface declares a single method, handleNotification(), which will be called when a notification is being delivered from a source the listener has registered with.

❷ After registering the MBean with the MBean server, the `HelloAgent` class adds itself to the `HelloWorld` MBean as a listener. To do this, it passes itself as the `NotificationListener` parameter to the MBean's `addNotificationListener()` method (inherited from its super class, `NotificationBroadcasterSupport`).

❸ As mentioned earlier, in order to receive notifications, an object must implement the `NotificationListener` interface. The interface declares a single method, `handleNotification()`, which is a callback method invoked by the sender to deliver notifications to the listener. For this implementation, the `HelloAgent` class just prints out some of the members of the incoming notification.

Getting results

To test the notification example, you need to compile the HelloAgent.java and HelloWorld.java files and execute the resulting `HelloAgent` class. (Look back at section 2.5 for a reminder.) Once the agent is running, open your web browser to http://localhost:9092 to see the Agent View of your `HelloAgent` class. To perform the test and receive a notification, follow these steps:

1   Navigate to the MBean View of the `HelloWorld` MBean by clicking on the corresponding object name in the list. Look back at section 2.5.2 for a refresher.

2   The `HelloWorld` MBean sends a notification when its greeting is changed, so enter a new value and click Apply. For example, enter **I have changed my greeting**.

3   Look at the output window of your `HelloAgent`. You should see the following:

```
Receiving notification...
jmxbook.ch2.helloWorld.test
I have changed my greeting
```

The output contains your printed message, "Receiving notification…", the notification type, and the message contained in the notification.

2.7 Summary

This chapter gave you some hands-on experience with much of the JMX framework. In this chapter you developed a manageable resource, and created and ran a simple JMX agent. We discussed how to register an MBean, ensure that it has a unique name, and create an MBean server.

In addition, you worked with the HTML adapter that comes with the Sun reference implementation. By constructing the `HelloWorld` example, you should now understand that MBean development is simple from the JMX point of view.

MBeans expose resources with just a few lines of code. Part 2 of this book covers instrumenting resources by walking you through numerous MBean examples.

Finally, to round out your JMX introduction, we gave you a crash course on JMX notifications. We will discuss notifications in greater detail in chapter 6 and make a stronger case for why notifications are an essential part of managing resources.

In chapter 3, you'll begin to develop a JMX agent that you'll enhance throughout the remainder of the book. This agent will be used for many of the examples in other chapters.

Building a foundation 3

This chapter's purpose is to lay the groundwork for many of the examples throughout the book. As you read the following chapters, most of your coding time will be spent writing and working with MBeans. Most examples in this book are executed within the chapter to demonstrate the working code. In all the examples, you will need to have a JMX agent to contain your MBeans. In order to spare you from repeatedly writing the same agent code, you'll construct your JMX agent in this chapter to use throughout the book. In addition, as the book progresses, you will add functionality to the agent by including other services or utilities.

3.1 *The scope of the agent*

Before you begin writing any code, you should understand that the agent you will write in this chapter will end up closely resembling the `HelloAgent` class from chapter 2. In fact, there will be only one major difference. The important point is that as the book moves along, you will add code to your agent as needed. Therefore, because we have not discussed any new topics, your agent code will closely resemble the `HelloAgent` example.

Your agent will be defined by the class `jmxbook.ch3.JMXBookAgent`. At this point in the book, it has two responsibilities:

- Create an MBean server
- Provide connectivity

Just like the `HelloAgent` from the previous chapter, your `JMXBookAgent` class must contain an MBean server. In addition, it too will create an HTML adapter so that you can examine and interact with MBeans residing on the agent. However, in addition to the HTML adapter, you will add a Java Remote Method Invocation (RMI) connector to the agent in order to provide your future code examples with a programmatic way of interacting with the agent. Figure 3.1 illustrates the two ways this agent will be used.

Looking at the figure, you can see that you will be able to interact with your agent both through a web browser and by using a Java RMI client. You will construct a factory class for creating RMI clients later in this chapter. Later examples that need an RMI client will use this factory class to acquire it.

3.1.1 *Using the HTML adapter*

Adding the HTML adapter to your agent will be useful for some of the reasons presented in chapter 2. It will give you a view into the agent, allowing you to see a list of MBeans residing in the MBean server. Not only that, but as you wit-

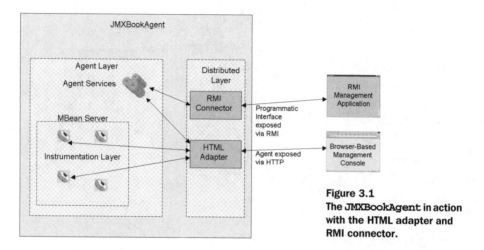

Figure 3.1
**The JMXBookAgent in action
with the HTML adapter and
RMI connector.**

nessed in chapter 2, you will be able to manipulate MBeans, add more MBeans, and remove MBeans from an agent. In future examples, you will typically use the HTML adapter for testing example MBeans by viewing and accessing their attributes and operations.

3.1.2 *Using the RMI connector*

The RMI connector serves the same purpose as the HTML adapter: it allows outside clients to contact and interact with a JMX agent. The RMI connector you will be using is provided by Sun Microsystems as a contribution to its JMX RI.

The RMI connector comes in two parts: a server and a client. The server part resides with the JMX agent in order to provide access to the MBean server. The RMI client resides with other client-side processes that wish to contact the JMX agent. The RMI client shields users from having to write Java RMI code. Figure 3.2 illustrates how the RMI connector can be used to create MBeans from remote locations.

In future examples, you will use the RMI connector to interact programmatically with your agent. Because the HTML adapter does not work with all class types, you will sometimes need to access the agent via example code. In these cases, you will use the RMI client.

For the purposes of this chapter, we won't discuss the features or API of the RMI connector—we will only explain how to add it to the agent and use it.

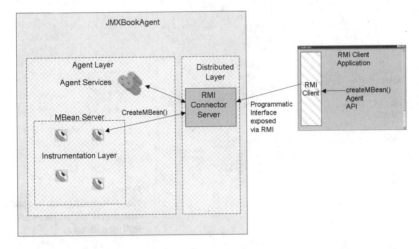

Figure 3.2 The JMXBookAgent showing the different parts of the RMI connector with example createMBean() method delegation from client to server.

3.2 *Writing the JMXBookAgent class*

Writing the JMXBookAgent class is not that difficult (as illustrated by the HelloAgent from chapter 2). The process of completing the class is broken into four parts:

- Writing the class definition and constructor
- Adding the HTML adapter
- Adding the RMI connector
- Adding the main() method

3.2.1 *Class definition and constructor*

The first step includes declaring the class and writing its constructor. Listing 3.1 shows the class body and constructor in the source file JMXBookAgent.java. Notice that the package is jmxbook.ch3.

Listing 3.1   The first part of JMXBookAgent.java

```
package jmxbook.ch3;

import com.sun.jdmk.comm.*;
import javax.management.*;

public class JMXBookAgent
{
```

```
    private MBeanServer server = null;

    public JMXBookAgent()                                    Create MBean
    {                                                            server
        System.out.println("\n\tCREATE the MBeanServer.");
        server = MBeanServerFactory.createMBeanServer("JMXBookAgent");  ◁┘

        startHTMLAdapter();      │ Add agent
        startRMIConnector();     │ connectivity
    }

}
```

At this point, you need to import only two packages for the agent: `javax.manage-ment.*` and `com.sun.jdmk.comm.*` (later in the book, you will add more packages as necessary). The latter package includes the classes for the HTML adapter and the RMI connector.

The constructor must initialize its MBean server. It does so using the domain name `JMXBookAgent`. In addition, the constructor invokes two methods: one starts the HTML adapter, and the other starts the RMI connector. The next two sections discuss the implementation of the connectivity invoked by the constructor.

3.2.2 Adding agent connectivity

To make your agent more useful, you'll add an adapter and connector that allow you to interact with the agent visually and programmatically. You need the HTML adapter in order to perform tasks similar to those in chapter 2: it is a quick way to view the contents of the agent (its MBeans). If you used the HTML adapter exclusively, you would not be able to register and receive MBean notifications.

However, in order to work with notifications (and for later examples), you need to interact with the agent programmatically. To do so, you will add the RMI connector to the agent. It will let you connect to the agent using an RMI client and directly through program code.

The next two sections walk you through adding the connectivity to the agent.

Adding the HTML adapter

You saw the code for adding the HTML adapter in chapter 2. In this chapter, this code is broken out into its own method called `startHTMLAdapter()`. Listing 3.2 shows the method implementation.

Listing 3.2   startHTMLAdapter() method that adds the HTML adapter to the agent

```
protected void startHTMLAdapter()
{
  HtmlAdaptorServer adapter = new HtmlAdaptorServer();
  ObjectName adapterName = null;

  try
  {
    adapter.setPort( 9092 );
    //create the HTML adapter
    adapterName = new ObjectName(
                     "JMXBookAgent:name=html,port=9092" );
    server.registerMBean( adapter, adapterName );
    adapter.start();
  }
  catch(Exception e)
  {
    ExceptionUtil.printException( e );
    System.out.println("Error Starting HTML Adapter for Agent");
  }

}
```

Remember from the previous chapter that the HTML adapter is an MBean and therefore must be registered with the agent like any other MBean. It needs an `ObjectName` instance, which you provide with the domain of the agent and a few descriptive properties. Once it is registered on the MBean server, you call its `start()` method to initialize it. If any errors occur, you print them out to the agent output.

Notice in the `catch` block that the method uses a class called `ExceptionUtil`; it's a utility class that you'll write at the end of this chapter. It contains a single static method, `printException()`, which prints `MBeanExceptions` and the exceptions wrapped within.

Adding the RMI connector

You have seen the HTML adapter created and registered twice in this book, but you have yet to see any code for the RMI connector. (Remember, we aren't covering the connector extensively in this chapter—we're only showing how to use it during a simple test. Later chapters use the connector to add and manipulate MBeans in the agent. For a detailed discussion of the connector, you can jump ahead to chapter 9.)

Listing 3.3 shows the `startRMIConnector()` method that is invoked by the agent constructor. Its purpose is to create and start the RMI connector for this agent.

**Listing 3.3   startRMIConnector() method that adds the RMI connector server
to the agent**

```
protected void startRMIConnector()
{
    RmiConnectorServer connector = new RmiConnectorServer();
    ObjectName connectorName = null;

    try
    {
      connector.setPort( 2099 );
      connectorName = new ObjectName(
                "JMXBookAgent:name=RMIConnector");
      server.registerMBean( connector, connectorName );
      connector.start();
    }
    catch(Exception e)
    {
      ExceptionUtil.printException( e );
    }
}
```

The implementation of this method is almost identical to the `startHTML-Adapter()` method we already examined. First, you create the `RmiConnectorServer` instance (which is the connector MBean) and register it on the `MBeanServer` using a new `ObjectName` instance. After registering the connector, you invoke its `start()` method, preparing it to receive clients. After we examine the `main()` method of the agent, you will create the RMI client factory class used to create clients for the RMI connector.

3.2.3 *Finishing with a main() method*

Listing 3.4 shows the `main()` method used to start this agent from a command-line prompt. It simply constructs an instance of the agent and print out messages for the user.

Listing 3.4   The main() method of the JMXBookAgent class

```
public static void main(String[] args)
{
    System.out.println("\n~~~~~~~~~~~~~~~~~~~~~~~~" +
    "~~~~~~~~~~~~~~~~~~~~~~~~~~~~~~~~~~~~~~~~~~~~~~~~~~~~");
    System.out.println("\n>>> START of JMXBook Agent");
    System.out.println("\n>>> CREATE the agent...");
    JMXBookAgent agent = new JMXBookAgent();
    System.out.println("\nAgent is Ready for Service...\n");
}
```

With the completion of the main() method, you have finished the agent code. As mentioned earlier, you still need to provide a way to create an RMI client when you want to interact with the agent using the RMI connector. The next section presents a utility class called RMIClientFactory that provides the solution.

3.3 *Writing the RMIClientFactory class*

The RMIClientFactory class is used as a convenient way to acquire an RMI client to connect to your JMX agent. Currently, the factory class returns a client with all the default values, which will connect to the agent. You will learn how to change the defaults for the RMI connector in chapter 9. Listing 3.5 shows the class.

Listing 3.5   RMIClientFactory.java

```java
package jmxbook.ch3;

import javax.management.*;
import com.sun.jdmk.comm.*;

public class RMIClientFactory
{
  public static RmiConnectorClient getClient()
  {
    RmiConnectorClient client = new RmiConnectorClient();
      RmiConnectorAddress address = new RmiConnectorAddress();
    address.setPort( 2099 );
      System.out.println("\t\tTYPE\t= "   +
      address.getConnectorType ());
      System.out.println("\t\tPORT\t= "   + address.getPort());
      System.out.println("\t\tHOST\t= "   + address.getHost());
      System.out.println("\t\tSERVER\t= " + address.getName());

      try
      {
        client.connect( address );
      }
      catch( Exception e )
      {
          ExceptionUtil.printException( e );
      }

    return client;
  }

}
```

To create a client, the `getClient()` method creates an `RmiConnectorClient` object and initializes it with an `RmiConnectorAddress` object. This method configures the address object to locate the RMI server on port 2099, which you used when starting the server.

3.4 *Writing the ExceptionUtil class*

`ExceptionUtil` is a simple class that lets you print out the entire exception hierarchy of an `MBeanException` exception class. `MBeanException` is the main exception class used to wrap all exceptions stemming from operations on MBeans or agents. Listing 3.6 shows the `ExceptionUtil` class.

Listing 3.6 ExceptionUtil.java

```java
package jmxbook.ch3;

import javax.management.*;

public class ExceptionUtil
{
  public static void printException( Exception e )
  {
    StringBuffer        exceptionName = new StringBuffer();
    Exception           exc = null;

    System.out.println("-------[ Exception ]-------");
    e.printStackTrace();
    if (e instanceof MBeanException)
    {
      boolean hasEmbeddedExceptions = true;
      Exception embeddedExc = e;
      while (hasEmbeddedExceptions)
      {
        embeddedExc = (( MBeanException )
                    embeddedExc).getTargetException();
        System.out.println("-------[ Embedded Exception ]-------");

        embeddedExc.printStackTrace();

        if (!(embeddedExc instanceof MBeanException))
        {
          hasEmbeddedExceptions = false;
        }
      }
    }
  }
}
```

You will see this class used in many of the examples throughout the book.

3.5 *Running the agent*

Now that you have constructed the agent and written a factory class that provides RMI clients, it is time to test the agent. In this section, you will test the agent by connecting to it with an HTML client and an RMI client.

Using one of the build environments created in chapter 2, compile the `JMXBookAgent`, `RMIClientFactory`, and `ExceptionUtil` classes. With the code compiled, you are ready to run the agent. To execute the agent, use the following command:

```
java jmxbook.ch3.JMXBookAgent
```

You should see the following output from the agent:

```
~~~~~~~~~~~~~~~~~~~~~~~~~~~~~~~~~~~~~~~~~~~~~~~~~~~~~~~~~~~~~~~~~~~~

>>> START of JMXBook Agent

>>> CREATE the agent...

        CREATE the MBeanServer.

Agent is Ready for Service...
```

With the `JMXBookAgent` running, you can now connect to it using the two methods you have set up (HTML and RMI).

3.5.1 *Connecting to the agent with the browser*

To connect to the agent's HTML adapter, open a web browser to http://local-host:9092 (opening on the same machine). The HTML adapter should display the Agent View in your browser. The Agent View should show you three MBeans: the adapter, the connector, and `MBeanServerDelegate`. (In fact, you could use this agent to redo the `HelloWorld` example in chapter 2.)

3.5.2 *Connecting to the agent with an RMI client*

To test the RMI connector, you need to write a little program to use an RMI client that reaches the agent. You'll take the `HelloWorld` MBean from chapter 2 and register it in the agent by using an RMI client. Listing 3.7 shows the `HelloWorld-Setup` class, which does just that. You'll use setup classes like this one throughout the book to register other MBeans, so this won't be the last time you see this type of simple program.

Listing 3.7   HelloWorldSetup.java

```java
package jmxbook.ch3;

import javax.management.*;
import jmxbook.ch2.*;
import com.sun.jdmk.comm.*;

public class HelloWorldSetup
{
  public HelloWorldSetup()
  {
    try
    {
      RmiConnectorClient client = RMIClientFactory.getClient();
      ObjectName hwName = new
                  ObjectName( "JMXBookAgent:name=helloWorld");

      client.createMBean( "jmxbook.ch2.HelloWorld",
                          hwName );

      client.invoke( hwName, "printGreeting", null, null );
    }
    catch( Exception e )
    {
      e.printStackTrace();
    }
  }

  public static void main( String args[] )
  {
    HelloWorldSetup setup = new HelloWorldSetup ();
  }
}
```

Just a reminder: don't worry about the particulars of the RMI client right now. Keep in mind that it lets you invoke the methods of the MBean server contained in the JMX agent. For instance, in the setup class, you invoke the createMBean() and invoke() methods. Both of these methods correspond directly to methods in the MBeanServer API.

Because the agent is already running, compile and run the setup class. You should see the following output:

```
TYPE    = SUN RMI
PORT    = 2099
HOST    = t8100x0232
SERVER  = name=RmiConnectorServer
```

Looking at the agent output, you should see an additional line:

```
Hello World! I am a Standard MBean.
```

3.6 *Summary*

In this chapter, we laid out the basis for many of the future examples in the book. By creating the `JMXBookAgent` and `RMIClientFactory` classes, you will save time and effort each time you need to use an example agent in later chapters. In addition, writing these classes provided the opportunity for us to introduce the RMI connector, which you will also use in later chapters.

The agent you created in this chapter is very simple; it is on par with the simple agent created in chapter 2. However, the `JMXBookAgent` class is only in foundation form for now; you will add to it as we progress to chapters that require the agent to have more features.

With the groundwork laid for future examples, you are ready to move to chapter 4. It begins the detailed discussion of MBeans by examining the Standard MBean type.

Part 2

Instrumenting manageable resources

In part 1, you learned about the JMX architecture and how it provides a simple, scalable management solution. Chapter 1 introduced you to the power and benefits of JMX, and also described how JMX components work together. You learned that JMX consists of three component layers: instrumentation, agent, and distributed. In chapter 2, you began using JMX for the first time by constructing a working example using an MBean, a simple JMX agent, and a simple notification. Now you are ready to begin dealing with each component layer in more detail and depth.

Part 2 of this book explores the instrumentation layer. The four chapters in this part of the book discuss different types of MBeans, as well as using notifications.

Chapter 4, "MBeans for Stable Resources," covers the Standard MBean. In this chapter, you will learn how to create and use Standard MBeans. Chapter 4 uses Standard MBeans to demonstrate how you can use MBeans to make your applications more componentized and configurable.

Chapter 5, "MBeans for Changing Resources," discusses the Dynamic MBean. In this chapter you will learn the differences between Dynamic and Standard MBeans, and how to create your own Dynamic MBeans. The examples in this chapter are centered around other Java technologies such as Enterprise JavaBeans and the Jini network technology.

Chapter 6, "Communication with MBeans Using Notifications," interrupts the coverage of MBeans to discuss using JMX notifications. In chapter 6, you learn more about notifications and the important role they play in the life of MBeans and application management.

Chapter 7, "MBeans on-the-fly," covers the Model MBean. The Model MBean is provided with a JMX implementation. You don't create the Model MBean class; rather, you instantiate it and configure it at runtime.

MBeans for
stable resources

- Understanding common development rules for all MBeans
- Examining rules specific to developing Standard MBeans
- Using the Standard MBean development patterns
- Exploring Standard MBean examples

65

In this chapter, we will discuss the simplest type of MBean: the Standard MBean. You created this type of MBean in chapter 2. Standard MBeans are intended for resources that have well-known, stable interfaces. This chapter shows how you can use Standard MBeans to configure application resources (a log utility and application properties) and to break applications into components. If you need the quickest way to implement a resource, the Standard MBean is for you. Standard MBeans expose a resource with an explicitly declared management interface that is unchanging.

In addition, because this is the first of three chapters on MBean types, we also discuss some of the common construction rules of all types of MBeans. After completing this chapter, you will know much more about Standard MBeans, including how to write them and when to use them.

4.1 Laying the MBean groundwork

As we just hinted, before diving into a discussion about writing Standard MBeans, we first need to describe certain traits that are required across all MBean types. Whether you are coding a Standard or Dynamic MBean, you must follow certain rules. After covering these common rules, we will explore the unique traits of a Standard MBean.

4.1.1 Common coding rules for all MBeans

When developing any MBean, you must adhere to the following rules:

- An MBean must be a concrete Java class. A *concrete* class is a Java class that is not abstract, and can therefore be instantiated. Remember from chapter 2 that you dynamically loaded the `HelloWorld` MBean into your simple JMX agent using the HTML adapter. For the agent to successfully create the MBean using reflection, the class name you used had to correspond to a concrete class.

- An MBean must have a public constructor. No additional rules apply to the constructor other than that it must be public. It can have arguments—and the class can contain as many constructors as needed.

- An MBean must implement either its own MBean interface or the `javax.man-agement.DynamicMBean` interface. An MBean interface is any interface that follows a naming scheme `ClassNameMBean`. We will cover MBean interfaces thoroughly in this chapter. MBeans using an MBean interface are Standard MBeans.

A Standard MBean is an MBean that implements its own MBean interface. As mentioned earlier, the `HelloWorld` MBean from chapter 2 was a Standard MBean. It was a concrete class, had a public constructor, and implemented an interface named `HelloWorldMBean`.

Enabling notifications

In addition to following the three rules we just listed, all MBeans can optionally implement the `javax.management.NotificationBroadcaster` interface. This interface allows MBeans to send notifications to interested listeners. Notifications are Java objects sent from JMX components to other objects that have registered as notification listeners. MBeans that implement the `NotificationBroadcaster` interface gain methods that allow objects to register with them to receive notifications. The notification delivery mechanism is very similar to the Java event model, and is covered in chapter 6.

4.1.2 Using Standard MBeans

Now that you know the rules that all MBeans must follow, let's more closely examine the Standard MBean. The Standard MBean is an MBean that uses an explicitly declared management interface to interact with a manageable resource. A *management interface* is the set of methods and attributes exposed by an MBean that management applications can use to manage a resource (via an MBean).

Standard MBean attributes are class members exposed for management by the use of *getter* and *setter* methods. Standard MBean operations are the public class methods in addition to the getters and setters. Operations and attributes are discovered by introspection at the JMX agent level.

Once created, the Standard MBean's management interface does not change. In addition, more than any other MBean type, it embodies one of the major benefits of using JMX: it is simple. Standard MBeans should be used when the interface to a managed resource is well defined or unlikely to change.

For example, Standard MBeans are good for resources that are still being developed, because the resource will have a well-known interface and the management interface can be written explicitly. If you plan to use an MBean to expose part of a new application in development, you should use a Standard MBean. The MBean is simple to develop, and you can create it concurrently with your application. In chapter 5, you will learn about writing MBeans that are not as straightforward as the Standard MBean. In the following sections, you will see that the Standard MBean is the simplest way to expose a resource for management.

4.2 *Composing the standard management interface*

All information about an MBean must be gathered from its management interface. In the previous section, you read that an MBean must implement an MBean interface or the `javax.management.DynamicMBean` interface. Standard MBeans are MBeans that implement a user-developed MBean interface.

An MBean interface is any interface that follows the naming convention `XMBean`, where *X* is some implementing class name (for example, `PrinterMBean`). An MBean interface declares methods that expose the attributes and operations of a manageable resource.

> **NOTE** One item of importance is that your MBean interfaces must be in the same package as your implementation class. For example, if the `PrinterMBean` interface was in the package `jmxbook.ch6` and the `Printer` class was in `jmxbook.ch4`, then you would not have a valid MBean.

Remember that a management interface includes the set of attributes and operations exposed by an MBean, allowing management applications to use the MBean. In addition, a management interface includes an MBean's constructors and notifications. The following section covers the composition of an MBean's management interface.

4.2.1 *Components of the management interface*

The management interface of an MBean is composed of the four following items:

- Its public constructors
- Its attributes
- Its operations
- Its notifications

The next few sections cover the details of each of the four components of the management interface of an MBean. The description of the management interface pertains to all types of MBeans. MBeans differ in the way the management interface is exposed, but all management interfaces are composed of the same four parts.

Public constructors

As you witnessed in chapter 2 when using the HTML adapter via a web browser, MBeans can be dynamically loaded into JMX agents. Agents do this using any of the public constructors exposed by the MBean. Constructors are included in the definition of the management interface because a particular constructor could define specific behavior over the life of the MBean object. For instance, one constructor may tell the MBean to log all of its actions, and another may make it silent. Any way of altering the behavior of an MBean is included as part of its management interface. For Standard MBeans, agents must use introspection to discover the public constructors.

Attributes

Attributes are a vital part of the management interface of an MBean. The attributes describe the manageable resource. Remember, a manageable resource is some application or resource exposed for management by an MBean. For instance, an MBean managing a device such as a printer might have attributes for the number of paper trays, job counts, and so forth.

With Standard MBeans, you expose attributes by declaring getter and setter methods. For an attribute `JobCount` of a printer MBean, there would be a method `getJobCount()`. Recall from chapter 2 that getter methods define read access to an attribute, and setter methods define write access. If both a setter and a getter exist, the MBean grants read/write access to that attribute.

Operations

Operations correspond to actions that can be initiated on the manageable resource. For Standard MBeans, exposed operations are simply the remaining operations that are not getters or setters. Staying with the printer example, in an MBean managing a printer, you might find an operation like `cancelPrintJob()`. Operations are methods like any other; they can have multiple parameters and optionally return a value.

Notifications

Notifications allow MBeans to communicate with registered listeners. You encountered them in chapter 2 when you added a notification to the `Hello-World` example.

In order to emit notifications, an MBean must implement the `javax.management.NotificationBroadcaster` interface. This interface provides methods for sending notifications, as well as methods for other objects to register as listeners on the implementing MBean. We will skip notifications for now, but we cover them in detail in chapter 6.

4.2.2 *Example: a printer MBean interface*

Now that you understand the four major parts of a management interface, let's look at an example of an MBean interface. Recall that a user-defined MBean interface indicates that an MBean is a Standard MBean.

The following is the MBean interface for an MBean managing a printer. Look through it before reading further, and try to determine the attributes and operations it exposes:

```
public interface PrinterMBean
{
    public int    getPrintJobCount();
    public String getPrinterName();
    public String getPrintQuality();
    public void   setPrintQuality( int value );
    public void   cancelPrintJobs();
    public void   performSelfCheck();
}
```

The `PrinterMBean` interface exposes three attributes and two operations. You can tell this by visually examining the interface. JMX agents use a process called *introspection* to read the interface. Introspection uses Java reflection to examine the MBean interface to determine its attributes and operations. After discovering all the public methods in this interface, the agent uses a small set of rules to determine what the MBean has exposed as part of its management interface.

To find attributes, a JMX agent looks for any method following the `getAttributeName()` or `setAttributeName()` naming scheme. In addition to the `getAttributeName()` pattern, you can optionally use the form `isAttributeName()`, which must return a `boolean` value. However, if an attribute is exposed with a getter method, it cannot also have an *is* method. Setter methods also have a unique rule: they cannot be overloaded. For example, this interface would be invalid if the method `setPrintQuality( String value )` was added, because it would imply that the attribute `PrintQuality` has two different types: `String` and `int`.

WARNING   When you're exposing attributes in a Standard MBean, remember that Java is case sensitive. For example, the method `setPrintQuality()` exposes an attribute `PrintQuality`, whereas `setprintQuality()` exposes a different attribute: `printQuality`.

Table 4.1 breaks down the `PrinterMBean` interface into the parts of the management interface it exposes.

Table 4.1 The exposed attributes and operations of the `PrinterMBean` interface. Attributes are defined by the getter and setter methods. The operations are the methods that are not attributes.

Declared method	Exposed part of management interface
`getPrintJobCount()`	Attribute `PrintJobCount` with read access
`getPrinterName()`	Attribute `PrinterName` with read access
`getPrintQuality()`	Attribute `PrintQuality` with read access
`setPrintQuality( int value )`	Attribute `PrintQuality` with write access
`cancelPrintJobs()`	Operation `cancelPrintJobs`
`performSelfCheck()`	Operation `performSelfCheck`

The two parts of a management interface that an MBean interface does not describe are the public constructors and optional notifications. Notifications are described by a separate interface, `NotificationBroadcaster`, and will be covered later (in chapter 6). Public constructors are found in the class that implements the MBean interface and are discovered by introspection at the agent level.

The MBean interface makes an MBean a Standard MBean. It follows the normal interface rules of the Java language with respect to inheritance and so forth. However, depending on the level at which the interface is implemented, a different management interface may be created for an MBean. The following section describes the different inheritance schemes you can use to create a Standard MBean.

4.3 Standard MBean inheritance patterns

As we've repeatedly mentioned, a Standard MBean is an MBean that implements its own MBean interface. However, you need to be able to recognize the design patterns associated with a Standard MBean. Most likely you have experience with Java, and you understand the ability of Java classes and interfaces to extend other classes and interfaces. However, what effect does subclassing have on the management interface of a Standard MBean?

This section breaks down all the possible inheritance scenarios and explains how each affects the management interface of a Standard MBean. The inheritance patterns are presented in this book because they can affect the management interface you are trying to create.

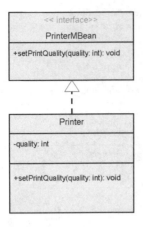

Figure 4.1
The simplest case: direct implementation of an MBean interface.
The resulting management interface is the methods contained in
the PrinterMBean interface.

4.3.1 *Direct implementation of an MBean interface*

The first scenario deals with an MBean that manages a printer. The pattern is described by figure 4.1, which shows the Printer class implementing the Printer-MBean interface described earlier.

This is the simplest scenario: a Standard MBean is created by implementing its own MBean interface. The management interface for the Printer class contains the methods and attributes exposed in the interface PrinterMBean. In this pattern, the PrinterMBean interface exposes only one attribute, PrintQuality (it is write only).

4.3.2 *Inheriting the management interface*

Similar to the previous case, a valid MBean can be created by extending another valid Standard MBean. Figure 4.2 depicts the CopierPrinter MBean.

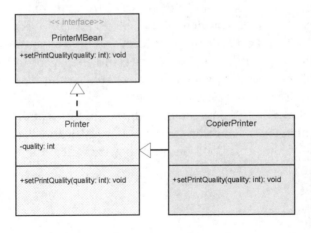

Figure 4.2
Inheriting a management interface by
extending another Standard MBean.
The CopierPrinter MBean will have
a management interface identical to
that of the Printer MBean.

In this case, the class `CopierPrinter` does not directly implement an MBean interface. However, its super class, `Printer`, does implement the `PrinterMBean` interface. The `CopierPrinter` class therefore is a `PrinterMBean`: it inherits the management interface of its super class.

This technique is useful if you want to change the behavior of an MBean but keep the interface unchanged. When you inherit the interface, you cannot add to it, but you can override methods in order to provide a new implementation in the subclass.

Keep in mind that the `CopierPrinter` class must still follow the other MBean rules. Thus it must not be an abstract class, and it must provide a public constructor because constructors cannot be inherited.

4.3.3 Overriding the management interface

The previous case mentioned overriding methods from an inherited MBean interface implementation. This scenario shows you how to override a management interface entirely with a new one (see figure 4.3).

Remember that one of the rules for writing an MBean is that it can only implement a single MBean interface. However, notice in this case that both the `Printer` and `CopierPrinter` classes implement an MBean interface. In this scenario, the `CopierPrinterMBean` interface replaces the management interface of the `PrinterMBean` interface. The `CopierPrinter` class still inherits the methods and implementation from its super class, but JMX agents will not recognize those methods as part of the `CopierPrinter` MBean's management interface. Only the

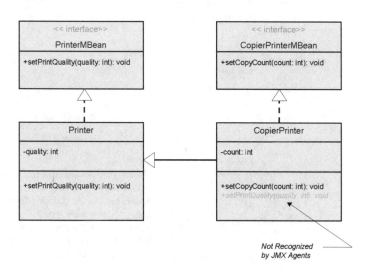

Figure 4.3
Overriding a management interface inherited from a super class. The management interface of the `CopierPrinter` MBean is declared by the `CopierPrinterMBean` interface. Nothing from the super class or the `PrinterMBean` interface is used.

methods and attributes exposed by the `CopierPrinterMBean` interface will be considered part of the management interface.

4.3.4 *Extending the management interface*

As you know, Java interfaces can extend other Java interfaces. This scenario presents the case when an MBean interface extends another MBean interface. The resulting management interface exposed is the combined methods of both interfaces. Figure 4.4 illustrates this concept with the `Printer` MBean.

Just as in the previous scenario, the `Printer` MBean can implement only a single MBean interface. However, the `PrinterMBean` interface can extend other MBean interfaces, adding more management capability. In this scenario, the `Printer` class is a `PrinterMBean`, not a `DeviceMBean`. This MBean's management interface includes the methods and attributes exposed by both the `DeviceMBean` and `PrinterMBean` interfaces, because a JMX agent will consider them part of the single MBean interface, `PrinterMBean`, implemented by the `Printer` class.

4.3.5 *Combination of extending and overriding*

By combining the last few scenarios, you can create the case shown in figure 4.5.

Looking at the figure, you can see that the `CopierPrinter` class inherits its management interface and implements its own MBean interface. In addition, the `CopierPrinterMBean` interface extends the `PrinterMBean` interface. The resulting management interface in this case is the same as the previous scenario. The management interface is always taken from the most closely related MBean interface. This means that if an MBean interface is implemented directly, it takes precedence over an inherited one. However, because `CopierPrinterMBean` extends

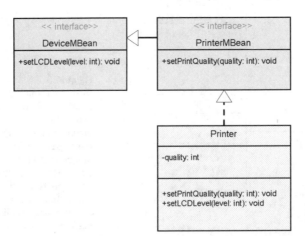

Figure 4.4
**Creating an MBean interface by
extending an existing MBean
interface. The `Printer` MBean
management interface is
composed of the methods from
both the `DeviceMBean` and
`PrinterMBean` interfaces.**

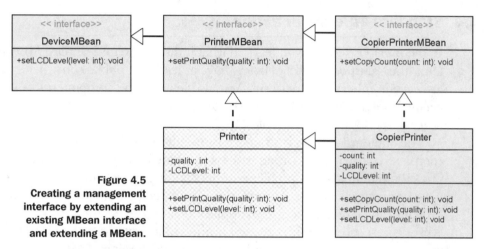

Figure 4.5
Creating a management
interface by extending an
existing MBean interface
and extending a MBean.

`PrinterMBean`, the management interface of the `CopierPrinter` class includes the attributes and operations from both MBean interfaces.

4.3.6 *Extending a non-MBean interface*

As we showed in section 4.3.4, the MBean interface can extend another MBean interface. It can also extend a non-MBean interface. Figure 4.6 depicts such a scenario.

When an MBean interface extends another interface that is not an MBean interface, the resulting exposed attributes and operations are determined by both interfaces because the MBean interface inherits all the methods of its parent. It does not matter that the `Device` interface does not follow the MBean interface naming pattern.

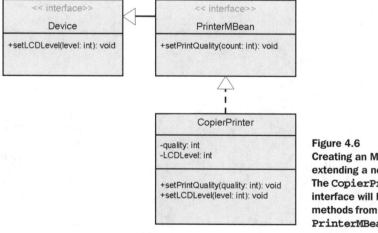

Figure 4.6
Creating an MBean interface by
extending a non-MBean interface.
The `CopierPrinter` management
interface will be composed of
methods from both the `Device` and
`PrinterMBean` interfaces.

4.4 *Standard MBeans in action*

In the previous section, you learned what it takes to write Standard MBeans. You know they must be concrete classes, have at least one public constructor, and follow certain inheritance patterns. You also learned the components of the management interface of a Standard MBean. At this point, you should be ready and eager to see some code examples.

The Standard MBean is straightforward and simple: you don't need to create complex data structures or algorithms to create a Standard MBean. Therefore, you should not have any problems understanding the examples presented in the next few sections. These examples are intended to help you understand how MBeans can be used in your own applications.

For this section, consider the application that contains its own instance of the `MBeanServer` class, or embedded JMX agent. Remember, a JMX agent is a Java class that acts as the container of MBeans. Agents have a small footprint and can be included easily into an application. When you include a JMX agent, the application can use MBeans for many purposes. This section describes using Standard MBeans to make your applications configurable and componentized. Figure 4.7 illustrates this concept.

You won't see any UML diagrams for the remaining examples in this chapter. Each MBean example implements its own MBean interface as described in the inheritance patterns in the previous section.

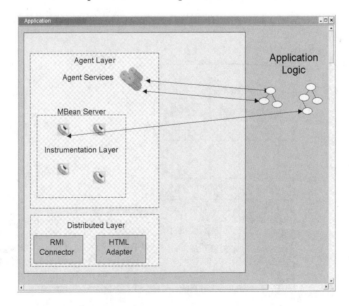

Figure 4.7
Embedding a JMX agent in an application. The application contains its own MBean server, which it can use to contain components of functionality. Doing so allows it to use and register its own MBeans.

4.4.1 *Making applications easily configurable*

In chapter 1, you read that one of the benefits of using JMX in your applications is that it can make them more configurable. With JMX, you can expose APIs from your application for management. By exposing certain operations, you can use MBeans to expose the behavior of your application at runtime. In other words, you can use MBeans to expose an API that configures your application. The configuration ability will give your applications more flexibility and can possibly save you downtime. The next section describes using MBeans to encapsulate your application properties.

Managing application properties

Many applications are configured by loading a set of properties from the file system. Unless the application chooses to monitor and reload the properties file, it can only be refreshed by being restarted. For many applications, it's not feasible to stop and start just for a minor reconfiguration. Applications that have the ability to be reconfigured during runtime are more flexible, powerful, and long lasting.

The `PropertyManager` Standard MBean example manages a set of properties. An application can acquire its configuration by using this MBean, and users can update the configuration by connecting to the embedded JMX agent. The first step in creating this MBean is to define its MBean interface:

```
package jmxbook.ch4;

import java.util.*;

public interface PropertyManagerMBean
{
  public String getProperty( String key );
  public void setProperty( String key, String value );
  public Enumeration keys();
  public void setSource( String path );
}
```

Now that you know how an MBean interface describes a Standard MBean's management interface, look at the `PropertyManagerMBean` interface to determine the management interface it describes. Judging by the fact that there is a `getProperty()` method and a `setProperty()` method, you might think the interface exposes a readable and writable attribute. However, the get method in this case is an operation, not an exposed readable attribute; a getter method cannot accept arguments. Likewise, the `setProperty()` method is not really a setter method—setter methods can take only a single argument. Therefore, although acceptable, this interface is misleading to a human reader. By definition, this interface exposes only one (writable) attribute: Source. All other methods are exposed operations.

Listing 4.1 shows the implementation of the PropertyManagerMBean interface.

```
package jmxbook.ch4;

import java.util.*;
import java.io.*;

public class PropertyManager implements PropertyManagerMBean
{
  private Properties props = null;

  public PropertyManager( String path )
  {
    try
    {
      //load supplied property file
      props = new Properties();
      FileInputStream f =  new FileInputStream( path );
      props.load( f );
      f.close();
    }
    catch( Exception e )
    {
      e.printStackTrace();
    }
  }

  public String getProperty( String key )
  {
    return props.getProperty( key );
  }

  public void setProperty( String key, String value )
  {
    props.setProperty( key, value );
  }

  public Enumeration keys()
  {
    return props.keys();
  }

  public void setSource( String path )
  {
    try
    {
      props = new Properties();
      FileInputStream f =  new FileInputStream( path );
```

```
      props.load( f );
      f.close();
    }
    catch( Exception e )
    {
      e.printStackTrace();
    }

  }

}//class
```

This MBean is straightforward and exposes only the methods present in the `java.util.Properties` class. The only attribute, `Source`, is used to reset the entire properties set with a new properties file.

Properties are the most obvious way to use MBeans to make applications configurable. However, you can also use an MBean to configure a single part of your application, such as database access.

Configuring a DataSource

Many applications need the services of a database. Java applications use the JDBC API to open database connections by creating a `Connection` object or by acquiring `Connection` objects from a `DataSource` object. In both cases, it might be useful to configure the creation of database connections. You can do so by encapsulating the acquisition of database connections inside an MBean.

The following example is a simple Standard MBean that acquires database connections from a `DataSource` object. It gets the `DataSource` object by using a Java Naming and Directory Interface (JNDI) lookup; it could just create the connection directly, as well. The following is the MBean interface for the `DBSource` MBean (to learn more about using JNDI or JDBC, go to http://www.javasoft.com):

```
package jmxbook.ch4;

import java.sql.*;

public interface DBSourceMBean
{
  public void resetDataSource( String name );
  public void setAutoCommit( boolean commit );
  public boolean getAutoCommit( );
  public Connection getConnection();
}
```

As you can see, the `DBSourceMBean` interface appears to expose one read/write attribute, `AutoCommit`, and one readable attribute, `Connection`. It also exposes an operation, `resetDataSource()`. Listing 4.2 shows the `DBSource` class.

Listing 4.2   DBSource.java

```java
package jmxbook.ch4;

import java.sql.*;
import javax.sql.*;
import javax.naming.*;

public class DBSource
{

  private DataSource ds = null;
  private boolean commit = false;

  public DBSource( String JNDIName )
  {
    try
    {
      //lookup data source using JNDI
      Context ctx = new InitialContext();
      ds = ( DataSource ) ctx.lookup( JNDIName );
    }
    catch( Exception e )
    {
      e.printStackTrace();
    }

  }

  public void resetDataSource( String name )
  {
    try
    {
      Context ctx = new InitialContext();
      ds = ( DataSource ) ctx.lookup( name );
    }
    catch( Exception e )
    {
      e.printStackTrace();
    }
  }

  public Connection getConnection()
  {
    Connection con = null;

    try
    {
      con = ds.getConnection();
      con.setAutoCommit( commit );
      return con;
    }
    catch( Exception e )
    {
```

❶ Expose getConnection() operation

```
        e.printStackTrace();
        con = null;
        return null;
    }
  }

  public boolean getAutoCommit( )
  {
    return commit;
  }

  public void setAutoCommit( boolean commit )
  {
    this.commit = commit;

  }
}
```

❶ The `getConnection()` method is unique because the implementation class does not contain a `Connection` attribute. In fact, it really returns a connection from the `DataSource` object. The `getConnection()` method is more like an operation than an exposed attribute. This situation illustrates again the importance of carefully naming methods for an MBean interface—for example, perhaps you should name this method `acquireConnection()`. By naming methods thoughtfully, you can avoid misunderstandings.

Testing the PropertyManager MBean

Before moving to the next section, let's run one of these MBeans in the JMXBook-Agent agent from chapter 3. (As we've mentioned, you will use this agent class at various times in the book.)

You can register an MBean into your agent two ways: you can use either the HTML adapter or the Remote Method Invocation (RMI) connector. You have already seen how to use the HTML adapter, so let's take this chance to use the RMI connector to register an MBean in the agent. To do so, you need to write a simple setup class that contacts an instance of the JMXBookAgent and registers an MBean. Listing 4.3 shows a setup class to create the PropertyManager MBean.

Listing 4.3 PropertyManagerSetup.java

```
package jmxbook.ch4;

import javax.management.*;
import com.sun.jdmk.comm.*;
import jmxbook.ch3.*;

public class PropertyManagerSetup
```

```
{
   public PropertyManagerSetup()
   {
     try
     {
        RmiConnectorClient client = RMIClientFactory.getClient();
        ObjectName propertyName = new
                   ObjectName( "JMXBookAgent:name=property");

        client.createMBean( "jmxbook.ch4.PropertyManager",
                             propertyName );
     }
     catch( Exception e )
     {
        ExceptionUtil.printException( e );

     }
   }
   public static void main( String args[] )
   {
      PropertyManagerSetup setup = new PropertyManagerSetup();
   }
}
```

The setup class uses the RMIClientFactory class to acquire an RMI client with which to contact your agent. Using the client, it invokes the createMBean() method of the MBeanServer. When you used the HTML adapter in chapter 2, you caused the same thing to happen by using the browser.

Before you run the setup class, make sure you have an instance of the JMX-BookAgent running—use the following command to do so:

```
javac jmxbook.ch4.JMXBookAgent
```

After the agent successfully starts, execute the PropertyManagerSetup class to create your PropertyManager MBean. Open your web browser to the address of the agent's HTML adapter, and you will see the new MBean registered in the agent.

The PropertyManager and DBSource MBeans are both good examples of using MBeans to make an application more configurable. The next section deals with making an application componentized.

4.4.2 *Breaking applications into components*

Chapter 1 explains that it is possible to use JMX to break applications into manageable components. *Componentization* is a development method that defines interfaces between components of an application, allowing their implementations to be changed or even replaced. With Standard MBeans, you can define unchanging MBean interfaces that an application uses to access certain imple-mentations of functionality it needs. With the MBean interfaces staying the same over time, you can change the MBean implementation as needed, preserving access to the functionality. The next example demonstrates this concept.

Abstracting a data layer

We already showed how an application can encapsulate the creation of data-base connections. Taking that concept a little further, an application can abstract its entire data access layer by using JMX. Figure 4.8 illustrates the data abstraction concept.

This example is presented as a Standard MBean because it would be devel-oped with a well-known interface. It would be developed along with the applica-tion, and its interface could be defined in advance. For this scenario to work, the application needs to send and receive data to the data layer in a form indepen-dent of the persistence mechanism. The interface to the data layer is dependent on the application, so a full code example is not too useful. However, you could expect the interface to resemble something like the following:

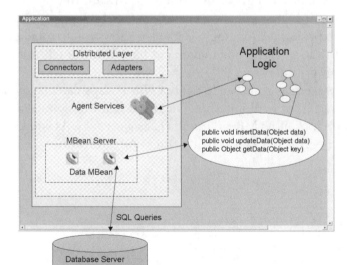

Figure 4.8
Abstracting a data layer using JMX. A Standard MBean shields the application from the actual implementation of the data layer.

```
public interface DataLayerMBean
{
  public boolean insertData( Object data );
  public boolean updateData( Object data );
  public boolean deleteData( Object data );
  public boolean retrieveData( Object data );
}
```

The data object should contain enough information for the persistence implementation to fulfill its task.

The logging MBean

Up to this point, the examples have pertained to Java resources such as properties and JDBC connections. One example had to do with application configuration, and the other introduced MBeans as components of an application. The final example of this section combines these concepts.

Most applications use logs to keep records of activity and occurrences of errors. In many cases, the log file also records developer debug statements for possible analysis. Like data repositories, logs can be kept in many different forms, such as a flat file or a database. By writing an MBean, you can both componentize the application's logging system and expose the logging system to a management tool. Exposing the logging mechanism allows you to tune it for certain behavior. For instance, using a management tool, you can tell the logging MBean to record only critical errors.

By defining the log system as an MBean, you not only encapsulate its implementation, but also expose it for configuration. The following example creates such an MBean. First, let's look at its MBean interface, LoggerMBean. As you know, the interface describes the MBean's exposed attributes and operations:

```
package jmxbook.ch4;

public interface LoggerMBean
{
  public void setLogLevel( int level );
  public int getLogLevel();
  public String retrieveLog( int linesback );
  public void writeLog( String message, int type );
}
```

Table 4.2 describes the management interface exposed by the LoggerMBean interface.

Table 4.2 The parts of the `LoggerMBean` interface. Attributes are described by the getter and setter methods, and operations are described by the remaining methods.

Declared method	Part	Description
setLogLevel()	Attribute	Declares write access to LogLevel
getLogLevel()	Attribute	Declares read access to LogLevel
retrieveLog()	Operation	Declares an exposed operation
writeLog()	Operation	Declares an exposed operation

The `Logger` class implements the `LoggerMBean` with a flat-file implementation. Listing 4.4 shows the `Logger` class.

Listing 4.4   Logger.java

```java
package jmxbook.ch4;

import javax.management.*;
import java.io.*;
import java.util.*;

public class Logger implements LoggerMBean
{
  public static final int ALL    = 3;
  public static final int ERRORS = 2;
  public static final int NONE   = 1;

  private PrintWriter out = null;
  private int logLevel = Logger.ALL;

  public Logger()
  {
    try
    {
      //open the initial log file
      out = new PrintWriter(
              new FileOutputStream
              ( "record.log " ) );
    }
    catch( Exception e )
    {
      e.printStackTrace();
    }
  }

  public void setLogLevel( int level )
  {
    logLevel = level;
  }
}
```

```
    public int getLogLevel()
    {
      return logLevel;
    }

    public String retrieveLog( int linesback )
    {
      //implementation here
      return null;
    }

    public void writeLog( String message, int type )
    {
      try
      {
        if( type <= logLevel )
          out.println( message );
      }
      catch( Exception e )
      {
        e.printStackTrace();
      }
    }
  }//class
```

Breaking applications into components as Standard MBeans is a valuable development advantage. In this manner, you can keep the interfaces between components stable, and shield the application from the implementation of specific functionality. Once the implementation is hidden, changing it will not impact the application. For example, if an application was using a logging MBean like the previous example, the logging implementation could persist messages to a file or a database. Neither method affects how an application would access its logging functionality.

4.4.3 *MBeans using other MBeans*

In the past two sections, we have discussed using Standard MBeans to componentize and configure your applications. We presented each of these concepts with a single MBean: you used an MBean to manage a property set that an application could use to access application settings, and you also used an MBean to handle an application's logging functionality.

You have created an application that uses MBeans to handle its configuration and certain components. However, as part of the application, the MBean components should have access to the configuration of the application. In this scenario, your MBean components need access to another MBean. Figure 4.9 illustrates this concept using the Logger MBean and PropertyManager MBean.

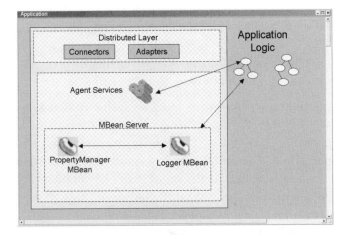

Figure 4.9
The `Logger` **MBean accessing the** `PropertyManager` **MBean. The** `Logger` **class can use another MBean because it has a reference to the MBean server. It acquires this reference by implementing the** `MBeanRegistration` **interface.**

For one MBean to use another MBean, it must be able to contact the MBean server. You could pass in an MBean as a parameter to another's constructor, but you don't want to create an unnecessary dependency on the MBean. You can implement an MBean to contain a reference to its MBean server two ways:

- Construct the MBean with an MBean server parameter.
- Implement the `MBeanRegistration` interface.

This section discusses the `MBeanRegistration` interface. This interface declares methods that are invoked before and after registration and deregistration on the MBean server. The following is the `MBeanRegistration` interface:

```
package javax.management;

public abstract interface MBeanRegistration
{
  public void postDeregister();
  public void postRegister( Boolean registrationDone );
  public void preDeregister();
  public ObjectName preRegister( MBeanServer server,
                                 ObjectName name );
}
```

This interface contains two methods that are called in conjunction with the MBean's registration on a MBean server, and two methods that are called with deregistration. These methods are invoked by the `MBeanServer` instance that is being asked to perform the registration or deregistration of a particular MBean instance. For example, if the `HelloWorld` MBean from chapter 2 implemented this interface, the MBean server would perform the following tasks when asked by the HTML adapter to create another `HelloWorld` MBean instance:

1 Create the MBean instance using the appropriate constructor.

2 Invoke the `preRegister()` method.

3 Register the MBean instance.

4 Invoke the `postRegister()` method.

The `postRegister()` method is invoked with a `Boolean` value passed as a parameter. This value indicates whether the registration of the MBean was successful. If the value is `true`, registration succeeded. The `preRegister()` method allows the MBean to find and use other MBeans. It takes two parameters: an `MBeanServer` instance and an `ObjectName` instance. If the `ObjectName` parameter is passed as null, the method should return an appropriate `ObjectName` value to use with the registration of this MBean.

Revisiting the `Logger` MBean, listing 4.5 shows how to implement the `MBean-Registration` interface to provide the `Logger` class with a mechanism to get the initial values for its attributes. The changes from the previous `Logger` MBean class (listing 4.4) are shown in bold.

Listing 4.5 Logger.java

```java
package jmxbook.ch4;

import javax.management.*;
import java.io.*;
import java.util.*;

public class Logger implements LoggerMBean, MBeanRegistration
{
  public static final int ALL    = 3;
  public static final int ERRORS = 2;
  public static final int NONE   = 1;

  private PrintWriter out = null;
  private int logLevel = Logger.ALL;
  private MBeanServer server = null;

  public Logger()
  {
    try
    {
      out = new PrintWriter(
              new FileOutputStream (
              "record.log" ) );
    }
    catch( Exception e )
    {
      e.printStackTrace();
```

```
    }
}

public void setLogLevel( int level )
{
    logLevel = level;
}

public int getLogLevel()
{
    return logLevel;
}

public String retrieveLog( int linesback )
{
    //implementation here
    return null;
}

public void writeLog( String message, int type )
{
    try
    {
        if( type <= logLevel )
            out.println( message );
    }
    catch( Exception e )
    {
        e.printStackTrace();
    }
}
public void postDeregister() {}
public void postRegister( Boolean registrationDone ) {}
public void preDeregister() {}

public ObjectName preRegister(
                MBeanServer server, ObjectName name )
{
    this.server = server;
    try
    {
        ObjectName name1 = new ObjectName(
            "JMXBookAgent:name=props" );
        Object[] params = { "loglevel" };
        String[] sig = { "java.lang.String" };
        String value = ( String )
            server.invoke( name1, "getProperty", params, sig );
        logLevel =
            Integer.parseInt( value );
    }
    catch( Exception e )
    {
```

Implement MBeanRegistration interface ❶

```
        e.printStackTrace();
        logLevel = 0;
    }
    return name;
}

}//class
```

❶

❶ The methods that appear in bold are declared in the `MBeanRegistration` interface. For the first three, the `Logger` MBean did not provide an implementation. However, the `preRegister()` method is implemented to get its initial `logLevel` attribute value from a `PropertyManager` MBean present in the MBean server passed in as an argument to this method.

To find the value for the `logLevel` attribute, the `Logger` MBean must invoke the `getProperty()` method of a registered `PropertyManager` MBean. For this example, the `Logger` MBean assumes that the object name `HelloAgent:name=props` will correspond to a `PropertyManager` MBean. In the code, the appropriate method signature is created to allow the MBean server to invoke the `getProperty()` method. The `Logger` MBean invokes the MBean server's `invoke()` method with the appropriate parameters.

WARNING   When you're creating an MBean that depends on the existence of another MBean, you need to implement some default behavior in case the necessary MBean does not exist. For example, the `Logger` MBean must ensure that its attributes have appropriate values if an exception occurs when invoking methods on the `PropertyManager` MBean.

The `MBeanRegistration` interface is useful for acquiring a reference to the containing MBean server. In addition, because it declares methods that are invoked before an MBean is removed from the MBean server, implementing MBeans can be informed when to clean up resources before the MBean is removed from the MBean server.

4.5 *Handling MBean errors*

In each example in this chapter, there is an opportunity to catch an exception. Each MBean contains a generic `try-catch` statement:

```
try
{
    //code
}
catch( Exception e )
{
    e.printStackTrace();
}
```

You can see the drawbacks of this approach. Imagine you are using management software to configure the `PropertyManager` MBean you created in section 4.3.1. You create that MBean by specifying a path to a properties file. During construction, the MBean attempts to open a file with that path and load it into a properties object. If that file does not exist, an exception is thrown and basically ignored. From the management tool, you would never know what had occurred, and your application's configuration would be in error.

To adequately manage an application, you must know if your management actions succeed or cause errors. Fortunately, JMX provides a way to avoid the situation we just described, by supporting runtime and declared exceptions. Declared exceptions are declared in a `throws` statement. Runtime exceptions are not expected and are not required to be in a `try-catch` statement.

Exceptions in JMX occur in two categories. First, exceptions occur as agent-level components (such as `MBeanServer`) perform operations on an MBean. For example, registration, lookup, and invoking methods on an MBean instance fall into this category. Second, exceptions occur as defined by MBean code. These include Java language exceptions and user-defined exceptions.

JMX supports a mechanism for handling exceptions in a meaningful way. The last sections of this chapter discuss exceptions at the MBean level.

4.5.1 *Throwing exceptions*

Figure 4.10 depicts the class hierarchy for JMX exceptions. The main class is `JMException`; all others are subclasses of it. It has three subclasses: `OperationsException`, `ReflectionException`, and `MBeanException`. Each of these exception types has subclasses, as well.

You can see that JMX exceptions at the MBean level are broken down into three categories, extending from one of three super classes:

- `OperationsException`—Subclasses define exceptions that occur when invoking operations on an MBean.

- `ReflectionException`—Wraps standard reflection exceptions of the Java language that occur when working with MBean classes.

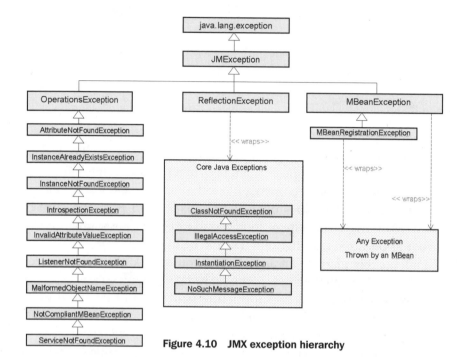

Figure 4.10   JMX exception hierarchy

- MBeanException—Wraps any other (user-defined or standard) exceptions thrown from an MBean. The MBean server constructs and throws this exception when an unknown exception is thrown by an MBean.

Table 4.3 describes the remaining exceptions. All these exceptions will propagate from the MBean server, because it is the object that will detect (and possibly wrap) the condition that causes a problem. Again, not all subclasses of JMException are listed here.

Table 4.3   JMX exceptions

Exception	Description
AttributeNotFoundException	Thrown when a specified attribute cannot be found (does not exist for the MBean specified)
InvalidAttributeValueException	Thrown when the specified attribute contains an invalid value for that attribute
InstrospectionException	Thrown if an error occurs when the MBean server is examining the management interface of an MBean
NotCompliantMBeanException	Occurs when attempting to register an MBean, if the MBean does not follow the applicable rules

Table 4.3 JMX exceptions *(continued)*

Exception	Description
`MBeanRegistrationException`	Wraps exceptions thrown by the `preRegister()` and `preDeregister()` methods of the `MBeanRegistration` interface
`ClassNotFoundException`	Thrown if the MBean server cannot find a specified MBean class when creating an MBean
`InstantiationException`	Thrown by the `newInstance()` method from the `Class` class when trying to create an MBean instance
`IllegalAccessException`	Thrown by the `Class.forName()` method when the MBean server is trying to create an MBean instance
`NoSuchMethodException`	Thrown when trying to invoke a non-existent method on an MBean

4.5.2 *Runtime exceptions*

Runtime exceptions are handled in the same manner as other exceptions. Operations performed on MBeans occur in a `try-catch` statement inside the JMX agent, allowing the agent to catch any runtime exceptions and wrap them in a JMX exception. The JMX framework defines a subclass of `java.lang.RuntimeException` called `JMRuntimeException`. In JMX, there are subclasses for runtime exceptions at the agent level and the MBean level. Figure 4.11 shows the class

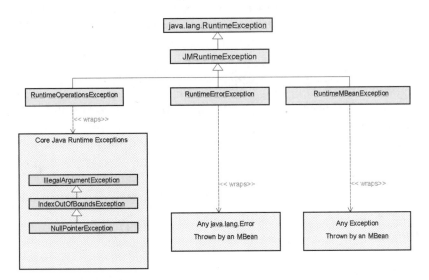

Figure 4.11 JMX runtime exception hierarchy

hierarchy of the JMX runtime exceptions for the MBean level. Note that JMX wraps both runtime errors and runtime exceptions in its own runtime exception.

Like JMX exceptions, JMX runtime exceptions at the MBean level are broken down into three categories:

- `RuntimeOperationsException`—Wraps Java runtime exceptions that occur during operations on an MBean
- `RuntimeErrorException`—Wraps standard runtime errors of the Java language that occur at the MBean level
- `RuntimeMBeanException`—Wraps any other (user-defined or standard) runtime exceptions thrown from an MBean

4.6 *Summary*

This chapter introduced the Standard MBean. The Standard MBean uses an explicitly declared management interface to interact with a manageable resource. The explicitly declared interface—the MBean interface—makes the Standard MBean a static, unchanging MBean used for well-known or pre-defined resources.

The examples in this chapter covered the three following topics:

- *Configuration*—Using MBeans to make your applications more configurable. The example was a Standard MBean used to manage a properties object.
- *Componentization*—Using MBeans to break your applications into components, allowing you to alter or replace component implementations. The `Logger` MBean demonstrated this concept.
- *MBeans using MBeans*—Combining both previous concepts, the `Logger` MBean used the `PropertyManager` MBean to initialize one of its member variables.

At the end of this chapter, you got your first look at the exception hierarchy for exceptions that occur when working with MBeans. JMX provides exceptions for many situations that may occur when reflecting upon or invoking MBean objects. In addition, JMX provides other exception classes to wrap core Java exceptions and user-defined exceptions.

Chapter 5 introduces the Dynamic MBean. The Dynamic MBean is used to manage evolving resources in situations where the Standard MBean may not be appropriate.

MBeans for
changing resources

- Exploring rules for creating Dynamic MBeans
- Understanding dynamic MBean development patterns
- Using the MBean metadata classes
- Managing a Jini service

You learned in chapter 4 that Standard MBeans are perfect for managing new resources or resources with well-known, static interfaces. Unfortunately, we all know that resources often evolve over time. Indeed, certain APIs may vary with each release.

Standard MBeans are not well suited for these situations because of their explicitly declared management interfaces. However, the Dynamic MBean is ideal for handling such cases because it defines its management interface at runtime in a generic fashion. Dynamic MBeans use metadata classes to describe their management interfaces. As a developer, you decide how much or how little of a resource to expose by describing it with the metadata objects.

In this chapter, you will manage a Jini service with a Dynamic MBean. The MBean will be responsible for changing how the Jini service advertises itself across a network. In addition, you will provide a Dynamic MBean super class to provide some code reuse for generating the metadata descriptions of future resources. After reading this chapter, you will know how to build and when to use Dynamic MBeans.

5.1 *Working with the DynamicMBean interface*

JMX agents recognize Dynamic MBeans because they must implement the `javax.management.DynamicMBean` interface. Recall from chapter 4 that MBeans cannot implement both their own MBean interface and the `DynamicMBean` interface. This limitation ensures that an MBean cannot be both Standard and Dynamic. The `DynamicMBean` interface is a predefined, standard interface that allows MBeans to describe their management interface at runtime. Remember that an MBean's management interface is the group of attributes, operations, constructors, and notifications that it exposes, enabling the management of a resource.

Because the interface to a Dynamic MBean does not change, you can use Dynamic MBeans to shield other applications from the evolving interface of a manageable resource. Figure 5.1 illustrates this scenario.

The best place to begin this chapter is a discussion of the `javax.management.DynamicMBean` interface. The next section breaks down the interface and examines its methods one by one.

5.2 *Examining the DynamicMBean interface*

To be a Dynamic MBean, a class must implement the `DynamicMBean` interface. As previously mentioned, the `DynamicMBean` interface declares predefined methods that let an MBean expose the interface to its manageable resource at runtime. By

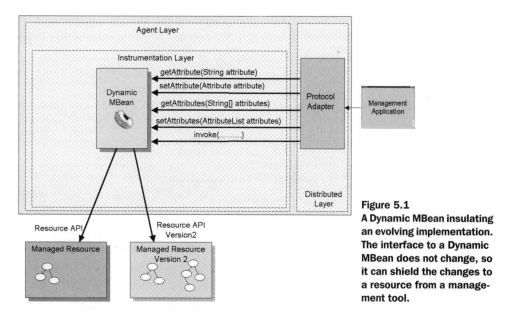

Figure 5.1
A Dynamic MBean insulating an evolving implementation. The interface to a Dynamic MBean does not change, so it can shield the changes to a resource from a management tool.

defining the management interface at runtime, Dynamic MBeans are flexible enough to handle dynamic and evolving resources. The following code listing shows the DynamicMBean interface. Notice that it contains methods for handling attributes and operations, and for acquiring a description of the MBean:

```
package javax.management;

public interface DynamicMBean
{
    public Object getAttribute( String attribute )
                throws AttributeNotFoundException, MBeanException,
                    ReflectionException;

    public void setAttribute( Attribute attribute )
                throws AttributeNotFoundException,
                    InvalidAttributeValueException,
                    MBeanException,
                    ReflectionException;

    public AttributeList getAttributes( String[] attributes );

    public AttributeList setAttributes( AttributeList attributes );

    public Object invoke( String actionName, Object[] params,
                    String[] signature ) throws MBeanException,
                    ReflectionExceptionn

    public MBeanInfo getMBeanInfo();
}
```

The next several sections discuss the methods declared in this interface. You might recognize some of the exceptions thrown by these methods from table 4.3 in chapter 4.

5.2.1 Acquiring the dynamic management interface

The DynamicMBean interface exposes the management interface of a resource in a generic manner by using a standard JMX class: MBeanInfo. JMX agents use the getMBeanInfo() method to get the description of the management interface of a Dynamic MBean.

Unlike Standard MBeans, Dynamic MBeans do not use explicitly declared methods to expose their management interface. Instead, the management interface is described by the MBeanInfo value returned from the getMBeanInfo() method at runtime. The MBeanInfo object is used as a container for standard JMX objects that describe various portions of the MBean's management interface. Therefore, the MBeanInfo instance contains all the information needed for a management tool to interact with the managed resource.

NOTE   Internally, the MBean server either acquires or constructs an MBeanInfo object for each MBean it contains. These objects aid the MBean server when it needs to perform operations on its MBean.

We will closely examine the javax.management.MBeanInfo object shortly. First, we need to finish discussing the methods of the DynamicMBean interface.

5.2.2 Working with dynamic MBean attributes

The last section revealed that the management interface of a Dynamic MBean is described by the return value of its getMBeanInfo() method. However, once you acquire the management interface, you still need the ability to access attributes and invoke operations. Because Dynamic MBeans define their management interface at runtime, there can be no explicit setter or getter methods for an exposed attribute.

In order for Dynamic MBeans to provide support for managing attributes, the DynamicMBean interface must provide a generic way of getting and setting any exposed attributes. The DynamicMBean interface has the following methods for getting attribute values: getAttribute() and getAttributes(). In addition, it has the following two setter methods: setAttribute() and setAttributes().

Getting attribute values

In order to get an attribute's value, you need to know the name of the attribute. This attribute name is provided in the `MBeanInfo` object returned from the `getMBeanInfo()` method. In the `getAttribute()` method, you pass a single attribute name. In the `getAttributes()` method, you pass an array of attribute names.

The `getAttribute()` method returns a value of type `Object` in order to generically encapsulate the actual value of the exposed attribute. The other method, `getAttributes()`, returns an instance of the `AttributeList` class. The `AttributeList` class is a subclass of `java.util.ArrayList` and is a collection of `Attribute` objects. Each `Attribute` object encapsulates an attribute name and its value, and provides support for an `equals()` method. Both `AttributeList` and `Attribute` are in the `javax.management` package.

Setting attribute values

The `setAttribute()` method accepts a single `Attribute` object as an argument. It attempts to set the value of the MBean attribute with the name returned by the `getName()` method from its `Attribute` argument. The `setAttributes()` method acts exactly like `setAttribute()`, but it operates over an `AttributeList` argument.

For all four methods, if an invalid attribute name is specified, an `AttributeNotFoundException` exception should be thrown. For the set methods, if an invalid attribute value is specified, an `InvalidAttributeValueException` exception should be thrown. We say "should" because this is only an interface—the actual implementation depends on the developer.

Before moving on, let's summarize some of the information presented in the last two sections. Table 5.1 provides a summary of setting and getting attribute values.

Table 5.1 Summary of information concerning setting and getting attribute values of a Dynamic MBean

Dynamic MBean method	Return value	Incoming arguments
`getAttribute()`	`Object`	`String` attribute name
`getAttributes()`	`AttributeList`	`String[]` of attribute names
`setAttribute()`	`void`	`Attribute`
`setAttributes()`	`AttributeList`	`AttributeList`

Now, let's move on and discuss how Dynamic MBeans expose operations.

5.2.3 *Invoking operations*

So far, you have seen how to acquire the management interface from a Dynamic MBean, and how to get and set attributes. The management interface is described by the `MBeanInfo` object returned by the `getMBeanInfo()` method, and attributes are managed via the `getAttribute(s)()` and `setAttribute(s)()` methods. At this point, we need to explain how the `DynamicMBean` interface provides a mechanism for invoking exposed MBean operations. Again, an MBean user gains knowledge of MBean operations by first acquiring an `MBeanInfo` object by invoking the `getMBeanInfo()` method of the Dynamic MBean.

For the same reason as attributes, operations cannot be explicitly defined by a Dynamic MBean (its management interface is provided at runtime). Therefore, another generic mechanism is needed to provide the ability to invoke Dynamic MBean operations. The `DynamicMBean` interface declares the `invoke()` method to provide such a mechanism.

The `invoke()` method takes three arguments:

- A `String` value containing the name of the method you want to invoke
- An array of `Object` instances that are the parameter values to the method being invoked
- An array of `String` values corresponding to the parameter class types of the invoking method

The last two arguments (the arrays) contain their values in the order they appear in the desired method declaration. For example, a method declared as `setPrint-Quality( Integer level )` would be described with an array of one element containing the `Integer` value, and another one-element array containing the value `java.lang.Integer`. Dynamic MBeans analyze these arguments, invoke the appropriate method, and return the result. The result of the underlying method invocation is returned in the `invoke()` method as an `Object` value.

5.3 *Understanding the MBeanInfo class*

In the previous section, you learned the purposes of the methods of the `Dynamic-MBean` interface and how they are used to manage a Dynamic MBean. However, the previous section only told you that the management interface of the MBean is contained in the `MBeanInfo` object returned by the method `getMBeanInfo()`.

The `MBeanInfo` class is the container for other objects that describe portions of the MBean's management interface. The `MBeanInfo` class and the classes it contains are collectively called MBean *metadata* classes.

The MBean metadata classes are created by Dynamic MBeans and also by the MBean server. The MBean server uses these objects internally in order for it to treat all MBeans equally regardless of the MBean type. In the case of Standard MBeans, the MBean server uses introspection to create a set of metadata objects that describe an MBean's management interface. For other MBeans (like the Dynamic MBean), the metadata objects are constructed by the MBean itself.

This section breaks down the `MBeanInfo` object and explains how Dynamic MBeans use it to provide a description of their exposed management interface.

5.3.1 *Metadata of the MBeanInfo class*

The `MBeanInfo` class is a standard JMX class containing classes that describe individual parts of the overall management interface. Recall from chapter 4 that management interfaces consist of exposed constructors, attributes, operations, and optional notifications. The `MBeanInfo` contains a metadata object for each of these parts. The following sections describe these metadata classes.

Table 5.2 identifies each metadata class and its corresponding management interface part.

Table 5.2 The metadata classes and the parts of a management interface they represent. These classes are contained in the **MBeanInfo** object that is the return value for the **getMBeanInfo()** method of the **DynamicMBean** interface.

Metadata class	Exposed part of the management interface
MBeanFeatureInfo	Super class to all other metadata classes
MBeanParameterInfo	Arguments passed to methods and constructors
MBeanConstructorInfo	Any exposed constructors
MBeanAttributeInfo	Readable and writable attributes
MBeanOperationInfo	Exposed MBean operations
MBeanNotificationInfo	The notifications an MBean can emit

In addition to containing the metadata objects, an instance of `MBeanInfo` provides the class name and description of the MBean. You can get these values by invoking the `getClassName()` method or the `getDescription()` method. In fact, all the metadata classes contain a description member variable that describes the metadata object. When writing Dynamic MBeans, you should use this description variable to adequately describe parts of the management interface. Management software that interacts with your Dynamic MBeans can use the descriptions to help users better understand how to use your MBeans.

5.3.2 *The MBeanFeatureInfo and MBeanParameterInfo classes*

Before we examine the metadata classes that describe the management interface, let's look at their base class (MBeanFeatureInfo) and a support class (MBeanParameterInfo). Every MBean metadata class is a subclass of the MBeanFeatureInfo class. The class contains a name and a human-readable description of the feature. This ensures that every feature described by a subclass has both a name and a description.

The MBeanParameterInfo class extends MBeanFeatureInfo and provides a description of arguments to constructors and operations. MBeanParameterInfo objects add a type field to the name and description fields provided by their super class. The type field contains the name of the class type of a parameter. With those three fields, you can adequately describe a method argument.

5.3.3 *The MBeanConstructorInfo class*

The MBeanConstructorInfo class is a metadata class that describes a single exposed constructor of an MBean. It is created by using a Constructor object parameter or by using an array of MBeanParameterInfo objects that describe a constructor's signature. Because a constructor is described solely by its signature, the MBeanConstructorInfo class contains only one method (in addition to its inherited methods)—getSignature(), which returns the constructor's signature as an Array of MBeanParameterInfo objects. The following are the class's two constructors:

```
public MBeanConstructorInfo( String description,
                            java.lang.reflect.Constructor
                            constructor )

public MBeanConstructorInfo( String name, String description,
                            MBeanParameterInfo[] signature )
```

5.3.4 *The MBeanAttributeInfo class*

The MBeanAttributeInfo class is a metadata class that describes an exposed attribute of an MBean. Remember that attributes are exposed with readable access, writable access, or both readable and writable access. In addition to describing an attribute's exposed access, the class contains the attribute's name, description, and type. The following are the two constructors for the MBeanAttributeInfo class:

```
public MBeanAttributeInfo( String name, String description,
                           java.lang.reflect.Method getter,
                           java.lang.reflect.Method setter )

public MBeanAttributeInfo( String name, String type, String
                           description, boolean isReadable,
                           boolean isWritable, boolean isIs )
```

You create an instance of `MBeanAttributeInfo` by either specifying all the details of an attribute (the second constructor) or passing in the `Method` objects for the getter and setter methods for the attribute.

The constructor that accepts the `Method` arguments only uses them to get the information it needs to describe the attribute. The `Method` parameters are not stored for invocation when it is time to access the attribute.

Objects access information from an `MBeanAttributeInfo` class by calling one of the provided convenience methods:

- `getType()`—Returns the attribute's class type (such as `java.lang.String`)
- `isReadable()`—Returns a `boolean` value indicating whether this attribute is readable
- `isWritable()`—Returns a `boolean` value indicating whether this attribute is writable
- `isIs()`—Returns a `boolean` value indicating whether this attribute is accessible using an *is* type method

5.3.5 *The MBeanOperationInfo class*

The `MBeanOperationInfo` class is the metadata class that encapsulates an operation exposed by an MBean. Just like some of the other metadata classes, it can be constructed in two ways: by using a `Method` object or by passing in a signature and a return value type. The following are its two constructors:

```
public MBeanOperationInfo( String description,
                           java.lang.reflect.Method method

public MBeanOperationInfo( String name, String description,
                           MBeanParameterInfo[] signature,
                           String type, int impact )
```

Notice that the second constructor takes an `int` argument called `impact`. The `MBeanOperationInfo` class defines four `public static final` member variables containing values for this argument. These values describe the impact of invoking the specified operation:

- INFO—The operation returns information, similar to a getter method.
- ACTION—The operation causes a change or action on the MBean.
- ACTION_INFO—The operation results in a combination of the INFO and ACTION impact.
- UNKNOWN—The impact of the operation is unknown.

The MBeanOperationInfo class provides a set of methods to access information about the operation it describes. The getReturnType() method returns the class type of the operation's return value, returning void if the operation does not have a return value. The getImpact() method returns an int value equal to one of INFO, ACTION, ACTION_INFO, or UNKNOWN. Finally, the getSignature() method returns an array of MBeanParameterInfo objects that describe the signature of the exposed operation.

5.3.6 *The MBeanNotificationInfo class*

The final metadata class is MBeanNotificationInfo. This class describes the notifications that a particular MBean can emit. We will avoid this class for now, because it is covered in chapter 6. However, rest assured, it is much the same as the previously described metadata classes.

5.4 *Inheritance patterns*

Unlike Standard MBeans, Dynamic MBeans cannot compose a management interface by adding additional methods through different inheritance patterns. This is true because the entire management interface of a Dynamic MBean is exposed by the single method: getMBeanInfo() from the DynamicMBean interface.

An MBean is identified as being Dynamic if the DynamicMBean interface is found anywhere up its inheritance hierarchy. Remember that MBeans cannot implement both the DynamicMBean interface and their own MBean interface; doing so will result in an exception when you attempt to register such an MBean.

Classes that extend a Dynamic MBean class have a special responsibility. As a subclass to a DynamicMBean interface implementation, a class can pick and choose which DynamicMBean methods to override. If a subclass changes the exposed management interface, it must also provide a new getMBeanInfo() implementation. It is assumed that a Dynamic MBean's getMBeanInfo() return value is an accurate depiction of an MBean's management interface.

5.5 *Dynamic MBeans in action*

Now that you have read about writing and working with the management interface of a Dynamic MBean, it's time to look at a few examples. The following examples involve the Jini network technology. Our discussion will mostly center around working with JMX, not the Jini technologies. However, if you need more information about Jini, go to http://www.javasoft.com.

5.5.1 *Managing a Jini service*

Jini network technology is another emerging Java technology. Programs that want to use a Jini service use a discovery technique that hides the network transportation layer and the location of the service.

Jini services make themselves available for discovery by registering with lookup registries all across a network. Services use a broadcasting system to find lookup registries and register on them. In turn, client programs find these service registries to get references to Jini services. Once a client has a reference to that service, it interacts with the service using Java Remote Method Invocation (RMI). For example, a Java program can search and find a Jini service that provides the ability to print documents.

Client programs wishing to use Jini services need a way to know which service will meet their needs. Jini services can *advertise*, or describe, their function and capabilities. When registering on a service lookup registry, a Jini service constructs a service template object that contains information about the service. Specifically, the template contains the interface type of the service and a set of `Entry` objects that describe attributes of the service. `Entry` objects could be something like a name, address, or type. (To read more about this technology, go to http://www.javasoft.com/jini.)

When the Jini service is created, it registers an MBean with a JMX agent. The MBean is now available for a management application to configure that Jini service without having to restart or bring down the service.

To start this example, imagine you have created a Jini service to perform a business function like calculating payroll. The service would implement a remote interface `Payroll`, for example, that would allow you to invoke methods upon it after discovery. In addition to the `Payroll` interface, you will have the service implement another remote interface, `ManagedJINIService`. This interface will contain any methods you want to expose with the MBean created by the Jini service. Figure 5.2 illustrates this relationship.

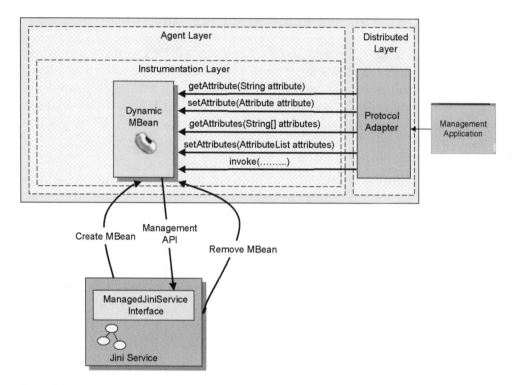

Figure 5.2 A Dynamic MBean managing a Jini service. The service creates the MBean when it is initialized and removes the MBean as it is shut down. The MBean can be used to change the service's description to the world by adding/removing Jini **Entry** objects.

A good place to begin Jini service management via an MBean is its set of Entry objects, which describe the service. You want to be able to add, modify, or delete Entry attributes at runtime in order to describe the Jini service in a different way. By changing the Entry objects, you change the way clients discover the Jini service. The following is the ManagedJINIService interface:

```
package jmxbook.ch5;

import java.rmi.*;
import java.util.*;

public interface ManagedJINIService extends Remote
{
  public void addEntries( Vector entry ) throws RemoteException;

  public void modifyEntries( Vector oldEntries, Vector newEntries )
                                      throws RemoteException;
}
```

The `ManagedJINIService` interface provides two operations:

- `addEntries()`—Lets you add additional entries to the Jini service's service template
- `modifyEntries()`—Lets you change existing `Entry` objects

For the sake of time and space, this book does not contain the code for the Jini service we are describing. However, it does contain the code for the MBean used to manage this service. Remember, the `ManagedJINIService` service (as it is called because it implements the `ManagedJINIService` interface) creates an MBean upon its creation. It should also destroy that MBean when it knows it is being shut down.

Let's begin the examination of the MBean that manages the Jini service. Listing 5.1 is the `JINIServiceManager` Dynamic MBean class.

Listing 5.1   JINIServiceManager.java

```
package jmxbook.ch5;

import net.jini.core.entry.*;      Import packages
import net.jini.discovery.*;       to support Jini
import net.jini.core.lookup.*;     interaction
import java.util.*;
import javax.management.*;
import java.rmi.*;
import java.lang.reflect.*;

public class JINIServiceManager implements DynamicMBean
{
    private ManagedJINIService serviceRef = null;
    private String jiniInterfaceName = null;
    private Entry initialAttribute = null;
    private String serviceName = null;

    public JINIServiceManager(Entry att )
    {
      jiniInterfaceName = "jmxbook.ch5.ManagedJINIService";
      serviceRef = ( jmxbook.ch5.ManagedJINIService )    Look up service
                            lookUpService();             reference
      initialAttribute = att;
    }

    public Object getAttribute( String name ) throws MBeanException,
                  AttributeNotFoundException, ReflectionException
    {
        throw new AttributeNotFoundException( name );     Expose MBean  ❶
    }                                                     attributes
    public AttributeList getAttributes( String[] names )
    {
```

```
            AttributeList rvalue = new AttributeList();
            return rvalue;
    }

    public void setAttribute( Attribute att ) throws MBeanException,
                    AttributeNotFoundException, ReflectionException,
                    InvalidAttributeValueException
    {
    throw new AttributeNotFoundException( "No attributes can be set" );
    }

    public AttributeList setAttributes( AttributeList list )
    {
        AttributeList rvalue = new AttributeList();
        return rvalue;
    }

    public Object invoke( String actionName,
                        Object args[], String sig[] )
                        throws MBeanException, ReflectionException
    {
        try
        {
          String methodName = actionName;
          Class types[] = new Class[ sig.length ];
          for( int i = 0; i < types.length; i++ )
            types[ i ] = Class.forName( sig[ i ] );

          Method m =
              serviceRef.getClass().getMethod( methodName, types );
          Object temp = m.invoke( serviceRef, args );
          return temp;
        }
        catch( Exception e )
        {
          throw new MBeanException( e );
        }
    }

    public MBeanInfo getMBeanInfo()
    {
        MBeanConstructorInfo[] cons  = new MBeanConstructorInfo[ 1 ];
        MBeanNotificationInfo[] nots = null;
        MBeanAttributeInfo[] atts    = null;
        MBeanOperationInfo[] ops = new MBeanOperationInfo[ 2 ];

        try
        {
          Class conargs[] = { Class.forName( "java.lang.String" ),
                    Class.forName( "net.jini.core.entry.Entry" ) };
          MBeanConstructorInfo cinfo =
                    new MBeanConstructorInfo( "Main constructor",
                    this.getClass().getConstructor( conargs ) );
          cons[ 0 ] = cinfo;
```

❶

```
      }
      catch( Exception e ){}

      MBeanParameterInfo[] sig0 = new MBeanParameterInfo[ 1 ];
      sig0[ 0 ] = new MBeanParameterInfo( "entries",
      "java.util.Vector", "Entries to Add" );
      ops[ 0 ] =  new MBeanOperationInfo(
             "addEntries", "Used to add service attributes",
             sig0, "void", MBeanOperationInfo.ACTION );

      MBeanParameterInfo[] sig1 = new MBeanParameterInfo[ 2 ];
      sig1[ 0 ] = new MBeanParameterInfo( "oldEntries",
         "java.util.Vector", "Old Entries to modify" );

      sig1[ 1 ] = new MBeanParameterInfo( "newEntries",
       "java.util.Vector", "New Entries" );

      ops[ 1 ] = new MBeanOperationInfo(
          "modifyEntries", "Modify service attributes",
                         sig1, "void",
                         MBeanOperationInfo.ACTION );

      MBeanInfo mbi =
                new MBeanInfo(  "jmxbook.ch5.JINIServiceManager",
                "Manages Service: " + initialAttribute.toString(),
                   atts, cons, ops, nots );
      return mbi;
   }
   private Object lookUpService()          ❷  Find Jini
   {                                           lookup service
     try
     {
       Class[] interfaces = { Class.forName( jiniInterfaceName ) };

       Entry[] ents = new Entry[ 1 ];
       ents[ 0 ] = initialAttribute;

       ServiceTemplate template = new
                 ServiceTemplate(null,interfaces,ents );

       ServiceRegistrar reg = RegistryFinder.getRegistry();
       ServiceMatches matches = reg.lookup( template,10000 );

       ServiceItem item = matches.items[ 0 ];
       return item.service;
     }
     catch( Exception e )
     {
        e.printStackTrace();
     }

     return null;
   }

} //class
```

❶ The `JINIServiceManager` Dynamic MBean doesn't provide much of an implementation for the get and set attribute methods. By examining the management interface of this MBean exposed by its `getMBeanInfo()` method, you can see that it does not expose any attributes. Therefore, the MBean should not support any methods that read or write attributes. In fact, both the `getAttribute()` and `setAttribute()` methods throw an `AttributeNotFoundException` exception when invoked.

❷ Because this MBean is intended to manage the Jini service that created it, it must be able to find that service. The MBean's constructor accepts a single argument: an `Entry` object that initially identifies the Jini service. The MBean also expects the Jini service to implement the `jmxbook.ch5.ManagedJINIService` interface. The MBean uses the interface, combined with the `Entry` object, to identify the Jini service. The `lookUpService()` method uses an object called `RegistryFinder` to find the nearest service registry. You should replace the implementation of this method with your own.

This example does not expose any operations or attributes from the Jini service; instead, it exposes the view of the Jini service.

5.5.2 *Rebuilding a management interface at runtime*

As described earlier in this chapter, Dynamic MBeans provide their management interface at runtime. This ability equips Dynamic MBeans to manage evolving resources over time. Developers can easily adapt Dynamic MBeans as their resources change. However, wouldn't it be useful to have an MBean that is truly dynamic? Consider the Dynamic MBean that reads a flat file to determine which of its manageable resource's methods to expose.

The MBean could monitor its flat file and watch for changes. When it detects a change, it could reload the file, rebuild its management interface (by creating a new `MBeanInfo` return value for the `getMBeanInfo()` method), and be ready to manage its resource in an entirely new way. However, this approach would pose a few problems.

Each time you tried using this Dynamic MBean, the attribute or operation you were trying to access could be different (or missing!). In fact, in order to ensure that you would not be incorrectly using a management interface, you would have to reacquire before every attempt.

JMX agents are not required by the JMX specification to ensure that a management interface does not change over the lifetime of an MBean. However, the specification does state that the management interface should not change, in order for management tools to better perform their function.

5.6 *Creating utility classes*

After examining only two Dynamic MBeans, you probably have noticed that it can sometimes be a tedious task to implement the getMBeanInfo() method. Depending on the management interface, you may spend some time writing the getMBeanInfo() method that constructs the MBeanInfo object. It can be tiring work constructing an object for every exposed constructor, operation, attribute, and notification. It would be nice not to have to write that method for every Dynamic MBean you create.

This section creates a super class for Dynamic MBeans that makes it easier to create MBeanInfo objects.

5.6.1 *Creating a dynamic MBean super class*

After you have written a few Dynamic MBeans, you begin to want to avoid writing the code that creates the MBeanInfo object. One way to solve this problem is to create methods that do it for you and reuse that code. You can do so by using a super class for Dynamic MBeans that provides a generic implementation of the DynamicMBean interface.

The super class contains generic getAttribute(), setAttribute(), and invoke() method implementations. In addition, it needs a mechanism for generically creating an MBeanInfo object to return in the getMBeanInfo() method. The DynamicMBeanSupport class in listing 5.2 is such a super class.

Listing 5.2   DynamicMBeanSupport.java

```
package jmxbook.ch5;

import javax.management.*;                          Implement
import java.lang.reflect.*;         javax.management.DynamicMBean
import java.util.*;

public class DynamicMBeanSupport implements DynamicMBean    <--┐
{
    protected MBeanInfo mbeanInfo = null;
    protected Hashtable attributes = new Hashtable();
    protected Hashtable notifications = new Hashtable();
    protected Hashtable constructors = new Hashtable();
    protected Hashtable operations = new Hashtable();;

    //exposed fields
    protected String description = "Description of the MBean";
```

```
public DynamicMBeanSupport()
{
    addMBeanAttribute( "description" , "java.lang.String",
        true, true, false, "Description of the MBean");
    addMBeanConstructor( this.getClass().getConstructors()[0],
                         "Default Constructor" );
}

public Object invoke( String method, Object args[],
                      String types[] )
                      throws MBeanException, ReflectionException
{
  try
  {
    Class c = this.getClass();
    Class sig[] = null;
    if( types != null )
    {
      sig = new Class[ types.length ];
      for( int i = 0; i < types.length; i++ )
      {
        sig[i] = Class.forName( types[i] );
      }
    }

    Method m = c.getDeclaredMethod( method , sig );

    Object returnObject = ( Object ) m.invoke( this, args );
    return returnObject;
  }
  catch( Exception e )
  {
    e.printStackTrace();
    return null;
  }
}

public Object getAttribute( String name )
             throws MBeanException, AttributeNotFoundException,
             ReflectionException
{
  try
  {
    Class c = this.getClass();
    Method m = c.getDeclaredMethod( "get" + name, null );
    return m.invoke( ( Object ) this, null );
  }
  catch( Exception e )
  {
    e.printStackTrace();
    return null;
  }
}
```

Begin building
MBeanInfo object

Implement ❶
DynamicMBean
interface

```
public void setAttribute( Attribute attribute )
              throws MBeanException,
              AttributeNotFoundException, ReflectionException,
              InvalidAttributeValueException
{
  String fname  = attribute.getName();
  Object fvalue = attribute.getValue();
  try
  {
    Class c = this.getClass();
    String type =  getType( fname, false, true );
    if( type == null )
      throw new AttributeNotFoundException( fname );

    Class[] types = { Class.forName( type ) };
    Method m = c.getDeclaredMethod( "set" + fname, types );

    Object[] args = { fvalue };
    m.invoke( ( Object ) this, args );
  }
  catch( AttributeNotFoundException ae )
  {
    throw ae;
  }
  catch( Exception e )
  {
    e.printStackTrace();
  }
}
public AttributeList setAttributes( AttributeList attributes )
{
  Attribute[] atts = ( Attribute[] ) attributes.toArray();
  AttributeList list = new AttributeList();
  for( int i = 0; i < atts.length; i++ )
  {
    Attribute a = atts[i];
    try{
      this.setAttribute( a );
    }catch( Exception e ) { e.printStackTrace(); }
  }//for

  return attributes;
}
public AttributeList getAttributes( String[] names )
{
  AttributeList list = new AttributeList();

  for( int i = 0; i < names.length; i++ )
  {
    try{
    list.add( new Attribute( names[i],
            this.getAttribute ( names[i] ) ) );
```

❶ Implement DynamicMBean interface

❶ Implement DynamicMBean interface

❶ Implement DynamicMBean interface

```
      }catch( Exception e ) { e.printStackTrace(); }
    }
    return list;
  }

  public MBeanInfo getMBeanInfo()   ◁─── Add parts to
  {                                       management
    try                                   interface
    {
      buildDynamicMBeanInfo();   ◁─── Build MBeanInfo
    }                                 object
    catch( Exception e )
    {
      e.printStackTrace();
    }
    return mbeanInfo;
  }

  protected void addMBeanOperation( String name,
      String[] paramTypes,
      String[] paramNames, String[] paramDescs, String desc,
      String rtype, int type )
  {
    MBeanParameterInfo[] params = null;
    if( paramTypes != null )
    {
      params = new MBeanParameterInfo[ paramTypes.length ];
      for( int i = 0; i < paramTypes.length; i++ )
      {
        params[i] = new MBeanParameterInfo( paramNames[i],
                  paramTypes[i], paramDescs[i] );
      }
    }

    operations.put( name, new MBeanOperationInfo( name, desc,
                                          params,
                                          rtype, type ) );

  }

  protected void addMBeanAttribute( String fname, String ftype ,
                boolean read, boolean write, boolean is,
                String desc )
  {
      attributes.put( fname, new MBeanAttributeInfo(fname, ftype,
                              desc,read,write,is) );
  }

  protected void addMBeanConstructor( Constructor c,
                  String desc )
  {
      this.constructors.put( c,
                  new MBeanConstructorInfo( desc, c ) );
  }
```

```java
    private void buildDynamicMBeanInfo() throws Exception
    {
        MBeanOperationInfo[] ops =
                new MBeanOperationInfo[ operations.size() ];
        copyInto( ops, operations );

        MBeanAttributeInfo[] atts =
                new MBeanAttributeInfo[ attributes.size()];
        copyInto( atts, attributes );

        MBeanConstructorInfo[] cons =
                new MBeanConstructorInfo[ constructors.size() ];
        copyInto( cons, constructors );

        mbeanInfo = new MBeanInfo(
                this.getClass().getName(), description,
                                atts, cons, ops, null );
    }
    private void copyInto( Object[] array, Hashtable table )
    {
      Vector temp = new Vector( table.values() );
      temp.copyInto( array );
    }
    private String getType( String attName,
                    boolean read, boolean write )
    {
        boolean allowed = true;

        if( attributes.containsKey( attName ) )
        {
            MBeanAttributeInfo temp = ( MBeanAttributeInfo )
                                        attributes.get( attName );
            if( read )
            {
              if( !temp.isReadable() )
                allowed = false;
            }
            if( write )
            {
              if( !temp.isWritable() )
                allowed = false;
            }
            if( !allowed )
              return null;
            else
              return temp.getType();
        }
        else return null;
    }
}//class
```

❶ The DynamicMBeanSupport class provides an implementation for all the methods from the DynamicMBean interface. Subclasses can override them, but these implementations should be good enough for most situations. The getAttribute() and setAttribute() methods use introspection (using the java.lang.reflect package) to get and set the value of class member variables. In addition, the setAttribute() method invokes the getType() method to discover the type of a member variable whether the requester has proper access to an attribute as defined by the MBean's management interface. If it is an invalid request, getType() returns null. The invoke() method does something similar in that it also uses introspection to invoke operations of the class.

The four methods that make using this class advantageous are addMBeanAttribute(), addMBeanConstructor(), addMBeanOperation(), and buildDynamicMBeanInfo(). The add methods allow subclasses to create their MBeanInfo object by adding portions of it as needed. For instance, look in the constructor of the class: it invokes the addMBeanAttribute() method in order to expose the description field of this MBean. Of course, it is not necessary to expose this field, but doing so serves as a good example. The constructor also adds itself to the MBeanInfo object. Finally, the buildDynamicMBeanInfo() method is called to put everything together in an MBeanInfo instance as needed.

5.7 *Summary*

This chapter introduced you to a more complex type of MBean: the Dynamic MBean. You learned that Dynamic MBeans are useful when managing evolving resources or resources with unstable interfaces. In addition, you learned that Dynamic MBeans generate their management interface at runtime using a standard set of JMX metadata classes. In addition to writing Dynamic MBeans, you created a super class that can save you time and effort in future Dynamic MBean development.

Chapter 6 covers the JMX notification model surrounding MBeans. That chapter will teach you about using standard JMX notifications, creating your own notifications, and receiving notifications from MBeans.

Communication with MBeans using notifications

- Introducing the notification framework
- Using notification filters
- Examining the AttributeChange notification classes

Before we move on to the last type of MBean, it is time you learned more about the JMX notification model. In chapters 4 and 5, we delayed covering JMX notifications in order to focus on the construction of the two basic types of MBeans. This chapter will show you how to make MBeans more beneficial by adding notifications. JMX notifications can be used to inform other objects or processes of important events, state changes, or statistical information from managed resources.

The JMX notification model is similar to the Java event model in that it provides a callback mechanism for interested listeners that have implemented specific interfaces. In this case, the notification model allows MBeans to send notification objects to interested listeners. Notifications are Java objects, like events; they contain information populated by an MBean, and are sent to other objects that have registered as listeners.

This chapter discusses sending and receiving notifications from MBeans. In subsequent chapters, you will begin including notifications into examples where appropriate.

6.1 *Using MBean notifications*

JMX is a powerful tool used to expose applications for management and monitoring. The first few chapters have given you a good feel for how you can use JMX to expose your own resources for management. However, exposing resources for management is only part of an application management solution. Management applications need to be informed about the *state*, or critical events, of a managed resource.

For example, imagine you have instrumented an application critical to your business (recall that instrumentation is the process of exposing a resource through MBeans). You are having success maintaining that application by using MBeans and a management tool, but you come to work one day and the application has crashed. The MBean should have been able to inform you that the application had gone into an error state and needed help.

In addition, consider MBeans used to control customer service applications. One particular MBean might need to send a notification when a specific customer help flag is raised.

The JMX notification model can help in such situations. By using notifications, you let your MBeans speak to the other objects, applications, and so forth. In turn, those notification receivers (or listeners) can take appropriate action: for example, they can contact pagers or other applications.

6.2 *Components of the JMX notification model*

If you have worked with the Java event model, then using the JMX notification model will come easily. MBean events are wrapped as notification objects and broadcast from MBeans. Notification listeners, like event listeners, register with MBeans in order to receive notifications. The notification model supports sending many different types of notifications, including user-defined notifications. One noticeable difference between the notification model and the event model is that notification listeners register only once with an MBean to receive all types of notifications. In addition, when registering for notifications, listeners can optionally provide a filter object that indicates the types of notifications in which the listener is interested (we talk about notifications filters in a moment).

Table 6.1 lists the four major components of the JMX notification model.

Table 6.1   The four components of the JMX notification model. Some of these components are similar to those found in the Java event model.

Component	Description	Section
Notification broadcaster	An object that implements the `javax.management.Notification-Broadcaster` interface, allowing it to send notifications	6.2.1
Notification	An object emitted from broadcasters that contain information for a listener	6.2.3
Notification listener	An object that implements the `javax.management.Notification-Listener` interface, allowing it to receive notifications	6.2.4
Notification filter	An object associated with a listener that can filter notifications, allowing only the desired notifications to be delivered to a listener	6.2.5

We discuss the four components in the following sections. After covering each component, you will begin writing some examples.

6.2.1 *Being a notification broadcaster*

A notification broadcaster is an MBean that implements the `javax.management.NotificationBroadcaster` interface. Classes can implement the interface or inherit the implementation from a super class. In the `HelloWorld` example from chapter 2, the `HelloWorld` MBean became a notification broadcaster when it extended the `javax.management.NotificationBroadcasterSupport` class. This support class provided the `HelloWorld` MBean with an implementation of the `NotificationBroadcaster` interface.

The NotificationBroadcaster interface

Figure 6.1 shows the UML diagram for the `NotificationBroadcaster` interface. This section introduces the methods of the interface.

The interface contains methods for adding and removing notification listeners. These methods allow objects to register as listeners for the notifications an MBean can emit. Listeners provide a callback method that broadcasters invoke in order to deliver a notification.

Notice in the `addNotificationListener()` method that one of the arguments is the `NotificationFilter` class. This object is the filter mentioned previously, and we discuss it in section 6.2.4. The last argument of this method is an `Object` instance called the *handback*. This value is sent back to the listener when a notification is delivered and should never be modified by the broadcaster. Both the filter and handback objects are optional and can be null.

The handback object can be used to provide a broadcaster with a context for the listener. For example, take the case of internationalization. Assume an MBean is sending out notifications that contain messages intended for human users. In order to internationalize this message, the MBean would need a resource bundle or language file to provide a translation. Each listener that registers for the notification could provide its own resource bundle that allows the MBean to

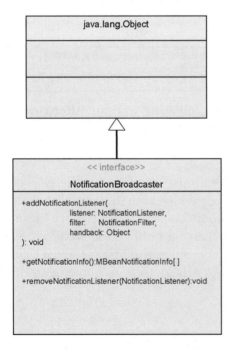

Figure 6.1
UML diagram of the
`NotificationBroadcaster` **interface**

translate the notification message for each listener. Alternatively, you could leave the handback object as null.

The last method in the interface, `getNotificationInfo()`, returns an array of objects of type `MBeanNotificationInfo`. You should recognize this object from chapter 5; it is a member of the set of metadata objects used to describe the management interface of an MBean. It is used here separately to ensure that broadcasters provide information about the types of notifications they emit. We examine the `MBeanNotificationInfo` class in section 6.2.2.

The NotificationBroadcasterSupport class

The other way to implement the `NotificationBroadcaster` interface is to extend the `javax.management.NotificationBroadcasterSupport` class. By extending this class, you inherit an implementation of the interface.

In addition, the `NotificationBroadcasterSupport` class provides an extra method called `sendNotification()`. The `sendNotification()` method provides a mechanism for sending a `Notification` object to registered listeners. This method attempts to send its notification argument to each registered listener after first applying that listener's filter object. If the filter indicates that the listener should receive that notification, then it is sent. A drawback of extending this class is that you don't have the opportunity to interact with the handback object before sending a notification.

The final method from the `NotificationBroadcaster` interface is `getNotificationInfo()`. A subclass of the `NotificationBroadcasterSupport` class should override the `getNotificationInfo()` method to provide information about the notifications it can broadcast. The return value of this method is an array of `MBeanNotificationInfo` objects. This class is a member of the metadata classes covered in chapter 5.

6.2.2 Describing notifications as part of a management interface

In chapter 5, which discussed Dynamic MBeans, you were introduced to the MBean metadata classes. These classes are used to describe the management interfaces of MBeans. One of the metadata classes that we didn't cover in detail is `MBeanNotificationInfo`. Now that we are discussing notifications, we need to examine this class.

The `javax.management.MBeanNotificationInfo` class is a metadata class used by MBeans that are notification broadcasters. MBeans provide this class in the following two ways:

- `DynamicMBean.getMBeanInfo()`—If the MBean is a Dynamic MBean, it must implement the `getMBeanInfo()` method. The `MBeanInfo` object returned by this method can contain an array of `MBeanNotificationInfo` objects.

- `NotificationBroadcaster.getNotificationInfo()`—When implementing the notification broadcaster interface, MBeans must implement this method. This method returns an array of `MBeanNotificationInfo` objects.

An instance of the `MBeanNotificationInfo` class contains information about the notifications that an MBean can emit. Just like the other metadata classes, it extends the `MBeanFeatureInfo` class.

An `MBeanNotificationInfo` object contains three things: the Java class name of the notification object being described (contained in the `name` class member variable), the notification types that can be sent using that class, and a description. The name and description fields are inherited from the `MBeanFeatureInfo` class. Each instance of `MBeanNotificationInfo` describes a specific Java class that is used as a notification. The class will be either `javax.management.Notification` or a subclass.

The class also contains a `getNotifTypes()` method that returns an array of `String` objects whose values are used to describe the types of notifications that could be sent using a particular notification class.

The *type* in this case does not refer to a Java class designation, but rather to a dot-separated `String` that identifies a notification instance. The identification `String`—its notification type—identifies a notification and conveys a sense of its purpose. For example, for a monitoring application developed by Acme Company, you might have a notification type like `acme.notif.statechange`. (Notification types tend to follow the pattern *company.resource.eventname*. This is only a suggested format; no rule specifies the exact format for the notification type `String`.)

6.2.3 *The Notification class*

JMX provides a standard notification class, `javax.management.Notification`. This class extends `java.util.EventObject` and is used as a super class for other notification classes.

The `Notification` class contains six member variables that are all accessible through getter methods. Table 6.2 describes these class members and their purposes.

The `Notification` class has several different constructors, each providing a different set of initialization arguments for these class members.

Table 6.2 The class members of the `javax.management.Notification` class

Class member	Purpose
`Message`	A `String` object representing a message. This could be the reason for the notification.
`SequenceNumber`	A number indicating the order in relation of events from the source. The source populates this field if it intends to give listeners the ability to sort incoming notifications. The notification model makes no guaranties that notifications will be received in the order they were sent.
`TimeStamp`	The timestamp of the notification, represented as a `long` value.
`Type`	The dot-separated `String` value indicating the type of the notification. Not a class type. For example:`acme.mbeanA.event1`.
`UserData`	An object used to contain any data that a source wants to send to a notification listener.
`Source`	The source of the notification. This object contains an `ObjectName` or a reference to the object that generated the notification.

6.2.4 *Being a notification listener*

Up to now, we have examined notification broadcasters, the `MBeanNotification-Info` class, and the `Notification` class. The last major component in the notification framework is the notification listener. In JMX, objects interested in receiving notifications must implement the `javax.management.NotificationListener` interface. You may remember this interface from chapter 2, where you implemented it in your `HelloAgent` class. Figure 6.2 shows the UML diagram for the `NotificationListener` interface.

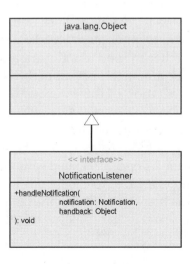

**Figure 6.2
UML diagram of the
`NotificationListener` interface**

The NotificationListener interface contains a single method: handleNotification(). It takes two arguments: an instance of Notification and an instance of Object. Notification broadcasters invoke this method when they are ready to deliver a notification to the listener. The instance of Notification is the notification being sent, and the Object instance is the handback object registered by the listener. Recall that when a listener registers to receive notifications using the addNotificationListener() method, it passes in an Object instance named *handback*.

NOTE   When implementing the handleNotification() method from the NotificationListener interface, you should have it return as soon as possible. Notification broadcasters invoke this method synchronously, meaning it will block until the method invocation is complete. Depending on the implementation and purpose of an MBean, this behavior could present a problem. You can avoid it by implementing the method that sends notifications (discussed later), which invoked the handleNotification() method asynchronously.

The only component remaining is the notification filter. Because MBeans can emit an infinite number of notification types, listeners can use a filter to ensure they receive only the specific notification types in which they are interested. Remember that listeners register once to receive all notifications from an MBean, and therefore need to be able to filter out notifications that are unwanted.

6.2.5 *Filtering notifications*

As stated earlier, notification filters give notification listeners a way to sort through a potential barrage of notifications to receive only those notifications that are important to them. To be more accurate, notification broadcasters use a registered listener's filter to determine whether to send a notification to a listener. Recall from section 6.2.1 that one of the arguments passed to the addNotificationListener() method is an implementation of the javax.management. NotificationFilter interface.

The NotificationFilter interface declares only one method: isNotificationEnabled(). This method accepts a Notification object that is about to be sent and returns a boolean value indicating whether the listener associated with this filter wants to receive the notification. Implementers are free to choose any way of filtering through notifications, but probably the best way to filter notifications is by their type. JMX contains a class called NotificationFilterSupport that does just that. You provide this object with acceptable notification types by invoking its enableType() method and passing it a String value notification type.

When you use filters, you usually assume that notification listeners have some knowledge of the notification meanings for a particular MBean, because filters must be able to decide whether they should accept a notification. In addition, the filter argument of the addNotificationListener() method can be left null, thereby indicating to the NotificationBroadcaster that a listener wants to receive all notifications.

NOTE   If you don't want to create a filter object that depends on having knowledge of notification types, you can alternatively have the isNotificationEnabled() method be a callback to the notification listener. The listener can decide whether it wants a notification to be sent.

6.3 *A notification polling example*

Now that you have an understanding of all the components involved in the notification model, let's put it all together in a short example. For this example, you will create a Standard MBean. (Remember that a Standard MBean is an MBean that implements an MBean interface that explicitly declares the MBean's management interface.)

The MBean for this example runs in a loop in its own thread. With every pass through the loop, it sends a notification. The following is the PollingMBean interface:

```
package jmxbook.ch6;

import javax.management.*;

public interface PollingMBean
{
  public void start();
  public void stop();
}
```

You can see that this MBean exposes only two operations—start() and stop()—and no attributes. These operations will start or stop a loop that sends a notification with each pass. Listing 6.1 shows the MBean that implements this interface; it creates the class Polling. In addition, the Polling class extends NotificationBroadcasterSupport in order to inherit an implementation of the NotificationBroadcaster interface.

Listing 6.1 Polling.java

```
package jmxbook.ch6;

import javax.management.*;

public class Polling extends NotificationBroadcasterSupport   ⊲─ Extend
                          implements PollingMBean, Runnable        support class
{                                                                  for sending
  private boolean stop = true;                                     notifications
  private int index = 0;

  public Polling()
  {
  }

  public void start()
  {
    try
    {
      stop = false;
      Thread t = new Thread( this );          Create Thread
      t.start();                              to run loop
    }
    catch( Exception e )
    {
      e.printStackTrace();
    }
  }

  public void stop()
  {
    stop  =  true;
  }

  public void run()
  {
    while( !stop )
    {
      try
      {
        Thread.sleep( 1000 );
        System.out.println( "Polling" );
      }
      catch( Exception e )
      {
        e.printStackTrace();
      }
      Notification notif = new Notification(
                      "ch6.PollingMBean.counter",        ❶ Create and send
                      this, index++ );                      notification
      sendNotification( notif );
```

```
        }//while
    }

    public MBeanNotificationInfo[] getNotificationInfo()      ➋  Expose
    {                                                             notifications
        String[] type = { "ch6.PollingMBean.counter" };
        MBeanNotificationInfo[] info = new MBeanNotificationInfo[ 1 ];

        info[ 0 ] = new MBeanNotificationInfo( type,
                                   "javax.management.Notification",
                                   "The Polling MBean counter" );
        return info;
    }

}//class
```

➊ As this MBean passes through its loop, it repeatedly executes these lines of code that build and send an instance of the `Notification` class. To build notifications in this example, you use the constructor of the `Notification` class that accepts values for the notification type, source, and sequence number. After constructing the notification, you send it using the `sendNotification()` method inherited from the `NotificationBroadcasterSupport` super class.

➋ Also inherited from the super class is the `getNotificationInfo()` method. You don't necessarily have to override this method, but you need to do so in order for the MBean to accurately describe the notifications it sends. The super class has no way of knowing what you intend to emit in the subclass. You must override this method in order to guarantee you are sending and describing the same types of notifications.

6.4 *Capturing MBean attribute changes*

After completing the previous example, you should have a good understanding of how the notification model works within JMX. Now it is time to move on to more specific notification types that are found throughout JMX. Recall that notifications can serve as events and usually contain information regarding an MBean event. A common event that occurs in a JMX application is the changing of MBean attributes.

For example, other components of an application might need to know when a particular attribute changes in order to perform some related action. Because attribute changes can be a common occurrence, JMX provides a standard notification class to encapsulate attribute changes: the `javax.management.Attribute-ChangeNotification` class.

The `AttributeChangeNotification` class extends the class `Notification`, and therefore inherits its class members for the notification message, timestamp, and so forth. However, it provides four additional fields that provide the receiver with all the information about an MBean attribute change. Table 6.3 lists the four additional class member variables by their access methods.

Table 6.3 The additional class members from the `AttributeChangeNotification` class

Class member	Purpose
`getAttributeName()`	Returns the name of the attribute that changed as a `String` object
`getAttributeType()`	Returns the class type of the attribute that changed as a `String` object
`getNewValue()`	Returns an `Object` instance containing the new value of the attribute that changed
`getOldValue()`	Returns the `Object` instance containing the old value of the attribute that changed

All `AttributeChangeNotification` notifications use the notification type `jmx.attribute.change`. This type is defined by the `public static` class member variable `AttributeChangeNotification.ATTRIBUTE_CHANGE`. This notification class provides a single constructor in which you pass all the arguments needed to populate the notification shown here:

```
public AttributeChangeNotification( java.lang.Object source,
    long sequenceNumber, long timeStamp, java.lang.String msg,
    java.lang.String attributeName, java.lang.String attributeType,
    java.lang.Object oldValue, java.lang.Object newValue )
```

With this new notification class comes a new concept surrounding filtering. All attribute change notification types are `jmx.attribute.change`, so you need a different method of filtering. This is the case because even though many notifications of the same type may be received, they could be encapsulating different attributes that have been altered. Filtering is needed because you may not want to receive all attribute-change events from an MBean.

6.4.1 *Filtering attribute change notifications*

As with any notification, listeners should be able to filter out attribute change notifications that are not desired. However, all `AttributeChangeNotification` notifications have the same type. Using the `NotificationFilterSupport` class examined earlier won't help, because it filters based on notification type. Therefore, if a listener only wanted to receive a notification for a specific attribute, the filter would need to examine the contents of the attribute notifications, not the type.

JMX provides another standard class that implements the `NotificationFilter` interface: the `javax.management.AttributeChangeNotificationFilter` class. This filter class implements the `NotificationFilter` interface and works similarly to the `NotificationFilterSupport` class. However, instead of enabling types of notifications, listeners enable attribute names.

For instance, to indicate to the filter that you are interested in attribute change notifications coming from the attribute named `State`, you would invoke the filter's `enableAttribute()` method and pass in the `String` value `State`.

Broadcasters use this filter just like any other by invoking the `isNotificationEnabled()` method, passing in the `Notification` to be sent, and receiving a `boolean` value indicating a listener's interest. The filter checks the notification to see if it encapsulates an attribute change in which its listener is interested.

6.4.2 *Revising the Polling MBean*

To further examine the attribute change notification class, let's modify the `Polling` MBean to use an `AttributeChangeNotification` notification. The first presentation of this MBean had no attributes, so you need to add one. The following interface declares a new attribute, `interval`, which indicates how long to pause between sending notifications. The changes to the interface are in bold:

```
package jmxbook.ch6;

import javax.management.*;

public interface PollingMBean
{
  public void start();
  public void stop();
  public void setInterval( long time );
}
```

The new method `setInterval()` accepts a `long` parameter used to set the amount of sleep time between sending notifications in the main loop. Listing 6.2 shows the new `Polling` MBean class. To demonstrate `AttributeChangeNotification`, the MBean will emit one notification each time the `setInterval()` is invoked. The changes to the class are in bold.

Listing 6.2 Polling.java

```
package jmxbook.ch6;

import javax.management.*;

public class Polling extends NotificationBroadcasterSupport
                     implements PollingMBean, Runnable
```

```
{
  private boolean stop = true;
  private int index = 0;
  private long interval = 1000;

  public Polling()
  {
  }

  public void setInterval( long interval )
  {
    long temp = this.interval;
    this.interval = interval;
    AttributeChangeNotification notif = new
        AttributeChangeNotification(
        this, 0, System.currentTimeMillis(),
        "Attribute Change",
        "interval", "long", new Long( temp ),
        new Long( interval ) );

    sendNotification( notif );

  }

  public void start()
  {
    try
    {
      stop = false;
      Thread t = new Thread( this );
      t.start();
    }
    catch( Exception e )
    {
      e.printStackTrace();
    }
  }

  public void stop()
  {
    stop  =  true;
  }

  public void run()
  {
    while( !stop )
    {
      try
      {
        Thread.sleep( interval );
        System.out.println( "Polling" );
      }
      catch( Exception e )
```

 **1** Create
AttributeChange
Notification

```
        {
          e.printStackTrace();
        }
        Notification notif = new Notification(
                "ch6.PollingMBean.counter",
                this, index++ );
        sendNotification( notif );
      }//while
   }

   public MBeanNotificationInfo[] getNotificationInfo()
   {
      String[] type = { "ch6.PollingMBean.counter" };
      String[] attChanges = {
              AttributeChangeNotification.ATTRIBUTE_CHANGE };

      MBeanNotificationInfo[] info = new MBeanNotificationInfo[ 2 ];

      info[ 0 ] = new MBeanNotificationInfo( type,
                            "javax.management.Notification",
                            "The Polling MBean counter" );

      info[ 1 ] = new MBeanNotificationInfo( attChanges,
                   "javax.management.AttributeChangeNotification",
                   "The Polling MBean counter" );
      return info;
   }
}//class
```

Add notification ❷ to management interface

❶ In order to create an AttributeChangeNotification object, you need to store the old value of the interval class member before changing it. The notification is created using the old and new values of the interval member variable. After you create the notification, it is sent the same way as the other notification in the main loop (using the sendNotification() method).

❷ In addition, the revised MBean adds another MBeanNotificationInfo object to the array return value of the getNotificationInfo() method. This additional object is the attribute change notification that is available to be received from this MBean.

6.4.3 *Testing the Polling MBean*

In order to round out your exposure to sending notifications, let's run the latest version of the Polling MBean in the JMXBookAgent agent. Remember from previous chapters that you created setup classes that registered MBeans in the agent. You will do the same thing in this chapter. Listing 6.3 shows the PollingSetup class, which contacts a JMXBookAgent instance and registers a Polling MBean with it.

Listing 6.3   PollingSetup.java

```
package jmxbook.ch6;

import javax.management.*;
import com.sun.jdmk.comm.*;
import jmxbook.ch3.*;

public class PollingSetup implements NotificationListener
{
   public PollingSetup()
   {
     try
     {
        RmiConnectorClient client = RMIClientFactory.getClient();
        ObjectName pollingName = new
                    ObjectName( "JMXBookAgent:name=polling");

        client.createMBean( "jmxbook.ch6.Polling", pollingName );
        client.addNotificationListener( pollingName, this,
                            null, null );
     }
     catch( Exception e )
     {
        ExceptionUtil.printException( e );
     }
   }

   public void handleNotification( Notification not, Object obj )
   {
     String type = not.getType();
     System.out.println( type );
   }

   public static void main( String args[] )
   {
     PollingSetup setup = new PollingSetup ();
   }
}
```

This setup class follows the format of the ones you created previously. However, in this case, after creating the MBean, it adds itself as a listener to receive any notifications the MBean emits.

Before running the setup class, you need to make sure you have an instance of the JMXBookAgent running. Use the following command to do so:

```
javac jmxbook.ch3.JMXBookAgent
```

After the agent successfully starts, execute the PollingSetup class to create your Polling MBean. Next, open your browser to http://localhost:9092, and you will see the `Polling` MBean registered in the agent. From the MBean View, you can change the `interval` attribute and execute the `start()` operation. If you do both, you should see output something like the following:

```
jmx.attribute.change
ch6.PollingMBean.counter
ch6.PollingMBean.counter
ch6.PollingMBean.counter
ch6.PollingMBean.counter
```

The attribute change notification was received when the `interval` attribute was altered, and the series of counter notifications was received after the `start()` operation was executed.

Writing this setup class also showed you one way of registering for notifications. The setup class invoked the `addNotificationListener()` of the MBean server. In the next section, we will summarize a few more details about registering as a notification listener.

6.5 *Registering as a notification listener*

If you remember from chapter 2, the `HelloAgent` class registered itself as a notification listener when it created the final version of the `HelloWorld` MBean. In that class, you used a method from the MBean server to register for notifications from the MBean. However, that is only one way to register with an MBean as a listener.

The next two sections describe how to register a listener with an MBean by using methods from the MBean or methods from the MBean server.

6.5.1 *Registering with an MBean*

If you have a class that creates an MBean object and registers it on an MBean server (using the `registerMBean()` method), then you can invoke methods on the reference at hand. If the MBean implements the `NotificationBroadcaster` interface in order to send notifications, then it also defines a method `addNotificationListener()`. Because you have manually created this MBean, you can also invoke its add listener method to add your own listener.

`Notification` objects received from an MBean after registering in this manner have their `source` class member set to contain an actual object reference to the MBean that emitted the notification. However, this is not the case if you register as a listener via the MBean server, as you did in chapter 2.

6.5.2 *Registering with the MBean server*

As just mentioned, the other way to register for notifications from an MBean is the method you used in chapter 2: invoking the addNotificationListener() method on the MBean server that contains the MBean. This method has the same signature as the same-named method in the NotificationBroadcaster interface, except for one additional argument: an instance of the ObjectName class.

This object name argument tells the MBean server the MBean in which to register the listener. If the MBean does not exist, the method will throw an InstanceNotFoundException exception. Notifications received after registering in this manner will contain a source class member variable containing the Object-Name of the MBean.

6.6 *Persisting MBean notifications*

You should realize by now that using notifications with your MBeans is not difficult. Emitting notifications is a powerful tool and can be used for communication, alerts, and more. Because notifications can contain important information and valuable data, it is a good idea to keep a record of them. In other words, you might want to *persist* your notifications.

Notifications can be persisted by the notification listener or by the broadcaster. For this chapter, we will consider the case of persisting notifications on the broadcaster side. By doing it on the agent side, you can create a sort of historical log of notification activity of MBean notifications. In fact, the next example shows how to persist notifications at the MBean level. To persist notifications, you can either create an MBean to act as a listener on every NotificationBroadcaster in the agent, or you can have each MBean manage its own notification persistence. We will discuss the latter option. Figure 6.3 illustrates the concept.

Normally, an MBean wanting to emit Notification objects would extend the NotificationBroadcasterSupport class. Listing 6.4 shows a new broadcaster support class that MBeans can use to inherit the ability to emit notifications. In addition, this class has the ability to store each notification sent by the MBean. This example persists notifications to a database; it assumes a table named Notifications already exists and has a column for each Notification class public member variable.

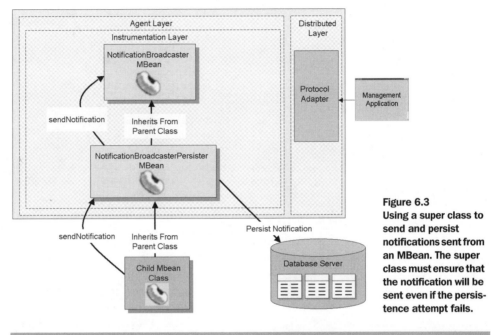

Figure 6.3
Using a super class to send and persist notifications sent from an MBean. The super class must ensure that the notification will be sent even if the persistence attempt fails.

Listing 6.4 NotificationBroadcasterPersister.java

```java
package jmxbook.ch6;

import java.sql.*;
import java.io.Serializable;
import javax.management.*;

public class NotificationBroadcasterPersister extends
                            NotificationBroadcasterSupport
{

    private Connection con = null;
    private boolean enable = false;

    public NotificationBroadcasterPersister( Connection con )
    {
        this.con = con;
    }

    public void setStorage( boolean enable )
    {
      this.enable = enable;
    }

    public boolean getStorage()
    {
      return enable;
    }
```

```
public void sendNotification( Notification notif )        ❶  Send
{                                                              notification
  try
  {
    String sql = "insert into Notifications ( message,
        sequence_number, " + " source, timestamp, type,
        user_data ) values ( ?,?,?,?,?,? )";

    PreparedStatement ps = con.prepareStatement( sql );
    ps.setString( 1, notif.getMessage() );
    ps.setLong( 2, notif.getSequenceNumber() );

    if( notif.getSource() != null &&
              notif.getSource() instanceof Serializable )
      ps.setObject( 3,notif.getSource() );
    else
      ps.setString( 3, "No Source" );

    ps.setLong( 4, notif.getTimeStamp() );
    ps.setString( 5, notif.getType() );

    if( notif.getUserData() != null &&
              notif.getUserData() instanceof Serializable )
      ps.setObject( 6,notif.getUserData() );
    else
      ps.setString( 6, "No User Data" );

    ps.executeUpdate();

    con.commit();

  }
  catch( Exception e )
  {
    e.printStackTrace();
  }

  super.sendNotification( notif );
}

}
```

❶ The `sendNotification()` method executes some simple JDBC code to persist the outgoing notification before sending it. Be sure to notice that an implementation like this one assumes the appropriate database tables already exist.

6.7 Notifications from the MBean server

When we first looked at the HTML adapter in chapter 2, you discovered that your `MBeanServer` contained an MBean that you did not create. That MBean was

MBeanServerDelegate. Apart from providing you with some information about the environment, this MBean serves to send notifications from the MBean server. An MBeanServer instance creates and registers this MBean in order to delegate the notification delivery, allowing the MBeanServer to go back to managing MBeans.

The delegate MBean performs the following two notification-related tasks:

- Emits an MBeanServerNotification when necessary (as described in the next section)
- Emits notifications that have been captured from other registered MBeans

6.7.1 *Notification types sent from the MBean server*

The MBean server's purpose is to provide a mechanism for managing MBeans. When working with an MBean server, you might find it important to know when new MBeans are registered or existing ones are removed. The MBean server emits the following notification types for these two events:

- jmx.mbean.registered
- jmx.mbean.unregistered

The two types correspond to registering and unregistering of MBeans. The important question, though, is how to register to receive these notifications. You know two facts that address this question: the MBean server delegates sending notifications to the MBeanServerDelegate MBean, and you can register to listen on any MBean that sends notifications. In order for the delegate MBean to send notifications, it must be a notification broadcaster. Therefore, just as the previous section described, you need to register as a listener with the delegate MBean. In order to do that, you need its object name. Again, recall from chapter 2 that the MBeanServerDelegate MBean's ObjectName value is JMImplementation:type= MBeanServerDelegate.

The notifications emitted by the MBean server are of the class MBeanServer-Notification. This class extends the Notification class and provides an additional operation, getObjectName(), which returns the object name of the MBean that caused the notification to be sent (by being registered or unregistered). The class also defines two public final static members—REGISTRATION_NOTIFICATION and UNREGISTRATION_NOTIFICATION—that correspond to the previously mentioned types.

In addition, JMX provides a filter for this type of notification. The MBean-ServerNotificationFilter class extends the NotificationFilterSupport class and provides methods that allow a listener to filter incoming MBeanServerNotification objects based on the object name that caused them to be sent. This functionality allows you to be informed when a particular MBean is registered or unregistered.

6.8 *Summary*

In this chapter, we discussed each of the components of the JMX notification model. We showed that MBeans must implement the `NotificationBroadcaster` interface in order to send notifications; this can be done directly or by extending the `NotificationBroadcasterSupport` class. You learned that notifications must be described by the `MBeanNotificationInfo` class, which is exposed by the management interface of an MBean. In addition, we examined the `Notification` class and how its members provide useful information such as notification type, source, timestamp, and so forth to notification listeners.

Along with sending notifications, this chapter also explained that classes interested in receiving notifications must implement the `NotificationListener` interface. In addition, notification listeners can register notification filters that reduce incoming notifications to only those in which a receiving object is actually interested. Filters are important because notification listeners would otherwise receive all types of notifications from a broadcaster. In JMX, listeners need to register only once to receive all notifications from a source.

Finally, we discussed some standard types of notifications that are already present in the JMX framework, including the `AttributeChangeNotification` and `MBeanServerNotification` classes. Attribute change notifications are sent by MBeans when they want to indicate that an attribute of their management interface has been altered. `MBeanServerNotification` notifications are sent by the MBean server to indicate that a particular MBean has been registered or unregistered.

The next chapter covers the final MBean type presented in this book: the Model MBean. Model MBeans are available for instantiation and configuration in every JMX-compliant agent.

MBeans on-the-fly

7

- Introducing the Model MBean classes
- Examining the various features of the Model MBean
- Discussing different uses for Model MBeans

In chapters 4 and 5, we covered Standard and Dynamic MBeans. This chapter discusses a new type of MBean: the Model MBean. The Model MBean is unique because developers do not have to write an MBean class. The classes and interface that make up the Model MBean are defined by the JMX specification and are guaranteed to be available in every JMX-compliant agent. Model MBeans are generic MBeans that can be instantiated in the MBean server and configured by a user to manage any resource.

In addition to resource management, the Model MBean provides several features that make it the most robust MBean, including MBean persistence, attribute value caching, and more. This chapter discusses how you can use Model MBeans to rapidly instrument a manageable resource.

7.1 *Working with the Model MBean*

Without considering the other features of the Model MBean (which we examine in the next section), the Model MBean's main difference from the Standard and Dynamic MBeans is that you do not develop the MBean class—the Model MBean is a required part of a JMX agent. The Model MBean is defined by the class `javax.management.modelmbean.RequiredModelMBean`.

As is the case for the Dynamic MBean, the management interface for a Model MBean is defined at runtime. In fact, the `RequiredModelMBean` class implements the `ModelMBean` interface, which extends the `DynamicMBean` interface. However, unlike usual Dynamic MBeans, the Model MBean's management interface is defined outside the MBean (by a management application or resource) and inserted into the MBean via a setter method.

To better understand how this works, let's walk through a few steps in a sample scenario that creates a Model MBean:

1   An application starts up and locates a JMX agent in order to expose itself for management by registering an MBean with the agent.

2   The application calls the `createMBean()` method of the agent's MBean server, telling it to create an instance of the `javax.management.modelmbean.RequiredModelMBean` class.

3   After the MBean is created, the application sets an object in the MBean to use as its managed resource.

4   The application creates an instance of the `ModelMBeanInfoSupport` class. This object, like the `MBeanInfo` class from chapter 4, encapsulates the

management interface of the new Model MBean (this object describes the Model MBean managed resource).

5   The application invokes an operation on the new Model MBean that sets the `ModelMBeanInfo` object.

At this point, the new Model MBean can be used to manage the application to the extent that its management interface allows. Using the Model MBean not only saves you development time, it also gives you the many features that come with the MBean. The next section highlights some of the most important Model MBean features and how they can be useful in a management environment.

7.2 *Features of the Model MBean*

The fact that Model MBeans can be created in any JMX-compliant agent is a great advantage for managing applications. It means that without writing any MBean code, you can instrument resources using a management tool interfacing with a JMX agent. Essentially, you can model a resource by describing its management interface in a Model MBean at runtime, exposing as much or as little as needed. That one advantage is enough to support the use of this type of MBean, but the Model MBean also has much more to offer.

The Model MBean has many features available for use; this section will highlight a few key ones. As you read this chapter, we'll discuss all the features of the Model MBean.

7.2.1 *MBean persistence*

One of the most valuable features of the Model MBean is its ability to persist itself. For a Model MBean, this means that it will not need to reset its managed resource and `ModelMBeanInfoSupport` objects. By using its persistence mechanism, a Model MBean can survive the cycling of the JMX agent that contains it. Each time a Model MBean is constructed, it checks to see if it can load its state from a specified location. When configuring a Model MBean, you can specify how often it should save its state.

The persistence mechanism of the Model MBean implementation provided in the Sun Reference Implementation (RI) uses Java Object Serialization to write the current state of the MBean's `ModelMBeanInfo` object out to a flat file location specified when the MBean was created. Other JMX implementations could provide different persistence mechanisms for their Model MBean implementations, such as JDBC.

7.2.2 Notification logging

Another valuable feature of the Model MBean is its ability to log each notification it emits. The Model MBean allows you to specify a log file location where it should write emitted notifications.

Using the notification logging mechanism lets you maintain an accurate record of all notifications sent by a particular MBean. This record is useful for keeping an audit trail of important management information from a particular resource.

7.2.3 Attribute value caching

A valuable performance feature built into the Model MBean is the ability to cache attribute values. The `ModelMBeanInfo` object associated with a Model MBean determines the attribute caching policy. For example, a Model MBean can be configured to locally store the value of an attribute after it is first acquired. Subsequent requests for this attribute can be satisfied with the local copy. How often the cache is updated is determined by the caching policy associated with the specific attribute, and configured by the user.

This ability can greatly increase a program's performance. If the operation that acquired the value of an attribute is costly, you can configure the caching policy to decrease the number of times the operation must be invoked to get the attribute. For instance, if the Model MBean manages a remote resource that has fairly static attributes, it could store their values locally in order to avoid repeatedly making a remote operation call to retrieve them.

7.2.4 Operation delegation

The Model MBean can have operations in its management interface that are invoked on objects other than its managed resource. When exposing a particular method for management, you can optionally include an `Object` reference in which to invoke the operation.

The delegation ability lets you expose operations that may interact with more than just your single manageable resource. For instance, you can delegate an exposed operation to an EJB, Java remote object, or any other `Object` reference. Currently, the Sun RI only supports `Object` references—other implementations (or your own subclass) could support the other types of delegation.

7.2.5 Generic notifications

The Model MBean also provides methods to send out generic, purely informational notifications. In the Model MBean implementation, there is a method that accepts a `String` argument to be sent out as a notification. The notification type is `jmx.modelmbean.general`.

7.3 *Examining the ModelMBean interface*

Now that we have examined the available features, let's discuss configuring the management interface of a Model MBean. Specifically, we need to explore the interfaces and classes that surround your use of Model MBeans. As with the Dynamic MBean, we'll first cover the interface to a Model MBean. Like the `DynamicMBean` interface, the `javax.management.modelmbean.ModelMBean` interface provides the methods necessary to work with a Model MBean. Figure 7.1 shows the `ModelMBean` interface with a UML diagram.

It is important to discuss the `ModelMBean` interface because it declares (or inherits) the methods you use to configure, access, and manage a Model MBean. These methods allow you to get and set attributes, invoke operations, and configure the overall management interface exposed by the MBean. In addition, the Model MBean provides the methods for MBean persistence and working with MBean notifications. After we cover this interface, we will discuss how to build the `ModelMBeanInfo` object for a Model MBean.

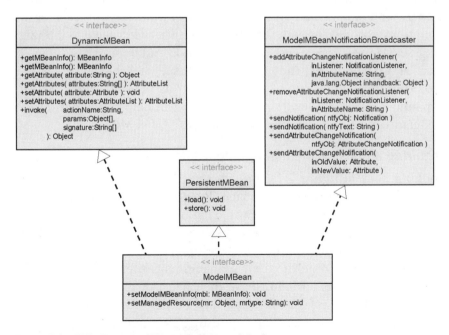

Figure 7.1   UML diagram of the `ModelMBean` interface

7.3.1 Configuring a Model MBean

As you read in the previous sections, a Model MBean manages an existing object: its managed resource. Developers choose how the MBean should use this object in order to provide the necessary management ability to the underlying managed resource. The Model MBean provides the following two methods that initialize the MBean for outside use:

- `setManagedResource( Object resource, String resourceType )`—This method sets the MBean's managed object. The object is the reference in which the operations will be invoked and attributes accessed. The `resource-Type` parameter tells the MBean what type of `Object` reference is being passed in. It can have the value `ObjectReference`, `Handle`, `IOR`, `EJBHandle`, or `RMIReference`; however, the Sun RI Model MBean implementation accepts only the `ObjectReference` type. Other JMX implementations may implement the other types.

- `setModelMBeanInfo( ModelMBeanInfo info )`—The `ModelMBeanInfo` parameter is the metadata object collection that describes the management interface of this Model MBean.

These two methods are very important for creating a Model MBean. They tell the MBean how to behave and what to interact with. You will see later that not all operations exposed through the `ModelMBeanInfo` object have to interact with the value set via the `setManagedResource()` method, but in most cases they do. In section 7.4, we will dissect the `ModelMBeanInfoSupport` class, which is the JMX RI provided implementation of the `ModelMBeanInfo` interface, as we did the Dynamic MBean's `MBeanInfo` class. Doing so will help you better understand all the features and configurations available to a Model MBean.

7.3.2 Acquiring and using the management interface

Looking back at figure 7.1, you can see that the `ModelMBean` interface also extends the `DynamicMBean` interface. By extending this interface, all Model MBeans are really Dynamic MBeans. That being so, a Model MBean defines its management interface at runtime like any other Dynamic MBean. However, where Dynamic MBeans are user-developed classes that construct their own `MBeanInfo` objects to define their management interface, Model MBeans are standard JMX classes and must have their `MBeanInfo` created and placed inside them (using the `setModelMBeanInfo()` method described earlier).

This requirement creates an interesting situation for Model MBean users. All MBeans are presented to clients in an identical format; in each case, the management application works with an MBeanInfo object. However, in the case of the Model MBean, its MBeanInfo object is actually the subclass of MBeanInfo: the ModelMBeanInfoSupport class. Management applications that know which MBeans are Model MBeans can then use the more specific MBeanInfo class to take advantage of the advanced capabilities of the Model MBean.

7.3.3 *Registering for notifications*

The second interface extended by the ModelMBean interface is ModelMBeanNotificationBroadcaster. This interface declares the notification-handling methods for Model MBeans. The methods declared by this interface register and remove notification listeners for Model MBean notifications. Model MBeans (based on their configuration) emit AttributeChangeNotifications notifications and generic informational notifications. In addition, the interface declares two sendNotification() methods that Model MBeans must implement. One of the methods is the regular sendNotification() method that you have seen in the past, and the other is an overloaded version that only accepts a String message to send out in a generic notification. When a generic notification is sent, its type is jmx.modelmbean.general. There is no need to list these methods here; you will see them in use later.

7.3.4 *MBean persistence*

The final interface extended by the ModelMBean interface is PersistentMBean. This interface declares two methods that initiate the persistence mechanism of a Model MBean: load() and store(). These methods are invoked based on the configuration of the Model MBean stored in its ModelMBeanInfo object. The load() method attempts to load an MBean state from a location specified in its ModelMBeanInfo instance. Alternatively, the store() method persists the current state of the MBean to a location specified in its ModelMBeanInfo instance. The Model MBean implementation in the Sun RI uses Java object serialization to a flat file for persistence.

7.4 *Understanding the Model MBean metadata*

As you just read, Model MBeans are Dynamic MBeans, and their management interfaces are created at runtime. The previous section showed that you can acquire and interact with the management interface the exact way you would a Dynamic MBean. (Look back at chapter 5 for more about Dynamic MBeans.) However, as stated earlier, if you know you are dealing with a Model MBean, you can take advantage of its additional capabilities. The behavior and configuration of these abilities lies within the `ModelMBeanInfo` object set in a Model MBean. This section will walk you through this class and all the features available to configure for a Model MBean.

Not only do Model MBeans use a subclass of the `MBeanInfo` class (`ModelMBean-Info`) to contain their metadata, each metadata class covered in chapter 5 also has a subclass used by Model MBeans. These subclasses provide the mechanisms to define the policies governing the behavior of a Model MBean. Table 7.1 lists the metadata classes and their parents.

Table 7.1   The metadata classes of the Model MBean used to describe its management interface

Class	Super class	Purpose
ModelMBeanAttributeInfo	MBeanAttributeInfo	Describes a Model MBean attribute
ModelMBeanConstructorInfo	MBeanConstructorInfo	Describes a Model MBean constructor
ModelMBeanNotificationInfo	MBeanNotificationInfo	Describes a Model MBean notification
ModelMBeanOperationInfo	MBeanOperationInfo	Describes a Model MBean operation
ModelMBeanInfo	MBeanInfo	Describes the policies of the MBean and contains the other metadata objects

We discussed the super classes of the Model MBean metadata classes in chapter 5, so we will not cover their methods again. For more information about how the metadata classes are used to describe exposed attribute, operations, and so forth, see chapter 5. The next several sections will walk you through each of the new metadata classes and what they offer to support the Model MBean.

7.4.1   Using descriptors

The next several subsections deal with the metadata objects that describe attributes, operations, notifications, and constructors in a Model MBean's management interface. But before we dive into the first class, it is important to explore what they all have in common. Each metadata class contains an instance of the `javax.management.Descriptor` interface: the `javax.management.model-mbean.DescriptorSupport` class.

The `Descriptor` objects help the metadata classes provide the additional configuration needed for the Model MBean's additional functionality. The `DescriptorSupport` class implements the methods of the `Descriptor` interface to create a class that can contain a number of *field name–field value* pairs. Each field name is represented by a `String` object, and each field value is represented by an `Object` instance. The methods defined in a `Descriptor` object deal with getting, setting, and removing these name-value pairs.

Each metadata object uses the descriptor to contain predefined fields that describe a particular piece of functionality. As you will see, each metadata class expects its `Descriptor` object to contain a field named `descriptorType` that indicates what the descriptor is being used to describe. The `descriptorType` field is expected to have the value `MBean`, `attribute`, `operation`, or `notification`. There are many more predefined fields for each metadata class, and we will discuss each as we go along.

In addition to containing a `Descriptor` object, each metadata class implements the `DescriptorAccess` interface, which provides the classes with the `setDescriptor()` and `getDescriptor()` methods. These metadata classes are treated exactly like the classes they extend, except for their inclusion of `Descriptor` objects. Therefore, the following sections will concentrate on their internal `Descriptor`—its features, configuration, and uses. For more information about their super classes, read the metadata section from chapter 5 (section 5.3).

7.4.2 *Constructing a ModelMBeanInfoSupport object*

As you already know, the `ModelMBeanInfoSupport` class extends the `MBeanInfo` class and therefore provides all the functionality described in chapter 5. However, this subclass provides the behavioral configuration of a Model MBean by use of its `Descriptor` object.

Table 7.2 displays the predefined attributes of the `Descriptor` object at the MBean level.

Table 7.2   The MBean-level descriptor attributes

Descriptor attribute	Possible values	Default value	Description
`name`	User-defined	mbeanName	The name of the MBean
`descriptorType`	`mbean, attribute, operation, notification`	mbean	The type of descriptor
`displayName`	User-defined	Classname	A name for this MBean to be used in the user display

Table 7.2   The MBean-level descriptor attributes *(continued)*

Descriptor attribute	Possible values	Default value	Description
persistPolicy	OnUpate, OnTimer, NoMoreOftenThan, Always, Never	never	How often to persist this MBean
persistPeriod	Seconds		Time value for a persist-Policy value of NoMore-OftenThan or OnTimer
persistLocation	Directory value		Directory of the persistent file
persistName	Filename		The filename of the persistent state
log	t, f	F	t logs all notifications; f logs none
logfile	Filename		Fully qualified file path for a log file
export	User-defined	F	Lookup name of the MBean, if it is to be exposed to an external registry
visibility	1, 2, 3, 4	1	1 means always visible; 4 means rarely visible
presentationString	XML format		Creates a rendering of the MBean for display purposes

You should be able to understand most of these attributes without much explanation. For instance, the attribute displayName is used only by applications that display information about a Model MBean; the JMX agent would not use this field to manage the MBean. The same is true for presentationString and visibility—the visibility attribute is intended for use by management applications to provide some level of viewing access for different users.

Examining the remaining attributes, we are left with those that describe the MBean's persistence policy and notification logging, and one called export. In this JMX RI, the export attribute is not used by the agent. However, it is intended to be used when exposing an MBean to the outside world via some lookup registry; the export value is the lookup name for this MBean.

JMX agents use the persistPolicy and persistPeriod attributes to determine how often to persist their state, and they use the persistLocation and persist-Name attributes to determine where to store it. Agents use these values to determine when to persist a Model MBean. Finally, you can use the log and logfile attributes to set up a log file tracking all the notifications emitted by an MBean. Doing so is useful because it lets you record the notification activity of your MBeans for later retrieval and analysis.

As we cover each of the metadata objects, we will focus on their descriptors. In their descriptors, you will see some of these attributes reproduced. If so, their values take precedence over the value at the MBean level, but apply only to the particular portion of the management interface being described.

7.4.3 *The ModelMBeanAttributeInfo class*

As you will recall, the MBeanInfo class (and therefore the ModelMBeanInfoSupport class) can expose many attributes for management using the MBeanAttributeInfo class. In the case of a Model MBean, the ModelMBeanAttributeInfo class is used. Again, in this section, we will focus on the Descriptor object that this class contains. Table 7.3 lists the predefined values of its descriptor.

Table 7.3 Attribute-level descriptor attributes

Descriptor attribute	Possible values	Description
name	User-defined	Attribute name
descriptorType	mbean, attribute, operation, notification	Type of descriptor
value	Value of the attribute	Current value of the attribute
default	User-defined	Default value of the attribute
getMethod	Method name of the getter for this attribute	Name of the method used to get the value of this attribute
setMethod	Method name of the setter for this attribute	Name of the method used to set the value of this attribute
prototcolMap		Object that provides a mapping to a different protocol
persistPolicy	Update, OnTimer, NoMoreOftenThan, Always, Never	How often to persist this attribute
persistPeriod	Seconds	Same as the MBean level
currencyTimeLimit	< 0 = never; 0 = always, > 0 = a seconds value	How long an attribute value is valid before needing to be refreshed
lastUpdatedTimeStamp	long value	When the value was last updated
iterable	T, F	Whether the attribute value object implements the Iterable interface
visibility	1 to 4	Same as the MBean level

Table 7.3 **Attribute-level descriptor attributes** *(continued)*

Descriptor attribute	Possible values	Description
`presentationString`	XML format	Same as the MBean level
`displayName`	User-defined	Display name for this attribute

You'll notice some duplicates from the MBean-level descriptor. As mentioned earlier, any duplicates override the MBean-level values but apply only to this particular attribute. The remaining attributes fall into three categories: describing the attribute, accessing the attribute, and storing the attribute value.

Describing the attribute

The descriptor attributes falling into this category are `name`, `default`, `protocolMap`, and `iterable`. The `name` value is simply the name of the attribute. The `default` attribute provides the MBean attribute with a default value. Remember, because the `Descriptor` class allows for name-`Object` pairs, the default value can be more than a `String` representation.

The `iterable` attribute indicates to a user whether the MBean attribute value is an iterable collection. This is a quick way to determine if the MBean attribute value is a list or some other class using the `java.util.Iterable` interface.

Finally, the `protocolMap` descriptor attribute is a unique attribute used only for MBean attributes. It contains an `Object` value that provides hints to a management application about how this MBean attribute value might be mapped to a different protocol. For example, you could use the `protocolMap` attribute to translate this value to Simple Network Management Protocol (SNMP) or a proprietary protocol.

Accessing the attribute

To describe how the MBean attribute is accessed, you need to use the `getMethod` and `setMethod` descriptor attributes. These two attributes contain the names of the methods used to get and set the value of the MBean attribute. In contrast to the other MBean types, these methods do not have to follow the naming scheme of *getName* and *setName*, where *Name* is the name of the MBean attribute. These method names can be any methods of the managed resource `Object` value contained in the Model MBean. Thus you can map an MBean attribute value to any method available in your object. Operations specified as getters and setter must also be described with an operation metadata object (shown in a moment).

Storing the attribute value

Each Model MBean attribute can be cached locally in the MBean. So, managed resources' attributes can be stored locally for quick retrieval. This behavior is configured on a per-MBean-attribute basis using the following descriptor attributes: `value`, `currencyTimeLimit`, and `lastUpdatedTimeStamp`.

The `value` attribute is the most current updated value of the MBean attribute. However, if you are depending on this being an accurate reflection of the MBean attribute value (because other processes besides the MBean could be changing it), you need to know when it was last acquired. The `currencyTimeLimit` descriptor attribute is used to configure how often the JMX agent will access this attribute and update the descriptor value. It can have one of three integer values: less than zero (never update), 0 (always update), and greater than zero (update every x seconds). In addition, the `lastUpdatedTimeStamp` descriptor attribute provides the timestamp of when the MBean was last used to update the attribute value.

Creating attributes not in the managed resource

Another interesting feature of Model MBeans is their ability to expose attributes of the MBean and attributes of its managed resource. To the management user, both attributes are from the same source (the resource being managed by the MBean); but in reality, you can add an attribute to a Model MBean that is not present in its managed resource. Essentially, such attributes have no getter or setter methods and are static values presented in the management interface.

7.4.4 The ModelMBeanOperationInfo class

Like the `ModelMBeanAttributeInfo` class, the `ModelMBeanOperationInfo` class provides some unique behavioral configuration for Model MBeans. With the Model MBean, you can expose operations for your management interface that belong to objects other than the one contained as the Model MBean's managed resource. In addition, you can configure the MBean to cache the return value of the operation. Table 7.4 lists the predefined descriptor attributes for operations.

Table 7.4 Operation-level descriptor attributes

Descriptor attribute	Possible values	Description
name	User-defined	Name of the MBean
descriptorType	mbean, attribute, operation, notification	Type of descriptor

Table 7.4 Operation-level descriptor attributes *(continued)*

Descriptor attribute	Possible values	Description
`class`	Class containing the method	Class where the method is defined
`role`	`getter, setter, operation, constructor`	Role of this operation
`targetObject`	`Object` value	Object on which to execute this operation
`targetType`	`ObjectReference, EJBHandle, IOR, RMIReference`	Type of `Object` held in the `targetObject` attribute
`displayName`	User-defined	Name used for display purposes
`lastReturnedValue`	Return value of the method	Cached return value for this operation
`currencyTimeLimit`	Same as attribute level	How long the return value is valid
`lastReturnedTimeStamp`	`long` value	Timestamp of the last returned value
`visibility`	1 to 4	Same as MBean level
`presentationString`	XML format	Same as MBean level

Let's examine the new descriptor attributes that help describe the exposed operation: `class`, `role`, `targetObject`, and `targetType`. The first two are simple enough: `class` contains the class name that defines this method, and `role` indicates the purpose of the method (setter, getter, operation, or constructor). The `targetObject` and `targetType` attributes are used to specify an object other than the Model MBean's managed resource in which to invoke the operation. This optional mechanism is useful if you want to delegate processing to other objects, or if you have such a distributed resource that you want to spread out operations among different application components. Currently, the Sun RI only supports the `ObjectReference targetType`.

Operations for attributes

When exposing an attribute in a Model MBean, you optionally specify the methods used as its getter and setter in the managed resource. Because methods invoked from a Model MBean can have configurable behavior, Model MBeans expect these getter and setter methods to be added to their `ModeMBeanInfo` objects with operation metadata. Therefore, when adding an attribute, you may also be adding two additional operations. You will see this in the example at the end of the chapter.

7.4.5 *The ModelMBeanConstructorInfo class*

The exposed constructor descriptor is similar to the exposed operation. In fact, it does not define any new descriptor attributes. Table 7.5 displays its predefined descriptor attributes.

Table 7.5 **Constructor-level descriptor attributes**

Descriptor attribute	Possible values	Description
name	User-defined	Name of the constructor
descriptorType	operation	Must be `operation`
role	constructor	Indicates this operation is a constructor
displayName	User-defined	Name used for displays
class		Class where the method is defined
visibility	1 to 4	Same as MBean level
presentationString	XML format	Same as MBean level

7.4.6 *The ModelMBeanNotificationInfo class*

The final metadata class is the `ModelMBeanNotificationInfo` class. It is used to describe and configure individual notifications that can be emitted by a Model MBean. The only behavior you can configure is if and where to log this notification type. Table 7.6 lists the descriptor attributes associated with this class.

Table 7.6 **Notification-level descriptor attributes**

Descriptor attribute	Possible values	Description
name	User-defined	Name of the notification
descriptorType	mbean, attribute, operation, notification	Type of descriptor
severity	1 to 5	1=fatal, 2=server, 3=error, 4=warning, 5=info
messageId		Unique key for the message text
messageText	User-defined	Text of the notification
log	T, F	Whether to log this notification
logFile	Fully qualified filename	Where to log this notification information; if not specified here, the MBean level value will be used

Table 7.6   Notification-level descriptor attributes *(continued)*

Descriptor attribute	Possible values	Description
`visibility`	1 to 4	Same as MBean level
`presentationString`	XML format	Same as MBean level

As you can see from the table, the descriptor provides attributes in order to store the pertinent information about a notification. For example, you can specify a generic notification `severity`, `messageId`, and `messageText`. The `messageId` is useful when logging notifications: when you come back to analyze the log file, you will be able to uniquely identify each message based on the notification id.

In addition, the `log` and `logfile` attributes specified here can override the ones specified at the MBean level, but will apply only to this particular notification.

7.5   *Model MBeans in action*

These metadata classes should feel familiar to you after learning about the metadata classes for the Dynamic MBean. However, as noted, the `Descriptor` objects enable the Model MBean's additional features. Now that we have covered each of the metadata objects and their descriptors, we can move into some examples.

7.5.1   *Building ModelMBeanInfo objects*

When building an instance of the `ModelMBeanInfo` class, you not only have to create arrays of metadata objects, but you also have to create corresponding `Descriptor` instances for the metadata. If you are modeling a resource with many operations, attributes, and notifications, you will have to write many lines of code. One way to help with this problem is to write a class similar to the Dynamic MBean super class you wrote in chapter 5.

Listing 7.1 shows the `ModelMBeanInfoBuilder` class. Like the `DynamicMBeanSupport` class in chapter 5, this class contains methods that help you build the metadata objects of the Model MBean's management interface. In addition, the `ModelMBeanInfoBuilder` class has methods to help construct some of the `Descriptor` instances you will need for `ModelMBeanInfo` objects.

Listing 7.1   ModelMBeanInfoBuilder.java

```
package jmxbook.ch7;

import javax.management.*;
import javax.management.modelmbean.*;
```

```
import java.lang.reflect.*;
import java.util.*;

public class ModelMBeanInfoBuilder
{
    protected Hashtable attributes = new Hashtable();
    protected Hashtable notifications = new Hashtable();
    protected Hashtable constructors = new Hashtable();
    protected Hashtable operations = new Hashtable();;

    public ModelMBeanInfoBuilder()
    {
    }
    public void addModelMBeanMethod( String name,
                            String[] paramTypes,
                            String[] paramNames,
                            String[] paramDescs,
                            String description, String rtype,
                            int type, Descriptor desc )
    {
      MBeanParameterInfo[] params = null;
      if( paramTypes != null )
      {
        params = new MBeanParameterInfo[ paramTypes.length ];
        for( int i = 0; i < paramTypes.length; i++ )
        {
          params[i] = new MBeanParameterInfo( paramNames[i],
                  paramTypes[i], paramDescs[i] );
        }
      }

      operations.put( name,
          new ModelMBeanOperationInfo( name, description,
                                  params, rtype, type, desc ) );
    }
    public void addModelMBeanNotification( String[] type,
                        String className,
                        String description, Descriptor desc )
    {
        notifications.put( className,
              new ModelMBeanNotificationInfo( type,
                        className, description, desc ) );
    }
    public void addModelMBeanAttribute( String fname,String ftype,
                        boolean read, boolean write,
                        boolean is,
                        String description, Descriptor desc )
    {
        attributes.put( fname, new ModelMBeanAttributeInfo(fname,
                        ftype,
```

Expose an operation

Expose an attribute

```
                               description,read,write,is, desc ) );
}

public void addModelMBeanConstructor( Constructor c,
                     String description,
                     Descriptor desc )
{
    this.constructors.put( c,
      new ModelMBeanConstructorInfo( description,
                         c, desc ) );
}

public ModelMBeanInfo buildModelMBeanInfo( Descriptor desc )
                                        throws Exception
{
   ModelMBeanOperationInfo[] ops =
      new ModelMBeanOperationInfo[ operations.size() ];
   copyInto( ops, operations );

   ModelMBeanAttributeInfo[] atts =
      new ModelMBeanAttributeInfo[ attributes.size() ];
   copyInto( atts, attributes );

   ModelMBeanConstructorInfo[] cons =
      new ModelMBeanConstructorInfo[ constructors.size() ];
   copyInto( cons, constructors );

   ModelMBeanNotificationInfo[] notifs =
   new ModelMBeanNotificationInfo[ notifications.size() ];
   copyInto( notifs, notifications );

   System.out.println( ops );

   return new ModelMBeanInfoSupport(
       "javax.management.modelmbean.ModelMBeanInfo",
                       "description",
                    atts,
                    cons,
                    ops,
                    notifs, desc );
}

public Descriptor buildAttributeDescriptor( String name,
                  String displayName, String persistPolicy,
                  String persistPeriod, Object defaultValue,
                  String getter, String setter,
                  String currency )
{
            Descriptor desc = new DescriptorSupport();
            if( name != null )
              desc.setField("name",name );
              desc.setField("descriptorType","attribute");
          if( displayName != null )
            desc.setField("displayName", displayName );
```

Build
MBeanInfo
object

```
              if( getter != null )
                desc.setField("getMethod", getter );
              if( setter != null )
                desc.setField("setMethod", setter );
              if( currency != null )
                desc.setField("currencyTimeLimit", currency );
              if( persistPolicy != null )
                desc.setField("persistPolicy", persistPolicy );
              if( persistPeriod != null )
                desc.setField("persistPeriod", persistPeriod );
              if( defaultValue != null )
                desc.setField("default", defaultValue );
              return desc;

      }

  public Descriptor buildOperationDescriptor( String name,
                      String displayName, String role,
                      Object targetObject, Object targetType,
                      String ownerClass, String currency )
      {
              Descriptor desc = new DescriptorSupport();
              if( name != null )
               desc.setField("name",name );

              desc.setField("descriptorType","operation");
              if( displayName != null )
                desc.setField("displayName", displayName );
              if( role != null )
                desc.setField("role", role );
              if( targetObject != null )
                desc.setField("targetObject", targetObject );
              if( targetType != null )
                desc.setField("targetType", targetType );
              if( ownerClass != null )
                desc.setField("class", ownerClass );
              if( currency != null )
                desc.setField("currencyTimeLimit", currency );

              return desc;
      }

  public Descriptor buildMBeanDescriptor( String name,
                      String displayName,
                      String persistPolicy,
                      String persistPeriod,
                      String persistLocation,
                      String persistName,
                      String log, String logFile )
      {
              Descriptor desc = new DescriptorSupport();
              if( name != null )
               desc.setField("name",name );
```

```
              desc.setField("descriptorType","mbean");
              if( displayName != null )
               desc.setField("displayName", displayName );
              if( persistLocation != null )
               desc.setField("persistLocation",
                             persistLocation );
              if( persistName != null )
               desc.setField("persistName", persistName );
              if( log != null )
               desc.setField("log", log );
              if( persistPolicy != null )
               desc.setField("persistPolicy", persistPolicy );
              if( persistPeriod != null )
               desc.setField("persistPeriod", persistPeriod );
              if( logFile != null )
               desc.setField("logFile", logFile );

              return desc;
        }

     private void copyInto( Object[] array, Hashtable table )
     {
        Vector temp = new Vector( table.values() );
        temp.copyInto( array );
     }
  }
```

No fancy code exists in this class. The `ModelMBeanInfoBuilder` class serves as a way to avoid repeating lines of code when creating `ModelMBeanInfo` objects. It contains methods for creating the metadata objects for attributes, operations, constructors, and notifications. In addition, the class contains methods for creating the `Descriptor` objects for the MBean, attribute, and operation metadata classes. The descriptor methods don't take all the predefined field names, but you can add more as needed to the method, or you can add them after the new `Descriptor` object is returned.

For a demonstration of using this utility class, look at listing 7.2. It shows the `ModeledClass` class, which defines a simple class with two methods. `ModeledClass` contains a `main()` method that you will use to test a Model MBean. The `main()` method uses the `ModelMBeanInfoBuilder` class to create a management interface for a Model MBean.

Listing 7.2   ModeledClass.java

```
package jmxbook.ch7;

import javax.management.*;
```

```java
import javax.management.modelmbean.*;
import jmxbook.ch3.RMIClientFactory;
import com.sun.jdmk.comm.*;

public class ModeledClass implements java.io.Serializable
{
  private String attribute = "My Attribute";
  public ModeledClass()
  {
  }

  public String getMyAttribute()
  {
    System.out.println( "Returning attribute to MBean" );
    return attribute;
  }

  public void printAttribute()
  {
    System.out.println( attribute );
  }

  public static void main( String[] args ) throws Exception
  {
    ModeledClass obj = new ModeledClass();
    ModelMBeanInfoBuilder builder = new ModelMBeanInfoBuilder();

    Descriptor attDesc =
            builder.buildAttributeDescriptor( "MyAttribute",
            null, "always", "10", null, "getMyAttribute",
            null, "10" );

    builder.addModelMBeanAttribute( "MyAttribute",
            "java.lang.String",
             true, false, false, "", attDesc );

    Descriptor opGetDesc = builder.buildOperationDescriptor(
            "getMyAttribute", null, "getter", null, null,
            "jmxbook.ch7.ModeledClass", "10" );

    builder.addModelMBeanMethod( "getMyAttribute", null,
            null, null, "",
            "java.lang.String" , MBeanOperationInfo.INFO,
             opGetDesc );

    Descriptor opDesc = builder.buildOperationDescriptor(
            "printAttribute",
            null, "operation", null, null,
            "jmxbook.ch7.ModeledClass", "10" );

    builder.addModelMBeanMethod( "printAttribute", null,
            null, null, "",
             "void" , MBeanOperationInfo.ACTION, opDesc );

    Descriptor mbeanDesc = builder.buildMBeanDescriptor(
```

Add attribute and getter ❶

```
                           "modeledClass",
                           "", "always", "10", "." ,"ModeledClass",        ❷  Build MBean
                           null, null );                                       descriptor

           ModelMBeanInfo info =
                      builder.buildModelMBeanInfo( mbeanDesc );

           RmiConnectorClient client = RMIClientFactory.getClient();

           ObjectName mName = new ObjectName("JMXBookAgent:name=Modeled");

           client.createMBean(
                      "javax.management.modelmbean.RequiredModelMBean",
                      mName );

           String[] sig = { "java.lang.Object", "java.lang.String" };
           Object[] params = { obj, "ObjectReference" };
           client.invoke( mName, "setManagedResource", params, sig );

           sig = new String[ 1 ];
           sig[ 0 ] = "javax.management.modelmbean.ModelMBeanInfo" ;
           params = new Object[ 1 ];
           params[ 0 ] = info;
           client.invoke( mName, "setModelMBeanInfo",  params, sig );

           //store the MBean                              Set resource   ❸
           client.invoke( mName,"store",null,null );      and MBean info
       }
   }                                                   Persist MBean
```

The `ModeledClass` class contains the method `getMyAttribute()`, which the created `ModelMBean` will use as an attribute. The class also contains the method
`printAttribute()`, which will be modeled as an operation. The `main()` method is
used to create a test of a `ModelMBean` managing an instance of this class.

❶ After creating an instance of the `ModeledClass`, the `main()` method uses the `Model-
MBeanInfoBuilder` utility class to build a `ModelMBeanInfo` object. The `main()` method
first adds the attribute `MyAttribute` to the builder. To do this, it creates a `Descrip-
tor` object using the `buildAttributeDescriptor()` method, passing in the various
values to initialize its predefined fields. In this case, the `main()` method must
describe the attribute and indicate that its getter method is named `getMyAt-
tribute()`. After the descriptor has been built, it is added to the builder to create
an attribute entry for the `ModelMBeanInfo` object under construction.

Because the attribute has been added, the `main()` method must now create an
operation entry in the builder for the attribute's getter method, `getMyAt-
tribute()`. You add operations to the builder much the way you add attributes: by
building the descriptor and then calling the correct add-metadata-object method.

❷ After all the operations and attributes are added to the builder object, the `main()` method builds an MBean `Descriptor` object in order to complete the `ModelM-BeanInfo` object being constructed by the builder. Finally, the `main()` method calls the `buildModelMBeanInfo()` method to acquire the constructed `ModelMBeanInfo` object for creating a Model MBean.

❸ To create the Model MBean, the `main()` method acquires an `RmiConnectorClient` in order to contact your `JMXBookAgent`. Every Model MBean is defined by the class `javax.management.modelmbean.RequiredModelMBean`. The `main()` method invokes the `createMBean()` method and passes in an `ObjectName` and the `RequiredModel-MBean` classname for the new MBean. After a Model MBean is registered in an agent, it must be initialized with a managed resource, the object it will manage, and an instance of `ModelMBeanInfo` that describes its management interface. To set these objects in the Model MBean, the `main()` method invokes the `setManage-dResource()` and `setModelMBeanInfo()` methods on the new Model MBean.

7.5.2 *Modeling with Model MBeans*

As you might gather even from this simple example, the main task in creating Model MBeans is generating the `ModelMBeanInfo` objects to adequately describe your needed behavior and management interfaces. Put differently, you need to be able to model your resource for the Model MBean. This requirement highlights one of the advantages of using Model MBeans.

Imagine that you have to instrument 50 different resources for a JMX agent. This seems like a daunting task if you are responsible for writing 50 different MBeans, all of which need to be tied in to their manageable resources in a specific manner. Now consider the scenario if each interface to the resource is described a flat file (properties, XML, and so forth). If you have a program that can parse these files and generate `ModelMBeanInfo` objects, you can instrument the resources in moments.

With Model MBeans, you can spend your time describing management interfaces and behavior, and then generate the code needed to create the MBean in an agent. We do not present such a generation tool in this book, because each environment will have specific requirements for the file or XML format needed to generate Model MBean info. However, the `ModelMBeanInfoBuilder` class we've presented in this chapter is a useful utility class.

7.6 *Summary*

In this chapter, you learned about the final MBean type presented in this book: the Model MBean. Model MBeans offer MBean developers management and configuration capabilities that the Standard and Dynamic MBeans do not. These features include configurable attribute caching, notification logging, and persistence.

The next chapter begins part 2 of this book, which covers the agent layer of JMX. Chapter 8 presents a detailed discussion of the MBean server.

Part 3

The JMX agent and distributed layers

Part 3 begins a detailed examination of the JMX agent layer. JMX agents contain MBeans by using one or more MBean servers and also provide access for management applications. Agents also provide a set of services that help with the manipulation of MBeans. The chapters in this part of the book discuss these agent-related topics.

Chapter 8 covers the MBean server. It starts with a brief review of the overall agent architecture, and then undertakes a detailed discussion of the MBean-Server interface. The second half of the chapter covers the query capability built into the MBean server, including the construction of queries and using queries to retrieve MBeans.

Chapter 9 examines protocol adapters and connectors. Specifically, the chapter covers the RMI connector contributed by Sun Microsystems in its JMX Reference Implementation. In addition, chapter 9 walks you through writing a Jini connector and TCP adapter.

Chapter 10 discusses the M-let agent service. This service can dynamically load MBeans at runtime from remote locations outside an agent's codebase. It is useful for expanding an agent's CLASSPATH as well as dynamically updating it with new MBeans at runtime.

Chapter 11 covers another agent service: the relation service. The relation service allows you to describe the relationships that may exist between MBeans. For example, MBeans may all belong to a single workflow. They are related by the order in which they must be used to complete the workflow. This chapter explains this service using an example that manages a telephone routing application.

Chapter 12 explores the remaining two agent services: the monitoring services and the timer service. The monitoring services are predefined MBeans that can monitor other MBean attributes. The timer service gives the agent the ability to emit notifications at intervals.

8

Working with an MBean server

- Exploring the MBean server API methods
- Introducing the MBean server querying mechanism
- Writing query examples

As you become more experienced with JMX and writing your own MBeans, you may envision a time when you have a JMX agent containing dozens of MBeans of different class types and purposes. Keeping track of all your MBeans, their purposes, and their management interfaces can be difficult as the number of MBeans in an agent increases. Fortunately, the `MBeanServer` class comes with a querying mechanism that allows you to build and execute custom MBean queries to identify specific MBeans.

You have used the MBean server in several of the previous chapters. In particular, you registered MBeans and used the HTML protocol adapter to access information from an instance of the `MBeanServer` class. This chapter discusses the MBean server in more detail, giving you a better understanding of its features. Specifically, we will cover two main areas:

- The `MBeanServer` interface
- Using the MBean server querying mechanism to find MBeans

However, before we begin exploring these topics, let's quickly review the overall JMX agent architecture information from chapter 1.

8.1 JMX agent architecture in review

Remember from chapter 1 that a JMX agent is a Java process that contains a set of MBeans and enables management applications to interact with them. JMX agents contain one or more MBean servers that act as registries for MBeans. Remember also that agents use one or more protocol adapters or connectors. Adapters and connectors make JMX agents available to different management applications.

Figure 8.1 depicts the agent-level components. After reviewing the figure, if you still have questions, look back to chapter 1.

8.1.1 Using protocol adapters and connectors

As you can see from figure 8.1, protocol adapters and connectors provide access to the MBean server. Adapters and connectors help you to interact with the MBean server as if you were working with it directly.

Management applications can interact with MBeans by using protocols such as Simple Network Management Protocol (SNMP) or HTTP. Essentially, protocol adapters let you use existing management applications to interact with JMX agents. You can map your existing protocols into a JMX agent, allowing you to interact with and manage its MBeans.

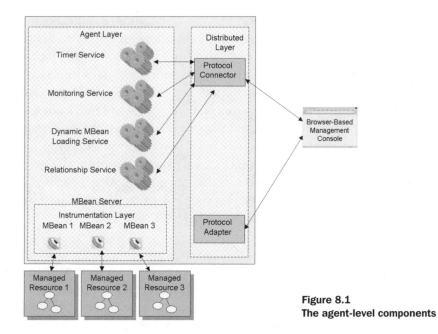

Figure 8.1
The agent-level components

In addition, management applications can use connectors in order to reach the MBean server with remote clients. For example, Sun provides a Remote Method Invocation (RMI) connector for remote access over Java RMI. Connectors are more useful when you're developing a management application. As mentioned, connectors provide you with a client portion, which enables seemingly direct calls into a JMX agent's MBean server.

Both protocol adapters and connectors are important to this chapter because each should provide a direct mapping to the methods of the MBeanServer interface. One way or another, you should be exposed to these methods. You will learn more about protocol adapters and connectors in chapter 9. Now it is time to turn our focus to the MBean server.

8.2 *The MBeanServer interface*

As previously mentioned, the MBean server acts a registry for MBeans. In addition to being the repository for MBeans, an MBean server provides a set of services for manipulating registered MBeans. For example, the MBean server gives you access to MBean attributes and operations. In addition, the MBean server provides more advanced services such as querying (discussed later in section 8.3) and MBean relationships (covered in chapter 10).

Up to this point in the book, you have used methods of the MBean server as necessary. However, you should have a good understanding of the entire set of methods available in the `MBeanServer` class. The methods available for use in any MBean server are declared by the `MBeanServer` interface. This interface declares methods for creating, registering, manipulating, and finding MBeans (and more). Each of the following sections will cover one method, set of overloaded methods, or set of related methods. Objects used as input parameters and return types are in the `javax.management` or `java.lang` package unless otherwise specified.

Rather than show the entire interface in a single diagram, the next several sections focus on a few specific methods that are related. After learning about the majority of methods in this chapter, you should look at the available javadoc API for overloaded or additional methods not covered.

8.2.1 *Registration methods*

The first set of methods we'll discuss deals with registering an MBean that you have created but not registered in the MBean server. For example, you used the `registerMBean()` method in chapter 2 to register your `HelloWorld` MBean.

Table 8.1 summarizes the registration methods.

Table 8.1   MBean registration-related methods of the `MBeanServer` interface

Method	Purpose
`registerMBean (Object mbean, ObjectName name )`	Registers an already created MBean in the MBean server
`isRegistered( ObjectName name )`	Checks to see if a particular MBean is registered on the MBean server
`unregisterMBean( ObjectName name )`	Removes an MBean from the MBean server

The registerMBean() method for existing objects

This method is intended for use when you have already created an MBean manually in code. It is useful if you have objects that serve as application components but also happen to be MBeans. At some point in their lifecycle, you might want to expose them for management by registering them in an MBean server.

The `registerMBean()` method takes the constructed MBean and an appropriate `ObjectName` instance for parameters. If the MBean conforms to the MBean rules and the `ObjectName` instance is valid, the MBean server will register the incoming MBean. For information on creating the different types of MBeans, look back at chapters 4, 5, and 7.

The `registerMBean()` method returns an instance of the `ObjectInstance` class. An `ObjectInstance` object contains the `ObjectName` of an MBean and its class-name. This method can throw the following exceptions (all contained in the `javax.management` package):

- `InstanceAlreadyExistsException`—An MBean with the given `ObjectName` value already exists in the MBean server.

- `MBeanRegistrationException`—The MBean being registered implements the `MBeanRegistration` interface and threw an exception in one of the registration methods.

- `NotCompliantMBeanException`—The object is not a compliant JMX MBean. See chapters 4 and 5 for the rules governing a compliant MBean.

- `RuntimeOperationsException`—This exception class wraps an `IllegalArgumentException` indicating that the `Object` parameter is `null` or that the object name is invalid or also `null`.

The isRegistered() method

If you need to know whether a particular MBean is registered, you can use the `isRegistered()` method. You would use this method to check to see if a particular MBean has already been created, or to determine whether a particular `ObjectName` value is already in use.

This method returns a `boolean` value indicating whether the supplied `ObjectName` instance corresponds to one of the registered MBeans in the MBean server. This method can throw a `RuntimeOperationsException` indicating that the `ObjectName` value supplied is invalid or `null`.

The unregisterMBean() method

When you need to remove an MBean from the MBean server, you can use the `unregisterMBean()` method. This method will unregister (remove) the MBean that corresponds to the supplied `ObjectName` instance. An `InstanceNotFoundException` will be thrown if the `ObjectName` instance does not correspond to a registered MBean. The following exceptions could arise from this method:

- `InstanceNotFoundException`—The requested MBean cannot be found in the MBean server.

- `MBeanRegistrationException`—The MBean being registered implements the `MBeanRegistration` interface and threw an exception in one of the deregistration methods.

- `RuntimeOperationsException`—This exception wraps an `IllegalArgument-Exception` indicating that the object name is invalid or `null`.

8.2.2 *Creation and registration methods*

The `registerMBean()` method shown in the previous section registers an MBean that is already created. The MBean server also has four methods that let you create and register an MBean with one method call. Table 8.2 shows two of these methods that we will discuss in the following sections.

Table 8.2 MBean creation-related methods of the **MBeanServer** interface

Method	Purpose
`createMBean( String className, ObjectName name )`	Creates and registers a new MBean of the given class
`createMBean( String className, ObjectName name, ObjectName loader )`	Creates and registers a new MBean of the given class using the class loader referenced by the given `ObjectName` *loader*

The remaining two methods are overloaded, adding additional parameters; you can look them up in the JMX javadoc available with the RI. Using the `createMBean()` methods tells the MBean server to instantiate a particular instance of an MBean class as well as register the new instance. This process allows clients of a JMX agent such as management applications or other programs to delegate the creation of MBeans to the agent. Outside processes need only supply the correct information and parameters, and the agent's MBean server will do the rest.

The createMBean(String className, ObjectName name) method

The first `createMBean()` method accepts the MBean's classname as a `String` and an `ObjectName` instance for registering the new MBean. This method uses Java reflection to instantiate an instance of the supplied classname. The class must contain a default constructor (a no-argument public constructor). In addition, the resulting MBean instance must conform to the MBean validation rules described in chapters 3, 4, 6, and 7. Also, the supplied `ObjectName` must be valid and unique. The various `createMBean()` methods can throw many exceptions, including:

- `ReflectionException`—The exception wraps a `ClassNotFoundException` or any exception that occurs while trying to invoke the class's constructor to instantiate the MBean.

- InstanceAlreadyExistsException—An MBean with the given ObjectName value already exists in the MBean server

- MBeanRegistrationException—The MBean being registered implements the MBeanRegistration interface and threw an exception in one of the register methods.

- NotCompliantMBeanException—The object is not a compliant JMX MBean. See chapters 4 and 5 for the rules governing a compliant MBean.

- RuntimeOperationsException—The exception wraps an IllegalArgument-Exception indicating that the Object parameter is null or that the object name is invalid or also null.

- MBeanException—This exception wraps any exception being thrown by the constructor of the MBean.

The createMBean(String className, ObjectName name, ObjectName loader) method

This version of the createMBean() method provides the same result as the previous method, but it uses the class loader identified by the supplied ObjectName instance. The class loader must be available in the MBean server and correspond to the supplied ObjectName instance. (You will learn more about the class loader version of this method when we discuss the M-let service in chapter 10. The M-let service is one of the JMX agent services responsible for dynamic loading of MBeans from remote locations; it can also be used for expanding the codebase of a JMX agent.)

The exceptions for this method are similar to those of the previous method. Check the javadoc for more information.

8.2.3 Notification methods

When dealing with notifications, you need to be able to add and remove notification listeners. The MBeanServer interface declares two addNotificationListener() methods for adding listeners and two removeNotificationListener() methods for removing listeners. (For more information about using notifications, look back at chapter 6.)

The addNotificationListener(ObjectName name, NotificationListener listener, NotificationFilter filter, Object handback) method

The first addNotificationListener() method accepts an ObjectName corresponding to the MBean emitting the notifications, a NotificationListener instance to register as the listener, and a handback Object to associate with the listener. You should use this method when adding a listener from outside the agent—a management application or other program.

The `ObjectName` argument must correspond to a registered MBean that is a `NotificationBroadcaster`. This method throws a single exception: an `Instance-NotFoundException` indicating that the broadcaster MBean could not be found given the `ObjectName` value.

The addNotificationListener(ObjectName name, ObjectName listener, NotificationFilter filter, Object handback) method

The second version of the `addNotificationListener()` method takes two `Object-Name` instances; the remaining arguments are the same as for the previous method. You would use this method when one MBean needs to listen for another MBean's notifications. This technique has many uses: for example, you might want to aggregate all notifications in one place, or you might have an MBean that listens for notifications and persists the ones it receives.

The first `ObjectName` argument corresponds to the MBean emitting notifications, and the second corresponds to another MBean registered in the MBean server. The second `ObjectName` must correspond to a registered MBean that is also a `NotificationListener`. This method has the same exceptions as the previous method.

The removeNotificationListener(ObjectName name, NotificationListener listener) method

The `removeNotificationListener()` method accepts an `ObjectName` corresponding to a registered MBean that is also a `NotificationBroadcaster`. The `NotificationListener` parameter indicates which listener the MBean must remove from its listener list. After invoking this method successfully, a listener will not receive any more notifications from this MBean.

The remove methods can throw an exception in addition to those thrown by the add listener methods: the `ListenerNotFoundException` exception indicates that the supplied listener could not be found on the supplied MBean.

The removeNotificationListener(ObjectName name, ObjectName listener) method

Similar to the second add listener method, this method tells a registered MBean `NotificationBroadcaster` to remove the `NotificationListener` registered with the MBean server with the supplied `ObjectName` instance.

8.2.4 *MBean manipulation*

The following sections describe the methods declared to manipulate MBeans. They include methods to get and set attributes, invoke MBean operations, and gather other MBean information. The methods available to manipulate MBeans produce the same results regardless of MBean type. All MBeans are described with MBean metadata objects internally in the MBean; therefore, the MBean type is not important when performing these methods. (For more information about MBean metadata objects, look back to chapter 4.)

The Object getAttribute(ObjectName name, String attribute) method

This method returns the value of the attribute with the name supplied in the `String` parameter from the MBean corresponding to the supplied MBean. The `ObjectName` must refer to a registered MBean, and the `String` value must be a readable attribute of that MBean. The value is returned as an instance of the `Object` class. In addition to some of the exceptions you have already seen (`MBean-Exception`, `InstanceNotFoundException`, `ReflectionException`, and `RuntimeOperationsException`), this method throws the `AttributeNotFoundException` exception. This exception indicates that the requested attribute could not be found on the given MBean.

The AttributeList getAttributes(ObjectName name, String[] attributes) method

The `getAttributes()` method performs the same function as the previous method, but operates over an array of attribute names (the `String` array parameter). The `ObjectName` must refer to a registered MBean, and the `String` values must be readable attributes of that MBean. The return value of this method is an instance of `AttributeList`. (The `AttributeList` class was covered in detail in chapter 4.) It contains a set of `Attribute` objects, each of which contains the name and value of an attribute.

In contrast to the `getAttribute()` method, this method throws only three exceptions: `InstanceNotFoundException`, `ReflectionException`, and `RuntimeOperationsException`.

The void setAttribute(ObjectName name, Attribute attribute) method

The `setAttribute()` method takes an `ObjectName` parameter and an `Attribute` parameter. The `ObjectName` corresponds to a registered MBean. The `Attribute` object must contain the name of a writeable MBean attribute and the value to which to set the attribute.

The `setAttribute()` method throws `InstanceNotFoundException`, `MBean-Exception`, `AttributeNotFoundException`, `ReflectionException`, and `Runtime-OperationsException`. In addition to these exceptions, the method throws `InvalidAttributeValueException`, indicating that the supplied attribute value cannot be assigned to the MBean attribute.

The AttributeList setAttributes(ObjectName name, AttributeList list) method

This method operates like the previous method, but over an `AttributeList` argument. The `AttributeList` parameter contains `Attribute` objects that contain names and values for writeable MBean attributes. This method throws the `InstanceNotFoundException`, `ReflectionException`, and `RuntimeOperationsException` exceptions.

The Object invoke(ObjectName name, String method, Object[] params, String[] sig) method

The `MBeanServer` interface declares the `invoke()` method in order to allow management applications to invoke the exposed operations of MBeans. To invoke an MBean operation, you need to pass in its `ObjectName`, the method name, and two arrays that contain the method's signature and input parameters. The result of the MBean operation will be returned as an instance of the `Object` class. The method name supplied by the `String` parameter must be a valid MBean operation. This method throws `InstanceNotFoundException`, `MBeanException`, and `ReflectionException`.

The MBeanInfo getMBeanInfo(ObjectName name) method

The `getMBeanInfo()` method will return an instance of the `MBeanInfo` class that describes the MBean corresponding to the supplied `ObjectName` instance. Management applications would use this method to discover everything about an MBean. With all the information from the `MBeanInfo` object, applications can create a view of the MBean for user interaction.

For more information about the `MBeanInfo` class and the other metadata objects, look back at chapter 4. Remember that the MBean server uses the MBean metadata objects (the `MBeanInfo` descriptions) to internally represent MBeans. Therefore, every MBean is described in the same manner regardless of its type.

In addition to the `InstanceNotFoundException` and `ReflectionException` exceptions, this method throws the `IntrospectionException` exception indicating that an error occurred while the MBean server was using reflection to build the `MBeanInfo` object for the MBean.

The ObjectInstance getObjectInstance(ObjectName name) method

The `getObjectInstance()` method returns the `ObjectInstance` object for the MBean corresponding to the supplied `ObjectName` instance. The `ObjectInstance` class contains both the `ObjectName` value and classname of a particular MBean. This method only throws an `InstanceNotFoundException` exception.

The boolean isInstanceOf(ObjectName name, String classname) method

To determine if a particular MBean is an instance of a particular class, use the `isInstanceOf()` method. This method takes an `ObjectName` instance of a particular MBean in the MBean server, and the `String` parameter specifies the classname in question. Only an `InstanceNotFoundException` exception is thrown from this method.

8.2.5 MBean server information

Some methods declared in the `MBeanServer` interface are for informational purposes. Two of these methods are declared in order to provide information about the MBean server.

The Integer getMBeanCount() method

This method returns the number of MBeans registered in the MBean server. The value is returned as an `Integer` object.

The String getDefaultDomain() method

The `getDefaultDomain()` method returns the domain name that identifies this MBean server.

8.2.6 Other methods

In addition to all the methods covered in the previous sections, there are some remaining methods that don't fall into any category. The following are utility methods for deserializing data and instantiating objects.

The java.io.ObjectInputStream deserialize(ObjectName name, byte[] data) methods

The `MBeanServer` interface actually declares three `deserialize()` methods, taking various additional parameters. The `deserialize()` methods take an array of `byte` data and the name of a registered class loader. The result is returned in an `ObjectInputStream` stream. This method is a useful utility for deserializing objects. For instance, you could use this method if you needed to load a persisted state from a serialized object file.

The Object instantiate(String classname) method

The `MBeanServer` interface also declares four `instantiate()` methods. Each accepts different parameters, but the result of each is an instance of the supplied classname. The result is returned as an instance of the `Object` class. This method can be used to create objects from classnames instead of using reflection code in your own MBeans.

8.3 Querying for MBeans

In a real-world situation, you may have a JMX agent that contains many MBeans. Consider a JMX agent that contains MBeans for a set of applications, each of which registers 10 MBeans in the agent. You could easily have 40 to 50 MBeans residing in a single agent. If you need to work with the MBeans for a particular application, you might not want to sort through the other applications' MBeans. In essence, when you interact with the agent through a management application, you could have some trouble viewing only the MBeans you need.

Even if you can filter the MBeans by their object names, you still might want to further restrict your MBean view by attribute values. For example, maybe each of the MBeans for an application has an identical attribute whose value indicates the component of the application that the MBean manages. It would be nice to be able to view just the specific MBean you are looking for.

In fact, it would be useful to be able to build a view like the following: *All MBeans from application A that have an attribute* `count` *whose value is greater than 10 but less than 20, or that have an attribute* `owner` *whose value equals* `ABC`.

Reading through that statement, you should notice the following important points:

- The MBean view is restricted by object name.
- The restricted set then must have a certain attribute.
- The attribute must meet a numeric range.
- Or, a different attribute must equal a `String` value.

JMX agents support a query mechanism that can build and execute complex queries like this one. Queries are submitted to a JMX agent for the purpose of retrieving a set of `ObjectInstance` objects. In essence, a query identifies all the MBeans that conform to the rules of a given query.

8.3.1   *The MBeanServer query methods*

In section 8.2, we covered the methods of the MBeanServer interface. However, we left out the two methods shown in table 8.3.

Table 8.3   The two remaining methods of the MBeanServer interface. These two methods are used to query the MBean server for a set of qualifying MBean object names.

Method	Return type	Description
queryMBeans(ObjectName, QueryExp)	java.util.Set	Returns the set of ObjectInstance objects identifying the set of MBeans that qualify, given the QueryExp object
queryNames(ObjectName, QueryExp)	java.util.Set	Returns the set of ObjectName objects identifying the set of MBeans that qualify, given the QueryExp object

The two methods, queryMBeans() and queryNames(), both accept an ObjectName instance and a QueryExp instance. The ObjectName instance defines the scope of the query, and the QueryExp instance defines the constructed query expression. The following sections describe the meaning of the parameters and how to use these two methods.

The queryMBeans() method returns a set of ObjectInstance objects. The ObjectInstance class contains the ObjectName of an MBean and the MBean's defining class type. The queryNames() method only returns a set of ObjectNames of MBeans. Both methods execute queries in the same manner; only their return type differs. You must choose to use one method over the other based purely on the amount of information you needed returned.

Defining the scope of a query

We will discuss the QueryExp class in a moment—it represents a query like the one we described in the first paragraph of section 8.3. However, let's first examine the first argument to the query methods, the ObjectName instance.

When executing a query, you need to describe a set of MBeans in which to apply the query. By defining the scope of a query, you are almost performing a pre-query. Defining the scope of the query is the role of the ObjectName argument passed to the two query methods. Table 8.4 lists the possible values for this parameter.

Table 8.4 Possible values for the `ObjectName` parameter passed into the two query methods of an MBean server

Possible value	Example	Description
`null`	`null`	Indicates that the query should be applied to all MBeans in the MBean server
Complete object name `String`	`HelloWorld:type=a`	Indicates that the query should be applied to only a single MBean (the MBean that has the `ObjectName` instance equal to the one passed to the query method)
Partial object name `String`	`Hello*:type=a,*`	Indicates that the query should be applied to all MBeans whose `ObjectName` matches the partial `ObjectName` passed to the query method

After examining the partial object name `String` in the previous table, you are probably wondering what the rules are for specifying partial object names. The following list contains the few rules for creating partial object names:

- `*` indicates a wildcard for any characters, including none at all.
- `?` represents any single character.
- Key properties (such as `type=a`) must always be complete, but the wildcard `*` can appear in the list.

In other words, you can use wildcards anywhere in the domain name, but you cannot use them in the value of a property in the property list. Just to clarify these rules, a few examples are presented in the table 8.5.

Table 8.5 Further examples of partial object name values that conform to the pattern-matching rules

Partial object name value	Matching MBeans
`HelloAgent:*`	All MBeans in the domain `HelloAgent`
`HelloAgent:type=a,*`	All MBeans in the domain `HelloAgent` whose names have at least the property `type=a`
`*:type=a`	All MBeans in any domain with the property `type=a`
`Hello???:type=a`	All MBeans in a domain that begins with `Hello` plus any three characters and that has a property `type=a`
`*:*`	All MBeans

Once the scope of the query has defined a set of MBeans, the query will be applied to each MBean in the set. The query will be applied to each MBean individually—currently, JMX has no way of forming a query across multiple MBeans. A query building a condition across two MBeans is impossible to represent using this querying service. For example, the following query is not supported: *If MBean A has an attribute* MyAttribute, *then return MBean B with attribute* TheAttribute *value of 5.* However, in chapter 11, we will discuss the relation service, which can provide for MBean relationships.

8.3.2 *Creating query expressions*

Let's revisit the query we described earlier: *All MBeans from application A that have an attribute* count *whose value is greater than 10 but less than 20, or that have an attribute* owner *whose value equals* ABC.

JMX provides the capability to perform many types of query expressions, including the ones in this query. In our query, we have attribute values that must be either greater than, less than, or equal to some value. In addition, the query combines these expressions by using an AND and an OR type expression.

JMX provides the class javax.management.Query as a mechanism for objects to build simple and complex queries. The Query class contains static methods to build expressions and to relate expressions into more complex expressions. Each method returns a type of expression, represented by one of the following classes:

- QueryExp
- ValueExp
- AttributeValueExp
- StringValueExp

The ValueExp and StringValueExp classes represent an attribute value. The AttributeValueExp represents the name of an attribute. The QueryExp class represents a query expression constructed of one or more other expressions. You should never need to create instances of the classes yourself; rather, you should use the methods of the Query class to build expressions.

As you will see in a moment, some of the methods of the Query class take other expressions as inputs in order to build more complex queries. For example, examine the following code that builds the query *MBeans with attribute* count *greater than* 10:

```
QueryExp exp = Query.gt( Query.attr( "count" ), Query.value( 10 ) );
```

The method gt() of the Query class indicates that a *greater-than* expression is being constructed. The code uses the attr() method to indicate that the attribute involved in the greater-than expression is called count and then uses the value() method to indicate the second half of the greater-than expression.

Before we create any more examples, examine the following tables, which show the methods of the `Query` class. Each table breaks out a few methods of the `Query` class into a category. Table 8.6 shows the methods that make new expressions out of `QueryExp` objects that were created by other `Query` methods.

Table 8.6 Methods of the `Query` class that relate `QueryExp` objects. The objects are returned by other `Query` methods.

Method	Return type	Description
`and( QueryExp, QueryExp )`	`QueryExp`	Returns a new expression that is an AND of the two input expressions
`or( QueryExp, QueryExp )`	`QueryExp`	Returns a new expression that is an OR of the two input expressions
`not( QueryExp, QueryExp )`	`QueryExp`	Returns a new expression that is a NOT of the input expression

Table 8.7 shows the `Query` class methods that operate over `String` values and indicate attributes or classnames of an MBean. These methods are used in conjunction with `ValueExp` objects to create `QueryExp` objects.

Table 8.7 Methods of the `Query` class that identify labels in an expression (attributes, classnames).

Method	Return type	Description
`attr( String name )`	`AttributeValueExp`	Returns a value that identifies an attribute name
`attr( String classname, String name )`	`AttributeValueExp`	Returns a value that identifies an attribute name for the given class
`classattr( String name )`	`AttributeValueExp`	Returns a value that identifies the classname of an MBean

Table 8.8 shows the methods that return a `ValueExp` object. `ValueExp` objects indicate the value for an MBean attribute that can be used in a `QueryExp` object.

Table 8.8 Methods of the `Query` class that return a `ValueExp` object indicating an attribute value to be used in a query expression.

Method	Return type	Description
`value( boolean )`	`ValueExp`	Returns a `ValueExp` indicating a `boolean` value
`value( double )`	`ValueExp`	Returns a `ValueExp` indicating a `double` value

Table 8.8 Methods of the `Query` class that return a `ValueExp` object indicating an attribute value to be used in a query expression. *(continued)*

Method	Return type	Description
value(float)	ValueExp	Returns a `ValueExp` indicating a `float` value
value(int)	ValueExp	Returns a `ValueExp` indicating a `int` value
value(long)	ValueExp	Returns a `ValueExp` indicating a `long` value
value(java.lang.Number)	ValueExp	Returns a `ValueExp` indicating a `Number` value
value(String)	ValueExp	Returns a `ValueExp` indicating a `String` value

Finally, Table 8.9 shows the methods used to create objects that can be used to form more complex query expressions. Arguments to these methods are Value-Exp objects—indicating that an expression is being created between two values.

Table 8.9 Methods of the `Query` class that create `QueryExp` objects (or subclasses) that can be used in more complex query expressions.

Method	Return type	Description
between(ValueExp, ValueExp, ValueExp)	QueryExp	Creates an expression that means one value is between two other values
div(ValueExp, ValueExp)	ValueExp	Creates a new `ValueExp` by dividing the first `ValueExp` by the second
minus(ValueExp, ValueExp)	ValueExp	Creates a new `ValueExp` by subtracting the second `ValueExp` from the first
plus(ValueExp, ValueExp)	ValueExp	Creates a new `ValueExp` by adding the first `ValueExp` to the second
times(ValueExp, ValueExp)	ValueExp	Creates a new `ValueExp` by multiplying the first `ValueExp` by the second
eq(ValueExp, ValueExp)	QueryExp	Creates an expression that means the first `ValueExp` should be equal to the second
geq(ValueExp, ValueExp)	QueryExp	Creates an expression that means the first `ValueExp` should be greater than or equal to the second
gt(ValueExp, ValueExp)	QueryExp	Creates an expression that means the first `ValueExp` should be greater than the second
in(ValueExp, ValueExp[])	QueryExp	Creates an expression that means the first `ValueExp` should be in the list of following `ValueExp` objects
leq(ValueExp, ValueExp)	QueryExp	Creates an expression that means the first `ValueExp` should less than or equal to the second

Table 8.9 Methods of the `Query` class that create `QueryExp` objects (or subclasses) that can be used in more complex query expressions. *(continued)*

Method	Return type	Description
`lt( ValueExp, ValueExp)`	QueryExp	Creates an expression that means the first `ValueExp` should be less than the second
`match( AttributeValue-Exp, StringValueExp)`	QueryExp	Creates an expression that means the first `ValueExp` should match the `String` expression represented by the second argument; for example, the second argument might be `va*lu?`
`initialSubString( AttributeValueExp, StringValueExp)`	QueryExp	Creates an expression that means the first `ValueExp` should have a prefix matching the `String` expression represented by the second argument; for example, the second argument might be `va*lu?`
`anySubString( AttributeValueExp, StringValueExp)`	QueryExp	Creates an expression that means the first `ValueExp` should contain the `String` expression represented by the second argument; for example, the second argument might be `va*lu?`
`finalSubString( AttributeValueExp, StringValueExp)`	QueryExp	Creates an expression that means the first `ValueExp` should have a suffix matching the `String` expression represented by the second argument; for example, the second argument might be `va*lu?`

If you are overwhelmed with all these methods right now, don't worry—the next section presents several examples to get you started.

8.3.3 *Constructing examples*

Now that you have seen the methods of the `Query` class that are used to create simple and complex queries, we can present some examples. To create meaningful query examples, let's first imagine the scenario in which the example queries might exist. Each query will be described in a textual sentence, and then shown in code using the methods of the `Query` class.

Imagine you have a JMX agent with the domain `Hardware`. The agent will contain five MBeans that monitor different pieces of hardware (modem, printer, and so forth). Each MBean has its own unique object name, but some MBeans have common attributes. Table 8.10 lists the devices being monitored, along with the object names and a few attributes of the MBeans.

Use this table as a reference as you develop the queries in the following paragraphs. As you can see, you have five devices ranging from modems to a fax machine. All the devices have a `status` attribute, and one has an `error` value. The printer, fax, and copier all have identical attributes with varying values (as

Table 8.10   Devices in a imaginary JMX agent used in the query examples in this section.

Device	MBean object name	Attributes and values
Modem1	`Hardware:type=com,location=office,name=modem1`	`status = OK, transferRate = 28800`
Modem2	`Hardware:type=com,location=office,name=modem2`	`status = ERROR, transferRate = 56000`
Printer	`Hardware:type=paper,location=network,name=printer`	`status = OK, paperCount = LOW, inkLevel = HIGH`
Fax	`Hardware:type=paper,location=network,name=fax`	`status = OK, paperCount = NORM, inkLevel = LOW`
Copier	`Hardware:type=paper,location=network,name=copier`	`status = OK, paperCount = LOW, inkLevel = LOW`

do the two modems). Each MBean object name provides some detailed information about the devices as well, including location, type (modem or paper), and name. These object name properties could be represented as attributes, but you will leave them in the object name because doing so gives you a good way to restrict the scope of a query.

Now that you are familiar with the set of MBeans involved in the examples, let's move on to the first query.

Query example 1

The first query is as follows: *All hardware with a* `LOW` `inkLevel`. The results of this query should return only MBeans that have an `inkLevel` attribute with a value of `LOW`. Remember, the MBean server's methods for performing queries have two arguments: the first argument (the object name) defines scope, and the second argument is the actual query. Let's define the scope first with the following partial object name:

```
Hardware:*
```

This partial object name defines the scope of the query to be all MBeans with a domain of `Hardware`.

The query expression itself is also simple. The following code constructs the necessary query expression and invokes the query method from your imaginary MBean server in the agent:

```
QueryExp query = Query.equals( Query.attr( "inkLevel" ),
                               Query.value( "LOW" ) );

mbeanServer.queryMBeans( new ObjectName( "Hardware:*" ), query );
```

The only two MBeans that meet the constraints of this query are the `Fax` and `Copier` MBeans.

The next example creates another simple query, but also restricts the scope using a partial object name.

Query example 2

The second query is as follows: *All communication devices with a transfer rate greater than 28800*. The results of this query should be only modem MBeans with a `transferRate` attribute greater than 28800. Again, the first thing you need to do is define the query scope. The following is the partial object name to define the scope of the query:

```
Hardware:type=com,*
```

This partial object name defines the scope of the query to be all MBeans with a domain of `Hardware` and an object name property `type` set to `com`. The following code constructs and executes the query:

```
QueryExp query = Query.gt( Query.attr( "transferRate" ),
                           Query.value( 28800 ) );

mbeanServer.queryMBeans( new ObjectName( "Hardware:type=com,*" ),
                         query);
```

The two modem MBeans are in the scope of the query; however, only `Modem2` has a transfer rate greater than 28800, so it is the only MBean that satisfies this query.

The next example creates a more complex expression by joining two expressions together.

Query example 3

The third query is as follows: *All hardware with a LOW inkLevel or LOW paper-Count*. First, let's show the partial object name to define the scope. This is the same as in the first example:

```
Hardware:*
```

Now, here's the code that constructs and executes the query:

```
QueryExp exp1 = Query.equals( Query.attr( "inkLevel" ),
                              Query.value( "LOW" ) );

QueryExp exp2 = Query.equals( Query.attr( "paperCount" ),
                              Query.value( "LOW" ) );

QueryExp finalExp = Query.or( exp1, exp2 );

mbeanServer.queryMBeans( new ObjectName( "Hardware:*" ), finalExp );
```

To construct this more complex query, you first create the subexpressions for `inkLevel` and `paperCount`. Once you have those expressions, you can create a final expression combining them with an OR. The resulting query expression should return the `Printer`, `Fax`, and `Copier` MBeans, because either their `inkLevel` or `paperCount` attribute has a `LOW` value.

The next example uses only a scope definition to get a result set.

Query example 4

The fourth query is as follows: *All hardware located on the network*. This example is not really a query. It reads like a query, but because you have created MBeans with detailed object names, you can simply execute the query method with only an object name parameter:

```
mbeanServer.queryMBeans( new ObjectName( "Hardware:*,
                        location=network" ),
                        null );
```

The resulting set of MBeans includes every MBean with *location=network* included in its object name.

The next example puts everything together.

Query example 5

The final query is as follows: *All hardware located on the network with a status of ERROR that does not have a LOW inkLevel or LOW paperCount*. With this example, you will need to build a few subexpressions, but it should not be too difficult. The following is the code for this query:

```
QueryExp statusQuery = Query.equals( Query.attr( "status" ),
                                     Query.value( "ERROR" ) );

QueryExp inkQuery = Query.equals( Query.attr( "inkLevel" ),
                                  Query.value( "LOW" ) );

QueryExp paperQuery = Query.equals( Query.attr( "paperCount" ),
                                    Query.value( "LOW" ) );

QueryExp orQuery = Query.or( inkQuery, paperQuery );

QueryExp notQuery = Query.not( orQuery );

QueryExp finalExp = Query.and( statusQuery, notQuery );

mbeanServer.queryMBeans(
                new ObjectName( "Hardware:*,location=network" ),
                finalExp );
```

As you can see, with the query mechanism of the MBean server, you can build complex and specific queries to return useful results about the MBean contained in an agent.

8.4 Summary

This chapter began by focusing more closely on the MBean server than previous chapters. You had already used the MBean server a little, but before we could move on to more agent-level material, we needed to cover the `MBeanServer` interface in greater detail. This chapter introduced you to every method in the interface (except some overloaded versions), including their purpose and exceptions.

After we discussed the `MBeanServer` interface, you learned how to turn query sentences into objects that can be used to filter through and identify MBeans in the MBean server. The query capability of the MBean server is a powerful tool when an MBean server contains a large number of MBeans. Using the querying mechanism, you can retrieve specific MBeans without manually examining the contents of each to discover the one you need. You learned not only how to construct queries, but also how to refine their scope through the use of partial object names. We presented several query examples to demonstrate how to build simple and complex expressions.

Chapter 9 focuses on using and building protocol adapters and connectors for JMX agents. In that chapter, you will be exposed to the RMI connector contributed by Sun Microsystems, and you will build your own Jini connector and TCP adapter.

Communicating
with JMX agents

- Using the RMI adapter from Sun
- Creating a Jini connector
- Creating a TCP adapter

You had your first exposure to working with an MBean server by using the HTML adapter you registered on the server. Previous chapters reminded you how JMX uses protocol adapters and connectors to enable a JMX agent for use by the outside world.

You studied the overall agent architecture in chapter 1 and explored the MBean server in greater detail in chapter 8. This chapter covers another component of JMX agents: protocol adapters and connectors. In this chapter, we will discuss two connectors that will enable you to distribute your agents across a network using Java Remote Method Invocation (RMI) and the Jini network technology. We will also spend some time discussing using TCP and Simple Network Management Protocol (SNMP) to enable access to JMX agents.

By allowing clients of your agent to contact the agent from remote locations, you greatly increase the agent's usefulness. By using connectors and adapters, you can collocate agents with managed resources and contact them from remote locations. Thus you can use web browsers, hand-held devices, and so forth to stay in contact with your managed resources.

As previously mentioned, such remote communication is particularly useful in a monitoring context. You can install a JMX agent in a hosted application environment and stay in communication with it over your network. This ability lets you maintain reliable, real-time status. Figure 9.1 depicts this scenario; you should recognize components of this figure from previous chapters.

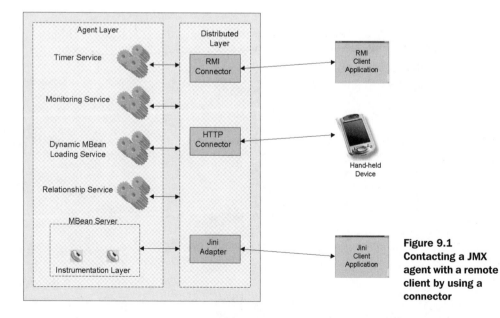

Figure 9.1
Contacting a JMX agent with a remote client by using a connector

When discussing protocol adapters and connectors as means of exposing your JMX agents to management tools, it is important to understand the differences between them.

9.1 Comparing connectors and protocol adapters

Protocol adapters and connectors are very similar in that they serve the same overall purpose: to open a JMX agent to managing entities. The difference between them is how they go about it. Protocol adapters generally must listen for incoming messages that are constructed in a particular protocol like HTTP or SNMP. In this sense, protocol adapters are made up of only one component that resides in the agent at all times.

Connectors, on the other hand, are made up of two components: one component resides in the JMX agent, and the other is used by client-side applications. Clients use the client-side connector component to contact the server-side component and communicate with a JMX agent. In this manner, connectors hide the actual protocol being used to contact the agent; the entire process happens between the connector's two components.

9.2 Connecting by using RMI

Recall from chapter 2's discussion of Sun Microsystems' JMX Reference Implementation (RI) that the RI includes a jmx folder and a contrib folder. The contrib folder contains the RMI connector that you included in the JMXBookAgent from chapter 3. This section is intended to make you more familiar with how the RMI connector works. It is unsupported in the RI, but it is also contained in Sun Microsystems' commercial JMX product, the Java Dynamic Management Kit (JDMK). (For more information about the JDMK, go to http://www.javasoft.com.)

9.2.1 Using the RMI connector

Figure 9.2 illustrates the components of the RMI connector. It is an MBean registered on an MBean server, just like the HTML adapter you have already used. However, whereas you used a web browser previously to contact the HTML adapter, the RMI connector comes with an RMI client.

You can use the RMI connector client to connect to the RMI server MBean and invoke methods that correspond directly to methods on the MBean server in which the MBean is registered. For example, after connecting to the server with an RMI connector client rmiClient, you could invoke the method

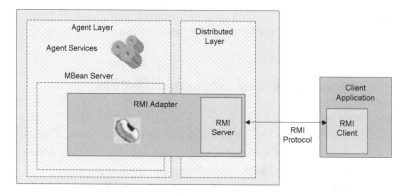

Figure 9.2   The components of the RMI connector included in the JMX RI from Sun Microsystems. The RMI connector uses both a server object and a client object.

`rmiClient.getMBeanCount()` to acquire the number of MBeans running on the remote MBean server. You will find every method on the RMI client that you would find in the `MBeanServer` interface.

9.2.2   *Creating the RMI server MBean*

The server portion of the RMI connector is contained in the `RmiConnectorServer` class. To create the server, you need to perform the following three steps:

1   Create an instance of `RmiConnectorServer` using one of its four constructors. The different constructors let you specify different values for the server registration port and service name.

2   Register the connector and the MBean server.

3   Invoke the connector's `start()` method. The `start()` method tells the server to bind to an RMI registry and prepare itself to receive client calls.

Reexamining the JMXBookAgent class

When you created the `JMXBookAgent` class in chapter 3, you gave it a `startRMI-Connector()` method that added the RMI connector MBean to the agent. However, in that chapter, we did not discuss what took place in code. Listing 9.1 shows the method again; let's examine it.

> **Listing 9.1   The startRMIConnector() method of the JMXBookAgent class**

```
protected void startRMIConnector()
{
    RmiConnectorServer connector = new RmiConnectorServer();
    ObjectName connectorName = null;
```

```
try
{
  connectorName = new ObjectName(
              "JMXBookAgent:name=RMIConnector");
  server.registerMBean( connector, connectorName );
  connector.start();
}
catch(Exception e)
{
  e.printStackTrace();
}

}
```

The JMXBookAgent class imports the com.sun.jdmk.comm package in order to obtain the RmiConnectorServer class. It contains the classes contributed by Sun Microsystems in Sun's JMX RI.

The class uses the default constructor of the RmiConnectorServer class. The constructor tells the server to use the default port and service name. However, as mentioned previously, this is not the RmiConnectorServer class's only constructor. Table 9.1 lists the constructors and their arguments.

Table 9.1   The constructors of the `RmiConnectorServer` class

Constructor	Description
RmiConnectorServer()	The default constructor
RmiConnectorServer(int port)	Specifies a new port for binding to an RMI registry
RmiConnectorServer(String name)	Specifies a name for the object registered on the RMI registry
RmiConnectorServer(int port, String name)	Specifies both a new registry port and new remote object name

By using one of the other constructors, you can control the RMI registry the server will bind to, and you can change the name of the remote object that will be registered on the registry.

9.2.3 *Connecting to the RMI server*

Now that we have examined a basic agent that uses an RMI connector, let's look at the RMI connector client contained in the class RmiConnectorClient. As mentioned earlier, this class declares methods that correspond to every method available on an MBean server. The following example shows you how to connect to the RMI connector server running on the JMXBookAgent.

Reexamining the RMIClientFactory class

In chapter 3, you created the RMIClientFactory class. Recall that you use this class to acquire an RMI client in which to contact your JMXBookAgent class. Listing 9.2 lists the class again.

Listing 9.2 RMIClientFactory.java

```
package jmxbook.ch3;

import javax.management.*;
import com.sun.jdmk.comm.*;

public class RMIClientFactory
{

  public static RmiConnectorClient getClient()
  {
    RmiConnectorClient client = new RmiConnectorClient();
      RmiConnectorAddress address = new RmiConnectorAddress();
    System.out.println("\t\tTYPE\t= "    +
              address.getConnectorType ());
      System.out.println("\t\tPORT\t= "    + address.getPort());
      System.out.println("\t\tHOST\t= "    + address.getHost());
      System.out.println("\t\tSERVER\t= " + address.getName());

      try
      {
        client.connect( address );
      }
      catch( Exception e )
      {
        e.printStackTrace();
      }

    return client;
  }

}
```

To tell the RmiConnectorClient object where to find the RmiConnectorServer, you need to use the RmiConnectorAddress class. This class encapsulates host, port, and lookup name values that tell the client object where to find the RMI registry and look up the remote object of the RMI connector. If you created the RmiConnectorServer using the default constructor, then you can create the address object with its default constructor. Both classes contain the same default values for host, port, and lookup name. The default values are the following:

- *Host*—Defaults to the local host value
- *Port*—Default value is contained in the static variable `ServiceName.RMI_CONNECTOR_PORT`
- *Lookup name*—Defaults to the value of `ServiceName.RMI_CONNECTOR_SERVER`

After creating the `RmiConnectorClient` object, you invoke its `connect()` method. This method tells the client object to make a connection with the server-side component of the RMI connector. After successfully connecting to the agent, you can return the client reference—ready for use.

9.2.4 *Additional uses for the RMI connector*

In addition to providing RMI connectivity to a JMX agent for invoking methods on a remote MBean server, the RMI connector offers some other useful features. The remaining features of the RMI connector are as follows:

- *Remote notifications*—The RMI connector will transmit notifications emitted from the remote server to the remote client.
- *Connector heartbeat*—Connector clients can emit a heartbeat to monitor the connection to the connector server. Doing so allows agents and client to retry or clean up bad connections.
- *Client context checking*—This feature allows the server to verify that a client has the correct context before invoking requested operations.

Recall that the RMI connector is contributed unsupported to the Sun JMX RI. The RMI connector is part of Sun's commercial product, the JDMK. With that in mind, the following sections briefly describe the three previously listed features in more detail.

Retrieving notifications

The RMI connector provides two ways to receive notifications from a remote MBean server. When an RMI connector client connects to an RMI connector server, it can specify a notification receiving mode via the client's `setMode()` method. The `setMode()` method takes a single parameter: either `ClientNotificationHandler.PUSH_MODE` or `ClientNotificationHandler.PULL_MODE`. The first value indicates that notifications from the remote JMX agent will be pushed to the RMI connector client, and the second value indicates that the RMI connector client will pull notifications from the remote agent.

To receive notifications from a particular MBean, you simply invoke the `add-NotificationListener()` method of the client. Because all `Notification` objects are serializable, they can be transmitted over RMI to interested clients.

Connector heartbeat

The RMI connector uses a notification system to detect the health of the client and/or server portions of the connector. When using an `RmiConnectorClient` object, you can add a notification listener for receiving `HeartBeatNotification` objects. A `HeartBeatNotification` object can indicate several conditions about a connection to the RMI connector server, as listed in table 9.2. The values in the Notification Type column are `public static` members of the `HeartBeatNotification` class.

Table 9.2   Notification types used by a **HeartBeatNotification** notification

Notification type	Description
CONNECTION_ESTABLISHED	A connection has been made between the client and server.
CONNECTION_LOST	A connection has died.
CONNECTION_REESTABLISHED	A connection was temporarily unavailable, but is now connected.
CONNECTION_RETRYING	The client is trying to reestablish a dead connection.
CONNECTION_TERMINATED	The connection has been closed.

You acquire the condition value by invoking the `getType()` method of the notification.

Client context checking

The last feature of the RMI connector covered in this chapter is the concept of a client context checker. A context checker ensures that a client passes a predefined test before it can invoke any methods on the remote MBean server.

The client must set an `OperationalContext` object into its `RmiConnectorClient` object. The connector client object will pass this context to the RMI connector server, which uses it to decide whether to complete a client's request on an MBean server. To do so, the server uses an instance of the class `MBeanServerChecker`.

An `MBeanServerChecker` object encapsulates an `MBeanServer` object and contains a check method for every method declared by the `MBeanServer` class. For instance, for a client that attempted to invoke `create Bean()` on a remote MBean server, the `MBeanServerChecker` would first invoke the method `checkCreate()`. This method would verify the client's `OperationalContext` in some way and, if it were valid, would invoke the method on the MBean server. To provide your own implementation for the check methods, you would provide a subclass to the `MBeanServerChecker` class.

9.3 *Connecting to agents using Jini*

The RMI connector we just discussed should give you a good idea what can be accomplished by making your JMX agents remotely accessible. As you discovered, the RMI connector not only gives you the ability to invoke MBean server methods, but also lets you receive notifications.

However, you might have noticed one drawback to using the RMI connector: you must know the address of the RMI connector server. That is, you have to be able to tell your `RmiConnectorClient` object where to look up the remote server object.

To get around this issue, you can build a Jini connector. By using Jini, you can distribute a JMX agent just like the RMI connector does, without requiring clients to know the exact location of the agent. Jini enables developers to write services that can describe themselves and can be discovered by clients.

For instance, clients wishing to interact with a JMX agent can construct a Jini connector client, enter a few search parameters, and locate the nearest matching agent, as illustrated in figure 9.3.

Your Jini connector will advertise itself by using the value of the default domain name of the MBean server in which it is registered. The Jini connector client will do a search for agents by using the domain name as a search parameter. Later, you can expand the search capabilities as needed. As the chapter continues,

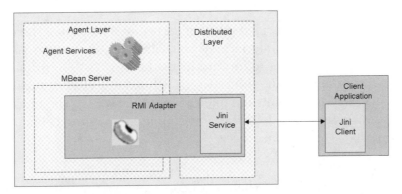

Figure 9.3 **The Jini connector makes the JMX agent available to a greater client audience by allowing itself to be discovered.**

we will discuss more connector scenarios that use the Jini connector. The connector will be made up of three components: an MBean, a Jini service, and a Jini client. The following section explores these three components in detail.

9.3.1 Components of the Jini connector

As the previous section mentioned, you need the following three components to create this connector:

- *MBean*—The MBean allows the connector to be managed through the MBean server (like the RMI connector and HTML adapter MBeans).
- *Jini service*—The service is created by the MBean. It allows clients to connect to the agent.
- *Jini client*—People use the client class to locate the Jini service from the agent.

The following sections describe the role each component plays in the connector. Then, we will begin to examine the code.

The MBean

The role of the MBean in the connector is to set up and manage the Jini service. The MBean gives the agent the capability to control the Jini service, including setting up its description and deciding when to make the service available for discovery. The MBean contains a reference to its MBean server, which allows the Jini service to perform callbacks to the MBean server methods. (You will learn more about this process when we examine the code.) The MBean component will be defined by the JINIServerMBean interface and the JINIServer class (which implements the JINIServerMBean interface).

The Jini service

The Jini service implements methods that correspond to each of the methods found in the MBean server interface. As you will see in the code to follow, this process allows the Jini client to forward its method invocations to the MBean server via the Jini service. The Jini service is defined in a class named JINIConnectorImpl, which implements the interface JINIConnector. The interface is a remote interface used in a Java RMI environment, enabling clients to make remote invocations on the Jini service.

The connector client

Client-side objects use the Jini client to discover and use the Jini connector service (and therefore use the JMX agent). Like the Jini service, it contains methods that correspond to the methods of the MBeanServer interface. Invocations of these methods are forwarded to the Jini service, which forwards them to the MBean server of the JMX agent. In addition, the connector client shields the developer from the process of finding the Jini service. The JINIConnectorClient class defines the Jini client.

9.3.2 *Writing the Jini connector*

Now that we have discussed the components that form the Jini connector, let's begin writing the code. You will create the components in the order they were presented: the MBean, the Jini service, and then the Jini client. All the classes are in the package jmxbook.ch9. After you write all the classes, we will go over what you need to do to compile and run them. To test the connector, you will need to write some code for your JMXBookAgent class to include an instance of the Jini connector.

Writing the MBean

With the MBean, you must decide what attributes and operations you want to expose in order to make the Jini service configurable and more useful. Table 9.3 lists the attributes and operations exposed by the JINIServerMBean interface. Remember from chapter 4 that this type of interface indicates you are creating a Standard MBean.

Table 9.3   Attributes and operations exposed by the `JINIServerMBean` interface

Attribute/operation	Description
Domain	Read-only attribute that indicates the domain of the agent that contains this connector.
EntryName	Read/write attribute that supplies the Jini service started by the MBean with an identifier. This attribute is optional, but providing a value gives clients a way to refine their search for the service (it makes the Jini service more unique).
Groups	Read/write attribute that indicates which lookup service groups the Jini service will register with. (For more information about the lookup service, go to http://www.javasoft.com.)
enableConnections	Operation that tells the MBean to start the Jini service.

Table 9.3 gives a good view of what the MBean will be like. Now that you know the exposed attributes and operations of the MBean, look at the JINIServer-MBean interface:

```
package jmxbook.ch9;

public interface JINIServerMBean
```

```
{
    public String getDomain();
    public String getEntryName();
    public void setEntryName( String name );
    public String[] getGroups();
    public void setGroups( String[] groups );
    public void enableConnections();
}
```

After creating the interface, you need to implement it with the `JINIServer`
MBean class. Recall from the previous sections that the `JINIServer` class will create the Jini service when requested by the JMX agent. Listing 9.3 shows the
`JINIServer` class. (Starting with this class, you will notice a lot of Jini-related
packages and classes; this discussion goes into detail for many but not all of the
Jini-related issues. If you need to take time to read more about Jini, check the
documents at http://www.javasoft.com.)

Listing 9.3   JINIServer.java

```
package jmxbook.ch9;

import javax.management.*;
import java.rmi.*;
import java.util.*;
import net.jini.discovery.*;
import net.jini.core.lookup.*;
import net.jini.lookup.*;                    ❶ Import Jini
import net.jini.lease.*;                        packages
import net.jini.core.discovery.*;
import net.jini.lookup.entry.*;
import net.jini.core.entry.*;

public class JINIServer implements JINIServerMBean,
                                   MBeanRegistration,      ❷ Implement
                                   ServiceIDListener          necessary
{                                                             interfaces
    private MBeanServer mbs = null;
    private JoinManager jm = null;
    private ServiceID id = null;
    private String domain = null;
    private ObjectName name = null;
    private String[] groups;
    private Name entry = null;
    private boolean enabled = false;

    public JINIServer()
    {
        groups = new String[ 1 ];
        groups[ 0 ] = "public";
    }
```

```
public String getDomain()
{
  return domain;
}

public String getEntryName()
{
  return entry.name;
}

public void serviceIDNotify( ServiceID id )
{
  this.id = id;
}

public ObjectName preRegister( MBeanServer server,
                               ObjectName name) throws Exception
{
  this.mbs = server;
  if( name == null )
  {
    name =
       new ObjectName( mbs.getDefaultDomain() +
                     ":connectorType=JINI" );
  }
  this.domain = name.getDomain();
  return name;
}

public void postRegister (Boolean registrationDone) {}
public void preDeregister() throws Exception {}
public void postDeregister(){}

public void setGroups( String groups[] )
{
  if( groups != null )
     this.groups = groups;
}

public String[] getGroups()
{
  return groups;
}

public void enableConnections()
{
   createService();
}

public void setEntryName( String name )
{
   Entry old = entry;
   this.entry = new Name( name );
   if( enabled )
```

```
            {
              Entry[] newlabels = { entry };
              Entry[] labels = { old };

              jm.modifyAttributes( labels, newlabels );
            }
        }

        private void createService()
        {
            try
            {
              JINIConnector connector =                      Set up Jini    ❹
                      new JINIConnectorImpl( this );           service

              Entry[] labels = { entry };

              LookupDiscoveryManager mgr =
                      new LookupDiscoveryManager( groups, null, null );

              jm = new JoinManager(connector, labels, this,   ❸  Create
                          mgr,                                    JoinManager
                          new LeaseRenewalManager());

              enabled = true;
            }
            catch( Exception e )
            {                              ❹  Set up Jini
              e.printStackTrace();             service
            }

        }

        /*
            call back methods      ❺  Implement
        */                             remaining methods
        public Integer getMBeanCount() throws Exception
        {
          return mbs.getMBeanCount();
        }

        public ObjectInstance createMBean(String className,
                                ObjectName name) throws Exception
        {
          return mbs.createMBean( className, name );
        }
    }
```

❶ These `import` statements import packages from the Jini toolkit. These packages contain the classes needed to find lookup services and manage and describe Jini services. All of these packages come with the downloadable Jini toolkit from Sun Microsystems.

2 The `JINIServer` class implements the following three interfaces:

- `JINIServerMBean`—This MBean interface declares the exposed attributes and operations for this MBean.

- `MBeanRegistration`—Recall from chapter 4 that this interface allows the MBean to acquire a reference to the MBean server. For more information, look back at that chapter.

- `ServiceIDListener`—This is a Jini interface that allows the Jini lookup service to perform a callback and inform the listener (the interface implementer) of the unique service id generated for a particular Jini service. It declares only one method: `public void serviceIDNotify()`.

With a reference to the MBean server, the MBean can propagate corresponding invocations from the Jini service to the MBean server. (More about this in a moment.)

3 The `JINIServer` class uses a Jini utility class, `JoinManager`, which handles the lookup, registration, and management of lookup services for a particular Jini service. You can see how it is created in the `createService()` method. The MBean keeps a reference to this class in order to manage the attributes of the `JINIConnectorImpl` service.

4 The `createService()` method is where all the action takes place in this MBean. This method is invoked when the JMX agent calls the `enableConnections()` method of the MBean. It is responsible for creating the Jini service class (`JINIConnectorImpl`) and registering it with available Jini lookup services. We will examine the `JINIConnectorImpl` class in the next code listing, but as you can see, all you have to do is use the constructor that accepts a reference to this MBean. The `JINIConnectorImpl` class will use that reference to make callbacks to the MBean.

Once the service is created, it must be made available to possible clients. As mentioned earlier, the `JINIServer` MBean uses a Jini utility class called `JoinManager` to handle all the logistics surrounding registration and management of a service on a lookup service. (For more information about the `JoinManager` class, refer to the javadocs bundled in the Jini download.)

5 All the methods after this point correspond to methods in the MBean server. These are the callback methods the Jini service invokes in order to perform an operation on the `MBeanServer` instance residing in the JMX agent. For the sake of space, only two methods are currently implemented: `getMBeanCount()` and `createMBean()`. You will use the latter method in your tests later.

Writing the Jini service

Now that you've written the JINIServer MBean, let's examine the JINIConnectorImpl class that the MBean uses to expose its JMX agent to Jini clients. With all Jini services, JINIConnectorImpl must implement a remote interface that declares the methods available to a client. The following code is the service interface, JINIConnector:

```
package jmxbook.ch9;

import java.rmi.*;
import javax.management.*;

public interface JINIConnector extends Remote
{
   public Integer getMBeanCount() throws JINIConnectorException;

   public ObjectInstance createMBean(String className,
              ObjectName name) throws JINIConnectorException;

}
```

As you can see, it contains only two methods. Recall from the previous code discussion that the Jini connector is left incomplete for the sake of space. For this connector to be complete, all the methods of the MBean server must be made available. This interface declares the methods available to your JINIConnector-Client class (discussed in a moment). Remember, however, that all methods declared in this interface will also be made available to the client, allowing the user to invoke the corresponding methods on the remote MBean server.

Notice also that the interface declares the methods as throwing an instance of the JINIConnectorException exception class. We'll define this exception class shortly; basically, it extends java.rmi.RemoteException and wraps server-side exceptions, enabling service clients to acquire the wrapped exception. You will see it thrown from the Jini service code to follow, and also used in the Jini connector client later.

Listing 9.4 shows the JINIConnectorImpl class. It contains the Jini service created by the JINIServer MBean.

Listing 9.4   JINIConnectorImpl.java

```
package jmxbook.ch9;

import java.rmi.*;
import java.rmi.server.*;
import javax.management.*;                              Extend    ❶
                                          UnicastRemoteObject class
public class JINIConnectorImpl extends
          UnicastRemoteObject implements JINIConnector  ◁
```

```
{
  private JINIServer server = null;

  public JINIConnectorImpl( JINIServer server )
                                    throws RemoteException
  {
    this.server = server;      ❷  Store reference
                                   to Jini service
  }

  public Integer getMBeanCount() throws JINIConnectorException
  {
    try
    {
      return server.getMBeanCount();
    }
    catch( Exception e )
    {
      throw new JINIConnectorException( "getMBeanCount", e );
    }
  }

  public ObjectInstance createMBean(String className,
                        ObjectName name) throws
                        JINIConnectorException
  {
    try
    {
      return server.createMBean( className, name );
    }
    catch( Exception e )
    {
      throw new JINIConnectorException( "createMBean", e );
    }
  }
}
}
```

❶ In order to be a Jini service, this class must be a remote class. That is, it must be available in a Java RMI environment. Toward this end, it extends the `UnicastRemoteObject` class, which provides the service with the capabilities of a remote object. In addition, it implements its remote interface, `JINIConnector`, which declares the methods that will be available to clients.

❷ The key feature of this class is that it contains a reference to the `JINIServer` MBean from the JMX agent. This reference allows the service to make callbacks to the MBean to perform the necessary invocations for a service client.

As you can see, the source is short. However, remember that you implemented only two corresponding methods to the MBean server—to finish this

Jini service, you would need to write the final methods that correspond to the remaining method of the MBean server. From the first two methods already implemented, you should be able to tell that this is not a difficult task.

Before moving on to the Jini connector client, let's look at the `JINIConnectorException` class to clarify its purpose. Listing 9.5 shows the exception class.

Listing 9.5   JINIConnectorException.java

```
package jmxbook.ch9;

import java.rmi.*;

public class JINIConnectorException extends RemoteException
{

    private Exception exception = null;

    public JINIConnectorException( String message, Exception ex )
    {
      super( message, ex );
      this.exception = ex;
    }

    public Exception getWrappedException()
    {
      return exception;
    }
}
```

This class extends `RemoteException` so that it can serve as the single exception thrown from the remote interface `JINIConnector`. However, `RemoteException` does not grant access to its wrapped exception, so this subclass does. In the constructor, the class stores the wrapped exception in a class member variable for later retrieval by the `getWrappedException()` method.

This exception class will let the client decipher the exact type of the exception being thrown from a service method (such as `createMBean()`) and throw the appropriate type on the client side.

The last component to cover is the connector client. The following section discusses the `JINIConnectorClient` class, which creates a Jini client.

Writing the Jini connector client

The first thing you will notice when examining the `JINIConnectorClient` class (listing 9.6) is the large section of stubbed-out MBean server methods at the end. The client does in fact implement the `MBeanServer` interface; it does so to provide client-side users with all the methods that would be available on the server side. We've stubbed out all but two of these methods for the sake of space. The remaining two MBeanServer methods are used to test the connector later. Examine the listing; the discussion follows.

Listing 9.6   JINIConnectorClient.java

```
package jmxbook.ch9;

import javax.management.*;
import java.rmi.*;
import java.util.*;
import net.jini.discovery.*;
import net.jini.core.lookup.*;
import net.jini.lookup.*;
import java.io.*;

public class JINIConnectorClient
            implements DiscoveryListener, MBeanServer
{
   private ServiceTemplate template = null;
   private LookupDiscovery reg = null;
   private JINIConnector server =null;

   public JINIConnectorClient()
   {
      System.setSecurityManager( new RMISecurityManager() );

      Class[] cls = { JINIConnector.class };
      template = new ServiceTemplate( null, cls, null );

      try
      {
        reg = new LookupDiscovery( new String[] { "" } );
        reg.addDiscoveryListener( this );

        while( server == null )
          Thread.sleep( 1000 );
      }
      catch( Exception e )
      {
        e.printStackTrace();
      }

   }

   public void discovered( DiscoveryEvent event )
   {
     if( server != null )
       return;
     ServiceRegistrar[] lookups = event.getRegistrars();
     try
     {
      ServiceMatches items = lookups[0].lookup( template,
```

① Begin search for Jini service

② Implement listener callback

```
                                  Integer.MAX_VALUE );
  server = ( JINIConnector ) items.items[ 0 ].service;
  System.out.println( "service found" );
  }
  catch( Exception e )
  {
    e.printStackTrace();
  }

}

public void discarded( DiscoveryEvent event ){}

public Integer getMBeanCount()
{
  try
  {
    return server.getMBeanCount();
  }
  catch( JINIConnectorException e )
  {
    return null;
  }
}

public ObjectInstance createMBean(String className,
                 ObjectName name)
        throws ReflectionException,
      InstanceAlreadyExistsException,
      MBeanRegistrationException, MBeanException,
      NotCompliantMBeanException
{
  try
  {
    return server.createMBean( className, name );
  }
  catch( JINIConnectorException e )
  {
    Exception ex = e.getWrappedException();
    if( ex instanceof ReflectionException )
       throw ( ReflectionException ) ex;
    else if( ex instanceof InstanceAlreadyExistsException )
       throw ( InstanceAlreadyExistsException ) ex;
    else if( ex instanceof MBeanRegistrationException )
       throw ( MBeanRegistrationException ) ex;
    else if( ex instanceof MBeanException )
       throw ( MBeanException ) ex;
    else
       throw ( NotCompliantMBeanException ) ex;
  }

}
/*
```

❸ Implement getMBeanCount() method

❹ Implement createMBean()

```
UNIMPLEMENTED METHODS BELOW    ⑤   Implement remaining
*/                                    methods
public Object instantiate(String className)
                throws ReflectionException,
                    MBeanException { return null; }
public Object instantiate(String className,
                    ObjectName loaderName)
                    throws ReflectionException, MBeanException,
                    InstanceNotFoundException { return null; }
public Object instantiate(String className, Object params[],
                    String signature[])
                    throws ReflectionException, MBeanException
                        { return null; }
public Object instantiate(String className,
                    ObjectName loaderName,
                    Object params[], String signature[])
                    throws ReflectionException, MBeanException,
                    InstanceNotFoundException { return null; }
public ObjectInstance createMBean(String className,
                    ObjectName name,
                    ObjectName loaderName)
                    throws ReflectionException,
                    InstanceAlreadyExistsException,
                    MBeanRegistrationException, MBeanException,
                    NotCompliantMBeanException,
                    InstanceNotFoundException { return null; }
public ObjectInstance createMBean(String className,
                    ObjectName name,
                    Object params[], String signature[])
                    throws ReflectionException,
                    InstanceAlreadyExistsException,
                    MBeanRegistrationException, MBeanException,
                    NotCompliantMBeanException  { return null; }
public ObjectInstance createMBean(String className,
                    ObjectName name,
                    ObjectName loaderName, Object params[],
                    String signature[])
                    throws ReflectionException,
                    InstanceAlreadyExistsException,
                    MBeanRegistrationException, MBeanException,
                    NotCompliantMBeanException,
                    InstanceNotFoundException { return null; }
public ObjectInstance registerMBean(Object object,
                    ObjectName name)
                    throws InstanceAlreadyExistsException,
                    MBeanRegistrationException,
                    NotCompliantMBeanException { return null; }
public void unregisterMBean(ObjectName name)
                    throws InstanceNotFoundException,
                    MBeanRegistrationException { return; }
```

```
public ObjectInstance getObjectInstance(ObjectName name)
        throws InstanceNotFoundException   { return null; }
public Set queryMBeans(ObjectName name, QueryExp query)
        { return null; }
public Set queryNames(ObjectName name, QueryExp query)
        { return null; }
public boolean isRegistered(ObjectName name) { return false; }
public Object getAttribute(ObjectName name, String attribute)
                    throws MBeanException,
                    AttributeNotFoundException,
                    InstanceNotFoundException,
                    ReflectionException
                    { return null; }
public AttributeList getAttributes(ObjectName name,
                    String[] attributes)
                        throws InstanceNotFoundException,
                        ReflectionException { return null; }
public void setAttribute(ObjectName name, Attribute attribute)
                    throws InstanceNotFoundException,
                    AttributeNotFoundException,
                    InvalidAttributeValueException,
                    MBeanException,
                    ReflectionException   { return; }
public AttributeList setAttributes(ObjectName name,
                    AttributeList attributes)
                        throws InstanceNotFoundException,
                        ReflectionException   { return null; }
public Object invoke(ObjectName name, String operationName,
                    Object params[], String signature[])
                    throws InstanceNotFoundException,
                    MBeanException,
                    ReflectionException { return null; }
public String getDefaultDomain() { return null; }
public void addNotificationListener(ObjectName name,
                    NotificationListener listener,
                    NotificationFilter filter,
                    Object handback)
                    throws InstanceNotFoundException
                { return; }
public void addNotificationListener(ObjectName name,
                ObjectName listener,
                NotificationFilter filter,
                Object handback)
                    throws InstanceNotFoundException
                    { return; }
public void removeNotificationListener(ObjectName name,
                    NotificationListener listener)
                    throws InstanceNotFoundException,
                    ListenerNotFoundException { return; }
public void removeNotificationListener(ObjectName name,
                    ObjectName listener)
```

```
                        throws InstanceNotFoundException,
                        ListenerNotFoundException { return; }
    public MBeanInfo getMBeanInfo(ObjectName name)
                        throws InstanceNotFoundException,
                        IntrospectionException,
                        ReflectionException
                        { return null; }
    public boolean isInstanceOf(ObjectName name, String className)
                        throws InstanceNotFoundException
                        { return false; }
    public ObjectInputStream deserialize(ObjectName name,
                        byte[] data)
                        throws InstanceNotFoundException,
                        OperationsException { return null; }
    public ObjectInputStream deserialize(String className,
                        byte[] data)
                        throws OperationsException,
                        ReflectionException
                        { return null; }
    public ObjectInputStream deserialize(String className,
                        ObjectName loaderName, byte[] data)
                        throws InstanceNotFoundException,
                        OperationsException, ReflectionException
                        { return null; }
    public static void main( String args[] )            ❻  Test in main()
    {                                                       method
      try
      {
        JINIConnectorClient client = new JINIConnectorClient();
        System.out.println(client.getMBeanCount() );
        client.createMBean( "jmxbook.ch2.HelloWorld",
                    new ObjectName(
                    "JMXBookAgent:name=hwtest" ) );
      }
      catch( Exception e )
      {
        e.printStackTrace();
      }
    }

}
```

❶ A good place to begin the examination of the code is the class constructor. The constructor is responsible for creating the search parameters that will find the Jini service portion of the Jini connector. It does so by creating an instance of the class ServiceTemplate. For now, the only parameter going into the template is the interface type name jmxbook.ch9.JINIConnector.

After creating the template, the constructor starts a lookup service–finding process by creating a `LookupDiscoveryManager` instance. This object actively searches for Jini lookup services across the network. The constructor adds the client class as a `DiscoveryListener` and will be notified via the `discovered()` callback when a lookup service is found. When a lookup service is found, the client is notified and can search that lookup service for an instance of the `JINIConnector` service.

❷ As mentioned in the previous paragraph, the `discovered()` method is invoked by the `LookupDiscoveryManager` when a lookup service is found. Now that the client has a reference to a lookup service, it uses the `ServiceTemplate` object created in the constructor to search for the `JINIConnector` service. Service matches are returned from the lookup service in a `ServiceMatches` object that contains an array of `ServiceItem` objects. A `ServiceItem` object contains the actual Jini service that matched the search (in this case, an instance of `JINIConnector`). At this point, your client acquires a reference to the Jini service for use. It stores the reference in a class member called `server`.

❸ The `getMBeanCount()` method is the first of two methods implemented on the client side to correspond to remote MBean server methods. It simply invokes the identically named method on the `JINIConnector` service and returns the result.

❹ The final method implemented in the `JINIConnectorClient` class is `create-MBean()` (which corresponds to the remote MBean server `createMBean()` method that is identically declared). This method is singled out here as an example of using the `JINIConnectorException` class.

When this method is invoked, like `getMBeanCount()`, it simply invokes the same method on the `JINIConnector` service. However, unlike the `getMBeanCount()` method, it must be prepared to throw a variety of exceptions back to the user. To accomplish this, you use the `JINIConnectorClient` exception class. When the method catches a `JINIConnectorException` exception, it acquires the wrapped server-side exception, casts it to the appropriate type (the `getWrappedException()` method returns the type `Exception`), and throws it.

❺ Recall that we stubbed out the remaining methods declared in the `MBeanServer` interface. They are included below the comment block in order to successfully compile the connector client class.

❻ We include a `main()` method to use in a quick test later. The `main()` method creates a `JINIConnectorClient` instance and uses it to connect to a remote MBean server, get the MBean count, and create an instance of the `HelloWorld` MBean.

9.3.3 *Outstanding issues*

This connector example leaves out some important features. For instance, there are important details to consider when implementing the connector's notification delivery mechanism. You should also make changes so that multiple agents running this type of connector are distinguishable from each other.

Handling notifications

In a normal notification scenario, an agent directly invokes an object that has registered as a notification listener in order to deliver notifications to it. However, in the distributed environment, the notification listener may be in a remote location, and direct invocation may not be possible.

Therefore, the implementation of the `addNotificationListener()` methods of the `JINIConnectorClient` must be different than the usual `server.method()` invocation seen in the two methods you implemented. The add-listener methods must take into account the distributed nature of the connector. The best way to solve this problem is to have the `JINIConnectorClient` instance store the listener reference locally and add itself as the notification listener instead. The client can alternatively be a remote object; in that case the remote MBean can deliver notifications to the client, which can distribute them as needed to local listeners.

Jini connector attributes

Consider the environment that has two active JMX agents, both of which are using a Jini connector to allow remote clients to discover them. These two agents need the ability to ensure that their respective Jini services (created by the Jini connector) are uniquely identifiable. The `JINIServer` MBean allows the agent to set a single attribute for the service. The `JINIServer` MBean should always construct the Jini service using these attributes to be as unique as possible. In addition, the `JINIConnectorClient` needs code to allow a user to enter possible attribute values when the client begins to search for the Jini service. This code will let client users refine their search for a remote JMX agent.

9.3.4 *Testing the Jini connector*

We have covered all the components of the Jini connector; it is time to use it in an example. To test the connector, you need to modify the `JMXBookAgent` class. For your agent, you will add the `startJINIConnector()` method. For the client, you will use the `JINIConnectorClient` class's main method. Typically, a client will construct an instance of the `JINIConnectorClient` class to use. The following section examines the `startJINIConnector()` method.

The startJINIConnector() method

In chapter 3, which introduced the `JMXBookAgent` class, you gave it a `startRMI-Connector()` method that added the RMI connector MBean to the agent. However, in that chapter, we did not discuss what took place in the code. Listing 9.7 shows the `startJINIConnector()` method.

Listing 9.7   The startJINIConnector() method of the JMXBookAgent class

```
protected void startJINIConnector()
{
    ObjectName connectorName = null;

    try
    {
      System.setSecurityManager( new RMISecurityManager() );

      JINIServer jini = new JINIServer();
      ObjectName jiniName = null;

      jiniName =
          new ObjectName( "JMXBookAgent:name=JINIConnector" );
        server.registerMBean( jini, jiniName );
      jini.enableConnections();
    }
    catch(Exception e)
    {
      e.printStackTrace();
    }
}
```

The method creates an instance of the connector MBean (the `JINIServer` class) and a new `ObjectName` instance for the MBean, and registers the MBean on the MBean server. Finally, it calls the `enableConnections()` method of the MBean to create and start the Jini service within.

Running the example

Now you have written all the code, you need to test this connector. To compile and run the connector, however, you must download the latest Jini developer kit from http://www.javasoft.com. Once you have it, complete the following steps to test the connector:

1 Compile the `jmxbook.ch9` package. You need the JMX JARs, the JMX_re-moting.jar file from the contrib/jars folder, and the Jini JAR files in your `CLASSPATH` in order to compile the agent. To compile the connector source files, you need the JMX JARs and the Jini JARs in your `CLASSPATH`.

In addition, you must use the `rmic` compiler to generate stubs for the `JINIConnectorImpl` class.

2 Set up the Jini environment. Doing so involves starting an HTTP server, starting the Java activation daemon (`rmid`), and starting a Jini lookup service. Read the Jini documentation to see how to perform these steps.

3 Start the JMX agent. You will need to start the agent with a policy file indicated by the `-Djava.security.policy` property in the `java` command.

4 Run the client class (`JINIConnectorClient`). Doing so will invoke the class's `main()` method. The method will use the `JINIConnector` to find the JMX agent, get its MBean count, and create a new `HelloWorld` MBean on the agent.

The best way to see the results of this simple test is to open your browser (while the agent is still running) to the location http://localhost:9092 (assuming you are on the same machine as the agent). You should see all three adapter/connector MBeans (HTML, RMI, and Jini) as well as a new `HelloWorld` MBean.

9.4 JMX and SNMP

A large number of vendors have distributed many devices with SNMP management capabilities. It would be ideal if you could use this existing management base with new applications and systems you are building today. For example, a networking application could acquire knowledge of the health of the hardware it requires before making routing decisions. For such situations, it makes sense to use the SNMP technology already in place. Fortunately, due to the JMX architecture, your JMX agents can expose MBeans using an SNMP adapter. This section will review SNMP and provide information about using JMX with SNMP.

9.4.1 What is SNMP?

SNMP is a monitoring standard that has been in wide use for several years. (SNMP stands for Simple Network Management Protocol, but most developers might argue that it is not that simple.) Two versions of SNMP (v1 and v2) already exist, and a third version is being defined by the Internet Engineering Task Force (IETF).

In an SNMP system, there are *managed devices* such as routers, hubs, computers, operating systems, and even applications. Basically, any device or system that can expose information about itself can become a managed device. SNMP agents exist to convert requests or messages from the SNMP protocol to a device.

A network management system (NMS) sends information to and listens for information from agents.

SNMP provides capabilities for the NMS to communicate with the managed device. The SNMP API has two commands: `read` and `write`. The `read` command is sent to the agent in order to get information about the current state of a managed device. The `write` command is used to set the state on the managed device. Likewise, the managed device can signal the NMS that something interesting has occurred by sending an SNMP *trap*. A trap is the SNMP equivalent of a JMX notification.

Recall from chapter 1 that information about managed devices is stored in a Management Information Base (MIB). The MIB is a hierarchical representation of information about devices. A managed device can be located on a MIB tree using an object name or object identifier—for example, organization.dod.enterprise.myenterprise.variables.theProduct. An object identifier is a set of numbers that translates to the textual name. (For more information about MIBs, read the SNMP specifications at http://www.ietf.org.)

Due to incompatibilities between machines on the Internet, data must be exchanged using a neutral representation. A standard called Abstract Syntax Notation One (ASN.1) was developed to enable this exchange. Using this notation, people created rules for defining the management information called the *Structure of Management Information (SMI)*. SMI defines simple types such as integers, octet strings, and object ids. It also defines application data types such as network addresses, counters, gauges, time ticks, opaques, integers, and unsigned integers.

9.4.2 *Using an SNMP protocol adapter*

As with any protocol or transport technology, the flexible JMX architecture enables agents to communicate with SNMP management applications. An SNMP adapter translates data from an MBean to an SNMP MIB and uses the SNMP protocol to transport the information to interested listeners.

Sun Microsystems provides an implementation of an SNMP adapter with a tool suite included with the JDMK. The toolkit provides the capability to develop a JMX agent using an SNMP protocol adapter. Using a tool called mibgen, you can generate MBeans that represent SNMP MIBs. The mibgen tool creates Java objects for you using your existing MIB definitions. There is even a toolkit to build an NMS using a management API.

The SNMP protocol adapter can work with SNMP v1 and SNMP v2 protocols. As the protocol adapter receives requests from the SNMP system, it maps the requests to specific MBean operations and executes them. In addition, the protocol adapter can send an SNMP trap to an NMS in place of JMX notifications.

Using the SNMP protocol adapter, an NMS can access the MBeans in the MBean server that represent various MIBs. SNMP does not support the richness of JMX capabilities, but MBeans can be built that support all the capabilities of SNMP. This means your MBeans may have more capabilities than can be accessed using SNMP, but existing NMS systems can take advantage of the exposed capabilities that adhere to the SNMP standard. Java Community Process (JCP) efforts are underway to standardize the mappings between JMX and existing SNMP standards.

For more information about the SNMP protocol adapter and the JDMK, visit the JDMK product page on the Sun web site (http://java.sun.com/products/jdmk).

9.5 *Connecting by using a TCP adapter*

Up to this point, you have seen how you can distribute access to your JMX agents with a number of different technologies. For example, you can use the RMI connector provided by Sun, or you can use Jini to allow your agents to be discovered. In this section, you will write a TCP protocol adapter.

Note that you won't use any object serialization—we don't want you to re-create an RMI-like connector. Instead, the TCP adapter is a socket-based adapter that allows any capable client to connect and send simple commands in order to interact with your agent. This command approach allows non-Java clients to connect to your agent and work with MBeans. For instance, a C++ program could open a socket to your remote agent and acquire attribute values from existing MBeans.

The TCP adapter presented in this section can create MBeans, get and set attributes, and invoke operations. It places a few restrictions on the order and manner that arguments are sent by the client, as you will see when we walk through the code. The adapter is modeled as an MBean that creates a `Server-Socket` object to listen to a particular port. Figure 9.4 illustrates the use of the TCP adapter MBean.

When a client connects, the MBean creates a `TCPAdapter` object in a new `Thread` to handle the client request, and continues listening.

9.5.1 *Writing the code*

To complete this new protocol adapter, you need to create three classes and one interface:

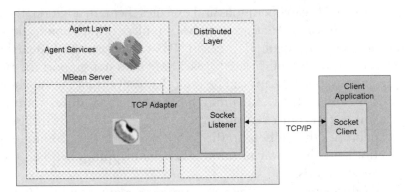

Figure 9.4 The `TCPServer` MBean handling incoming requests. Each time a client connects, a new `TCPAdapter` object is created.

- `TCPServerMBean`—MBean interface that declares the methods exposed for the adapter
- `TCPServer`—Implements the MBean interface and creates the `ServerSocket`
- `TCPAdapter`—Created by the `TCPServer` to handle each incoming client
- `TCPTester`—Class used to test the TCP adapter

The first step to create the adapter is to write the MBean interface for the `TCP-Server` MBean. The MBean is a Standard MBean (look back to chapter 4 if necessary), and its interface follows:

```
package jmxbook.ch9;

public interface TCPServerMBean
{
    public void setPort( int port );
    public int getPort();
    public boolean start();
    public boolean stop();
}
```

The `TCPServerMBean` interface declares two operations and one read/write attribute. The `Port` attribute is the port number to which the `ServerSocket` will listen for incoming clients. The `start()` method initiates the `ServerSocket` and tells the MBean to begin listening. Alternatively, the `stop()` method closes the `Server-Socket` and stops the `TCPServer` MBean from receiving any new clients. Existing clients will continue to have access to the agent until they close their connection.

Listing 9.8 shows the implementation of the `TCPServerMBean` interface in the `TCPServer` class.

Listing 9.8   TCPServer.java

```
package jmxbook.ch9;

import javax.management.*;
import java.net.*;

public class TCPServer implements TCPServerMBean,
                        MBeanRegistration, Runnable    ◁┐
{
   private int port = 1555;                            Implement
   private boolean stopped = false;            MBeanRegistration and
   private ServerSocket ss = null;               Runnable interfaces
   private MBeanServer mbs = null;

   public TCPServer()
   {
   }

   public void setPort( int port )
   {
     this.port = port;
   }

   public int getPort()
   {
     return port;
   }

   public boolean start()
   {
     stopped = false;
     Thread t = new Thread( this );
     t.start();
     return true;
   }

   public boolean stop()
   {
     stopped = true;
     return true;
   }

   public void run()
   {
     try
     {
       System.out.println( "Binding to port: " + port );
       ss = new ServerSocket( port );   ◁┐
                                          Create
       while( !stopped )                 ServerSocket
       {                                 instance
         Socket client = ss.accept();
         System.out.println( "Client being accepted" );
```

```
        Thread t = new Thread( new TCPAdapter( client, mbs ) )
        t.start();
    }

    ss.close();                                         Create TCPAdapter
                                                           object to handle
  }                                                             new client
  catch( Exception e )
  {
     e.printStackTrace();
     stopped = true;
  }
}

public void postDeregister()
{}
public void postRegister( Boolean done )
{}
public void preDeregister()
{}

public ObjectName preRegister(
    MBeanServer server, ObjectName name )
{
  this.mbs = server;
  return name;
}
}
```

As you can see in the code, upon invocation of the start() method, the TCPServer MBean runs continuously in a Thread until told to stop (via the stop() method). Once inside the run() method, the MBean opens the ServerSocket object to the specified port (the default value is 1555) and begins listening for clients.

When a socket is accepted, the MBean creates a new TCPAdapter instance, gives it the new client and a reference to the MBeanServer, and runs it in a new Thread. Each instance of the TCPAdapter class needs a reference to the MBean-Server in order to work with MBeans on behalf of its client.

The real work of the TCP adapter is done in the TCPAdapter class. It defines the commands clients can send, as well as the order in which it expects them to be sent. Table 9.4 lists the possible commands that can be sent by a TCP client.

Table 9.4 The possible commands used by the TCP client

TCPAdapter variable	Actual value
CREATE_MBEAN	create mbean
ARGS	args

Table 9.4   The possible commands used by the TCP client *(continued)*

`TCPAdapter` variable	Actual value
GET_ATTRIBUTE	`get attribute`
SET_ATTRIBUTE	`set attribute`
INVOKE	`invoke`
SHUTDOWN	`shutdown`

Not every message sent from a client will be one of the commands from table 9.4. Other messages might be a classname or argument value, for instance. Table 9.5 lists the tasks the TCP adapter can perform, along with the messages needed to perform the tasks. The messages and commands are listed in the order they must be received. Messages in bold are expected values from the client (for example, **classname** is an actual classname `String`). Those in italic are optional.

Table 9.5   Commands to send to complete a function of the adapter

Adapter function	Command order
Create an MBean	CREATE_MBEAN, **classname**, **objectname**, *ARGS*, *arglist*, *siglist*
Get attribute	GET_ATTRIBUTE, **attname**, **objectname**
Set attribute	SET_ATTRIBUTE, **attname**, **objectname**, ARGS, **arglist**, **siglist**
Invoke an operation	INVOKE, **operation**, **objectname**, *ARGS*, *arglist*, *siglist*

For each object name sent, the adapter expects the whole `String` value (such as a `String` like `JMXBookAgent:name=myValue`). The `arglist` and `siglist` messages are expected to be comma-separated lists of arguments. The `arglist` parameters must correspond to the types in the `siglist` message. In addition, each object value being passed in the `arglist` must be able to create an `Object` from the `String` value. This is similar to what the HTML adapter expects from clients.

Listing 9.9 shows the `TCPAdapter` class. After examining this class, you will add the TCP adapter to your `JMXBookAgent` class and write a simple test program.

Listing 9.9   TCPAdapter.java

```
package jmxbook.ch9;

import java.net.*;
import javax.management.*;
import java.io.*;
```

```java
import java.lang.reflect.*;
import java.util.*;

public class TCPAdapter implements Runnable
{
  private MBeanServer server = null;
  private Socket socket = null;
  private BufferedReader in = null;
  private PrintWriter out = null;

  public static String SHUTDOWN        = "shutdown";
  public static String CREATE_MBEAN    = "create mbean";
  public static String GET_ATTRIBUTE   = "get_attribute";
  public static String SET_ATTRIBUTE   = "set_attribute";
  public static String INVOKE          = "invoke";
  public static String ARGS            = "args";

  public TCPAdapter( Socket socket, MBeanServer server )
  {
    this.socket = socket;
    this.server = server;
    try
    {
      this.out = new PrintWriter( socket.getOutputStream() );
      this.in  = new BufferedReader(
             new InputStreamReader( socket.getInputStream() ) );
      System.out.println( "TCP Adapter CREATED" );
    }
    catch( Exception e )
    {
      e.printStackTrace();
    }
  }

  public void run()
  {
    try
    {
      System.out.println( "TCP adapter starting..." );
      String line = in.readLine();

      while( !line.equals( SHUTDOWN ) )           ❶ Read until
      {                                             shutdown
        if( line.equals( CREATE_MBEAN ) )
        {
          try
          {
            createMBean(  );
            out.println( "SUCCESS" );
            out.flush();
          }
          catch( Exception e )
          {
```

```
        e.printStackTrace();
        out.println( "ERROR " + e.getMessage() );
        out.flush();
      }
    }
    else if( line.equals( GET_ATTRIBUTE ) )
    {
      try
      {
        out.println( getAttribute(  ) );
        out.flush();
      }
      catch( Exception e )
      {
        e.printStackTrace();
        out.println( "ERROR " + e.getMessage() );
        out.flush();
      }

    }
    else if( line.equals( SET_ATTRIBUTE ) )
    {
      try
      {
        setAttribute(  );
        out.println( "SUCCESS" );
        out.flush();
      }
      catch( Exception e )
      {
        e.printStackTrace();
        out.println( "ERROR " + e.getMessage() );
        out.flush();
      }
    }
    else if( line.equals( INVOKE ) )
    {
      try
      {
        out.println( invoke() );
        out.flush();
      }
      catch( Exception e )
      {
        e.printStackTrace();
        out.println( "ERROR " + e.getMessage() );
        out.flush();
      }
    }

    line = in.readLine();
}
```

```
        in.close();
        out.close();
        socket.close();
    }
    catch( Exception e )
    {
        e.printStackTrace();
    }
}
private void createMBean() throws Exception
{
    String classname = null;
    String objectName = null;
    String line = in.readLine();
    String arglist = null;
    String siglist = null;

    classname = line;
    objectName = in.readLine();

    line = in.readLine();
    if( line.equals( ARGS ) )
    {
        arglist = in.readLine();
        siglist = in.readLine();
    }

    String[] sig = createSignature( siglist );
    Object[] args = createObjectList( arglist, sig );

    System.out.println( "NOW CREATING MBEAN" );

    server.createMBean( classname, new ObjectName( objectName ),
                        args, sig );

}
private String getAttribute() throws Exception
{
    String attname = null;
    String objectName = null;
    String line = in.readLine();
    attname = line;

    objectName = in.readLine();

    System.out.println( "GETTING ATTRIBUTE " + attname
                        + " FROM " + objectName );

    Object obj = server.getAttribute( new ObjectName( objectName ),
                                      attname );
    return obj.toString();
}

private void setAttribute() throws Exception
```

Implement createMBean() ➋

```
{
  String attName = null;
  String objectName = null;
  String line = in.readLine();
  String arglist = null;
  String siglist = null;

  attName = line;
  objectName = in.readLine();

  line = in.readLine();
  arglist = in.readLine();
  siglist = in.readLine();

  String[] sig = createSignature( siglist );
  Object[] args = createObjectList( arglist, sig );

  System.out.println( "SETTING ATTRIBUTE " + attName
                    + " FROM " + objectName );
  server.setAttribute( new ObjectName( objectName ),
                    new Attribute( attName, args[0] ) );
}

private String invoke() throws Exception
{
  String operation = null;
  String objectName = null;
  String line = in.readLine();
  String arglist = null;
  String siglist = null;

  operation = line;
  objectName = in.readLine();

  line = in.readLine();
  if( line.equals( ARGS ) )
  {
      arglist = in.readLine();
      siglist = in.readLine();
  }

  String[] sig = createSignature( siglist );
  Object[] args = createObjectList( arglist, sig );

  System.out.println( "INVOKING OPERATION " + operation
                    + " FROM " + objectName );
  Object result = server.invoke( new ObjectName( objectName ),
                    operation, args, sig );
  return result.toString();
}

private String[] createSignature( String siglist )
{
  if( siglist == null )
     return null;
```

Implement invoke() ❸

```
            StringTokenizer toks = new StringTokenizer( siglist, "," );
            String[] result = new String[ toks.countTokens() ];

            int i = 0;
            while( toks.hasMoreTokens() )
            {
                result[ i++ ] = toks.nextToken();
            }

            return result;
        }

    private Object[] createObjectList( String objects,
                                        String[] sig ) throws Exception
    {
        if( objects == null )
            return null;

        Object[] results = new Object[ sig.length ];
        StringTokenizer toks = new StringTokenizer( objects, "," );

        int i = 0;
        while( toks.hasMoreTokens() )
        {
            String object = toks.nextToken();
            Class conSig[] = { Class.forName( sig[i] ) };
            Object[] conParams = { object };

            Class c = Class.forName( sig[i] );
            Constructor con = c.getConstructor( conSig );
            results[ i ] = con.newInstance( conParams );
            i++;
        }

        return results;
    }

}
```

❶ Once the TCPAdapter object has been created by the TCPServer MBean, it is continuously in its run() method until it reads the SHUTDOWN message from the client. Upon receiving that message, the adapter object closes the socket and stops communication.

In the run() method, the adapter reads messages from the client until it finds one of its four available tasks (CREATE_MBEAN, GET_ATTRIBUTE, SET_ATTRIBUTE, or INVOKE). When it reads a valid command, it invokes the appropriate private method to complete the task. Because the output and input streams are class variables, they can be used in every method.

❷ The createMBean() method allows clients to create new MBeans in the agent. If any exceptions occur during this process, the method fails and returns an error to the client. When creating an MBean, clients should expect either the SUCCESS message or an error returned.

To complete this task, the client must send the classname of the MBean, a String value for an object name, and the arguments and signature if a constructor with arguments is to be used. If arguments are sent, the method breaks them into the needed Object and String arrays for the MBean server's createMBean() method. After acquiring all the necessary information from the client, the createMBean() method invokes the createMBean() method on the MBean server to complete the task. If no exception is thrown, the task completes.

3 The invoke() method works similarly to the createMBean() method. For this task, the adapter must gather the operation name, object name, and possible arguments from the client in order to invoke an MBean operation. After doing so, the invoke() method calls the invoke() method of the MBean server and prepares the return value to be sent back to the client. The return value is put into String form via the toString() method to be sent over the socket. No object serialization is used.

Adding the adapter to the JMXBookAgent class

Before you write the test program, let's add the code to the JMXBookAgent class that will create TCP adapter when the agent is started. Listing 9.10 shows the new startTCPAdapter() method for the agent class.

Listing 9.10   The startTCPAdapter() method

```
protected void startTCPAdapter()
{
    TCPServer tcp = new TCPServer();
    ObjectName adapterName = null;

    try
    {
      adapterName = new ObjectName(
                "JMXBookAgent:name=TCPAdapter");
      server.registerMBean( tcp, adapterName);
      tcp.start();
    }
    catch(Exception e)
    {
      e.printStackTrace();
    }

}
```

Be sure to invoke the new method from the agent's constructor. In addition, you will need to import the jmxbook.ch9 package. It is like all the other connectivity methods of the agent—it creates the MBean, registers it on the MBean server, and invokes its start() method. Use the HTML adapter (via a web browser) if you need to change the port value of the adapter.

9.5.2 *Testing the TCP adapter*

With everything else completed, it is time to write a simple test program for the TCP adapter (see listing 9.11). The test program is defined by the class TCPTester, and it performs all four tasks available to the adapter.

Listing 9.11   TCPTester.java

```java
package jmxbook.ch9;

import java.net.*;
import javax.management.*;
import java.io.*;

public class TCPTester
{

  public TCPTester( String port ) throws Exception
  {
    Socket s = new Socket( "localhost", Integer.parseInt( port ) );
    PrintWriter print = new PrintWriter( s.getOutputStream() );

   //create a Hello World MBean

      print.println( TCPAdapter.CREATE_MBEAN );
      print.flush();
      print.println( "jmxbook.ch2.HelloWorld" );
      print.flush();
      print.println( "JMXBookAgent:name=TCPCreatedHW" );
      print.flush();
      print.println( TCPAdapter.ARGS );
      print.flush();
      print.println( "This is my greeting" );
      print.flush();
      print.println( "java.lang.String" );
      print.flush();

      BufferedReader in  = new BufferedReader(
                     new InputStreamReader(
                     s.getInputStream() ) );

      System.out.println( in.readLine() );
      Thread.sleep(10000);

     //reset the greeting
```

```
        print.println( TCPAdapter.SET_ATTRIBUTE );
        print.flush();
        print.println( "Greeting" );
        print.flush();
        print.println( "JMXBookAgent:name=TCPCreatedHW" );
        print.flush();
        print.println( TCPAdapter.ARGS );
        print.flush();
        print.println( "This is my greeting after being changed" );
        print.flush();
        print.println( "java.lang.String" );
        print.flush();

        Thread.sleep(10000);

      //get the greeting
        print.println( TCPAdapter.GET_ATTRIBUTE );
        print.flush();
        print.println( "Greeting" );
        print.flush();
        print.println( "JMXBookAgent:name=TCPCreatedHW" );
        print.flush();

        System.out.println( in.readLine() );

      //invoke printGreeting
        print.println( TCPAdapter.INVOKE );
        print.flush();
        print.println( "printGreeting" );
        print.flush();
        print.println( "JMXBookAgent:name=TCPCreatedHW" );
        print.flush();
        print.println( TCPAdapter.SHUTDOWN );
        print.flush();

        System.out.println( in.readLine() );

    }

    public static void main(String args[]) throws Exception
    {
        TCPTester t = new TCPTester( args[0] );
    }
}
```

The output on the agent and from the test program should tell you everything
you need to know. In addition, you can check out the HTML adapter view to see
the results of running the test program.

9.6 *Summary*

Previous chapters made it clear how JMX uses protocol adapters and connectors to provide connectivity to JMX agents through all manner of technologies and protocols. This chapter covered the RMI connector more thoroughly, discussed SNMP, and showed you how to write a Jini connector and a TCP adapter.

The RMI connector is contributed to developers in Sun Microsystems' JMX Reference Implementation. It lets you connect to remote JMX agents using Java RMI. In addition, it provides excellent handling of remote notification delivery and heartbeat functionality.

The Jini connector you wrote took the RMI connector one step further by allowing you to connect to a JMX agent using the Jini network technology. The connector still operates over Java RMI, but clients do not have to know the address of a potential JMX agent. Using the Jini discovery mechanism, you were able to provide an agent discovery capability to remote clients.

Finally, you created a TCP adapter to provide access to JMX agents from non-Java clients. Even though the TCP adapter is limited by its inability to translate complex objects to simple commands, it does provide the core functionality of a JMX agent to TCP clients. In fact, the TCP adapter is much like the HTML adapter.

Chapter 9 not only provided you with the examples for agent connectivity, it also showed you some guidelines for writing your own custom classes in order to provide connectivity for other technologies or protocols that you have in your environment.

Agent services provide important functionality to every JMX agent. Chapter 10 covers the first of four agent services that are present in every JMX-compliant agent: the M-let service, which is used to load MBeans from remote locations outside an agent's codebase.

10

Advanced
MBean loading

- Introducing the M-let service
- Explaining the M-let MBean and M-let files
- Loading MBeans and expanding the codebase of JMX agents

This chapter is the first of three chapters that discuss the standard JMX agent services. In this chapter, you will find coverage of a JMX agent's ability to create MBeans from dynamically loaded class files from remote locations.

When developing a Java application intended to run for an extended period of time, you have probably encountered the need to restart the application to include new classes in its CLASSPATH. In fact, think of any JMX agent that is running: you'll need to add MBeans of a new class type currently not in the agent's codebase. The Management Applet (M-let) service was designed to solve this problem, as well as to provide other useful functionality.

Dynamic MBean loading, provided via the JMX M-let service, allows the agent, other MBeans, and management applications to create MBeans by downloading class files from remote locations. In addition, the M-let service lets agents expand their codebase at runtime.

10.1 *Understanding the M-let service*

Consider the situation of a JMX agent serving as a monitor to hosted applications in the same environment. Now imagine that you add more applications to the hosted environment, and that, for monitoring purposes, they require very specialized MBeans. Due to the nature of the applications already being monitored, you don't want to restart your JMX agent. Figure 10.1 illustrates such an environment.

How can you make the new MBeans available to the agent without having to first stop the JMX agent and update its CLASSPATH in order for new MBeans class types to be loaded? In addition, you may need to add other classes to the agent's codebase without creating MBeans. Simply use the agent's dynamic class-loading service: the M-let service.

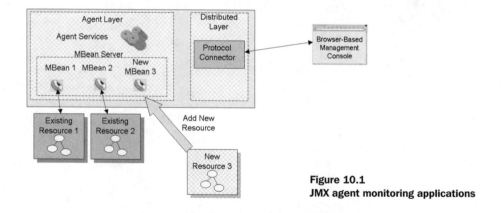

Figure 10.1
JMX agent monitoring applications

As mentioned in the chapter introduction, JMX agents have the ability to load remote class files and create MBeans. This agent service lets an agent use classes that are not in its original startup CLASSPATH.

First, you place the new MBean class files in a downloadable location; then you use the M-let loading service to access them. Now the agent can instantiate the new MBeans without being restarted. In addition, the dynamic loading service provides a mechanism to add to the agent's codebase at runtime, allowing you to make classes available without necessarily creating MBeans at the same time.

The next section starts the discussion of the JMX M-let service. This agent service provides the mechanism to dynamically load classes into the agent.

10.2 Using the M-let service

You will notice that all the agent services provided in this and the next chapter are also MBeans. This is the case so that the services can be instantiated and configured as needed. The M-let agent service handles the dynamic loading of MBeans; it must reside in every JMX agent compliant with the JMX specification.

To load new MBeans, users point the service to a remote M-let text file. An M-let text file is an XML-like file that contains information about loading classes and creating MBeans. The M-let service loads this file, processes the information it contains, and downloads the named classes in order to create one or more MBeans. Figure 10.2 illustrates how the M-let service works.

Remember, because the M-let service is also a registered MBean in the agent, it can be used by the agent itself, other MBeans, or remote management applications. The M-let service lets you load MBean classes and their resources from remote locations by using M-let files; it also acts as a class loader, providing the ability to expand an agent's codebase.

Before we discuss the M-let service MBean, let's examine the contents of an M-let file.

10.2.1 Writing M-let files

This section will walk you through the possible contents of an M-let file. After we cover this topic and the M-let MBean class, you will begin writing some concrete examples.

The M-let service finds M-let files by being provided a URL to the file. So, there are no restrictions on the name of an M-let file.

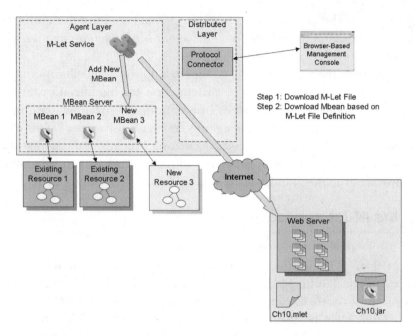

Figure 10.2   JMX agent creating MBeans by loading an M-let file

The contents of an M-let file closely resemble XML. If you have XML experience, you will recognize the content structure; if you don't, it will still be easy to understand.

The following is a simple entry from an M-let file. It does not contain all the possible attributes, but it shows the MLET tag used to encapsulate an entire entry in an M-let file:

```
<MLET CODE=jmxbook.ch2.HelloWorld ARCHIVE=test.jar
NAME=hello:type=HelloWorld>
</MLET>
```

This MLET entry tells the agent to load the test.jar file, look for the jmxbook.ch2.HelloWorld class, and create and register a HelloWorld MBean with an object name of hello:type=HelloWorld.

As you can see, the MLET tag contains attributes that specify a classname, a location for the class, and an object name for a new MBean to be created. Every M-let file can contain any number of MLET entries. Before going any further, let's examine each MLET tag attribute in the following sections.

The CODE attribute

CODE is a mandatory attribute used to specify the specific class that contains an MBean implementation. In the previous simple example, the CODE attribute specified jmxbook.ch2.HelloWorld as the MBean class for the MLET entry. The classname must include the package name, and the compiled class must be contained in one of the JAR files specified in the ARCHIVE attribute.

The OBJECT attribute

The OBJECT attribute specifies a path to a serialized object file. This attribute is only used in place of the CODE attribute. The serialized object file must contain the serialized form of an MBean to be loaded into the agent. Just like the CODE attribute value, the file must be contained in one of the JAR files listed in the ARCHIVE attribute. The attribute value can be a path and filename in order to traverse a possible directory hierarchy in one of the JAR files.

The ARCHIVE attribute

The only other mandatory attribute is ARCHIVE. Its value is either a single JAR file or a list of JAR files that contain the classes, objects, and resources needed to support a specified MBean class or serialized object file. If the value is a list of JAR files, the list must be enclosed in quotation marks (") and the filenames must be comma separated.

The agent will assume that all specified JAR files are in the same directory as the M-let file, unless the MLET tag contains a CODEBASE attribute.

The CODEBASE attribute

This attribute is used to specify a codebase URL value for JAR files listed in the ARCHIVE attribute. If this attribute is not specified, the JAR files are assumed to be in the same directory as the M-let file.

Because the codebase is a URL value, you could specify any network-locatable value. Thus an M-let file can be loaded from a remote location, and the JAR files it lists can be in a different remote location. The value of this attribute should be a fully qualified, reachable URL.

The NAME attribute

This attribute specifies a value for the object name for the agent to associate with the new MBean this MLET entry describes. The value must have a domain and at least one property value (see the previous MLET tag for a NAME example).

The VERSION attribute

The VERSION attribute specifies a version number for the MBean and JAR files to be loaded into the agent. The value of this attribute must be a dot-separated list of decimal numbers (for example, 1.4).

The ARGLIST tag

This tag lets you specify a particular constructor for the M-let service to use when instantiating the MBean described by this MLET tag. However, the use of this tag is restricted to describing constructors with arguments that can be represented as String values. In the ARGLIST attribute, you use an additional attribute to specify type–value pairs describing arguments to a constructor. The following is an example:

```
<ARGLIST>
 <ARG TYPE=java.lang.Integer VALUE=5 >
</ARGLIST>
```

The M-let service will parse an argument list to build a constructor signature. It will look for a constructor with a matching signature to use to instantiate the MBean.

MLET tag rules

After being introduced to the possible attributes to an MLET tag entry, you should recognize that each MLET entry must contain at least two attributes: it must contain a CODE or OBJECT attribute, and an ARCHIVE attribute. In addition, remember that each M-let file can contain as many MLET entries as you wish—there is no upper limit. Table 10.1 summarizes the attributes.

Table 10.1   A summary of the available MLET tag attributes

MLET tag attribute	Required	Description
CODE	Yes	Required unless OBJECT is used; specifies the class of the MBean
OBJECT	Yes	Required unless CODE is used; specifies a serialized object
ARCHIVE	Yes	Specifies JAR files containing the MBean classes and resources
CODEBASE	No	Used if the ARCHIVE JAR files are not in the same directory as the M-let file
NAME	No	Object name value for the new MBean
VERSION	No	Specifies a version number for the MBean and JAR files

Using table 10.1, you can quickly recall the mandatory attributes and their purpose. Now that we have covered how to create M-let files, let's examine the MLet

MBean. This MBean and its supporting classes and interfaces are contained in the `javax.management.loading` package.

10.2.2 *Examining the MLet MBean*

The `MLet` MBean is implemented in the `MLet` class, which implements the `MLet` MBean interface. In addition, the `MLet` class implements the `MBeanRegistration` interface and extends the `java.net.URLClassLoader` class. Figure 10.3 shows a UML diagram of the `MLet` MBean.

The `java.net.URLClassLoader` super class provides the MBean with the implementation of a class loader for convenience. Shortly, you will see that this super class provides the `MLet` MBean with its ability to load remote classes. Using the M-let service boils down to understanding its available methods. The next sections cover the methods available in the `MLet` MBean.

M-let methods

You have already examined the contents of the M-let file, and you know how to interact with MBeans, so let's move ahead and examine the methods of the `MLet-MBean` interface. This interface declares the methods the `MLet` MBean uses to expose its attributes and operations. Table 10.2 lists the methods of the interface. The following sections discuss the most commonly used methods in more detail.

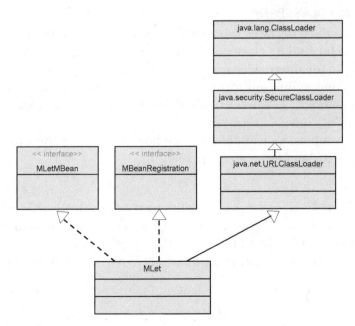

Figure 10.3
UML diagram of the `MLet`
MBean interface and its
class hierarchy

Table 10.2 The methods declared by the `MLetMBean` interface

Declared method	Description
`addURL( String url )`	Appends the specified URL to the list of URLs to be searched for classes and resources
`addURL( URL url )`	Appends the specified URL to the list of URLs to be searched for classes and resources
`getLibraryDirectory()`	Returns the directory in which native libraries are stored before loading them into memory
`getMBeansFromURL( String url )`	Tells the MBean to load an M-let file at the specified URL
`getMBeansFromURL( URL url )`	Tells the MBean to load an M-let file at the specified URL
`getResource( String name )`	Finds the specified resource
`getResourceAsStream( String name )`	Finds the specified resource and returns an `InputStream` for reading it
`getResources( String name )`	Finds all the resources with the specified name
`getURLs()`	Returns the list of URLs being used to search for classes and resources
`setLibraryDirectory( String path )`	Sets the native library directory

Adding URLs to the CLASSPATH

The `MLetMBean` interface declares two `addURL()` methods that add URLs to the search list of URLs for finding classes and resources. These methods simply add the specified URL to the internal list used by the MBean's class loader. These two methods (each taking a different form of a URL) add to the agent's codebase, allowing it to find more classes. You can use these methods to make more classes available to the agent.

Later, in the examples, we will demonstrate how you can use the URL list to load MBean classes without using an M-let file.

Creating MBeans

The interface declares two `getMBeansFromURL()` methods for loading M-let files. When the MBean loads an M-let file, it loads all the classes and resources contained in the listed JAR files. Just like the `addURL()` methods, the `createMBean()` method is overloaded to accept either a URL object or a `String` representation of a URL.

Acquiring resources

Finally, the MBean interface declares several methods that expose the class loader capability of the MBean's super class. The resource acquisition methods like `getResource()` are declared to expose some of the functionality inherited from the MBean's super class, `java.net.URLClassLoader`. You can use these methods to acquire resources outside the normal CLASSPATH of the JMX agent containing the MLet MBean.

You can use the resource-loading capability to download a new internationalization file into the agent and thereby provide internationalized notification messages.

10.3 *Using the M-let service to load MBeans*

Now that we have examined the M-let service, let's create some examples. In this section, you will build two examples. The first example loads MBeans with the M-let service, using an M-let file. The second example shows you that by using the M-let service to expand the agent's codebase, you can also load MBeans without using an M-let file.

10.3.1 *Adding to the JMXBookAgent class*

The first step in writing your M-let examples is to add the M-let service to your `JMXBookAgent` class. You will do this by adding the method `startMletService()` to the agent and invoking it in the agent's constructor. Once you've made the agent class changes, you will be able to use the agent for the examples. Listing 10.1 shows the `startMletService()` method.

Listing 10.1 The startMletService() method

```
protected void startMletService()
{
    ObjectName mletName = null;

    try
    {
      mletName = new ObjectName( "JMXBookAgent:name=mlet" );

      server.createMBean( "javax.management.loading.MLet",
                          mletName );
        }
    catch( Exception e )
    {
        ExceptionUtil.printException( e );
    }

  }
```

You use the MBean server's `createMBean()` method to create an instance of the `MLet` MBean. This MBean will be your focus for the M-let service examples. The MBean is registered with the `ObjectName` value `JMXBookAgent:name=mlet`.

10.3.2 Example: using an M-let file

The first example involves the main feature of the M-let service: creating MBeans by loading M-let files. You begin by creating an M-let file.

The example M-let file

Using the attributes we examined earlier in section 10.2.2, you will create an M-let file to load and create an instance of the `HelloWorld` MBean you used in chapter 2. The following is the `MLET` entry for the file:

```
<MLET CODE=jmxbook.ch2.HelloWorld
      ARCHIVE=ch2. jar
      NAME=MLetAgent:name=hello1>
</MLET>
```

This entry is saved in a file called ch10.mlet in your jmxbook/ch10 directory.

Setting up the environment

You need to ensure you have the correct environment before trying to load this M-let file. Before you start the agent, make sure you don't have the `jmxbook.ch2.HelloWorld` class in your `CLASSPATH` (but keep your `jmxbook.ch10` package in the `CLASSPATH`). Next, create the ch2.jar file that contains the `jmxbook.ch2.Hello-World` class and copy it to the same directory as your M-let file. Use the following command to create the JAR file (from the parent directory of your jmxbook package structure):

```
jar -cvf ch2.jar jmxbook\ch2\HelloWorld.class
```

To be sure you do not have the `HelloWorld` class in the `CLASSPATH`, delete the class file before executing your environment setup script. After your environment is ready, you can start the `JMXBookAgent` class with the following command:

```
java jmxbook.ch3.JMXBookAgent
```

For this example, you won't see any output from the agent. After starting the agent, open your web browser and connect to the agent's HTML adapter.

Loading the M-let file

When you connect to the HTML adapter of the agent and select the `MLet` MBean, the first thing you will notice is that the HTML adapter does not support all the methods of the M-let MBean. Fortunately, it supports all the methods you need for this example. Follow these steps to load the example M-let file:

1. If you haven't already, select the `MLet` MBean.
2. Put the cursor in the blank for the `getMBeansFromURL()` method.
3. Type in the URL to your M-let file. In our case, the URL is file://c:/jmx-book/ch10/ch10.mlet.
4. Click the button to execute the method. You should get a success message.
5. Go back to the Agent View, and you should see a new `HelloWorld` MBean registered in the MBean server.

Stop the agent. You will use it for again in the next example, which creates an MBean without using an M-let file.

Reusing loaded classes

After you have loaded classes specified in an M-let file, they are available for use again. However, you would need to specify the `MLet` MBean as the class loader when creating an MBean from a previously loaded JAR file (from using an M-let file).

In chapter 8, we discussed the MBean server's overloaded version of the `createMBean()` method, which adds an `ObjectName` parameter that specifies a class loader. The overloaded method uses this class loader to search for the MBean class needed to instantiate the requested MBean. The value of this parameter should be the `ObjectName` value of the M-let service. The method invocation to load another `HelloWorld` MBean would look like the following:

```
ObjectName helloName = new ObjectName( "MLetAgent:name=hello2" );
ObjectName mletName = new ObjectName( "MLetAgent:name=mlet" );
    mbeanServer.createMBean( "jmxbook.ch2.HelloWorld",
                        helloName, mletName );
```

This code results in a new `HelloWorld` MBean with the specified `ObjectName` value. The MBean server relies on the M-let service to act as the class loader for the `jmxbook.ch2.HelloWorld` class.

10.3.3 *Example: expanding the agent's codebase*

At this point, you might be telling yourself that you want to load classes from a remote location without creating MBeans at the same time. Any time you want to add classes or add to your codebase, you don't want to have to create an MBean (for instance, to use an M-let file to load a JAR file).

As mentioned earlier, the M-let service provides for this situation by allowing you to expand its codebase. By using its addURL() methods, you can add to the list of searchable URLs for classes and resources. After URLs are added, you can access classes at the new locations, even in order to create MBeans. For example, follow these steps to create the HelloWorld MBean again without using an M-let file:

1   Make sure the agent process is stopped.

2   Restart the agent using the command from section 10.3.2.

3   Connect to the HTML adapter of the agent and select the MLet MBean.

4   Invoke the MBean's addURL() method with the file URL pointing to the ch2.jar file. In our case, this value is file://c:/jmxbook/ch10/ch2.jar.

5   After receiving the success message, go to the Admin View of the adapter.

6   Enter the appropriate parameters to create a HelloWorld MBean. For the Class Loader entry, enter the ObjectName value for the M-let service: MLetAgent:name=mlet.

7   Execute the create request. You should receive a success message.

8   Go back to the Agent View, and you should see the new HelloWorld MBean in the MBean list.

If you experience any errors with the MBean create request, be sure you typed in the correct value for the added URL pointing to the ch10.jar file. You can verify the value you entered by viewing the URLs attribute of the MLet MBean.

10.4 Wrapping the M-let service to provide notifications

You should know enough about the M-let service now that you could begin including it in your JMX applications to expand their codebases and increase their usefulness. However, if you used the M-let service with any frequency, you might notice that the service does not emit any notifications. For example, you cannot emit a notification indicating that a remote class was loaded. If your agent persists notifications for later analysis of the agent's activity, you will probably want to include the activity of the M-let service. Otherwise, you will be missing valuable information from the activity log of your agent.

This section builds an MBean that wraps the M-let service to provide notifications for the M-let events that could occur. Figure 10.4 illustrates this idea.

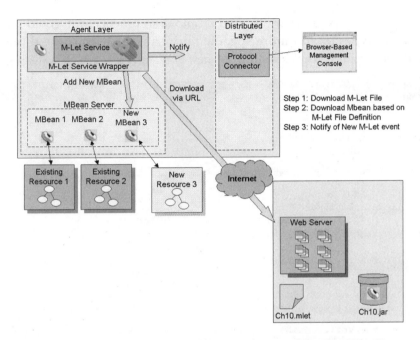

Figure 10.4 Using an MBean to wrap the M-let service to provide notifications

You wrap the M-let service as an MBean in order to shield users from any implementation change. Using this wrapped M-let service is the same as using the M-let service. To create this MBean "wrapper," you must write an MBean and a notification class. Let's begin with the notification class.

10.4.1 Writing the MLetNotification class

The notifications used in this example are defined by the `MLetNotification` class. To keep it simple, the notification will contain the three notification types shown in table 10.3.

Table 10.3 The notification types used by the `MLet` wrapper

Notification type	Description
`jmxbook.mletwrapper.urlAdded`	Indicates that a URL value was added successfully
`jmxbook.mletwrapper.mbeanCreated`	Indicates that an MBean was created successfully from an M-let file
`jmxbook.mletwrapper.error`	Indicates that an error occurred in some M-let service operation

Three types will serve to create a good example; in practice, you could use more notification types to add more specific notifications. With these three types defined, let's examine the code for your new `MLetNotification` class (listing 10.2).

Listing 10.2　MLetNotification.java

```java
package jmxbook.ch10;

import javax.management.*;
import java.util.*;

public class MLetNotification extends Notification
{
  public static final String URL_TYPE   =
                     "jmxbook.mletwrapper.urlAdded";
  public static final String MBEAN_TYPE =
                     "jmxbook.mletwrapper.mbeanAdded";
  public static final String ERROR_TYPE =
                     "jmxbook.mletwrapper.error";

  private String url = null;
  private Set objectInstances = null;

  public MLetNotification( String type, Object source,
                           long sequence )
  {
    super( type, source, sequence );
  }

  public void setObjectInstances( Set oi )
  {
    this.objectInstances = oi;
  }

  public void setURL( String url )
  {
    this.url = url;
  }

  public String getURL()
  {
    return url;
  }

  public Set getObjectInstances()
  {
    return objectInstances;
  }
}
```

Looking over the code for the notification class, you can see that it does not contain anything complex. It declares the three notification types as public static final member variables for convenience. In addition, it adds methods for setting and getting a URL and an `ObjectInstance` object. The URL methods allow the `MLetWrapper` MBean to send the URL that was added successfully or that caused an error. The `ObjectInstance` variable will be set whenever an MBean is created successfully using the M-let service.

10.4.2 *Writing the MLetWrapper MBean*

Now that the notification is defined, you can move on to the `MLetWrapper` MBean class. This MBean is a Standard MBean (look back at chapter 3 for more information about Standard MBeans); because you will wrap the M-let service entirely, the new `MLetWrapper` MBean class will have the same management interface as the MLet MBean.

The `MLetWrapper` MBean class implements the MBean interface `jmxbook.ch10.MLetWrapperMBean`. This MBean interface extends the `javax.management.loading.MLetMBean` interface. Thus an implementing MBean has the same interface as the M-let service, ensuring that it has the same attributes and operations.

In addition, the `MLetWrapper` MBean class implements the `MBeanRegistration` interface to interact with the M-let service and extends the `NotificationBroadcasterSupport` class to provide support for sending notifications.

The following code shows the `MLetWrapperMBean` interface:

```
package jmxbook. ch10;

import javax.management.loading.*;

public interface MLetWrapperMBean extends MLetMBean
{
}
```

The `MLetWrapper` MBean will emit notifications for every MBean it creates and for every URL that is added. The basic behavior of the MBean is to delegate all method calls to the M-let service and capture return values in order to generate notifications. Listing 10.3 shows the `MLetWrapper` class.

Listing 10.3 MLetWrapper.java

```
package jmxbook.ch10;

import javax.management.*;
import javax.management.loading.*;
```

```
import java.util.*;
import java.io.*;
import java.net.*;

public class MLetWrapper extends NotificationBroadcasterSupport
                implements MLetWrapperMBean, MBeanRegistration
{
  private ObjectName mletName = null;
  private MBeanServer mbs     = null;

  public MLetWrapper( String mletServiceName )
  {
    try
    {
     this.mletName = new ObjectName( mletServiceName );
    }
    catch( Exception e )
    {
     //do nothing
    }
  }

  //MBeanRegistration methods
  public void postDeregister(){}
  public void preDeregister(){}
  public ObjectName preRegister( MBeanServer server,
                                 ObjectName name )
                            throws Exception
  {
    this.mbs = server;

    //check for the existence of the M-let service.
    if( mletName == null || !mbs.isRegistered( mletName ) )
      throw new
         Exception( "M-let service not present in MBean Server" );

    return name;
  }

  public void postRegister( Boolean done ){}

  //MLetMBean methods

  public Set getMBeansFromURL( String url )
             throws ServiceNotFoundException
  {
    Set rvalue = null;
    MLetNotification notif = null;

    Object[] obj = { url };
    String[] sig = { "java.lang.String" };

    try
    {
```

1 Store object name of actual M-let service

Find M-let service 2

3

```
            rvalue = ( Set ) mbs.invoke( mletName,
                                "getMBeansFromURL",
                                obj, sig );
            notif = new MLetNotification( MLetNotification.MBEAN_TYPE,
                                this, -1 );
            notif.setURL( url );
            notif.setObjectInstances( rvalue );

            sendNotification( notif );
            return rvalue;
        }
    catch( Exception e )
    {
            notif = new MLetNotification( MLetNotification.ERROR_TYPE,
                                this, -1 );
            notif.setURL( url );
            sendNotification( notif );
            throw new ServiceNotFoundException( e.getMessage() );
    }

}

public Set getMBeansFromURL( URL url ) throws
            ServiceNotFoundException
{
    Set rvalue = null;
    MLetNotification notif = null;

    Object[] obj = { url };
    String[] sig = { "java.net.URL" };

    try
    {
            rvalue = ( Set ) mbs.invoke( mletName,
                        "getMBeansFromURL", obj, sig );
            notif = new MLetNotification( MLetNotification.MBEAN_TYPE,
                        this, -1 );
            notif.setURL( url.toString() );
            notif.setObjectInstances( rvalue );

            sendNotification( notif );
            return rvalue;
    }
    catch( Exception e )
    {
            notif = new MLetNotification( MLetNotification.ERROR_TYPE,
                        this, -1 );
            notif.setURL( url.toString() );
            sendNotification( notif );
            throw new ServiceNotFoundException( e.getMessage() );
    }
}

public void addURL( String url ) throws ServiceNotFoundException
```

Build and send notification when loading MBean ❸

```
  {
    Set rvalue = null;
    MLetNotification notif = null;

    Object[] obj = { url };
    String[] sig = { "java.lang.String" };

    try
    {
      mbs.invoke( mletName, "addURL", obj, sig );
      notif = new MLetNotification( MLetNotification.URL_TYPE,
               this, -1 );
      notif.setURL( url );

      sendNotification( notif );
    }
    catch( Exception e )
    {
      notif = new MLetNotification( MLetNotification.ERROR_TYPE,
               this, -1 );
      notif.setURL( url );
      sendNotification( notif );
    }
  }
  public void addURL( URL url )
  {
    Set rvalue = null;
    MLetNotification notif = null;

    Object[] obj = { url };
    String[] sig = { "java.net.URL" };

    try
    {
      mbs.invoke( mletName, "addURL", obj, sig );
      notif = new MLetNotification( MLetNotification.URL_TYPE,
               this, -1 );
      notif.setURL( url.toString() );

      sendNotification( notif );
    }
    catch( Exception e )
    {
      notif = new MLetNotification( MLetNotification.ERROR_TYPE,
                this, -1 );
      notif.setURL( url.toString() );
      sendNotification( notif );
    }
  }

  public URL[] getURLs()                    ❹
  {
    try
```

```
  {
    return ( URL[] )mbs.invoke( mletName, "getURLs", null, null );
  }
  catch( Exception e )                        Forward method    ❹
  {                                          invocations to M-let
    //do something                                     service
    return null;
  }
}
public URL getResource( String name )
{
  Object[] obj = { name };
  String[] sig = { "java.lang.String" };
  try
  {
    return ( URL ) mbs.invoke( mletName, "getResource",
                          obj, sig );
  }
  catch( Exception e )
  {
    //do something
    return null;
  }
}

public InputStream getResourceAsStream( String name )
{
  Object[] obj = {. name };
  String[] sig = { "java.lang.String" };
  try
  {
    return ( InputStream ) mbs.invoke( mletName,
                                  "getResourceAsStream",
                                  obj, sig );
  }
  catch( Exception e )
  {
    //do something
    return null;
  }
}

public Enumeration getResources( String name )
{
  Object[] obj = { name };
  String[] sig = { "java.lang.String" };

  try
  {
    return ( Enumeration ) mbs.invoke( mletName,
                  "getResources", obj, sig );
```

```
    }
    catch( Exception e )
    {
      //do something
      return null;
    }
  }

  public String getLibraryDirectory()
  {
    try
    {
      return ( String ) mbs.invoke( mletName, "getLibraryDirectory",
                                    null, null );
    }
    catch( Exception e )
    {
      //do something
      return null;
    }
  }

  public void setLibraryDirectory( String path )
  {
    Object[] obj = { path };
    String[] sig = { "java.lang.String" };

    try
    {
      mbs.invoke( mletName, "setLibraryDirectory", obj, sig );
    }
    catch( Exception e )
    {
      //do something
    }
  }

  public MBeanNotificationInfo[] getNotificationInfo()
  {
    MBeanNotificationInfo[] info = new MBeanNotificationInfo[ 1 ];

    String[] types = { MLetNotification.MBEAN_TYPE,
                       MLetNotification.URL_TYPE,
                       MLetNotification.ERROR_TYPE };

    info[ 0 ] = new MBeanNotificationInfo( types,
                    "jmxbook.ch10.MLetNotification",
                    "Notifications from the
                    MLetWrapper" );
    return info;

  }
}
```

❶❷ The only constructor of the `MLetWrapper` MBean accepts an object name `String` value that should correspond to an instance of the M-let service already present in the MBean server at the time of construction. The `preRegister()` method is invoked before the MBean will be registered in the MBean server. In this method, the `MLetWrapper` MBean attempts to locate the M-let service with the `ObjectName` value specified in its constructor.

If the M-let service is not found, the `preRegister()` method throws an `Exception` in order to stop the registration process. The exception will ensure that an `MLetWrapper` MBean will not operate without an M-let service in the agent. Instead of throwing an `Exception` when it doesn't find an M-let service, the MBean could tell the MBean server to create one.

❸ The `getMBeansFromURL( URL url )` method provides a pattern for the methods that emit notifications (`getMBeansFromURL()` and `addURL()`). This method can emit one of two possible notification types represented by the public final static variables `MLetNotification.MBEAN_TYPE` and `MLetNotification.ERROR_TYPE`. The method delegates the work to the M-let service MBean and, depending on the result, sends either a success-type notification or an error-type notification.

If the method succeeds, it builds an `MLetNotification` with the returned `Set` of `ObjectInstance` objects and the URL that was specified as a parameter. For any error, including exceptions thrown while working with the MBean server, the `getMBeansFromURL()` method emits a notification populated with an error type and the URL specified in the incoming parameter.

❹ The `getURLs()` method demonstrates how the remaining methods are implemented. They do not emit notifications—they only delegate the method call to the M-let service and return the result where appropriate. In addition, these methods capture any exception arising from the interaction with the MBean server. If an exception is thrown by the MBean server, each method simply catches it and returns (null where appropriate).

10.4.3 *Using the MLetWrapper MBean*

To register for notifications, you need to create and register the new `MLetWrapper` MBean. However, instead of using the HTML adapter as you did for the examples in section 10.3, you will write a setup class to register the new wrapper MBean in your agent. Listing 10.4 shows the `MLetWrapperSetup` class. This class will use the `RMIClientFactory` class from chapter 3 to contact the agent and create an instance of the `MLetWrapper` MBean. It also adds itself as a notification listener.

Listing 10.4   MLetWrapperSetup.java

```java
package jmxbook.ch10;

import javax.management.*;
import com.sun.jdmk.comm.*;
import jmxbook.ch3.*;

public class MLetWrapperSetup implements NotificationListener
{
    public MLetWrapperSetup()
    {
      try
      {
        RmiConnectorClient client = RMIClientFactory.getClient();

        Object[] args = { "JMXBookAgent:name=mlet" };
        String[] sig = { "java.lang.String" };

        ObjectName wrapperName =
                new ObjectName( "JMXBookAgent:name=mletwrapper");
        client.createMBean( "jmxbook.ch10.MLetWrapper",
                    wrapperName, args, sig );
        client.addNotificationListener( wrapperName, this,
                    null, null );
      }
      catch( Exception e )
      {
        ExceptionUtil.printException( e );
      }
    }

    public void handleNotification( Notification not, Object obj )
    {
      String type = not.getType();
      System.out.println( type );
    }

    public static void main( String args[] )
    {
      MLetWrapperSetup setup = new MLetWrapperSetup();
    }

}
```

You can add more code to the handleNotification() method to output more information about the received notifications if desired. For now, the method only prints out each notification type. After compiling this class, start the JMXBook-Agent and execute the setup class with the following command:

```
java jmxbook.ch10.MLetWrapperSetup
```

The next section walks you through loading the `HelloWorld` MBean again, but this time using the `MLetWrapper` MBean.

Testing the MLetWrapper MBean

Testing the `MLetWrapper` MBean is a simple task. All you need to do is follow the steps from the first example in section 10.3.2. Go back and follow those exact steps to compile and start the `MLetAgent`. Then, follow the remaining steps as you did before, but instead of interacting with the `MLet` MBean, use the `MLet-Wrapper` MBean. It has the same attributes and operations as the `MLet` MBean, so the steps will match.

If you successfully execute the `getMBeansFromURL()` and `addURL()` methods, you should see the following output from the agent:

```
jmxbook.mletwrapper.mbeanAdded
jmxbook.mletwrapper.urlAdded
```

If you experience an error in one of the methods, you should see the following notification type appear in the agent output:

```
jmxbook.mletwrapper.error
```

10.5 Summary

In this chapter, you learned about the first of the JMX agent services found in compliant JMX agents: the M-let service. The M-let service gives JMX agents the ability to dynamically load MBeans from remote locations outside the agent's codebase. In essence, the service lets you expand the CLASSPATH of the agent, while at the same time constructing MBeans described in an M-let file. The M-let file is an XML-like file that describes to the service how to create the MBean contained by each M-let entry in the file. This is a powerful advantage for JMX over other management environments: using the M-let service, you can ensure that your agent will remain running even through code updates.

At the end of this chapter, you wrote an example that demonstrates how you might wrap the M-let service in another MBean to provide detailed notifications about its behavior. Using the wrapped service, you can ensure that other parts of your JMX system are informed of new classes and MBean types available to the agent.

Chapter 11 discusses the relation service, which helps you to create management relationships between MBeans.

11

Working with the relation service

- Defining a relation
- Understanding the components of the relation service
- Using the relation service in a real-world example

In the previous chapter, we discussed the first agent service: the M-let service. This chapter continues the coverage of agent services by examining the relation service. Consider the fact that a typical JMX agent may contain numerous MBeans, managing many resources. In fact, applications can expose components or resources through the use of several MBeans.

Additionally, multiple MBeans might be needed to solve a particular problem. For instance, imagine that you receive an alert telling you that your customer service application needs attention. You use its MBean to read a new customer query, but then you must use a different MBean to process the query. In management environments like this, keeping track of MBeans may be difficult. MBean management in cases of executing an ordered workflow is different than the MBean querying problem presented in chapter 8. The MBean querying service will help you find specific MBeans, but it cannot help you determine the order in which specific MBeans should be used to complete a task (or even which exposed operation to invoke).

This chapter will show you how to manage MBeans that are intended to have relationships. They can be related by the resource they manage or by being members of the same workflow. The JMX relation service provides a way to validate and manage MBeans as related groups, called *relations*.

11.1 *Using the JMX relation service*

Relations are objects that contain information describing the relationship between two MBeans. Each relation object must conform to a particular *relation type*. A relation type is an object that resides in the relation service and allows the service to validate relations. Relation types define the specific *roles* that MBeans represent in a relationship.

The JMX relation service, like the M-let service described in chapter 10, is an MBean registered in an agent. The service manages a group of registered relations that users can query. Rather than look for many MBeans residing in an agent that make a logical unit, you can query the relation service for an existing relation that will provide the MBean information you need (the `ObjectName` value).

In addition, the relation service maintains the consistency of registered relations against their particular relation types. As MBeans are added and removed from an agent, the relation service will continuously check its registered relations to ensure they still validate against their particular relation types. For example, consider a relation type that defines a relation as having one MBean of type A and one of type B. If an MBean of type A is removed from an existing relation of that type, the relation will no longer validate. In this case, the relation service will remove the relation from the group of registered relations. The relation service is "aware" of the relations and the MBeans that correspond to the roles and ensures that the integrity of the relations remains intact.

The service also acts as the source of notifications, providing information about the relations it contains. If a relation is created, updated, or deleted, the relation service will send a notification containing information about the modification.

11.1.1 *Components of the relation service*

In the previous section, we introduced some new terms: *relation*, *relation type*, and *role*. These terms correspond to some of the classes that make up the relation service. Throughout this chapter, we will use these terms and their classes to describe the relation service and construct examples. Therefore, you need to have a good understanding of these and other terms. This section will help you round out your knowledge of the following terms:

- Relation service
- Relation type
- Role information
- Relation
- Role

The relation service is a complex agent service. When you're working through the examples in this chapter, you can come back to this section to refresh your knowledge of these terms. Likewise, the relation framework being described may be difficult to envision. As you work through the example step by step, these concepts should become clearer.

Relation service

The relation service is an MBean that defines the methods used to create and remove relation types and relations. In addition, the relation service provides methods for finding a particular relation.

The relation service lets you create *internal* and *external* relations. Internal relations are relations that exist only within the relation service MBean. This type of relation only provides information about the MBeans that create a relationship. In contrast, external relations are registered with the relation service, but also exist as MBeans registered in the agent. In this chapter, you will create an external relation. This type of relation has some unique advantages that we will expose shortly.

Relation type

The relation type is an object that acts as a template for relations. It contains a list of role information objects that describe the members of a relation. The relation service uses relation types to validate relations by examining the relation type role information and comparing it to the role values in the relation. The relation type is defined by the class `javax.management.relation.RelationType`.

Role information

As we mentioned earlier, role information objects are contained within `Relation-Type` objects. The role information distinctly defines a member of a relation. An instance of the `RoleInfo` class contains a unique name of a role as well as the multiplicity of the MBeans for that role. The role name cannot be null and must be unique for a given relation type. The multiplicity defines the number of MBeans that can be referenced by the role.

For example, a `FamilyCar` relation type might have a `RoleInfo` object `wheels` with a multiplicity of four `Wheel` MBeans, whereas a `Tricycle` relation type would have a multiplicity of three `Wheel` MBeans. In addition, a `CookieJar` relation type might have a multiplicity of 0 to 100 `Cookie` MBeans, depending on how hungry you were.

A `RoleInfo` object also specifies two more constraints for a relation type: the class name of the MBeans that can act as a role in a relation of the type that contains the `RoleInfo` object, and the access mode of the role. The access mode determines the read and write permissions of the role.

Relation

Relations are represented by the `Relation` class. Every relation is an object representing an instance of a particular relation type (not an actual instance of the `RelationType` class, but the `Relation` class). The relation is an object, registered in the relation service, that defines an association between existing MBeans in an agent. A relation can reference several different classes of MBeans and present them in such a way that the user can clearly understand the association between them.

MBeans participating in a relation are said to be a *role* of a relation. A role is validated against the `RoleInfo` object of the `Relation`'s relation type. As we mentioned earlier, a relation is either *internal* or *external*. An external relation exposes methods that can operate of any `number` of its member MBeans; this functionality provides a powerful way to manage your enterprise's collection of existing MBeans.

Role

The `Role` class represents the roles of a relation; it consists of a role name and a role value. The role value is a list of MBeans that are acting as a role in a given relation. The role value must conform to the definition of its corresponding `RoleInfo` object. The role name corresponds to the `RoleInfo` name defined in the relation type of the `Relation` instance.

11.2 Using the relation service to manage a phone system

We've given you a lot of information to process all at once. A good example will help you understand all these classes and terms. In this section, you will model a real-world phone system using MBeans and their relationships. You'll see how relations are useful to associate MBeans and operate on them as a single unit.

The first thing we need to do is describe the scenario of the example. We will describe a system modeled with MBeans that presents a problem, and use the relation service to solve that problem.

11.2.1 Defining the scenario

Consider a system that sends and receives phone and fax messages. It consists of an application that controls the incoming and outgoing calls and faxes. In this system, the controller application can work with up to 10 phone cards and 1 fax card. In addition, the application uses a routing table to control the flow of calls. The routing table is the means by which the application makes decisions about whether to put a phone or fax board in the receive or send state. Figure 11.1 illustrates this system.

As operators of this system, you want a way to disable a device card and update the routing table in a single, efficient step. To do this, you will instrument the application using a JMX environment. To manage the system, you will define the following three types of MBeans:

- A phone card MBean
- A fax card MBean
- A routing table MBean

Managing phone and fax cards

To control the phone and fax devices, you need to define an MBean for each card. For phone cards, you will create an MBean represented by the `PhoneCard`

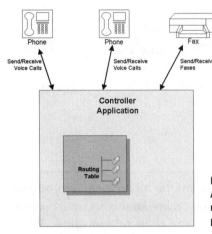

Figure 11.1
A controller application
maintains the state of
phone and fax cards.

class. Because your environment can have more than one phone card, each Phone-Card MBean will have a unique card id. In this case, you will use an integer to represent the slot number for the phone card. This example will use two Phone-Card MBeans.

For fax cards, you will define the FaxCard class. You can have only one fax card present in a deployment, and it will be represented by a FaxCard MBean. With only one fax card to manage, this MBean does not need any special identifiers.

Both the phone and fax card MBeans will have a single exposed method called disable(). This method prevents the card from sending or receiving calls or faxes.

Managing a routing table

Keep in mind that upon disabling either type of card, you'll need to notify the controller application that it should no longer attempt to route calls to or from the disabled card. To do so, you will expose a routing table MBean for disabling the route. The RoutingTable MBean will expose two important operations. The first operation allows the removal of the routing information for one of the phone cards; it will accept an integer representing the phone card slot. The second operation removes a fax card route from use.

11.2.2 *The phone system management example*

We have defined the system: it consists of some hardware devices and a component of a software application. For the relation example you'll create, assume that this JMX environment already exists. There are two PhoneCard MBeans and

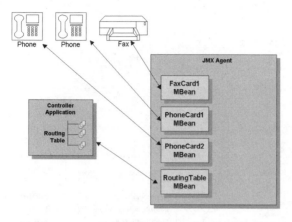

**Figure 11.2
Telephony system managed
with MBeans**

one `FaxCard` MBean registered in a JMX agent. In addition, you will register an instance of the `RoutingTable` MBean. This system is described in figure 11.2.

Here lies the problem: disabling a device (phone or fax) takes two steps. First you have to invoke the `disable()` method of a particular device MBean, and then you must invoke the appropriate operation of the `RoutingTable` MBean to update the routing table. If you treat this problem as representative of larger or more complex systems, you can imagine more problematic scenarios. For instance, in this example only two steps are necessary to perform the disable task, but what if 15 steps were required? To solve this problem, you will define an MBean relationship that can provide a mechanism to reduce this process to a single step, essentially allowing you to treat multiple MBeans as a unit.

11.2.3 *Defining an external relationship with an MBean*

As we described earlier, it would be nice if you could define an MBean that would behave like a single unit equivalent to the whole system. It would be useful to expose such an MBean to a management system in an abstracted manner so that the management system could effectively work with only one object, as opposed to requiring a manager to deal with each individual MBean.

You will do this by defining a relationship between the `PhoneCard` and `FaxCard` MBeans and the `RoutingTable` MBean. The relation is represented by an MBean, and users will only need to interact with it in order to update the phone system. An external relation is said to be a *relation MBean*. A relation MBean is registered as an MBean in an agent, and as a relation in the relation service. Figure 11.3 shows how a relation MBean can help your phone system.

The figure shows a relation MBean that exposes a method, `disablePhoneCard (integer)`. In the figure, the method is being invoked with an integer 1 that

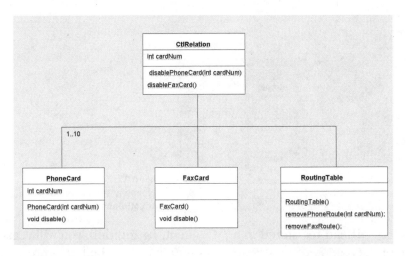

Figure 11.3
Telephony system
managed using a
relation MBean

indicates the phone card in slot 1 should be disabled and then updates the routing table. The relation MBean looks up the corresponding phone card MBean and calls its `disable()` method. The relation MBean next calls the appropriate route-removal method on the `RoutingTable` MBean. Figure 11.4 displays the JMX diagram relating all the MBeans. In this diagram, the relation MBean is named `CtlRelation`. So, your two device MBeans and the `RoutingTable` MBean have a relationship provided by the controller application represented by the `CtlRelation` MBean.

The `CtlRelation` MBean will associate the `PhoneCard`, `FaxCard`, and `RoutingTable` MBeans. You can see that the relation references 1 to 10 `PhoneCards`, 1 `FaxCard`, and 1 `RoutingTable` MBean.

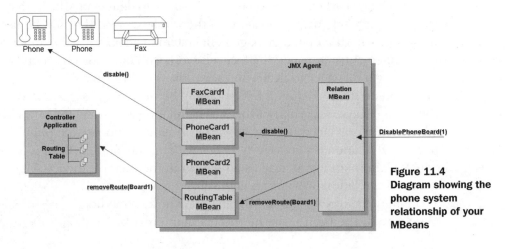

Figure 11.4
Diagram showing the
phone system
relationship of your
MBeans

Up to this point, we have defined the problem and presented a solution. You now need to write the code for all the MBeans, as well as the code for building the relation and adding the relation service to your JMXBookAgent class. The following sections will walk you through writing the code to build this example.

11.3 Constructing the MBean relationship

As you have in previous chapters, you will use the JMXBookAgent class constructed in chapter 3. You will add the relation service and your MBeans to the agent. Finally, you will execute a test using the HTML adapter to disable the fax and phone cards. To complete this example, you must write code to complete the steps shown in the following list:

1 Create the MBeans. Before any relation can be created, the MBeans that will participate in the relation must be created in the current agent. These are Standard MBeans, and they must be registered in the agent.

2 Create the RelationType object that will declare the role information and constraints about your relation.

3 Create role objects to participate in the new relation.

4 Create the relation object that corresponds to the situation described.

5 Add a method to your JMXBookAgent class that adds the relation service to the agent when it is started.

6 Write code that will add your new relation to the relation service for retrieval.

Let's begin this process by writing the code for all your MBeans.

11.3.1 Creating the MBeans

The first step is to write the MBeans that model each component of the scenario, including the PhoneCard, FaxCard, and RoutingTable MBeans. You will create them as Standard MBeans. (For more information about Standard MBeans, refer back to chapter 4.)

The listings in the following sections show the classes for these MBean classes, as well as their interfaces.

Writing the PhoneCard MBean

Each MBean will be placed in the jmxbook.ch11 package. The PhoneCardMBean interface for the PhoneCard class is as follows. It declares a single method, disable(), which disables the managed phone card from operation:

```
package jmxbook.ch11;

public interface PhoneCardMBean
{
  public void disable();
}
```

Listing 11.1 shows the implementation of the `PhoneCardMBean` interface by the `PhoneCard` class.

Listing 11.1   PhoneCard.java

```
package jmxbook.ch11;

public class PhoneCard implements PhoneCardMBean
{
  private int cardNum=0;

  public PhoneCard( int cardNum )
  {
    this.cardNum = cardNum;
  }

  public void disable()
  {
    System.out.println( "PhoneCardMBean::PhoneCard #" +
                        cardNum+" has been disabled" );
  }
}
```

This MBean exposes one method and a constructor. The constructor takes an `int` parameter that identifies the phone card slot this MBean represents. In the constructor, you store a reference to this card's slot number so that you can use it when the `disable()` method is called. The `disable()` method would typically execute some code that would disable the phone card. You do not have an actual phone card, so you will just display a message indicating the card number that is being disabled.

Writing the FaxCard MBean

Next, let's write the interface and implementation for the `FaxCard` MBean. The interface for this class looks similar to the `PhoneCardMBean` interface:

```
package jmxbook.ch11;

public interface FaxCardMBean
{
  public void disable();
}
```

Listing 11.2 shows the MBean class. It is also a simple class, like `PhoneCard`.

Listing 11.2   FaxCard.java

```
package jmxbook.ch11;

public class FaxCard implements FaxCardMBean
{
  public FaxCard(){}

  public void disable()
  {
    System.out.println(
        "FaxCardMBean::The FaxCard has been disabled");
  }

}
```

Like the `PhoneCard` MBean, this class exposes a single method and a constructor. Like the previous MBean, in the real world it would interface to a fax board and, when called, take the card out of service. For this example, you will print an informative message to the screen. Because you can have only one fax board per system, you do not include a card number with this MBean.

Writing the RoutingTable MBean

Now that you have the code for the two types of device card MBeans, you need to write the MBean that represents the routing table. The `RoutingTable` MBean contains the routing information for both the fax and phone cards. The interface for the `RoutingTable` MBean is as follows:

```
package jmxbook.ch11;

public interface RoutingTableMBean
{
  public void removePhoneRoute(Integer cardNum);
  public void removeFaxRoute();
}
```

The interface exposes two methods: `removePhoneRoute()` and `removeFaxRoute()`. The method for removing a phone route accepts a phone card number to identify the correct phone card. Listing 11.3 shows the implementation class, `RoutingTable`.

Listing 11.3   RoutingTable.java

```
package jmxbook.ch11;

public class RoutingTable implements RoutingTableMBean
{
```

```
public RoutingTable(){}

public void removePhoneRoute(Integer cardNum)
{
   System.out.println( "RoutingTableMBean::PhoneCard" +
                        cardNum.intValue() + " removed from "
                        + " routing table");
}

public void removeFaxRoute()
{
   System.out.println( "RoutingTableMBean::FaxCard removed "
                        + " from routing table");
}
}
```

This MBean manages a routing table that has both fax and phone board references, so it includes two user methods. The first method removes a phone card from the routing table and takes an integer as a parameter; this integer describes the slot of a phone card. The second method removes the fax card from the routing table; it requires no parameter, because there can be only one fax card per system. For this example, both methods will print a message to the screen, because you do not really have a routing table implemented for the phone and fax cards.

Registering the MBeans in the agent

Now that you have created the MBeans, you need to write code that will add them to the agent. The remaining code in this chapter comes from a main class built to create and register MBeans in the agent. The methods being described will form a class called RelationMain. This class will be similar to the setup classes you have written in previous chapters. However, in addition to registering your MBeans, this class will eventually contain the code that creates your relation. The method in listing 11.4 is extracted from the RelationMain class. You can find the complete source listing for this class on the book's web site at http://www.manning.com/.

Listing 11.4 The createMBeans() method from RelationMain.java

```
public void createMBeans()
{
   try
   {
      //register the first PhoneCard
         Object[] params = new Object[1];
         params[0] = new Integer(1);
         String[] sig = new String[1];
         sig[0] = "int";
```

```
        System.out.println("\n>>> REGISTERING PhoneCard1 MBean");
    ObjectName phoneCard1Name = new
            ObjectName("JMXBookAgent:name=phoneCard,slot=1");

    client.createMBean( "jmxbook.ch11.PhoneCard",
                        phoneCard1Name,
                        params,
                        sig );

    //register the second PhoneCard
    params[0] = new Integer(2);
    System.out.println("\n>>> REGISTERING PhoneCard2 MBean");
    ObjectName    phoneCard2Name = new
ObjectName( "JMXBookAgent:name=phoneCard,slot=2" );
    client.createMBean( "jmxbook.ch11.PhoneCard",
                        phoneCard2Name,
                        params,
                        sig );

    //register the FaxCard
    System.out.println("\n>>> REGISTERING FaxCard MBean");
    ObjectName    faxCardName = new
                ObjectName( "JMXBookAgent:name=faxCard" );

    client.createMBean( "jmxbook.ch11.FaxCard",faxCardName );

    //register the RoutingTable
    System.out.println("\n>>> REGISTERING RoutingTable MBean");
    ObjectName    routingTableName = new
                ObjectName( "JMXBookAgent:name=routingTable" );
    client.createMBean("jmxbook.ch11.RoutingTable",
                    routingTableName);

    }
    catch(Exception e)
    {
      e.printStackTrace();
      System.out.println("Error Registering MBeans");
    }
  }
```

In this method, you create four MBeans in the agent (two `PhoneCard` MBeans, one `FaxCard` MBean, and one `RoutingTable` MBean). Notice that the `create-MBean()` invocation for the phone cards requires more parameters than the fax or routing table MBeans. This is the case because the `PhoneCard` MBean constructor requires an integer to define the slot number for the card.

Also note that an `Integer` object, not an `int`, is used as the parameter for the constructor to the phone card. This is a different signature than that of the constructor defined in the object itself. The reflection capabilities used in the agent will reconcile the object to the primitive type where required.

In addition, the `client` object being used is an `RmiConnectorClient` instance acquired from the `RMIClientFactory` class that you have been using throughout the book. It is a global reference in the `RelationMain` class.

Now that the code for MBeans representing the system components is finished, you will proceed to define the objects required for the relation. We won't dissect particular classes and interfaces in the `javax.management.relation` package; rather, we will introduce them as we need them in code. In addition, the relation package contains more classes than we will discuss; you can examine the API in the javadoc later.

11.3.2 Defining the relation

Now it is time to create the objects that will help you create the relationship we have described for this scenario. Before you can create a `Relation` object, you need to create a `RelationType` object. And before you can create the `Relation-Type`, you must be able to populate it with an array of `RoleInfo` objects that represent the role information of the relation type. In the next section, you will create an array of role information needed to build your controller application relationship.

Creating the RoleInfo objects

For this example, you need to describe three roles: `VoiceProcessor`, `FaxProcessor`, and `CallRouter`. The `VoiceProcessor` role can include from 1 to 10 `PhoneCard` MBeans. The `FaxProcessor` role is restricted to one `FaxBoard` MBean, and the `CallRouter` is limited to one `RoutingTable` MBean. This follows the architectural model as described in the example description.

The relation service will use this role information to ensure that the roles used in a relation follow their constraints. Listing 11.5 is the `createRoleInfoArray()` method from the `RelationMain` class. It creates the three named `RoleInfo` objects and places them into an array. An array is used because that is the form needed to later create the `RelationType` object for this example.

Listing 11.5 The createRoleInfoArray() method from RelationMain.java

```
public RoleInfo[] createRoleInfoArray()
{
  RoleInfo[] roleInfoArray = new RoleInfo[3];

  try
```

```
            {
              roleInfoArray[0]= new RoleInfo("VoiceProcessor",
                                     "jmxbook.ch11.PhoneCard",
                                     true,
                                     true,
                                     1,
                                     10,
                                     "The Role for Phone Card");
              roleInfoArray[1] = new RoleInfo("FaxProcessor",
                                     "jmxbook.ch11.FaxCard",
                                     true,
                                     true,
                                     1,
                                     1,
                                     "The Role for Fax Card");
              roleInfoArray[2] = new RoleInfo("CallRouter",
                                     "jmxbook.ch11.RoutingTable",
                                     true,
                                     true,
                                     1,
                                     1,
                                     "The Role for Routing Table");
            }
            catch(Exception e)
            {
              System.out.println(
                  "Error Creating the Relation Service MBean");
              e.printStackTrace();
            }

            return roleInfoArray;
        }
```

The role information array describes the roles that will form the relation. Each RoleInfo instance contains the role name and the MBean class name that can act as this type of role. In addition, it describes whether the role is readable and writeable (the two boolean values).

It also includes the minDegree and maxDegree values that describe the multiplicity of this role. The minDegree value (1 in the case of the VoiceProcessor role) indicates the minimum number of MBeans that can exist for this role. The maxDegree value (10 in the case of the VoiceProcessor role) indicates the maximum number of MBeans that can exist for this role. The last parameter to the constructor is the description of the role. With the RoleInfo objects in hand, you can create the RelationType object.

Creating the RelationType object

Listing 11.6 shows the `createRelationTypes()` method from the `RelationMain` class. Its responsibility is to take the `RoleInfo` objects you just created and create a `RelationType` object to register in the relation service found in the `JMXBookAgent` class.

Listing 11.6 The createRelationTypes() method from the RelationMain class

```
public void createRelationTypes( RoleInfo[] roleInfoArray )
{
  try
  {
    Object[] params = new Object[2];
    params[0] = "myRelationType";
    params[1] = roleInfoArray;
    String[] signature = new String[2];
    signature[0] = "java.lang.String";
    try {
      signature[1] = (roleInfoArray.getClass()).getName();
    }
    catch (Exception exc)
    {
      throw exc;
    }
    client.invoke(relationServiceName, "createRelationType",
                params, signature);
  }
  catch (Exception e)
  {
    System.out.println("Error Creating the RelationType");
    e.printStackTrace();
  }
}
```

This method creates a relation type with an array of `RoleInfo` objects provided as a parameter. After creating an instance of `RelationType`, the method registers it in the relation service found in the agent connected by the `client` object (remember that the `client` object is a global instance of the `RmiConnectorClient` from the `RelationMain` class).

The parameters needed to create a relation type in the relation service are the name of the relation type and the array of `RoleInfo` objects. This method uses a global `ObjectName` to find the relation service on the `JMXBookAgent` and invoke its `createRelationType()` method, passing in the name and `RoleInfo` array for the new type. If the relation type name already exists in the relation service, an exception will be thrown indicating what happened. In this case, the relation type is named myRelationType.

11.3.3 *Creating the role objects*

Once the relation type is added to the relation service, you can successfully create a Relation object that represents an instance of that type. In order to create a Relation instance, you must be able to specify the roles that participate in the relation. Using the role information as a template, let's define the roles.

Remember from the previous section that you have three roles for this example: VoiceProcessor, FaxProcessor, and CallRouter. Just like the RelationType, you will need an array of Role objects in order to create the Relation instance. You will create your role array list in the method shown in listing 11.7. This method is also taken from the RelationMain class.

Listing 11.7   The createRoles() method from the RelationMain class

```
public void createRoles()
{
  ArrayList    voiceRoleValue = new ArrayList();
  ArrayList    faxRoleValue = new ArrayList();
  ArrayList    routingTableRoleValue = new ArrayList();

  try
  {
    voiceRoleValue.add( new
        ObjectName("JMXBookAgent:name=phoneCard,slot=1" ) );
    voiceRoleValue.add( new
        ObjectName("JMXBookAgent:name=phoneCard,slot=2")   );

    Role voiceProcessorRole = new Role("VoiceProcessor",
        voiceRoleValue);

    faxRoleValue.add(
  new ObjectName("JMXBookAgent:name=faxCard") );

    Role faxProcessorRole =
     new Role("FaxProcessor", faxRoleValue);

    routingTableRoleValue.add( new ObjectName(
        "JMXBookAgent:name=routingTable" ) );

    Role routingTableRole = new Role("CallRouter",
        routingTableRoleValue);

    roleList.add(voiceProcessorRole);
    roleList.add(faxProcessorRole);
    roleList.add(routingTableRole);
```

```
      }
      catch (Exception e)
      {
        System.out.println("Error Creating Roles");
        e.printStackTrace();
      }
    }
```

The Role class's constructor takes a role name and a role value that is a list of ObjectName instances that reference the MBeans belonging to this role. The array list of ObjectName instances must match the names allowed by the RoleInfo objects you created earlier with the same name. Note that the VoiceProcessor role has two PhoneCard MBeans (the role could contain up to 10) and that the other two roles contain a single ObjectName. This arrangement matches the RoleInfo classes created earlier. Once the roles are created, you add each of the roles to a list to be used when you create your Relation object.

11.3.4 *Creating the Relation MBean*

Up to this point, you have modeled all the scenario devices with MBeans and created a RelationType and Role instances. Now it is time to create the Relation object. As mentioned earlier in the chapter, relations can be either internal or external. You're creating an external relation, so you must create a relation MBean. A relation MBean implements the RelationSupportMBean interface and represents the actual relationship between existing MBeans participating as roles. External relations are useful because they can perform operations on their role values (the participating MBeans). The relation MBean will associate the roles and expose methods that work on those associations.

The RelationSupport class provides methods that the relation service will use to validate the relation against its relation type. You will see this process shortly.

The CtlRelationMBean interface is as follows:

```
package jmxbook.ch11;

import javax.management.*;
import javax.management.relation.*;

public interface CtlRelationMBean extends RelationSupportMBean
{
  public void disablePhoneCard(int cardNum)throws MBeanException;
  public void disableFaxCard()throws MBeanException;
}
```

This interface defines two methods that will be exposed in the external relation. The first method disables the phone card, and the second method disables the fax card. Invoking these methods will cause the relation MBean to look up the device MBean (phone or fax) and disable it. The relation MBean will also update the routing table by using the `RoutingTable` MBean. Notice the use of the `RelationSupportMBean` interface, which exposes certain operations so that the relation service can access the roles of the relation represented by this MBean. The relation service needs access to this information so that it can validate relations represented by this MBean. Listing 11.8 shows the MBean implementation.

Listing 11.8   CtlRelation.java

```
package jmxbook.ch11;

import javax.management.*;
import javax.management.relation.*;
import java.util.*;

public class CtlRelation extends RelationSupport
                    implements CtlRelationMBean, MBeanRegistration
{
  private MBeanServer server = null;

  public CtlRelation(String relationId,
                    ObjectName relationServiceName,
                    String relationTypeName,
                    RoleList roleList)
        throws InvalidRoleValueException, IllegalArgumentException
  {
    super(relationId, relationServiceName,
        relationTypeName, roleList);
  }

  public void disablePhoneCard( int cardNum )
                    throws MBeanException
  {
    System.out.println("Relation MBean::Disabling Phone Card");
    try
    {
      ObjectName phoneCardName = new ObjectName(
              "JMXBookAgent:name=phoneCard,slot="+cardNum);
      ObjectName routingTableName = new ObjectName(
              "JMXBookAgent:name=routingTable");

      server.invoke(phoneCardName, "disable", null, null);

      Object[] params = new Object[1];
      params[0] = new Integer(cardNum);
      String[] sig = new String[1];
      sig[0] = "java.lang.Integer";
```

❶ Set up MBean in constructor

❷ Implement disablePhoneCard() method

```
          server.invoke(routingTableName, "removePhoneRoute",
                         params, sig);
      }
      catch(Exception e)                                        ❷
      {
        System.out.println("Relation MBean::Error Removing "
                         +" Phone Card:"+e);
        throw new MBeanException(e);
      }
    }

    public void disableFaxCard() throws MBeanException
    {
      System.out.println("Relation MBean::Disabling Fax Card");
      try
      {
        ObjectName faxCardName = new ObjectName(
                        "JMXBookAgent:name=faxCard");
        ObjectName routingTableName = new ObjectName(
                        "JMXBookAgent:name=routingTable");

        server.invoke(faxCardName, "disable", null, null);
        server.invoke(routingTableName, "removeFaxRoute", null, null);
      }
      catch(Exception e)
      {
        System.out.println("Relation MBean::"
          + "Error Removing Fax Card:"+e);
        throw new MBeanException(e);
      }
    }

    public ObjectName preRegister( MBeanServer server,
           ObjectName name )
                   throws Exception
    {
      this.server = server;
      return name;
    }
  }
```

❶ The CtlRelation class is the MBean class in the scenario description that allows the user to disable device cards and update the routing table in a single step. It extends the RelationSupport class in order to provide an implementation for the RelationSupportMBean interface extended by the CtlRelationMBean interface. The RelationSupport methods provide a mechanism for the relation service to validate this external relation against its relation type.

The constructor of this MBean requires the parameters needed to call the constructor of its super class. The constructor requires an id for the relation, the relation service's ObjectName value, the name of the relation type, and a Role list. The id for the relation must be a unique value that identifies the relation within the relation service. The relation type name corresponds to the name of the relation type, which describes the constraints for this relation. The Roles that participate in this relation are contained within the Role list passed to the constructor. The Role objects will be validated against the RoleInfo objects once this relation is added to the relation service.

❷ Notice that this MBean implements the MBeanRegistration interface in order to get a handle on the MBean server that contains it. This implementation allows the MBean to interact with the MBeans participating as roles in the relation. This MBean needs to contact a particular PhoneCard or FaxCard MBean and the RoutingTable MBean.

The first method exposed for the user is disablePhoneCard(). In this method and the disableFaxCard() method, the CtlRelation MBean contacts the correct participating MBean in order to disable a particular device and update the routing table. The disablePhoneCard() method takes an Integer as a parameter in order to look up the appropriate PhoneCard MBean.

11.3.5 *Adding the relation service to the JMXBookAgent class*

Now that all the code is written to instantiate the Relation, you need to add the relation service to your JMXBookAgent before you can execute your test. Listing 11.9 is a method added to the JMXBookAgent class definition that will be invoked by the JMXBookAgent constructor. You will need to modify the constructor to invoke the new method.

Listing 11.9   createRelationService() method added to JMXBookAgent

```
public void createRelationService()
{
  ObjectName relationServiceName = null;

  try
  {
    relationServiceName = new ObjectName(
          "JMXBookAgent:name=relationService" );

    Object[] params = new Object[1];
    params[0] = new Boolean(true);
    String[] signature = new String[1];
    signature[0] = "boolean";
```

```
       server.createMBean( "javax.management.relation."
                           +"RelationService",
                           relationServiceName,
                           params,
                           signature);
    }
    catch(Exception e)
    {
      System.out.println("Error Creating the Relation"
      + " Service MBean");
      e.printStackTrace();
    }
  }
```

You create the relation service by registering the `RelationService` MBean (`javax.management.relation.RelationService`) with the `JMXBookAgent`. The MBean constructor takes a single argument, a `boolean`, which indicates whether the service should immediately purge a relation that has become invalid due to an invalid `Role`. Remember, a relation is invalid when a participating MBean of the relation is removed from the agent. If you set this value to `true`, whenever the relation service notices that an MBean associated with a relation has been unregistered, it will also remove the MBean reference from the role values. If the role is no longer valid according to the cardinality of the `RoleInfo`, the relation will also be removed. If you set this `boolean` value to `false`, the relation will be purged only if the `purgeRelations()` method is called on the `RelationService` MBean.

11.3.6 *Adding a new relation to the relation service*

You have created all the necessary MBeans and set up the services to start a relation. The final step is to instantiate an instance of the `CtlRelation` MBean and add it to the relation service (as well as register it in the agent). Listing 11.10 creates the relation by using the `addRelation()` method of the `RelationService` MBean. Again, the listing is from the `RelationMain` class that will execute the entire example.

> **Listing 11.10   createRelation() method from RelationMain**

```
public void createRelation()
{
  System.out.println("\n>>> CREATE EXTERNAL RELATION  of "
                    + " type myRelationType");
  try
  {
    //register the relation MBean
```

```
ObjectName relationMBeanName = new ObjectName(
        "JMXBookAgent:type=RelationMBean");

Object[] params = new Object[4];
params[0] = "RelationId1";
params[1] = relationServiceName;
params[2] = "myRelationType";
params[3] = roleList;

String[] sig = new String[4];
sig[0] = "java.lang.String";
sig[1] = relationServiceName.getClass().getName();
sig[2] = "java.lang.String";
sig[3] = roleList.getClass().getName();

client.createMBean( "jmxbook.ch11.CtlRelation",
        relationMBeanName, params, sig );

//add the new relation
params = new Object[1];
sig = new String[1];
params[0] = relationMBeanName ;
sig[0] = "javax.management.ObjectName";

client.invoke( relationServiceName, "addRelation",
        params, sig );
}
catch(Exception e)
{
  System.out.println("Could not create the relation");
  e.printStackTrace();
}
}
```

❶ Create relation MBean

❷ Invoke addRelation() method of MBeanServer

❶ The first thing you do in this method is instantiate the `CtlRelation` MBean and add it to the `JMXBookAgent`. You pass the arguments to use in its constructor to the `createMBean()` method of the `client` object. Remember that you must pass it a relation unique id, the relation service `ObjectName` value, and the list of `Role` objects participating in the relation.

❷ The `addRelation()` method in the relation service can throw exceptions for several reasons. If the relation service is not registered or a role does not exist in the relation type, an exception will be thrown. If the id chosen is already used by another relation, or if the relation type does not exist in the relation service, an exception will occur.

The relation service will do validity checks when the relation is added to ensure that the multiplicity for the roles matches that defined in the `RoleInfo` objects. In addition, it will ensure that the MBeans referenced in the roles are the expected ones, and that they exist in the MBean server. The relation service will also ensure that the same role name is not used for two different roles. If any of these criteria are not met, the service will throw an exception when you attempt to add the relation to the service.

11.3.7 *The RelationMain main() method*

The last listing from the RelationMain class is its main() method. The Relation-Main class now contains methods to create the relation type, role information, and roles, and also to create the relation service within a running JMXBookAgent. The main() method coordinates the steps in the correct order. Listing 11.11 shows the main() method.

Listing 11.11 Class definition and main() method from RelationMain

```
package jmxbook.ch11;

import jmxbook.ch3.RMIClientFactory;
import java.util.*;
import java.io.*;
import java.net.*;
import com.sun.jdmk.comm.*;
import javax.management.*;
import javax.management.relation.*;

public class RelationMain
{
  ObjectName        relationServiceName = null;
  Role              voiceProcessorRole = null;
  Role              faxProcessorRole = null;
  RoleList          roleList = new RoleList();
  RmiConnectorClient client = null;

  public RelationMain()
  {
    client = RMIClientFactory.getClient();
    try
    {
        relationServiceName=new
         ObjectName("JMXBookAgent:name=relationService");
    }
    catch(Exception e)
    {
        e.printStackTrace();
        System.exit(0);
    }
  }
}
```

```
public static void main( String[] args )
{
  System.out.println("\n>>> START of Relation Service example");

  RelationMain example = new RelationMain();

  example.createMBeans();
  RoleInfo[] roleInfo = example.createRoleInfoArray();
  example.createRoles();

  example.createRelationTypes(roleInfo);
  example.createRelation();

  System.exit(0);
}
}
```

11.4 *Running the example*

You need to perform two tasks to complete the example: run the JMXBookAgent class and the RelationMain class. To run both, execute the following commands in this order:

```
java jmxbook.ch3.JMXBookAgent

java jmxbook.ch11.RelationMain
```

With the agent still running, and having executed the RelationMain class, it is time to examine what has occurred.

11.4.1 *Viewing the MBeans*

The easiest way to see if the MBeans are registered in the agent is to connect to the agent using the HTML adapter. You should see something similar to figure 11.5 when you connect to the agent using the URL http://localhost:9092. If you don't see the correct MBeans, go back and verify all the MBean creation code. Also check your agent for exceptions. (To review how to use the HTML adapter, see chapter 2, where it is described in detail.)

Notice that MBeans now exist for the fax card, two phone cards, and the routing table. Also present are the relation service MBean and the CtlRelation MBean (under the object name "type=RelationMBean"). Click on your relation MBean and view its available methods.

11.4.2 *Viewing exposed methods*

After clicking on the correct link, you should see the screens shown in figures 11.6 and 11.7.

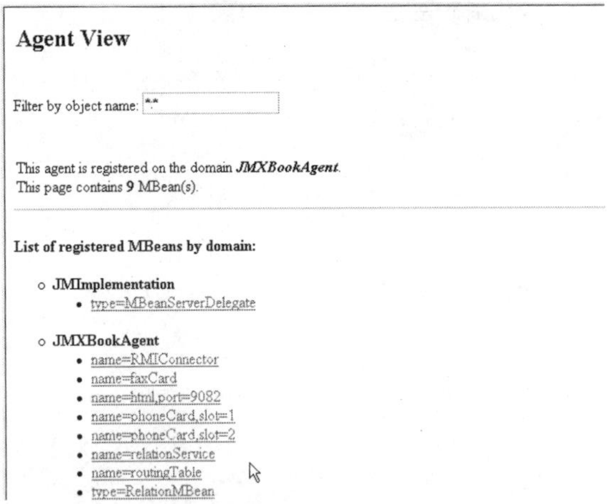

Agent View

Filter by object name: *:*

This agent is registered on the domain *JMXBookAgent*.
This page contains **9** MBean(s).

List of registered MBeans by domain:

- o JMImplementation
  - type=MBeanServerDelegate

- o JMXBookAgent
  - name=RMIConnector
  - name=faxCard
  - name=html,port=9082
  - name=phoneCard,slot=1
  - name=phoneCard,slot=2
  - name=relationService
  - name=routingTable
  - type=RelationMBean

**Figure 11.5
Agent View presented by
the JMXBookAgent's
HTML adapter**

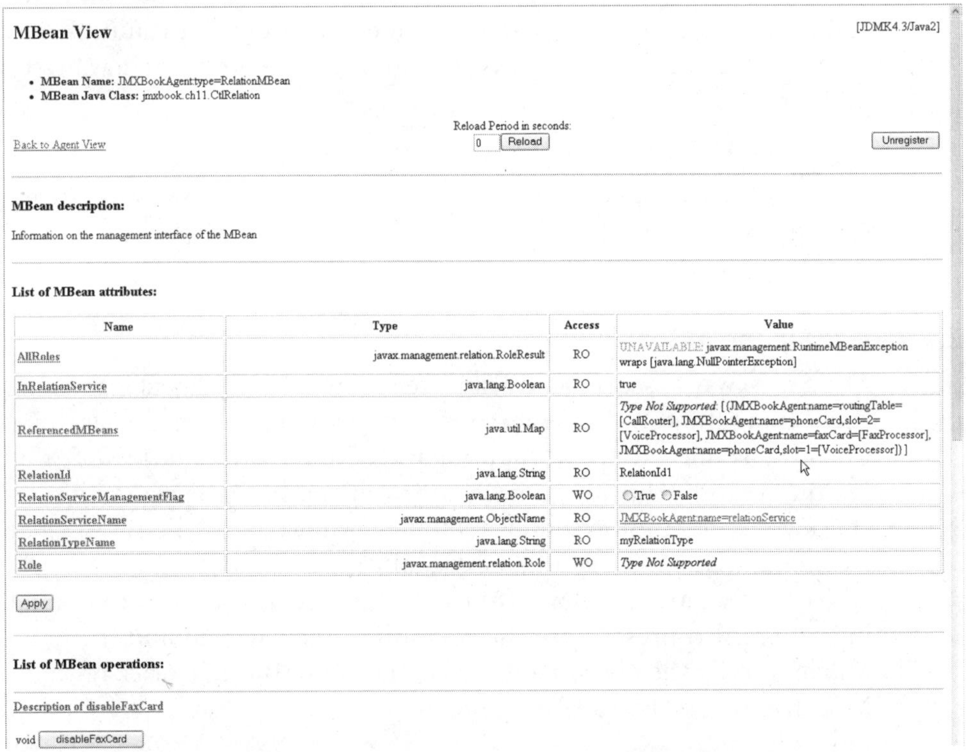

MBean View

[JDMK4.3/Java2]

- **MBean Name**: JMXBookAgent:type=RelationMBean
- **MBean Java Class**: jmxbook.ch11.CtlRelation

Back to Agent View

Reload Period in seconds:
0 [Reload]

[Unregister]

MBean description:

Information on the management interface of the MBean

List of MBean attributes:

Name	Type	Access	Value
AllRoles	javax.management.relation.RoleResult	RO	UNAVAILABLE: javax.management.RuntimeMBeanException wraps [java.lang.NullPointerException]
InRelationService	java.lang.Boolean	RO	true
ReferencedMBeans	java.util.Map	RO	Type Not Supported: [(JMXBookAgent:name=routingTable=[CallRouter], JMXBookAgent:name=phoneCard,slot=2=[VoiceProcessor], JMXBookAgent:name=faxCard=[FaxProcessor], JMXBookAgent:name=phoneCard,slot=1=[VoiceProcessor])]
RelationId	java.lang.String	RO	RelationId1
RelationServiceManagementFlag	java.lang.Boolean	WO	○True ○False
RelationServiceName	javax.management.ObjectName	RO	JMXBookAgent:name=relationService
RelationTypeName	java.lang.String	RO	myRelationType
Role	javax.management.relation.Role	WO	Type Not Supported

[Apply]

List of MBean operations:

Description of disableFaxCard

void [disableFaxCard]

Figure 11.6   The top half of the MBean View for the CtlRelation MBean

The first half of the screen, shown in figure 11.6, lists the attributes of the MBean. Notice the section labeled ReferencedMBeans. There is a `RoutingTable` MBean with the role name `CallRouter`, a `FaxCard` MBean with the role `FaxProcessor`, and two `PhoneCard` MBeans with the role `VoiceProcessor`.

These values match those you defined in your code. Now let's look at operations that are exposed for the MBean. Scrolling down the screen, you'll expose the list of operations for the MBean as shown in figure 11.7.

You can see your two methods exposed for disabling card devices: the `disableFaxCard()` method and the `disablePhoneCard()` method.

For a test, let's disable the phone card in slot 2.

11.4.3 Disabling a phone card

To disable the phone card in slot 2, you invoke the `disablePhoneCard()` method and pass in the number 2. Your relation MBean will disable the phone card and

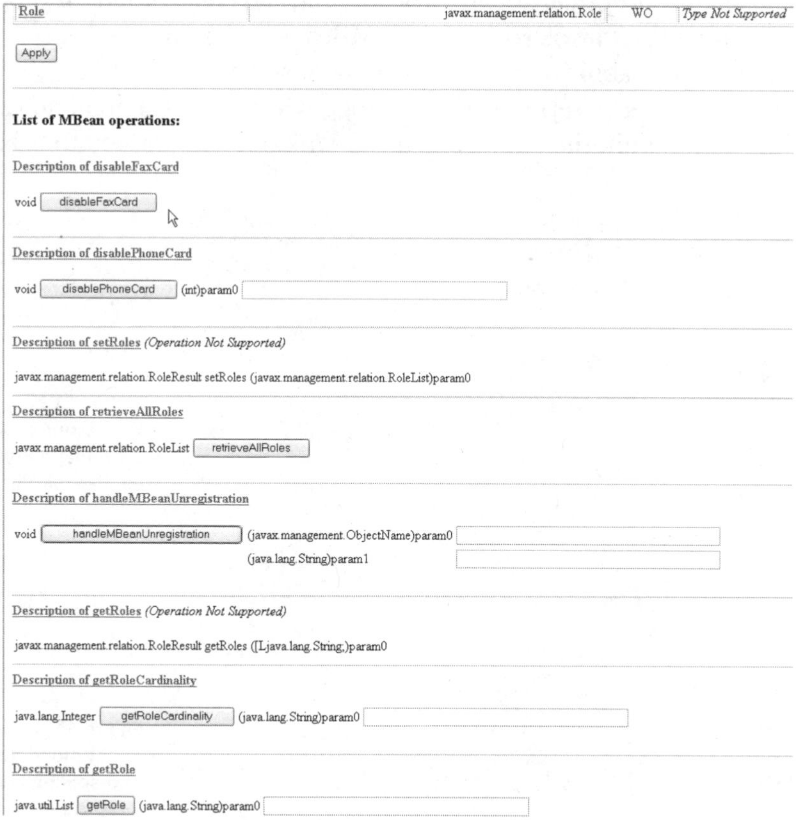

Role		javax.management.relation.Role	WO	*Type Not Supported*

[Apply]

List of MBean operations:

Description of disableFaxCard

void [disableFaxCard]

Description of disablePhoneCard

void [disablePhoneCard] (int)param0 [   ]

Description of setRoles *(Operation Not Supported)*

javax.management.relation.RoleResult setRoles (javax.management.relation.RoleList)param0

Description of retrieveAllRoles

javax.management.relation.RoleList [retrieveAllRoles]

Description of handleMBeanUnregistration

void [handleMBeanUnregistration] (javax.management.ObjectName)param0 [   ]
(java.lang.String)param1 [   ]

Description of getRoles *(Operation Not Supported)*

javax.management.relation.RoleResult getRoles ([Ljava.lang.String;)param0

Description of getRoleCardinality

java.lang.Integer [getRoleCardinality] (java.lang.String)param0 [   ]

Description of getRole

java.util.List [getRole] (java.lang.String)param0 [   ]

**Figure 11.7
The bottom
half of the
MBean View
from the
`CtlRelation`
MBean**

remove it from the routing table. You should see the success message shown in figure 11.8.

The web browser indicates that the phone card was disabled successfully. If it was not successfully disabled, you would see an exception notice returned. In addition to the web browser output, you should see the standard output from the JMXBookAgent similar to that in figure 11.9.

Notice that the first line of output is from the relation MBean; it reports that it is disabling a phone card. The next output line comes from the PhoneCard MBean itself; it indicates that it is the phone card in slot 2 and that it's being disabled. Finally, the report from the RoutingTable MBean indicates that the route for phone card 2 is being removed from the table.

11.5 *Summary*

This chapter introduced you to the relation service. The relation service provides a mechanism to conceptually relate MBeans. You can create relations modeled as MBeans to provide a way of working with MBeans as a group. Doing so increases the flexibility and usability of your management system.

If a user can collect a series of MBeans together in a logical unit and can operate on that logical unit, the management system can be developed to behave in a

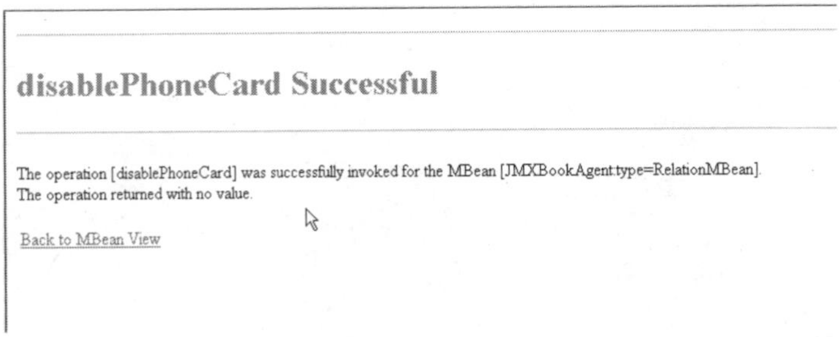

---

disablePhoneCard Successful

The operation [disablePhoneCard] was successfully invoked for the MBean [JMXBookAgent:type=RelationMBean].
The operation returned with no value.

Back to MBean View

Figure 11.8
Web browser view of disabling phone card 2 via the relation MBean

---

```
D:\Source\jmxbook>java jmxbook.ch3.JMXBookAgent

>>> START of JMXBook Agent

>>> CREATE the agent...

        CREATE the MBeanServer.

Agent is Ready for Service...

Relation MBean::Disabling Phone Card
PhoneCardMBean::PhoneCard #2 has been disabled
RoutingTableMBean::PhoneCard2 removed from  routing table
```

Figure 11.9
Agent standard output of disabling phone card 2 via the relation MBean

fashion that more readily models a real-world scenario. Typically, operators like to work at a logical level that closely resembles the business model they understand, as opposed to being required to have intimate knowledge of the internal implementation of the individual components. The relation MBean provides that capability.

Chapter 12 discusses the two remaining agent services: the monitoring and timer services.

More agent services: monitors and timers

- Examining the monitoring services provided by JMX
- Introducing the JMX timer service
- Extending the monitoring service to correct application faults

In the previous two chapters, we covered two important agent services: the relation service and the M-let service. This chapter continues coverage of agent services by examining the remaining two services: monitoring services and the timer service. Monitoring services are a valuable resource when you want to be informed of a state or behavioral change in a managed resource. The standard JMX monitors can observe MBean attributes and emit notifications when necessary to inform other objects or processes of a change. JMX-compliant agents provide three types of monitors, built as MBeans, which can monitor `String` and numeric MBean attributes.

In addition to the monitoring services, compliant agents provide a timer service. The JMX timer service allows users to send user-defined notifications at a given time, or at given intervals.

A robust management environment needs to be able to monitor itself and communicate with interested observers about its health, behavior, and important statistics. Using these last two agent services will increase the usefulness of your JMX environments. This chapter discusses all three JMX monitoring MBeans and the timer service. We'll examine their classes and purpose, and present some examples. Up first are the monitoring services.

12.1 *Monitoring MBean attributes with JMX*

JMX-compliant agents provide a set of Standard MBeans that together are considered the JMX monitoring services. Because these monitors are implemented as MBeans, users can instantiate and change them at runtime as needed. The monitored targets of these monitoring MBeans are other MBean attributes. Monitoring MBeans watch MBean attributes for predefined events and send notifications based on their own configuration. You can use these monitors to keep informed about state changes, workflow completions, or error messages.

For example, you can monitor something as critical as an MBean managing a real-time application's state, or as simple as a log file being rolled over. JMX monitors watch MBean attributes (the *observed value*) at user-configurable intervals (the *granularity period*). Each monitor creates a value called a *derived gauge* based on its observations of the observed MBean attribute, which it uses to determine whether to send and what type of notifications to send to its listeners.

Table 12.1 describes the three monitor types along with their main classes. You can see from the monitor classnames that we will be examining classes in a new package, `javax.management.monitor`. Based on the remaining information in table 12.1, you probably have more questions. However, before we move on to

Table 12.1 The three JMX monitor types

Monitor type	Classname	Description
String	`javax.management.monitor.StringMonitor`	Monitors a `String` attribute of an MBean
Gauge	`javax.management.monitor.GaugeMonitor`	Monitors MBean attributes of type `Float` or `Double` that can move within a set range of values (increasing or decreasing)
Counter	`javax.management.monitor.CounterMonitor`	Monitors MBean attributes of type `Byte`, `Integer`, `Short`, or `Long` that act as incremental counters

the specifics and examples of each monitor, we need to examine two things they all have in common: their super class and notification class.

12.1.1 *The monitoring foundation*

All JMX monitor MBeans have a common monitor base class and emit notification types contained in a common notification class. Before we examine each specific monitor type, we need to discuss these two classes. The following section covers the `javax.management.monitor.Monitor` class, which is the base class for all the provided JMX monitors.

The Monitor class

As already mentioned, this `Monitor` class (`javax.management.monitor` package) is the base class for JMX monitor MBeans. It defines common methods that all monitors need to function properly. In addition, it is defined as an MBean, allowing subclasses to interact with the MBean server to monitor observed MBean attributes.

The `Monitor` class also extends the `NotificationBroadcasterSupport` class and implements the `MBeanRegistration` interface. This ensures that all subclasses can emit notifications, and that they have a reference to the `MBeanServer` instance to which they belong (the reference is gained from the `preRegister()` method invocation of the `MBeanRegistration` interface; we discussed this interface in previous chapters).

However, the `Monitor` class is declared as an abstract class; therefore you must extend it in order to use it. Let's look at the methods of the class before we move forward. Table 12.2 lists its available methods. Notice that the table leaves out the methods implemented from the `MBeanRegistration` interface.

Table 12.2 The methods defined by the `javax.management.monitor.Monitor` class. This class is the base class for all JMX monitor MBeans.

Method	Description
`long getGranularityPeriod()`	Returns the observation interval of this monitor.
`String getObservedAttribute()`	Returns the name of the observed attribute.
`ObjectName getObservedObject()`	Returns the object name of the observed MBean.
`boolean isActive()`	Determines if this monitor has been started.
`void setGranularityPeriod( long period )`	Sets the observation interval of this monitor.
`void setObservedAttribute( String name )`	Sets the name of the attribute that will be monitored from the given MBean (set in the next method).
`void setObservedObject( Object-Name name )`	Sets the MBean that contains an attribute to observe. Only the object name of the MBean is needed; the monitor will interact with the MBean server to get the attribute value when set.
`abstract start()`	Starts observation of the set attribute.
`abstract stop()`	Stops observation of the set attribute.

All these methods are declared in the `javax.management.monitor.MonitorMBean` interface. Because this class implements its own MBean interface, it would be a Standard MBean if it were not an abstract class. (For more information about Standard MBeans, look back at chapter 4.)

Notice that two of the methods are undefined (declared abstract): `stop()` and `start()`. These two methods are implemented by subclasses, allowing each subclass to determine how the MBean monitors its observed value. As you might expect, these methods correspond to starting and stopping the monitor.

We should highlight two methods from this class: `setObservedObject()` and `setObservedAttribute()`. The first method tells the monitor which MBean in the MBean server to observe. You need only pass it an object name—it will use this object name value, combined with the attribute name set by the `setObservedAttribute()` method, to find the value of an MBean attribute. It does so at every monitoring interval (granularity period).

Also note that each monitor subclass provided by JMX monitors an attribute of a particular type, such as `String` or `Double`. However, the monitor MBeans do not validate the type of the attribute, only the type of the value returned from the `getAttribute()` method of the MBean server. In essence, this process lets you monitor an attribute whose value type is determined by its getter method (and possibly is different from the attribute's declared type).

The MonitorNotification class

Now let's examine the notification class used by all monitors: `javax.management.monitor.MonitorNotification`. This section will describe the notification class and some of the common notification types it contains. Sections discussing a specific monitor MBean will add any further notification types as they pertain to the particular monitor MBean. All of the notification types are presented as class member variables in the common notification class, but we will cover each type only as we need to. If you need to refresh your knowledge of the JMX notification mechanism, please look back at chapter 6.

The `MonitorNotification` class extends the basic `javax.management.Notification` class and therefore inherits the basic notification methods. In addition, it defines four more methods:

- `public Object getDerivedGauge()`—Returns the value computed from the monitor's last observation from the observed MBean attribute
- `public String getObservedAttribute()`—Returns the name of the observed MBean attribute
- `public ObjectName getObservedObject()`—Returns the object name of the observed MBean
- `public Object getTrigger()`—Returns the value (of the observed attribute) that triggered this notification to be sent

Remember that instances of this class are sent from monitors based on certain observed events (which are configured in the specific monitor)—that is why these methods are declared in this class. These methods give the listener much of the information it needs to make informed decisions. The last piece of information a listener would need from a notification is its notification type.

Recall that a notification type is a dot-separated `String` value that indicates the purpose of a notification. Each monitor MBean uses its own specific notification types, but the `MonitorNotification` class provides four types that are shared across all monitor MBeans. The `MonitorNotification` class also declares some public static final class members to denote the type values. Table 12.3 lists the types, along with their class members and short descriptions of when they should occur.

Table 12.3 Notification types that are common across all monitor MBeans, and the class members that represent them in the `MonitorNotification` class.

Notification type	Public static final class member	Description
`jmx.moni-tor.error.attribute`	OBSERVED_ATTRIBUTE_ERROR	The attribute is not found in the observed MBean.
`jmx.moni-tor.error.type`	OBSERVED_ATTRIBUTE_TYPE_ERROR	The attribute value type is not correct.
`jmx.moni-tor.error.object`	OBSERVED_OBJECT_ERROR	The observed MBean cannot be found.
`jmx.moni-tor.error.runtime`	RUNTIME_ERROR	A runtime error has occurred during monitoring.

If you look at the API reference for the `MonitorNotification` class, you will see more notification types than are listed in table 12.3. However, the remaining types are common to a subset of the JMX monitor MBeans, so we'll list them in the appropriate section.

Now that we have covered the foundations of the monitor MBeans available in all agents, it is time to look at the individual MBeans.

12.1.2 *Monitoring String values*

The first monitoring MBean we will discuss is the String monitor, which is represented by the class `javax.management.monitor.StringMonitor`. As mentioned in the previous section, all monitor MBeans extend the base class `Monitor`—the `StringMonitor` class is no exception.

This monitor type is the simplest of the three we will cover. A String monitor is used to observe an MBean attribute with a `String` value. The monitor compares the observed attribute with a preconfigured `String` pattern. This pattern is an actual `String` value; no wildcards can be used. The monitor can gather two events from its observed attribute:

- The observed `String` attribute matches the monitor's pattern.
- The observed `String` does not match the monitor's pattern.

However, even though the String monitor takes an observation at every observation interval, it may not observe an event. These two events are significant only if the observed attribute's value is different than the value from the previous observation interval. That means the monitor is interested only when the observed attribute changes to a match or a mismatch (unless it is the first observation by the monitor).

Remember that all monitors create a derived gauge value based on the value of their observations. In the `String` monitor case, the derived gauge value is always the value of the observed attribute.

Using the String monitor

You will develop a working example of this monitor after we discuss the remaining two monitors. However, we will mention its important methods now. A `StringMonitor` MBean's behavior is based on three values configured by the user. These values are configured by the invocation of the following methods:

- `setStringToCompare( String )`—Sets the internal `String` value to compare with the observed attribute
- `setNotifyDiffer( boolean )`—Tells the monitor to send a notification when the observed attribute changes to a non-matching value
- `setNotifiyMatch( boolean )`—Tells the monitor to send a notification when the observed attribute changes to a matching value

After setting the monitor MBean's `StringToCompare` attribute (and after configuring the observed MBean and attribute), you can invoke the monitor's `start()` method to begin observations. Remember, the monitor will send notifications (based on its configuration) only when the attribute transitions from a match to a non-match or vice versa. It will not continuously send notifications if the value always matches or always differs.

StringMonitor notifications

Based on the two events described in section 12.1.2, String monitors can send two more notification types in addition to the common notification types described in section 12.1.1. Recall that all monitors use the `MonitorNotification` class for sending notifications.

The following two types could be sent from a `StringMonitor` MBean that's operating normally:

- `jmx.monitor.string.matches`—Indicates that the monitor's observed attribute has changed to a matching value
- `jmx.monitor.string.differs`—Indicates that the monitor's observed attribute has changed to a differing value

You will see an example of the String monitor shortly. The next section covers the Gauge monitor MBean.

12.1.3 Monitoring a value range

The GaugeMonitor class is said to cover a range of values because it is observing an MBean attribute that could possibly cross a predefined threshold in the monitor. In order to prevent a possible flood of notifications, the Gauge monitor uses a range of values to cover the threshold. In this way, notifications won't be sent out when the observed attribute makes many small changes repeatedly over the threshold.

You accomplish such monitoring by configuring a GaugeMonitor MBean with a low threshold value and a high threshold value. The monitor sends notifications the first time the derived gauge (computed from the observed attribute value) crosses the low or high threshold after crossing the opposite threshold (unless it is the first occurrence of either).

For example, if the observed derived gauge crosses the high threshold, a notification is sent. If it then goes below the high threshold, and then rises above it again, no notification is sent. The observed attribute must first decrease below the low threshold (a notification could be sent for this event) and then cross the high threshold again in order for another high-threshold notification to be sent.

Computing the derived gauge

The Gauge monitor can compute its derived gauge value two ways. First, the derived gauge can be the value of the observed attribute at the current observation interval. Second, you can configure the GaugeMonitor MBean to compute its derived gauge by comparing the last two values of the observed attribute. The two values are stored from the last two observation intervals. Therefore, the derived gauge value is equal to the observed attribute's last observed value minus the observed value from the previous interval:

```
Derived Gauge = value now - value before
```

If the GaugeMonitor MBean is in its first observation interval, the derived gauge for the monitor is zero.

Using the Gauge monitor

Just like the String monitor, the Gauge monitor must be configured properly in order to operate. Table 12.4 lists the methods that implement the features described in the previous discussion of the Gauge monitor's behavior.

Note that table 12.4 shows only setter methods for the GaugeMonitor MBean's exposed attributes. However, the class also defines getter methods for the same attributes. For more information, look at the API reference for the GaugeMonitor class.

Table 12.4 The important methods of the `GaugeMonitor` class and their purpose. For each setter method, there is a corresponding getter method.

Method	Purpose
`setThresholds( Number high, Number low)`	Sets the high and low threshold values for the monitor using the `java.lang.Number` class
`setDifferenceMode( boolean )`	If true, tells the MBean to compute its derived gauge using the subtraction scenario already described
`setNotifyHigh( boolean )`	Tells the monitor to send notifications when a high-threshold event occurs
`setNotifyLow( boolean )`	Tells the monitor to send notifications when a low-threshold event occurs

Only two constraints exist on a `GaugeMonitor` MBean. First, the high and low threshold values must be of the same type as the observed attribute's value. Second, the high threshold value must be greater than or equal to the low threshold value. (Recall that Gauge monitors operate on `Float` and `Double` attribute value types.)

GaugeMonitor notifications

In our discussion of the `MonitorNotification` class, we left out one common notification type defined by that class. Both the `GaugeMonitor` class and the following `CounterMonitor` class can send notifications with the type `jmx.monitor.error.threshold`. However, this type has a different meaning for the two monitors. For the Gauge monitor, it means that either the low or high threshold value is not the same type as the observed attribute value. The Counter monitor is explained in the next section.

In addition to the common notification type, the Gauge monitor can send out two more notification types:

- `jmx.monitor.gauge.high`—Sent when the derived gauge has exceeded the high threshold value
- `jmx.monitor.gauge.low`—Sent when the derived gauge has exceeded the low threshold value

The following section discusses the final monitor MBean: the previously mentioned `CounterMonitor`.

12.1.4 *Monitoring a counted value*

The final monitor MBean we'll discuss is the CounterMonitor MBean. The CounterMonitor class defines an object that observes a numeric MBean attribute, watching for it to exceed a threshold value. The observed attribute is assumed to be positive and to have an increasing value (because it is a counter).

The observed counter attribute is allowed to have a maximum value that, when reached, causes the counter to roll over to its starting position. In order for the counter to roll over, the Counter monitor must know the maximum value, which it stores as its modulus value.

The Counter monitor will send a notification each time the observed counter crosses its threshold value. This does not mean a notification will be sent for every observation interval where the counter is above the threshold—the counter must go below the threshold after each notification in order to send another notification.

The Counter monitor also supports an offset value that is added to the threshold value when the observed counter exceeds the threshold. This offset allows users to monitor a counter moving through increments. After the counter has exceeded the threshold value, if the monitor contains an offset value, the monitor will keep adding the offset value to the threshold value until it is greater than the counter. If the monitor also contains a modulus value (the observed counter's maximum value before rollover), and if adding the offset value exceeds the modulus, the threshold will reset to its original value.

Computing the derived gauge

Just like the previous monitor, the CounterMonitor MBean can compute its derived gauge two ways. The method it uses depends on the monitor's configuration by the user. If the monitor's DifferenceMode attribute is true, then the derived gauge is calculated like the GaugeMonitor MBean's. That is, the monitor subtracts the previous observed counter value from the current value. If the result is negative, the monitor will then add the modulus value. Otherwise, if the result is positive, it is the final value of the derived gauge.

If the DifferenceMode is false, the derived gauge value is simply the value of the counter in the latest observation interval.

Using the Counter monitor

Table 12.5 lists the methods of the CounterMonitor MBean class that support the behavior described in the previous section. Like the previous tables, this one doesn't include the getter methods.

Table 12.5 The important methods of the `CounterMonitor` class and their purpose. For each setter method, there is a corresponding getter method.

Method	Purpose
`setDifferenceMode( boolean )`	Tells the monitor which method to use (see previous description) to compute its derived gauge
`setModulus( Number )`	Sets the observed counter's maximum value
`setNotify( boolean )`	Tells the MBean whether to send notifications
`setOffset( Number )`	Sets the offset value of the monitor
`setThreshold( Number )`	Sets the threshold value of the monitor for comparison to the observed counter

The final aspect of the Counter monitor to discuss is its notification types.

CounterMonitor notifications

The `CounterMonitor` class shares a common notification type with the `GaugeMonitor`: the type `jmx.monitor.error.threshold`. This type indicates that the monitor's threshold, offset, or modulus is not the same type as the observed counter attribute value.

In addition to the common notification types, the `CounterMonitor` class adds the notification type `jmx.monitor.counter.threshold`. This notification type indicates that the observed counter attribute has reached or exceeded the monitor's threshold value.

12.2 *Monitor examples*

We have discussed each monitor MBean's behavior and important methods and examined the `StringMonitor`, `GaugeMonitor`, and `CounterMonitor` classes. Now it is time to work through some examples.

To test these monitors, you need to create a subject MBean to monitor. You will use the `JMXBookAgent` class as your agent to contain your monitors and the subject MBean. Your monitoring subject MBean will be called `ObservableObject`; it implements the interface `ObservableObjectMBean`. The following section creates the MBean and the agent.

You will also create a simple startup program—the `MonitoringSetup` class—that uses the RMI connector to create three monitors and to act as a notification listener for each. In addition, the `MonitoringSetup` class will add the `ObservableObject` to the agent. After you create all the MBeans, you will use the HTML adapter to change the values of the target MBean in order to produce events in the monitoring MBeans.

12.2.1 *Creating the example agent and MBean*

The first thing you need to do is make the ObservableObject MBean. Remember that this MBean will be the target of all the monitor MBeans. Your MBean in this case is a Standard MBean, because it will implement its own MBean interface. This MBean is designed to be observable by all three types of JMX standard monitors (String, Gauge, and Counter), so you will give it an attribute applicable to all three types of monitors. Here is the MBean interface for the MBean:

```
package jmxbook.ch12;
public interface ObservableObjectMBean
{
  public String getString();
  public void setString( String value );
  public Float getGauge();
  public void setGauge( Float value );
  public Integer getCounter();
  public void setCounter( Integer value );
}
```

As you can tell, this MBean will have three read/write attributes. Each attribute corresponds to the particular type of monitor that will test it. The initial values for these attributes will be set through the HTML adapter of the agent.

Listing 12.1 shows the implementing MBean class for the ObservableObject-MBean. It is a simple class, so we won't examine it too closely. It stores the attributes passed to the setter methods and returns the attributes through the getter methods.

Listing 12.1 ObservableObject.java

```
package jmxbook.ch12;

public class ObservableObject implements ObservableObjectMBean
{
    private Integer counter = null;
    private Float   gauge   = null;
    private String  string  = null;

    public ObservableObject()
    {
      counter = new Integer( 0 );
      gauge   = new Float( 0 );
      string  = "abc";
    }
```

```
     public String getString()
     {
       return string;
     }

     public void setString( String value )
     {
       string = value;
     }

     public Float getGauge()
     {
       return gauge;
     }

     public void setGauge( Float value )
     {
       gauge = value;
     }

     public Integer getCounter()
     {
       return counter;
     }

     public void setCounter( Integer value )
     {
       counter = value;
     }

}
```

All changes to the MBean's attribute take place via the HTML adapter. Once you have the agent created and running, you will alter the values of this target MBean and watch the different types of notifications that are received from the monitors.

The next thing you need to do is write the MonitoringSetup class. Recall that this class will register your target MBean and an MBean for each type of monitor MBean. In addition, this simple program will remain active to act as a notification listener to the monitors. Listing 12.2 shows the MonitoringSetup class.

Listing 12.2 MonitoringSetup.java

```
package jmxbook.ch12;

import jmxbook.ch3.*;
import javax.management.*;
import javax.management.monitor.*;
import com.sun.jdmk.comm.*;

public class MonitoringSetup implements NotificationListener
```

```
 {
    public MonitoringSetup()
    {
     try
     {

       RmiConnectorClient client = RMIClientFactory.getClient();

       ObjectName sm = new ObjectName( "JMXBookAgent:name=string");
       client.createMBean( "javax.management.monitor.StringMonitor",
                           sm);
       client.addNotificationListener( sm, this, null, null );

       ObjectName gm = new ObjectName( "JMXBookAgent:name=gauge");
       client.createMBean( "javax.management.monitor.GaugeMonitor",
                           gm );
       client.addNotificationListener( gm, this, null, null );

      ObjectName cm = new ObjectName( "JMXBookAgent:name=counter");
      client.createMBean( "javax.management.monitor.CounterMonitor",
                           cm );
      client.addNotificationListener( cm, this, null, null );

       ObjectName oo = new ObjectName( "JMXBookAgent:name=subject");
       client.createMBean( "jmxbook.ch12.ObservableObject", oo );

       }
     catch( Exception e )
     {
       ExceptionUtil.printException( e );
     }
       }

    public void handleNotification( Notification not, Object obj )
    {
      String type = not.getType();
      System.out.println( type );
    }

    public static void main( String args[] )
    {
      MonitoringSetup setup = new MonitoringSetup();
    }
 }
```

This setup class registers all four MBeans exactly like the other setup classes you have already examined. It does not contain any code that differs from what you have seen, so we leave the examination for you.

After successfully starting the agent and running the MonitoringSetup class, you need to open a web browser to http://localhost:9092. You should see the Agent View page presented by the HTML adapter. In addition to the MBean-

`ServerDelegate` MBean, you should see the `ObservableObject` MBean (the subject MBean) and the three monitor MBeans. If you do not see all the MBeans in the Agent View, refresh the page after a few moments.

To test the monitors, you need to set a few attributes for each one so it can observe your subject MBean. The following sections explain what you need to do.

12.2.2 *Testing the String monitor*

The `StringMonitor` MBean operates over the `String` attribute of the `Observable-Object` MBean. Table 12.6 lists the attributes of the `StringMonitor` MBean that you need to set, along with the appropriate values.

Table 12.6 The attributes you need to configure in the `StringMonitor` MBean in order to monitor the `String` attribute of the `ObservableObject` MBean.

Monitor attribute	Value	Description
NotifyDiffer	true	Tells the MBean to send notifications when the observed attribute differs from the monitor's value
NotifyMatch	true	Tells the MBean to send notifications when the observed attribute differs from the monitor's value
ObservedAttribute	String	Name of the observed attribute from the subject MBean
ObservedObject	JMXBookAgent:name=subject	Object name of the subject MBean that will be monitored by this String monitor
StringToCompare	Abc	The value the monitor will compare to the observed attribute (you can pick any value)

Select the `StringMonitor` in the HTML adapter and set the attributes as described in table 12.6 (don't forget to click the Apply button). After all the values are set, click the Start button to invoke the `start()` method. To receive notifications from the String monitor, set the `String` attribute of your subject MBean to match the value set in the String monitor. You should see the following appear in the agent output:

```
jmx.monitor.string.matches
```

If you again return to the `StringMonitor` MBean View, you can see that the String monitor's derived gauge is equal to the value set in the subject MBean's `String` attribute. Now go back and change the `String` parameter of the subject MBean to a value different than the value in the String monitor. You should eventually see the following notification type appear in the agent output:

```
jmx.monitor.string.differs
```

Play around with the different attributes of the String monitor before moving on the next section, which discusses the GaugeMonitor MBean.

12.2.3 *Testing the Gauge monitor*

The GaugeMonitor MBean operates over the Gauge attribute of the ObservableObject MBean. Table 12.7 lists the attributes of the GaugeMonitor MBean that you need to set, along with appropriate values.

Table 12.7 The attributes you need to configure in the GaugeMonitor MBean in order to monitor the Gauge attribute of the ObservableObject MBean.

Monitor attribute	Value	Description
NotifyHigh	true	Tells the MBean to send a notification if the observed attribute reaches or exceeds the high threshold
NotifyLow	true	Tells the MBean to send a notification if the observed attribute reaches or moves below the low threshold
ObservedAttribute	Gauge	Name of the observed attribute from the subject MBean
ObservedObject	JMXBookAgent:name=subject	Object name of the subject MBean that will be monitored by this Gauge monitor
HighThreshold	4.1	High threshold value
LowThreshold	2.1	Low threshold value

You will test this monitor just like the previous MBean. Select the GaugeMonitor in the HTML adapter and set the attributes as described in table 12.7, and then invoke the start() method by clicking the Start button. Now go back to the ObservableObject and set the Gauge attribute to a value above the high threshold of the Gauge monitor. You should see the following appear in the agent output:

```
jmx.monitor.gauge.high
```

Once again, go back to the ObservableObject MBean and change the Gauge attribute to a value below the low threshold value of the GaugeMonitor MBean. The agent will receive the following notification type:

```
jmx.monitor.gauge.low
```

Spend some time working with the Gauge monitor so you fully understand its derived gauge value; you can see that value in the monitor's MBean View. Then move on to the following section, which discusses the Counter monitor.

12.2.4 *Testing the Counter monitor*

The `CounterMonitor` MBean operates over the `Counter` attribute of the `ObservableObject` MBean. Table 12.8 lists the attributes of the `CounterMonitor` MBean that you need to set, along with appropriate values.

Table 12.8 The attributes you need to configure in the `CounterMonitor` MBean in order to monitor the `Counter` attribute of the `ObservableObject` MBean.

Monitor attribute	Value	Description
Notify	true	Tells the MBean to send a notification if the observed attribute reaches or exceeds the threshold
ObservedAttribute	Counter	Name of the observed attribute from the subject MBean
ObservedObject	JMXBookAgent:name=subject	Object name of the subject MBean that will be monitored by this Gauge monitor
Threshold	3	Threshold value
Offset	3	Value of the offset that will be added to the threshold each time the observed attribute reaches or exceeds the threshold
DifferenceMode	False	Tells the monitor not to compute the derived gauge as simply the value of the observed attribute

Select the subject MBean again and set its `Counter` attribute to 4 (a value above the threshold of the `CounterMonitor` MBean). You should see the following notification type in the agent output:

```
jmx.monitor.counter.threshold
```

After receiving this notification, go back and look at the MBean View of the `CounterMonitor` MBean and notice that the threshold is now 6. The monitor has incremented the threshold with the offset value. Every time the observed attribute reaches or exceeds the threshold, the monitor increases the threshold with the offset.

With that last test, we have completed our coverage of the JMX monitoring services. Because the monitoring services are considered a mandatory part of

JMX agents as defined by the JMX specification, you can always use them with your JMX applications. The next section discusses the final agent service defined by the JMX specification that must be present in all JMX agents.

12.3 *Taking corrective measures*

Monitors are typically used to send alerts that inform listeners about critical events, state changes, and so forth, so that other processes or users can take a particular action. In chapter 1, we stated that an ideal management environment would be able to take corrective action on its own (and still inform its listeners about the triggering event). One way to do this is to subclass a JMX monitor (or use one) and, upon observing the triggering event, take appropriate action before involving an outside process via a notification.

To demonstrate this idea, you will do something a little simpler. The `CorrectiveStringMonitor` MBean subclasses the JMX `StringMonitor` MBean and adds the functionality that if the observed attribute reaches the "differs" state, a particular method on a particular MBean will be invoked. This added functionality is little more than you can accomplish by receiving the monitor notification and executing a method, but it demonstrates how you can configure an MBean to take some corrective measures before sending out an alerting notification to a user.

The following code is the `CorrectiveStringMonitor` MBean. It declares one additional method that allows users to set the `ObjectName` value and method name that should be invoked when the observed `String` differs:

```
package jmxbook.ch12;

import javax.management.*;
import javax.management.monitor.*;

public interface CorrectiveStringMonitorMBean extends
    StringMonitorMBean
{
    public void setExecutableMethodOnDiffer(
                    ObjectName name, String methodName );
}
```

Notice that the interface also extends the `StringMonitorMBean` interface. It does so to ensure that the `CorrectiveStringMonitor` MBean includes the management interface of the `StringMonitor` MBean. Listing 12.3 shows the MBean class implementing the interface.

Listing 12.3 CorrectiveStringMonitorMBean.java

```java
package jmxbook.ch12;

import javax.management.*;
import javax.management.monitor.*;

public class CorrectiveStringMonitor extends StringMonitor
                            implements CorrectiveStringMonitorMBean
{
    private ObjectName executeName = null;
    private String executeMethod = null;

    public CorrectiveStringMonitor()
    {
        super();
    }

    public void setExecutableMethodOnDiffer(
                    ObjectName name, String methodName )
    {
        this.executeName = name;
        this.executeMethod = methodName;
    }

    public void sendNotification( Notification not )
    {
        if( not.getType().equals(
            MonitorNotification.STRING_TO_COMPARE_VALUE_DIFFERED ) )
        {
          try
          {
            server.invoke( executeName, executeMethod, null, null );
          }
          catch( Exception e )
          {
            e.printStackTrace();
          }
        }

        super.sendNotification( not );
    }
}
```

❶ Override sendNotification() to take corrective step

❶ The `CorrectiveStringMonitor` class overrides its parent's `sendNotification()` method in order to watch for the `String`-differ notification. For this demonstration, this notification tells the MBean to take its corrective measure. When an instance of the class notices a notification being sent of the differ type, it invokes the method on the MBean with the given `ObjectName` value. Notice that the class uses the `server MBeanServer` reference from its parent.

This class may be overly simple, but it highlights the possibility of implementing MBeans that can be preconfigured to take corrective steps when system errors occur. By using JMX monitors to observe managed attributes, you can design MBeans to reroute messaging, reconfigure services, or start new processes.

12.4 *Sending dated notifications: the timer service*

Now that we have discussed the JMX monitoring services, let's switch gears and cover the JMX timer service. The timer service is an MBean class available to every JMX agent that emits user-defined notifications at specific times. Each notification from the timer service contains a date and time when it should be emitted. Alternatively, the timer service can continue to send a particular notification at intervals once a date has been reached.

Other MBeans can use a service such as the timer to send notifications of any type. For instance, if an MBean is not a `NotificationBroadcaster`, it cannot emit notifications. However, by using the timer service, it can send notifications at will. Such a scenario does not take into account the timing abilities of the timer, but it shows a simple use of the service.

In this part of this chapter we will examine the classes in the `javax.management.timer` package, including the `Timer` MBean and its notification class. You will also create some examples showing the various features of the timer service.

12.4.1 *Examining the timer*

The first class we need to discuss is `javax.management.timer.Timer`. The `Timer` class is a JMX class that defines a Standard MBean containing the JMX timer service. Before we begin examining individual methods, you need to understand more about how the timer works.

Timer behavior

As you read in the introductory section, the timer service is an MBean that emits dated notifications once, or repeatedly at intervals. The timer service is given the dated notifications by the user. Every notification emitted by a `Timer` MBean is an instance of the class `TimerNotification`, but the notification type is user defined. In this manner, many notification types are emitted by the service even though they are all of the same Java type.

Users add notifications to the timer by invoking one of its `addNotification()` methods. (We will examine these methods more closely in a moment.) Through these methods, a user configures the behavior of the timer surrounding a particular notification.

For example, you add a notification to the timer by specifying a notification type, a message, user data, and a date. Apart from the normal notification data (type, message, and user data) the date is the only behavior-controlling parameter: it tells the timer to send a notification with the provided data on the provided date. In addition to the date, you can specify the following:

- *Period*—If specified, indicates that a notification is to be sent repeatedly. This value supplies the timer with an interval in milliseconds between notification occurrences. If no period is given, the timer assumes that the notification should be sent only once.

- *Number of occurrences*—Tells the timer how many times to send a particular notification once its date has been reached.

Each notification added to a `Timer` MBean should have a date later than the current date (where *date* refers to date and time). If you add a notification with an earlier date, one of three things will happen, depending on the configuration supplied with the notification:

- If a period was specified for the notification, the timer will keep adding the period to the notification date until the date is later than the current date. When the date is corrected, the notification is added to the timer for sending.

- If a period and a number of occurrences were specified for the notification, then the timer will add the period value to the date as many times as the number of occurrences value will allow. Each time the period value is added to the date, the number of occurrences is reduced by one. If the number of occurrences is reduced to zero, and the date is still earlier than the current date, an `IllegalArgumentException` is thrown.

- An `IllegalArgumentException` is thrown if no period was specified for the notification. Without a period value, the timer cannot correct the date.

When a notification is finally added to the timer's notification list, a unique id is returned to the user. This id identifies the newly added notification and is sent with each emitted occurrence of the notification. In addition, this id should be used when retrieving information about a notification to be sent via the other `Timer` methods. You will see this as we examine the methods of the `Timer` class.

One last interesting part of the timer's behavior is best described with an example. You start and stop `Timer` MBeans the same way as monitor MBeans: by using the `start()` and `stop()` methods. Imagine that you add many notifications to a `Timer` MBean before you invoke its `start()` method, and some of the added notifications' dates have already been reached. You can configure the timer to send all past notifications by setting its `SendPastNotifications` attribute to `true`.

If the timer's `SendPastNotifications` attribute is `true`, all one-time notifications with a date before the current date are sent. The timer then sends all periodic notifications that could not be sent by updating their dates with previously described updating rules. If a periodic notification with an earlier date must be sent, then it will be sent as many times as it would have been if it had a correct date. The `SendPastNotifications` attribute only applies to notifications whose time has come and passed before the timer was started. The timer will ignore any notification added with a date earlier than the date when the `addNotification()` method was invoked.

The Timer class

Now that you understand the `Timer` MBean's behavior, let's examine some of the methods available in the `Timer` class. Rather than examine every method from the `Timer` class, we've listed them in table 12.9. Most of the methods in the table correspond to pieces of the behavior described in the previous section.

Table 12.9 The public methods of the `Timer` class

Method	Description
`Integer addNotification( String type, String message, Object user-data, Date date )`	Adds a notification with the specified date. This notification will be sent only once.
`Integer addNotification( String type, String message, Object user-data, Date date, long period )`	Adds a notification with the specified date and period. This notification will be sent once every period after the start date.
`Integer addNotification( String type, String message, Object user-data, Date date, long period, long nbOccurrences )`	Same as the previous method, but the notification will be sent only `nbOccurrences` times.
`Vector getAllNotificationIDs()`	Returns all the notification ids contained in the timer.
`Date getDate( Integer id )`	Returns the date for the notification with the id specified.
`Long getNbOccurrences ( Integer id )`	Returns the number of occurrences for the notification with the id specified.

Table 12.9   **The public methods of the `Timer` class** *(continued)*

Method	Description
`Vector getNotificationIDs( String type )`	Returns the ids of all the notifications with the supplied notification type.
`String getNotificationMessage ( Integer id )`	Returns the message for the notification with the id specified.
`String getNotificationType( Integer id )`	Returns the type for the notification with the id specified.
`Object getNotificationUserData ( Integer id )`	Returns the user data for the notification with the id specified.
`Long getPeriod( Integer id )`	Returns the period for the notification with the id specified.
`boolean getSendPastNotifications()`	Returns the value of the `SendPastNotifications` attribute.
`void removeNotification( Integer id )`	Removes the notification with the id supplied.
`void removeNotifications( String type )`	Removes notifications with the specified notification type.
`void setSendPastNotifications ( boolean value )`	Sets the `SendPastNotifications` attribute.
`void start()`	Starts the timer.
`void stop()`	Stops the timer.

As you can tell, the timer service is a fairly simple concept, and we don't need to cover each method. The best way to get a better understanding of the timer is to write an example. The following section presents an example of using the timer service.

12.5 *Using the timer service*

To build a working example of the timer service, you will again use your JMX-BookAgent class. Listing 12.4 shows a new method to add to the JMXBookAgent class. The `startTimerService()` method creates and registers a timer service for your agent.

Listing 12.4   The startTimerService() of the JMXBookAgent class

```
protected void startTimerService()
{
    Timer timer = new Timer();
```

```
ObjectName timerName = null;

try
{
  timerName =
      new ObjectName( "JMXBookAgent:name=timer" );

  server.registerMBean( timer, timerName );
  timer.setSendPastNotifications( true );

  //start timer
  timer.start();

    }
  catch( Exception e )
  {
      ExceptionUtil.printException( e );
  }
}
```

After creating and registering a `Timer` MBean, you set its `SendPastNotifications`
attribute to `true`. Recall that a `true` value for this attribute tells the MBean, once
started, to send any notification whose date has already passed. By setting it to
`true`, you are assured that your notifications will be sent. In addition to adding
this method, you need to import the `javax.management.timer` package and
invoke the method from the agent's constructor.

Listing 12.5 shows the `TimerSetup` class, which is used to test the newly added
timer service. This setup class adds an instance of the `Timer` MBean to your
agent. In addition, it adds two notification types to the `Timer` MBean.

Listing 12.5 TimerSetup.java

```
package jmxbook.ch12;

import jmxbook.ch3.*;
import javax.management.*;
import com.sun.jdmk.comm.*;
import java.util.*;

public class TimerSetup implements NotificationListener
{
  public TimerSetup()
  {
    try
    {
      RmiConnectorClient client = RMIClientFactory.getClient();
      ObjectName timerName = new ObjectName(
                    "JMXBookAgent:name=timer");
```

```
        Object[] args2 = { "ch12.timer.periodic", "message", "data",
                           new Date(), new Long( 6000 ) };
        String[] sig2  = { "java.lang.String", "java.lang.String",
                    "java.lang.Object", "java.util.Date", "long" };

        client.invoke( timerName, "addNotification", args2, sig2 );

        Object[] args3 = { "ch12.timer.periodic20", "message", "data",
                  new Date(), new Long( 2000 ), new Long( 20 )  };

       String[] sig3  = { "java.lang.String", "java.lang.String",
                          "java.lang.Object", "java.util.Date",
                          "long", "long" };

        client.invoke( timerName, "addNotification", args3, sig3 );

        client.addNotificationListener( timerName, this, null, null );
          }
      catch( Exception e )
      {
        ExceptionUtil.printException( e );
      }

    }

    public void handleNotification( Notification not, Object obj )
    {
      String type = not.getType();
      System.out.println( type );
    }

    public static void main( String args[] )
    {
      TimerSetup setup = new TimerSetup();
    }
  }
```

You use two of the three overloaded addNotification() methods to add a notification. You add a repeating notification to be sent every six seconds and a repeating notification to be sent every two seconds with 20 occurrences. The notification types are ch12.timer.periodic and ch12.timer.periodic20. All notifications are added with the current date as their sending date.

12.5.1 *Testing the timer service*

After running the new JMXBookAgent and the TimerSetup class, you should expect something like the following for output:

```
ch12.timer.periodic20
ch12.timer.periodic
ch12.timer.periodic20
```

```
ch12.timer.periodic20
ch12.timer.periodic
ch12.timer.periodic20
ch12.timer.periodic20
ch12.timer.periodic20
ch12.timer.periodic
```

This is just a sample of the generated output. The notification type `ch12.timer.peri-odic` should print out every six seconds, and the `ch12.timer.periodic12` type should print out 20 times, once every two seconds.

12.6 *Summary*

This chapter finished the agent services portion of the book by discussing the monitoring and timer services that are present in all JMX-compliant agents. This chapter showed how you can use the monitoring services to observe MBean attributes with `String` and numeric value types. In addition, you can use the monitors to send notifications based on the events generated from observing their target MBean attributes. The chapter presented all three monitor types: String, Gauge, and Counter. In addition, we presented an example that demonstrates how you might use monitors to take corrective action upon observing a certain condition in the watched MBean attribute.

The second half of the chapter examined the timer service. The timer service allows you to emit custom notification types at predefined intervals. You can tell the timer to send the dated notifications once, or to send them periodically after their due date has been reached. In addition, if notifications have passed their due dates before the timer has started, you can optionally ask the timer to send all past-due notifications so that none are lost.

This chapter concludes the third part of the book. Part 4 of the book discusses using JMX with Java J2EE.

Part 4

Using JMX with the J2EE platform

Part 4 of this book presents some examples of using JMX with the J2EE platform. As both JMX and J2EE are adopted by the developer community, you will begin to see JMX used to manage and support enterprise applications. Toward this end, we present two chapters in this part that discuss the Java Message Service and Enterprise JavaBeans.

Chapter 13 begins the coverage by introducing using JMX with the Java Message Service. This chapter examines a home theater system that combines the two technologies. In this chapter, you use the Publish-Subscribe mode of JMX combined with an MBean to provide macros for an automated lighting system.

Chapter 14 uses JMX with Enterprise JavaBeans. In this chapter, you use MBeans to provide visibility into the user login component of an application. From a management console, you can disable a user's account and retrieve the number of login attempts.

Using JMX with the
Java Message Service

- Introducing the Java Massage Service
- Exploring ways to use JMX and JMS together
- Creating a JMS subscriber MBean
- Publishing a JMS message from an MBean

In this chapter, you will combine JMX technology with the Java Message Service (JMS). JMS is part of the J2EE platform and provides enterprise messaging for J2EE applications. This chapter uses a simple example to show how you can add functionality to JMS applications using MBeans. In addition, the example shows how MBeans can give you a view into the messaging of a JMS application for diagnostics and management.

13.1 *The Java Message Service*

Enterprise messaging is an essential tool for building enterprise applications. It provides a standard way for applications to communicate in an asynchronous fashion. JMS supports two models of messaging: Point-to-Point and Publish-Subscribe. Point-to-Point messaging lets a sender send a message to a single recipient, whereas Publish-Subscribe allows a sender to "broadcast" a message to several recipients. In both cases, the message sender and message receiver behave in an asynchronous manner, meaning that the receiver does not necessarily have to be present when the message is sent.

In the Point-to-Point model, the message is queued for later consumption. In Publish-Subscribe mode, a consumer can choose two different types of subscription. A *durable* subscription ensures a consumer will receive all messages that are published, because all published messages will be queued by the JMS provider until retrieved. Alternatively, with a *normal* subscription, the subscriber must be present and subscribed to receive published messages. In this chapter, we will use Publish-Subscribe with a normal subscription.

In Publish-Subscribe mode, applications observe *topics*. A topic is the destination for a set of messages. JMS clients publish and/or subscribe to a particular topic for message connectivity.

JMS implementations adhere to the interfaces defined in the J2EE platform. When developing JMS applications, you write your code according to the interfaces. The only difference between JMS implementations is the way you deploy your applications. (If you need more information about JMS, go to http://www.javasoft.com.)

13.2 *Combining JMX with JMS*

Combining JMS and JMX opens many possibilities for Java applications. Using JMS, you can transform your management system so that it acts as a driver for your applications. It can also receive messages indicating the health of an application. With an application built using JMS in the Publish-Subscribe mode, you can use JMX to build a management application that uses the messaging capabilities in a non-intrusive manner.

For example, imagine that an integration workflow tool drives a set of applications in a sequenced manner by using JMS messaging to signal the start of the next step in a workflow. If the tool uses the Publish-Subscribe method for driving the workflow, you can create an MBean that subscribes to the messages sent out by the tool. In this manner, you can monitor the status of the tool and workflow without interfering or accessing it directly. An MBean used this way can acquire knowledge of the internal operations of the workflow tool without your having to write any special access code. The MBean can be a generic JMS subscriber, and therefore can work with many different types of message-publishing applications.

In addition, you can rapidly construct a management application that takes control of the workflow system for cases of debugging or testing. A management application can start workflows directly from the management system, or even change the operation of the workflow by publishing its own messages. JMS provides a convenient mechanism for you to integrate your management system with other applications.

13.3 *Driving a home theater system*

To demonstrate how you can combine JMX with a JMS application, we will describe an automated home theater system. Suppose you work for a company that develops home theater control applications. Your company is a value-added provider of a lighting control system. The lighting control system uses JMS messaging to drive components based on control commands received from a remote control. The software that receives the lighting commands also allows macros to be defined. Macro capability allows scenes to be defined and executed—for example, a "romantic" macro might dim the lights and play soft music.

JMX is used not only to provide the macro capability, but also to provide management access into the home theater system. The application uses a controller MBean that listens for all messages from the lighting system and publishes device control messages that execute different functions that make up a macro. These messages are published to a message bus using JMS. Figure 13.1 shows the architecture for this application.

As you can see, the controller MBean will subscribe to control messages just like the lighting control command processor. When receiving a particular message, it will check to see if it has a macro defined for that message. If so, it will then

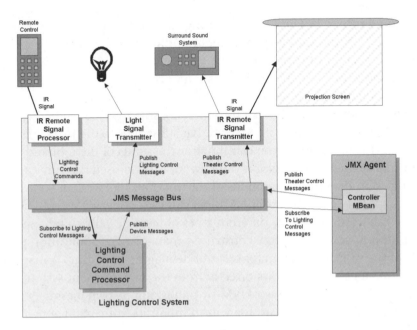

Figure 13.1 Lighting control system with JMX management application

publish messages that provide the added functionality. The lighting controller does not even know the added functionality exists—the MBean is truly a nonintrusive solution.

For this example, you want to add functionality to the system when the homeowner sends the MOVIELIGHTSOn command. The MOVIELIGHTSOn message sets the lights to a certain level, and also tells the controller MBean to publish a command to lower the projection screen and turn on the surround-sound system. Similarly, upon receipt of the MOVIELIGHTSOff command, the MBean raises the projection screen and turns off the surround-sound system.

Based on figure 13.1, this example needs one MBean, a JMS subscriber, and a JMS publisher. For debugging capabilities, the JMS subscriber will act as the IR signal transmitter that sends the final messages to the appropriate devices. For our purposes, this process will print the messages to standard out. The JMS publisher will send the control messages that simulate the IR signal processor that forwards commands received from the remote control.

The MBean will listen for commands published to the message bus of the lighting control system. Upon receipt of a recognized command, the MBean will determine the appropriate macro to execute and issue the messages needed to complete it. Not only will the MBean perform valuable functions in the home theater system, but it will also provide access into the system for outside management tools.

13.3.1 *Writing the example*

For this example, you will use the JBoss open-source J2EE container as the provider for JMS. You will configure the JBoss environment after writing all the code. For this JMS system, you need to configure two *topics* for message publishing. The system has one topic called `controlMessages` and another called `deviceMessages`.

The MBean will subscribe to the `controlMessages` topic in order to observe lighting commands from the remote control. The debugging client (IR signal transmitter) for the devices will subscribe to the `deviceMessages` topic. When the MBean recognizes the `MOVIELIGHTSOn` control message, it will publish the `SurroundOn` and `ScreenDown` messages to the `deviceMessages` topic. Alternatively, when the MBean sees the `MOVIELIGHTSOff` message, it will send the `SurroundOff` and `ScreenUp` device messages.

The following list shows the tasks you must complete to construct this example:

- Create the application's MBean.
- Construct the IR signal transmitter (your debugger).
- Write the setup class to register the MBean in a JMX agent.
- Construct the IR signal processor (your publisher).

The next section begins the example by constructing the controller MBean.

Constructing the main controller MBean

The MBean for this application will listen to all messages published to the `controlMessages` topic. It will make decisions based on the messages received and publish messages to each device in order to complete a designated macro. In addition, its management interface will provide direct access to its macros for a management application. Listing 13.1 shows the interface for the MBean.

Listing 13.1 JMSControllerMBean.java

```
package jmxbook.ch13;

public interface JMSControllerMBean
{
  public void turnOnHomeTheater();
  public void turnOffHomeTheater();
}
```

The two methods declared by this interface represent the two macros you have defined for the MBean. The turnOnHomeTheater() method makes the MBean publish the messages that cause the sound system to activate and the projector screen to drop. The turnOffHomeTheater() method sends the messages to deactivate the sound system and raise the screen. These two methods grant management applications the ability to invoke their macros without the use of messages from the lighting application (remote control).

Listing 13.2 shows the class for the controller MBean. It implements the JMX-ControllerMBean interface as well as the MessageListener interface from the javax.jmx package. The MessageListener interface declares the onMessage() method that is invoked when a message is sent to the topic to which the MBean is subscribed (controlMessages).

Listing 13.2   JMSController.java

```java
package jmxbook.ch13;

import javax.naming.Context;
import javax.naming.InitialContext;
import javax.naming.NamingException;

import javax.jms.TopicPublisher;
import javax.jms.TopicConnectionFactory;
import javax.jms.TopicConnection;
import javax.jms.TopicSession;
import javax.jms.TopicSubscriber;
import javax.jms.Topic;
import javax.jms.Message;
import javax.jms.TextMessage;
import javax.jms.Session;
import javax.jms.MessageListener;
import javax.jms.JMSException;

public class JMSController implements MessageListener,
                                      JMSControllerMBean
{
    private TopicConnection         topicConnection=null;
    private TopicSession            topicSession=null;
    private TopicSubscriber         topicSubscriber=null;
    private Topic                   topic=null;
    private TopicConnectionFactory  topicFactory=null;
    private int                     count_=0;
    private Context                 context=null;

    public JMSController() throws JMSException, NamingException
    {
        String          factoryJNDI="TopicConnectionFactory";
        String          topicJNDI="topic/controlMessages";
```

```
    // Get the initial context
    System.out.println("Getting Initial Context:");
    context = new InitialContext();
    System.out.println("Got Initial Context:"+context);

    // Get the connection factory
    System.out.println("Getting Topic Factory:");
    topicFactory = (TopicConnectionFactory)
                context.lookup(factoryJNDI);
    System.out.println("Got Topic Factory:"+topicFactory);

    // Create the connection
    topicConnection = topicFactory.createTopicConnection();

    // Create the session
    topicSession=topicConnection.createTopicSession(false,
                            Session.AUTO_ACKNOWLEDGE);

    // Look up the destination
    topic = (Topic)context.lookup(topicJNDI);

    // Create a subscriber
    topicSubscriber =
        topicSession.createSubscriber(topic);

    // Set the message listener,
    // which is this class.since we implement
    // the MessageListener interface
    topicSubscriber.setMessageListener(this);

    topicConnection.start();
}
public void onMessage( Message m )
{
  Topic            topic=null;
  TopicPublisher   topicPublisher=null;
  TopicSession     sendTopicSession=null;
  TextMessage      message=null;
  String           msg=null;
  String           msg2=null;

  try
  {
    msg = ((TextMessage)m).getText();
    if( msg.equals("MOVIELIGHTSOn")  )
    {
      msg="SurroundOn";
      msg2="ScreenDown";
      publishMessages(msg,msg2);
    }
    else if( msg.equals("MOVIELIGHTSOff")  )
    {
      msg="SurroundOff";
      msg2="ScreenUp";
```

❶ Create a subscriber

❷ Process message

```
        publishMessages(msg,msg2);
    }
    else
    {
      System.out.println("This message is not handled" +
                         "  by this MBean");
      return;
    }
  }
  catch(Exception ex)
  {
    System.err.println("Could not handle message: " + ex);
    ex.printStackTrace();
  }

}
public void publishMessages(String msg,String msg2)
{
  Topic            topic=null;
  TopicPublisher   topicPublisher=null;
  TopicSession     sendTopicSession=null;
  TextMessage      message=null;

  try
  {
    System.out.println("Will publish "+msg
                  +" Message to Device topic");
    // Look up the destination
    topic = (Topic)context.lookup("/topic/deviceMessages");
    System.out.println("Found the deviceMessages Topic");
    // Create a publisher
    sendTopicSession = topicConnection.createTopicSession(
                      false, Session.AUTO_ACKNOWLEDGE);
    topicPublisher = sendTopicSession.createPublisher(topic);

    // Create a message
    message = sendTopicSession.createTextMessage();
    message.setText(msg);
    // Publish the message
    topicPublisher.publish(topic, message);
    System.out.println("Published "+msg
                  +" to deviceMessages Topic");

    // Create a message
    message = sendTopicSession.createTextMessage();
    message.setText(msg2);
    // Publish the message
    topicPublisher.publish(topic, message);
    System.out.println("Published "+msg2
            +" to deviceMessages  Topic");

  }
```

2

Post messages **3**

```
      catch(Exception ex)
      {
        System.err.println("Could not handle message: " + ex);
        ex.printStackTrace();
      }
    }
    public void close() throws JMSException {
       topicSession.close();
       topicConnection.close();
    }

    public void turnOnHomeTheater()
    {
      System.out.println("Turning On Home Theater System");
      publishMessages("SurroundOn","ScreenDown");
    }
    public void turnOffHomeTheater()
    {
      System.out.println("Turning Off Home Theater System");
      publishMessages("SurroundOff","ScreenUp");
    }

  }
```

❸

❹ Expose macro methods

❶ In the constructor, the MBean attempts to subscribe to the `controlMessages` topic in the JMS container. The first step to do this is to get the Java Naming and Directory Interface (JNDI) context in order to access the classes required to connect to the JMS messaging provider. After getting a `Context` object, the MBean looks up an instance of the `TopicConnectionFactory` class for the `controlMessages` topic. From the topic factory, the MBean creates a topic connection, which it uses to create a `TopicSession` object. The session will allow the MBean to receive messages on the topic in which it is interested. In this example, it is listening for MOVIE-LIGHTSOn and MOVIELIGHTSOff.

After it creates a topic session, the MBean looks up the actual `Topic` object using its `Context` instance and JNDI name. After acquiring the `Topic` instance, the MBean creates a `TopicSubscriber` from its `TopicSession` instance. The MBean tells the subscriber which class to call back when JMS messages arrive. In this case, the class to be called is the MBean itself. The MBean uses the `setMessageListener()` method of the subscriber to indicate this. When messages arrive to the subscriber, it will invoke the `onMessages()` method implemented from the `MessageListener` interface.

After the connections are established and the subscriber is configured, the connection must be started using the `start()` method in order to have messages received. At this point, the MBean is ready to receive messages from the JMS message bus.

❷ The onMessage() method handles messages as they are published to the MBean. Remember that this MBean is interested in only two messages. If either the MOVIE-LIGHTSOn or MOVIELIGHTSOff message is received, the MBean will execute a macro. If any other message is received, the MBean will print a message indicating that it is not interested. To complete a macro, the MBean will invoke its publishMessages() method, passing in the two messages to be sent.

❸ The publishMessages() method uses the JMS bus to send device control messages. In this method, the MBean looks up the topic in which it will publish messages. After the topic lookup, it creates a topicPublisher so that it can publish the message. After acquiring the topicPublisher, it needs to create a message to publish. In this case, it will only be using a text message returned from a call to the Topic-Session object. Before publishing the message, it sets the value of the text message using the setText() method. After it has the topic, message, and publisher, it can publish the message. Using the publish() method in the topicPublisher, the MBean publishes both messages to the deviceMessages topic.

❹ Finally, the MBean implements the two methods exposed by its MBean interface. These methods are directly accessible from the management system by connecting the JMX agent containing the MBean. If you want to turn on or off the home theater system, you can do so from a management application. These methods will be useful for testing or diagnosing problems with the message bus.

Constructing the debugging device message listener (the IR signal transmitter)

Now it is time to write the subscriber class that simulates the IR signal transmitter. This class, shown in listing 13.3, subscribes to the deviceMessages topic and prints to the screen when it receives messages. This class looks very similar to the previous MBean class. It will be executed from the command line.

Listing 13.3 DebugSubscriber.java

```
package jmxbook.ch13;

import javax.naming.Context;
import javax.naming.InitialContext;
import javax.naming.NamingException;

import javax.jms.TopicPublisher;
import javax.jms.TopicConnectionFactory;
import javax.jms.TopicConnection;
```

```java
import javax.jms.TopicSession;
import javax.jms.TopicSubscriber;
import javax.jms.Topic;
import javax.jms.Message;
import javax.jms.TextMessage;
import javax.jms.Session;
import javax.jms.MessageListener;
import javax.jms.JMSException;

public class DebugSubscriber implements MessageListener
{
    private TopicConnection           topicConnection=null;
    private TopicSession              topicSession=null;
    private TopicSubscriber           topicSubscriber=null;
    private Topic                     topic=null;
    private TopicConnectionFactory    topicFactory=null;
    private int                       count_=0;
    private Context                   context=null;

    public DebugSubscriber() throws JMSException, NamingException
    {
      String            factoryJNDI="TopicConnectionFactory";
      String            topicJNDI="topic/deviceMessages";

      // Get the initial context
      System.out.println("Getting Initial Context:");
      context = new InitialContext();
      System.out.println("Got Initial Context:"+context);

      // Get the connection factory
      System.out.println("Getting Topic Factory:");
      topicFactory=(TopicConnectionFactory)
          context.lookup(factoryJNDI);
      System.out.println("Got Topic Factory:"+topicFactory);

      // Create the connection
      topicConnection = topicFactory.createTopicConnection();

      // Create the session
      topicSession=topicConnection.createTopicSession(false,
          Session.AUTO_ACKNOWLEDGE);

      // Look up the destination
      topic = (Topic)context.lookup(topicJNDI);

      // Create a subscriber
      topicSubscriber = topicSession.createSubscriber(topic);

      // Set the message listener,
      // which is this class since we implement
      // the MessageListener interface
      topicSubscriber.setMessageListener(this);

      System.out.println("DeviceSubscriber subscribed to topic: "
        + topicJNDI);
```

```
        // OBS! For the message listener to receive any messages
        // the connection has to be started
        topicConnection.start();
    }

    public void onMessage(Message m) {

        try {
            String msg = ((TextMessage)m).getText();
            System.out.println("DeviceSubscriber got message: " + msg);
        }
        catch(Exception ex) {
            System.err.println("Device Could not handle message: " + ex);
            ex.printStackTrace();
        }
    }

    public void close() throws JMSException {
        topicSession.close();
        topicConnection.close();
    }

    public static void main(String[] args){
        DebugSubscriber            subscriber=null;

        try{
            System.out.println("Starting Debugging Subscriber");
            subscriber=new DebugSubscriber();
        }
        catch(Exception e){
            System.out.println("Error Starting Device DebugClient");
            e.printStackTrace();
        }
    }
}
```

This class operates similarly to the MBean you just wrote. It looks up a particular topic, subscribes to it, and begins to listen for applicable messages. When a message is received, the `onMessage()` method from the `MessageListener` interface is invoked. If this class represented an actual device controller for the example, the `onMessage()` method would contain the code for communicating the messages to the appropriate devices. In this case, the method simply prints the message to standard out. In addition, this class's `main()` method creates an instance of the class and prints an error if the subscription fails.

Registering the MBean in the JMXBookAgent

Recall from previous chapters that you have created setup classes in order to place MBeans into your JMXBookAgent agent. Listing 13.4 shows the JMSSetup class, which registers an instance of the JMSController MBean.

Listing 13.4   JMSSetup.java

```java
package jmxbook.ch13;

import jmxbook.ch3.RMIClientFactory;
import java.util.*;
import java.io.*;
import java.net.*;
import com.sun.jdmk.comm.*;

import javax.management.Attribute;
import javax.management.ObjectName;
import javax.management.MBeanServer;
import javax.management.MBeanServerFactory;
import javax.management.MBeanInfo;
import javax.management.MBeanAttributeInfo;
import javax.management.MBeanConstructorInfo;
import javax.management.MBeanOperationInfo;
import javax.management.MBeanNotificationInfo;
import javax.management.MBeanParameterInfo;

import javax.management.MalformedObjectNameException;
import javax.management.MBeanException;    `

public class JMSSetup
{
  private RmiConnectorClient client = null;

  public JMSSetup()
  {
    System.out.println("\n\tCONNECT to the MBeanServer.");
    client = RMIClientFactory.getClient();
    System.out.println("\n\tGot RMI Client.");
  }

  public void createMBeans()
  {
    try
    {
      System.out.println("\n>>> REGISTERING JMS MBean");
      //register the JMS Controller MBean
      System.out.println("\n>>> REGISTERING JMS Controller MBean");
      ObjectName JMSBeanName=new ObjectName(
          "JMXBookAgent:name=JMS_Controller_Bean" );
      client.createMBean( "jmxbook.ch13.JMSController",
          JMSBeanName );
    }
```

```
      catch(Exception e)
      {
        e.printStackTrace();
        System.out.println("Error Registering MBeans");
      }

  }

  public void close()
  {
    client.disconnect();
  }

  public static void main(String[] args)
  {
    System.out.println("\n~~~~~~~~~~~~~~~~~~~~~~~~~~~~~~~~~~~~~~~");
    System.out.println("\n>>> START of JMS MBean example");
    JMSSetup agent = new JMSSetup ();
     agent.createMBeans();
     agent.close();

     System.exit(0);
  }

}
```

By this chapter, you have seen similar code many times. This class registers the JMSController MBean in the agent by providing an ObjectName and the class-name of the MBean.

Writing the MOVIELIGHTSOn and MOVIELIGHTSOff publisher

Now that you have written the MBean and subscriber code, you need a way to publish the control commands to the JMS bus. The class in listing 13.5 publishes three messages: MOVIELIGHTSOn, MOVIELIGHTSOff, and doNOTHING. This class represents the IR signal process receiving commands from a remote control.

Listing 13.5   JMSPublisher.java

```
package jmxbook.ch13;

import javax.naming.Context;
import javax.naming.InitialContext;
import javax.naming.NamingException;

import javax.jms.TopicConnectionFactory;
import javax.jms.TopicConnection;
import javax.jms.TopicSession;
import javax.jms.TopicPublisher;
import javax.jms.Topic;
import javax.jms.TextMessage;
```

```
import javax.jms.Session;
import javax.jms.JMSException;

public class JMSPublisher
{
    private TopicConnection          topicConnection=null;
    private TopicSession             topicSession=null;
    private TopicPublisher           topicPublisher=null;
    private Topic                    topic=null;
    private TopicConnectionFactory   topicFactory = null;

    public JMSPublisher( String factoryJNDI, String topicJNDI )
                    throws JMSException, NamingException {
        // Get the initial context
        Context context = new InitialContext();

        // Get the connection factory
        topicFactory=(TopicConnectionFactory)
              context.lookup(factoryJNDI);

        // Create the connection
        topicConnection = topicFactory.createTopicConnection();

        // Create the session
        topicSession=topicConnection.createTopicSession(false,
                                    Session.AUTO_ACKNOWLEDGE);

        // Look up the destination
        topic = (Topic)context.lookup(topicJNDI);

        // Create a publisher
        topicPublisher = topicSession.createPublisher(topic);
    }

    public void publish(String msg) throws JMSException {

        // Create a message
        TextMessage message = topicSession.createTextMessage();
        message.setText(msg);

        // Publish the message
        topicPublisher.publish(topic, message);
    }

    public void close() throws JMSException {
        topicSession.close();
        topicConnection.close();
    }

    public static void main(String[] args) {
        JMSPublisher           publisher=null;
        try{
          publisher= new JMSPublisher("TopicConnectionFactory",
                "topic/controlMessages");

            String msg = "MOVIELIGHTSOn";
```

```
          System.out.println("Publishing message: "+msg);
          publisher.publish(msg);
   try{Thread.sleep(2000);}catch(InterruptedException e){}
          msg = "MOVIELIGHTSOff";
          System.out.println("Publishing message: "+msg);
          publisher.publish(msg);
   try{Thread.sleep(2000);}catch(InterruptedException e){}
          msg = "doNothing";
          System.out.println("Publishing message: "+msg);
          publisher.publish(msg);

       // Close down your publisher
       publisher.close();

     }
     catch(Exception ex) {
       System.err.println("An exception occurred "
         + "while testing Publisher: " + ex);
       ex.printStackTrace();
     }
   }

 }
```

You will use this class to publish the control messages in which the MBean is interested, allowing you to test the system. This class simulates the sending of messages from the remote control of the home theater system. Looking at its main() method, you can see that it publishes three messages. The first message is MOVIELIGHTSOn; after sleeping for two seconds, the class publishes the MOVIE-LIGHTSOff message. The third message it publishes is doNothing; the subscriber MBean should print out a message indicating that it contains no macro for this type of message.

13.4 *Running the example*

Now that you have built the MBean and other necessary classes, let's run the example. You will need to have the JBoss J2EE container running to provide the JMS message bus. Additionally, you must start an instance of the JMXBookAgent class. After running the agent, execute the setup class to register the MBean. The following list shows the tasks you must perform to run the example:

- Start and configure the JBoss server.
- Start the agent and register the MBean.
- Run the debugger (IR signal transmitter).
- Publish the control messages (the IR signal processor).

The first task to tackle is configuring the JBoss server.

13.4.1 *Starting and configuring the JBoss server*

Starting the JBoss server is simple. You can download the free JBoss server from http://www.jboss.org (you should download version 2.4 to run the examples in this book). After installing the server, go to the bin directory of the JBoss home directory and execute the run.bat file. Doing so will produce several screens of output to the JBoss console.

After the JBoss server has started, you need to set up the topics for the JMS message bus. JBoss uses JMX as the backbone of its architecture. Therefore, you can access the JBoss configuration using your web browser (most likely http://localhost:8082 will work) to contact the server's HTML adapter. Figure 13.2 shows the main view page of the MBean server running in JBoss. Notice the section under the heading JBossMQ. You can add topics by clicking on the service=Server link.

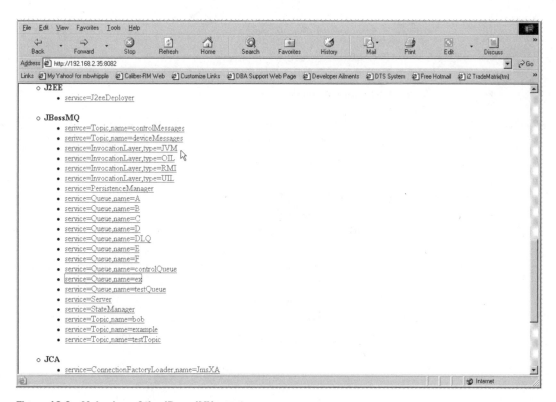

Figure 13.2   Main view of the JBoss JMX agent

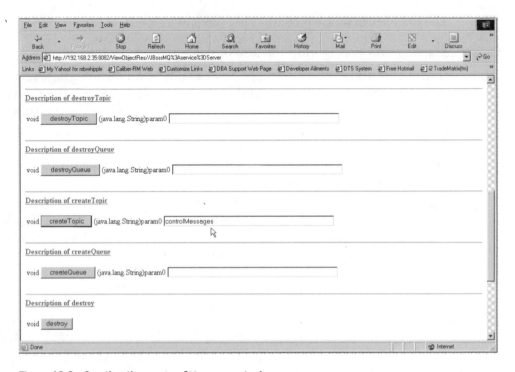

Figure 13.3   Creating the `controlMessages` topic

Clicking on the service=Server link causes the screen in figure 13.3 to appear. On this screen, you can add a new topic by clicking the createTopic button. You need to create both the `deviceMessages` and `controlMessages` topics. Figure 13.3 shows how you would create the `controlMessages` topic.

After you create both topics, you will notice a change on the main Agent View. If you look under the JBossMQ heading, you will see two new topics. Figure 13.4 shows the updated main page of the JBoss server, including the two topics you created.

Your JBoss J2EE messaging provider is ready to handle the Publish-Subscribe messaging you require.

Now that you have the JMS messaging operational and configured, you need to run your own JMX agent. The JMXBookAgent process must include the JAR files from the JBoss JMS provider in order to execute your examples.

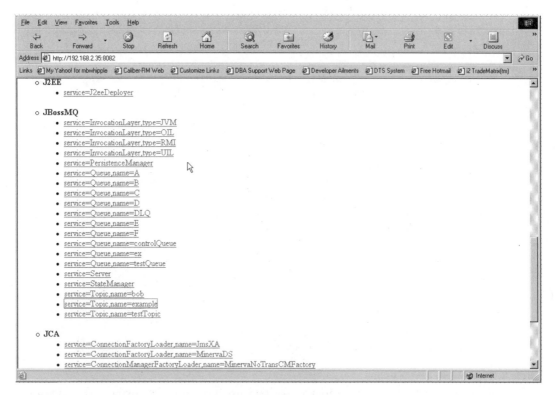

Figure 13.4 JBoss Agent View after creating the message topics

13.4.2 *Starting the agent and registering the MBean*

This section defines the command scripts needed to set up your environment and run the examples. However, before executing anything, you must create a resources folder in the location where you plan to run the example. In the resources folder, create a file called jndi.properties that contains the following items:

```
java.naming.factory.initial=org.jnp.interfaces.NamingContextFactory
java.naming.factory.url.pkgs=org.jnp.interfaces
java.naming.provider.url=localhost
```

Listing 13.6 shows a command script that adds the necessary JAR files to the classpath of the JMXBookAgent in order to support the JMS client. It will let you connect to the JMS server running in the JBoss container. In addition to setting the environment, the command script starts the JMX agent.

Listing 13.6   runSubscriber.bat

```
@echo OFF

set CLIENT_CLASS_DIR=c:\JMXbook\build
set JNDI_RESOURCE_DIR=resources
set JBOSS_DIST=d:\JBoss-2.4.4

REM Required libs to run JMS client
set CLASSPATH=%JBOSS_DIST%\client\jbossmq-client.jar
set CLASSPATH=%CLASSPATH%;%JBOSS_DIST%\client\jnp-client.jar
set CLASSPATH=%CLASSPATH%;%JBOSS_DIST%\client\jta-spec1_0_1.jar
set CLASSPATH=%CLASSPATH%;%JBOSS_DIST%\client\jboss-j2ee.jar
set CLASSPATH=%CLASSPATH%;%JBOSS_DIST%\lib\ext\oswego-concurrent.jar
set CLASSPATH=%CLASSPATH%;%JBOSS_DIST%\client\log4j.jar

set CLASSPATH=%CLASSPATH%;%JMX_HOME%\jmx\lib\jmxri.jar
set CLASSPATH=%CLASSPATH%;%JMX_HOME%\jmx\lib\jmxtools.jar
set CLASSPATH=%CLASSPATH%;%JMX_HOME%\contrib
       \remoting\jar\jmx_remoting.jar
set CLASSPATH=%CLASSPATH%;%JBOSS_DIST%\lib\ext\jboss-j2ee.jar
set CLASSPATH=%CLASSPATH%;% CLIENT_CLASS_DIR %\build

REM Aggregated classpath
set CLASSPATH=%CLASSPATH%;%CLIENT_CLASS_DIR%;%JNDI_RESOURCE_DIR%

echo "Running with classpath %CLASSPATH%"
%JAVA_HOME%\bin\java -classpath %CLASSPATH% jmxbook.ch3.JMXBookAgent
```

In the previous listing (and the following), you should replace the variables JMX_HOME with the values for your specific environment.

Executing this script starts the agent with the proper JARs to enable your MBean to subscribe and publish to the JMS message bus in the JBoss server. You will notice a reference to the JAR files in the JBoss distribution. After running the JMX agent, you need to register the MBean in the agent. The following command does this:

```
java jmxbook.ch13.JMSSetup
```

You should now have the JBoss J2EE application server running in one window and JMXBookAgent in a second window. The MBean you wrote should be subscribed to the topics in which it is interested. The output from your JMX agent console will look like that shown in figure 13.5.

The JMS bus is operational, your agent is running your MBean, and the MBean is subscribed to the control messages. The next thing you need to do is to run the debugger subscriber that simulates the IR signal transmitter.

```
D:\Source\jmxbook\ch13>runSubscriber.cmd
"Running with classpath d:\JBoss-2.4.4\client\jbossmq-client.jar;d:\JBoss-2.4.4\client\jnp-client.jar;d:\JBoss-2.4.4\cli
ent\jta-spec1_0_1.jar;d:\JBoss-2.4.4\client\jboss-j2ee.jar;d:\JBoss-2.4.4\lib\ext\oswego-concurrent.jar;d:\JBoss-2.4.4\c
lient\log4j.jar;d:\jmx\jmx\lib\jmxri.jar;d:\jmx\jmx\lib\jmxtools.jar;d:\jmx\contrib\remoting\jar\jmx_remoting.jar;d:\JBo
ss-2.4.4\lib\ext\jboss-j2ee.jar;d:\JBoss-2.4.4\lib\ext\jboss-mq.jar;d:\Source\jmxbook\build;d:\Source\jmxbook\build;reso
urces"


>>> START of JMXBook Agent

>>> CREATE the agent...

        CREATE the MBeanServer.

Agent is Ready for Service...

Getting Initial Context:
Got Initial Context:javax.naming.InitialContext@16ab4e
Getting Topic Factory:
Got Topic Factory:org.jboss.mq.SpyConnectionFactory@7e748f
_
```

Figure 13.5 Output from your JMX agent, showing the MBean subscribed to a JMS topic.

13.4.3 *Running the debugger subscriber*

The IR signal transmitter simulator class is also started with a command script, shown in listing 13.7. It sets up the `classpath` to include the JMS JARs from the JBoss provider before starting the class process.

Listing 13.7 runDeviceDebug.bat

```
@echo OFF

set CLIENT_CLASS_DIR=c:\JMXbook\build

REM Directory where jndi.properties is located
set JNDI_RESOURCE_DIR=resources

set JBOSS_DIST=d:\JBoss-2.4.4

REM Required libs to run client
set CLASSPATH=%JBOSS_DIST%\client\jbossmq-
client.jar;%JBOSS_DIST%\client\jnp-client.jar
set CLASSPATH=%CLASSPATH%;%JBOSS_DIST%\client\jta-
spec1_0_1.jar;%JBOSS_DIST%\client\jboss-j2ee.jar
set CLASSPATH=%CLASSPATH%;%JBOSS_DIST%\lib\ext\oswego-
concurrent.jar;%JBOSS_DIST%\client\log4j.jar

REM Aggregated classpath
set CLASSPATH=%CLASSPATH%;%CLIENT_CLASS_DIR%;%JNDI_RESOURCE_DIR%

echo "Running with classpath %CLASSPATH%"
%JAVA_HOME%\bin\java -classpath %CLASSPATH%
jmxbook.ch13.DebugSubscriber
```

After executing this command script, you now have everything running for your test application. In order to see things work, you need to publish control messages to the message bus. The next section describes the process of running the JMSPublisher class that you built to publish control messages.

13.4.4 *Publishing the control messages*

Your publisher class will publish three messages to the message bus. The first two messages drive your MBean functionality, and the third message causes your MBean to print a message to the screen indicating that it is not interested in the message. Listing 13.8 shows the command script required to run the publisher. Again, notice the reference to the JMS JARs from the JBoss provider.

Listing 13.8   runPublisher.bat

```
@echo OFF

REM JMSPublisher class
set CLIENT_CLASS_DIR=c:\JMXbook\build

REM Directory where jndi.properties is located
set JNDI_RESOURCE_DIR=resources

set JBOSS_DIST=d:\JBoss-2.4.4

REM Required libs to run client
set CLASSPATH=%JBOSS_DIST%\client\jbossmq-
client.jar;%JBOSS_DIST%\client\jnp-client.jar
set CLASSPATH=%CLASSPATH%;%JBOSS_DIST%\client\jta-
spec1_0_1.jar;%JBOSS_DIST%\client\jboss-j2ee.jar
set CLASSPATH=%CLASSPATH%;%JBOSS_DIST%\lib\ext\oswego-
concurrent.jar;%JBOSS_DIST%\client\log4j.jar

REM Aggregated classpath
set CLASSPATH=%CLASSPATH%;%CLIENT_CLASS_DIR%;%JNDI_RESOURCE_DIR%

echo "Running with classpath %CLASSPATH%"
%JAVA_HOME%\bin\java -classpath %CLASSPATH%
            jmxbook.ch13.JMSPublisher
```

Congratulations—you just successfully integrated JMX with JMS.

13.5 *Summary*

This chapter presented the idea of integrating JMX MBeans into your Java Message Service applications. Due to the non-intrusive nature of JMX, you can build a window into your JMS applications using JMX MBeans. By writing MBeans that can subscribe to JMS messages, you can listen to the activity of an operating JMS application. These messages can provide a management application with statistical or health information about the JMS application.

More importantly, you can use MBeans to give management applications direct access to the JMS message bus. Using MBeans, a management application can send and receive JMS messages. With MBeans providing message capabilities (sending and receiving), you can debug portions of your JMS applications; in addition, MBeans can become the drivers for certain workflows within the application.

MBeans can also expose the methods of an object that are usually invoked in response to JMS messages. By exposing these operations, you give a management system the ability to directly invoke portions of the application without the need to send a message. This technique can be useful for debugging, application configuration, or handling special cases within the application.

The next chapter discusses another J2EE technology: Enterprise Java-Beans. In chapter 14, we describe why and how to integrate MBeans into your EJB applications.

Using JMX with Enterprise JavaBeans

- Exploring the benefits of using JMX with Enterprise Java Beans
- Using JMX to manage user logins for systems built with EJBs
- Managing the lifecycle of EJBs using JMX MBeans in a workflow manager

In the previous chapter, you learned about using JMX with the Java Message Service (JMS), one of the components of the J2EE platform. In this chapter, you will learn about using JMX with Enterprise JavaBeans (EJB), a technology that enables you to access and manipulate enterprise data.

When people speak of J2EE, Enterprise JavaBeans immediately come to mind, because EJBs are the most robust, scalable way to create enterprise applications. However, like other applications, EJB applications can suffer from a lack of management and inability to be configured at runtime. Without additional custom development, EJB applications often cannot easily provide a high level of observation and modification at runtime.

By combining JMX with your EJBs, you can provide a distributed, simple way to gather information about, alter the behavior of, and monitor your enterprise applications. Using JMX, you can easily tap into the functionality of an EJB; in return for a little additional work, you gain significant advantages. As in chapter 13, which demonstrated this same advantage by using JMX with JMS, you can use JMX to open a window into the enterprise application.

Note that this chapter won't help you understand EJBs completely if you don't already have some exposure to them. For more information about EJBs, go to http://www.javasoft.com.

14.1 An EJB review

As we just stated, this chapter isn't an EJB tutorial. However, before diving into working with EJBs and JMX, we do need to review a little information about EJBs. If you have no experience with EJBs, we suggest you check out some of the documentation at http://www.javasoft.com.

14.1.1 The EJB model

As we've mentioned, EJBs are an ideal way for applications to access enterprise data. The EJB specification defines a pattern for creating EJBs such that they can be deployed in different containers without any code modification. The EJB container provides services such as database persistence and an execution JVM. To contain the EJBs in this chapter, you will again be using JBoss.

The EJB specification currently defines three types of EJBs: session beans, entity beans, and message-driven beans. Each type of EJB gives you different capabilities for reading or manipulating data.

Session beans

A session bean exposes operations to the user. The session bean exists in memory until the client removes the bean or disconnects from the server, terminating the session. A session bean can either be *stateless* or *stateful*. A stateless session bean exposes service APIs without ever storing a state—many people equate the exposed methods on this type of bean to using `static` methods. A stateful session bean, as its name implies, stores a state temporarily during its execution. However, even though it has a state, it is not persisted and is therefore discarded when the bean is removed or the client terminates the connection.

Entity beans

An entity bean provides access to persistent enterprise data. The bean is mapped to a row in a database table. For example, a purchase order management system would typically use an entity bean to provide access to an individual purchase order.

Combining session beans with entity beans using common software patterns provides a robust solution for accessing data. For example, a session bean could expose an interface that would provide employee information. The session bean could return an `EmployeeInfo` object that would be built from an `Employee-Address` object and an `EmployeeSalary` object. The `EmployeeAddress` object and the `EmployeeSalary` object would be persistent entity beans. The session bean would build the information object by combining the data that came from both entity beans.

Message-driven beans

Message-driven beans are used to handle messages from JMS. These beans are similar to stateless session beans in that they do not keep a client's state and retain no data between operations. Message-driven beans are used specifically to handle JMS messages in an asynchronous matter to avoid tying up application resources.

14.1.2 Why combine JMX with EJBs?

Combining EJBs with a JMX management system provides a powerful way to monitor data flow and manage an enterprise application. If your management system has visibility into the enterprise business model, you can present data in a fashion that might make certain decision processes simpler and more efficient. You can build additional client access into your back-end EJBs, but doing so takes time and additional resources for development and testing. By using JMX, you can quickly instrument your EJBs in order to provide direct access to their functionality and data.

For example, suppose you have built an order management system using EJBs. These beans provide the persistence layer and the access mechanism for manipulating your purchase order data. If you wanted your important customers to receive special treatment based on order size, you could tie MBeans into the EJBs that could introspect on the data and send alerts to a manager when the dollar value of an order exceeded a particular level. Figure 14.1 illustrates this concept.

Such a system could ensure that large orders received the special treatment they needed faster than a manual review process could provide. Using JMX, this application would be quicker, simpler, and more manageable.

14.1.3 *Accessing enterprise data with JMX*

MBeans can get enterprise information two ways:

- An MBean can retrieve data directly from an EJB by invoking its access methods.

- An MBean can receive data being pushed from EJBs.

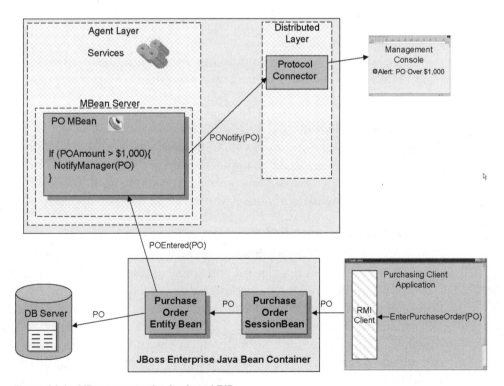

Figure 14.1   MBeans accessing back-end EJBs

Suppose you have been hired to develop a point-of-sale system and a back-office system that will allow visibility to data throughout the day. The store manager may want to monitor the cash and credit sales on a particular cash register at a given time of day, and this information needs to be presented on the manager's console upon request.

For this situation, you could develop MBeans that access the application entity beans for each of the registers and display that information to the manager. In this case, the MBeans retrieve the information directly from the entity beans (see figure 14.2).

However, the manager would also like to know when the cash amount in the till has reached a particular level, so he can remove the money and put it in the safe. In this case, the entity bean can signal your MBean when the cash level is reached, at which time the MBean will automatically signal the manager that the till needs to be emptied. By pushing data to an MBean, the EJB can use the MBean's ability to send notifications to outside listeners.

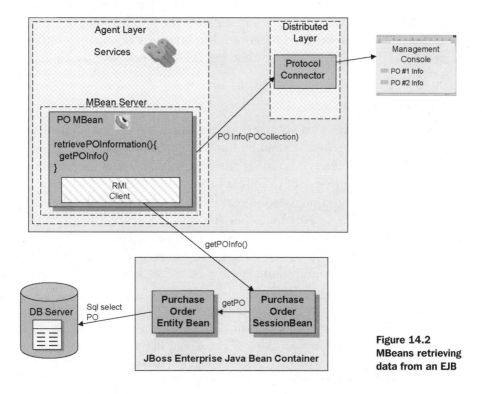

**Figure 14.2
MBeans retrieving
data from an EJB**

14.2 *Example: managing user logins*

Now that we have discussed some ways of using JMX with Enterprise JavaBeans, let's develop some examples. A friend called us recently with the following interesting dilemma, which can be resolved through the use of JMX.

14.2.1 *The problem*

Our friend was building an enterprise system that provided inventory tracking. He was working with an EJB system that uses entity beans to work with the application data. The EJBs ran in a J2EE-compliant container, and he provided a UI via a web browser. In addition, session beans provided the link between the user interface and the entity beans.

To ensure that a user could not log in from two browsers simultaneously, our friend needed a way to track the number of times a particular user attempted to log in to the system. In addition, he wanted to be able to enable or disable the login rights for a particular user. This capability lets an application administrator manage the set of users that can log in to the application.

Our friend had decided to write additional functionality into the system to create an administration application, but then did not have the time or desire to do so.

14.2.2 *The JMX solution*

Combining MBeans with entity EJBs can easily solve this problem. The next several sections construct an example to solve our friend's problem.

First, you will need to build an entity bean that tracks the number of logins for a user and is capable of disabling or enabling the user's account. Then, you can build an MBean that uses the entity EJB to retrieve the number of logins for a user, or to disable and enable a user account. In essence, the MBean will expose the entity bean's business methods as a management interface.

From the management console (the web browser), our friend will then be able to query user login attempts and get and set a user's permissions.

NOTE   To simplify this example, you will not build the persistence mechanism, but will rely on the activate and passivate capabilities of the EJB container to persist your data. If you would like to learn more about building persistence in EJBs, begin by looking at some of the examples provided in the JBoss server's free distribution.

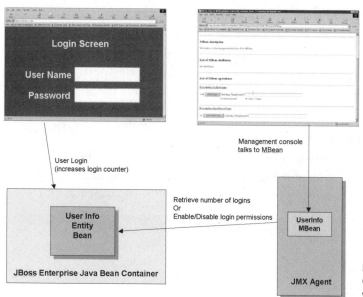

Management console
talks to MBean

User Login
(increases login counter)

Retrieve number of logins
Or
Enable/Disable login permissions

User Info
Entity
Bean

UserInfo
MBean

JBoss Enterprise Java Bean Container

JMX Agent

Figure 14.3
Combining an entity EJB
with JMX MBean

Figure 14.3 shows how the pieces of our solution fit together.

The entity bean runs in the JBoss container and accepts login requests from the UserLogin screen. Each time users successfully log in, their login count is incremented.

An MBean running in a JMX agent can request the login count from the entity bean and expose it in the management console. In addition, the MBean exposes the operations of the EJB that enables and disables a user's login permission.

14.3 *Developing the login monitor*

Now that we have explained the example, it is time to write some code. The following list shows all the tasks we will be discussing as you build the solution to this problem:

- Creating the application's entity bean
- Constructing the MBean
- Creating a client test class

After you complete these three tasks, we will move on to setting up the application environment in JBoss and deploying the EJB. The first thing you need to do is construct the entity bean that users will contact when logging in to the application.

14.3.1 *Constructing the user information entity bean*

The single entity bean—the user information EJB—will provide the persistence mechanism for the user data. Remember from the problem description that this EJB counts the number of user logins and provides permissions for the user. Every entity bean needs a primary key, which references the EJB's row in the database. For the user information EJB, the primary key is a user name value.

The home interface

Listing 14.1 is the home interface for the entity bean. The home interface declares methods for creating and locating this type of EJB. (Again, for more information about using and constructing EJBs, go to http://www.javasoft.com.)

Listing 14.1 UserInfoHome.java

```
package jmxbook.ch14;

import javax.ejb.*;
import java.rmi.*;
import java.util.*;

public interface UserInfoHome extends EJBHome
{
  public UserInfo create( String userName )
              throws CreateException, RemoteException;
  public UserInfo findByPrimaryKey( String userName )
              throws FinderException, RemoteException;

}
```

The home interface provides a `create()` method for creating a new instance of the EJB and a `findByPrimaryKey()` method for locating an existing instance. Because the EJB's primary key is a user name, it is passed in to both the `create()` and `findByPrimaryKey()` methods.

The remote interface

Listing 14.2 shows the remote interface for the entity bean. The remote interface declares the methods an EJB client uses to interact with an entity bean. The EJB `create()` and `findByPrimaryKey()` methods of the home interface return an instance of the EJB's remote interface. The remote interface declares the business methods of the application.

Listing 14.2   UserInfo.java

```
package jmxbook.ch14;

import java.rmi.*;
import javax.ejb.*;

public interface UserInfo extends EJBObject
{
   public int getNumberOfLogins() throws RemoteException;
   public boolean login() throws RemoteException;
   public void logout() throws RemoteException;
   public void setLoginAllowed( boolean isAllowed )
                           throws RemoteException;
}
```

The methods of a remote interface are used to manipulate the data represented by the entity bean. Every EJB remote interface declares the methods that will implement business logic. This remote interface declares a `login()` method and a `logout()` method that are invoked when the user performs the applicable action. The `setLoginAllowed()` method sets the login permissions for the user. For this example, the only permission for a user is whether the user can successfully log in. Essentially, this method disables or enables the user's account.

By writing the two interfaces for your EJB, you have declared the methods for creating, finding, and manipulating the EJB.

UserInfoBean code

Listing 14.3 shows the entity bean implementation. This class must implement all the methods necessary to adhere to the EJB specification, as well as the methods necessary for the business logic declared in the remote interface. Typically, the entity bean implementation would provide the persistence mechanism; but in this case, you will store the data in the object and rely on the container activation to maintain it in memory.

Listing 14.3   UserInfoBean.java

```
package jmxbook.ch14;

import java.io.*;
import java.sql.*;
import java.util.*;
import javax.ejb.*;
import javax.naming.*;
import javax.management.*;
import javax.sql.*;
```

```
import java.rmi.*;

import jmxbook.ch3.RMIClientFactory;
import com.sun.jdmk.comm.*;

public class UserInfoBean implements EntityBean
{
  private EntityContext ctx = null;
  private String userName = null;
  private int count=0;
  private boolean loginIsAllowed=true;

  public int getNumberOfLogins(){
    System.out.println("Return Number Of Queries:"+count);
    return count;
  }

  public boolean login()throws RemoteException{
    if(!loginIsAllowed) {
      System.out.println("User does not have "
                  + "permissions to login");
      return false;
    }
    this.count++;
    System.out.println("User has successfully logged in");
    return true;
  }

  public void logout()throws RemoteException{
    System.out.println("User has successfully logged out");
  }

  public void setLoginAllowed(boolean isAllowed){
    this.loginIsAllowed=isAllowed;
    System.out.println("Setting login isAllowed:"+loginIsAllowed);
  }

  public void ejbLoad(){
    System.out.println("EJBLoad::Loading New UserInfo Bean:");
  }

  public void ejbStore(){
    System.out.println("EJBStore::Storing UserInfo Bean:"+userName);
  }

  public String ejbCreate( String userName ) throws CreateException{
    System.out.println("EJBCreate::Creating New UserInfo"
                        + " Bean for:"+userName);
   return userName;
  }

  public void ejbPostCreate( String userName)
  {
    System.out.println( "Post create called" );
  }
```

Retrieve login count

Increase login count

Disable or enable user's account

```
public void ejbRemove()
{
   System.out.println("EJBCreate::Removing New UserInfo Bean");
}

public String ejbFindByPrimaryKey( String userName )
            throws FinderException,RemoteException
{
   System.out.println("find::Current Count:" + count++);
   this.userName=userName;
   return userName;
}

public void setEntityContext( EntityContext ctx )
{
   this.ctx = ctx;
}

public void unsetEntityContext()
{
   this.ctx = null;
}

public void ejbActivate()
{
   System.out.println( "Activate called:"+userName );
}

public void ejbPassivate()
{
   System.out.println( "Passivate called" );
}

}
```

You can see from the listing that the entity bean saves the number of logins for a particular user. It also contains the permissions to log in (in this case, a `boolean`).

The `login()` method checks to see if the user has login permission and returns that status to the calling program. It also increments the number of logins the user has completed.

As stated earlier, the `setLoginAllowed()` method enables or disables a user's account, based on the value of the `boolean` input parameter.

The methods that appear after the `setLoginAllowed()` method are required by the EJB specification, but you don't need to provide an implementation for this example. All in all, the code for the entity bean is quite simple—it just contains some information and behavior about the login process for an application.

That concludes the construction of the EJB. Now it is time to move on to the construction of the MBean you will use to interact with the `UserInfo` EJB.

14.3.2 *Constructing the user information management MBean*

By using an MBean to access the EJB, you have an elegant way to manage the login process of particular users. The MBean will be able to disable and enable user accounts, as well as retrieve information from the account.

The MBean interface

Listing 14.4 shows the MBean interface for the UserInfoMgr MBean class.

Listing 14.4   UserInfoMgrMBean.java

```
package jmxbook.ch14;

public interface UserInfoMgrMBean{

  public int getQueryCount( String userName );
  public void allowLogin( String userName,boolean isAllowed );

}
```

The MBean will expose two methods in its management:

- getQueryCount()—Exposes a read-only attribute that stores the number of successful logins for a particular user.

- allowLogin()—Exposes an operation to enable or disable a user's account. This method takes a user name and a boolean (the boolean value indicates the account status change).

UserInfoMgr MBean code

Listing 14.5 shows the MBean implementation class. This MBean is different from others you have created in that it uses a main() method to register itself into your JMXBookAgent class. In this chapter, you do not need a process to receive any notification, so you don't necessarily need a separate class to register this MBean in the agent.

Listing 14.5   UserInfoMgr.java

```
package jmxbook.ch14;

import com.sun.jdmk.comm.*;
import javax.management.*;
import jmxbook.ch3.RMIClientFactory;

import javax.naming.*;
import java.util.Hashtable;
import javax.rmi.PortableRemoteObject;
```

```
public class UserInfoMgr implements UserInfoMgrMBean{

  public UserInfoMgr(){
    System.out.println("Creating UserInfoMgr MBean");
  }

  public UserInfo getUserInfo( String userName ){
    int                   count=0;
    UserInfo              userInfo=null;

    System.out.println("Getting UserQueryInfo:");
    System.setProperty("java.naming.factory.initial",
                "org.jnp.interfaces.NamingContextFactory");
    System.setProperty("java.naming.provider.url",
                      "localhost:1099");

    try{
      InitialContext jndiContext = new InitialContext();
      System.out.println("Got context");
      Object ref  = jndiContext.lookup("jmxbook/ch14/UserInfo");
      System.out.println("Got reference");
      UserInfoHome home = (UserInfoHome)
      PortableRemoteObject.narrow (ref, UserInfoHome.class);
      userInfo=home.findByPrimaryKey(userName);
    }
    catch(Exception e){
      System.out.println(e.toString());
    }

    return userInfo;
  }

  public int getQueryCount( String userName ){
    int                   count=0;
    UserInfo              userInfo=null;

    try{
      userInfo=getUserInfo(userName);
      count=userInfo.getNumberOfLogins();
      System.out.println("Number of Logins:"+count);
    }
    catch(Exception e){
      System.out.println(e.toString());
    }

    return count;
  }

  public void allowLogin( String userName, boolean isAllowed ){
    UserInfo              userInfo=null;

    try{
      userInfo=getUserInfo(userName);
      userInfo.setLoginAllowed(isAllowed);
      System.out.println("Set isLoginAllowed:"+isAllowed);
```

Look up EJB ❶

```
      }
      catch(Exception e){
        System.out.println(e.toString());
      }

    }

  public static void main( String[] args ){
    System.out.println("\n\tCONNECT to the MBeanServer.");
    RmiConnectorClient client = RMIClientFactory.getClient();
    System.out.println("\n\tGot RMI Client.");

    try{
      //register the JMX_MBean
      Object[] params = new Object[0];
      String[] sig = new String[0];
      System.out.println("\n>>> REGISTERING JMX MBean");

      //register the JMX Controller MBean
      System.out.println("\n>>> REGISTERING JMX Controller MBean");
      ObjectName   JMXBeanName = new ObjectName(
                  "JMXBookAgent:name=EJB_UserInfo_Bean" );
      client.createMBean( "jmxbook.ch14.UserInfoMgr",
                  JMXBeanName );
      client.disconnect();

    }                                      Register MBean with  ❷
    catch(Exception e)                      JMXBookAgent
    {
      e.printStackTrace();
      System.out.println("Error Registering MBeans");
    }

  }

}
```

❶ In order for the methods exposed in the MBean's management interface to accomplish their tasks, the MBean must be able to look up the EJB that represents the user name and was passed in as a parameter. The `getUserInfo()` method accepts a user name as an argument and returns a `UserInfo` EJB reference. Remember from the entity bean implementation that the `UserInfo` object is the remote interface instance that contains the business methods of the entity bean.

The `getUserInfo()` method obtains a reference to the remote object using the naming service from the application server containing the EJB. It then obtains the entity bean for the particular user using the user name as the primary key. Once you have the entity bean for a user, you can either get the number of successful logins or modify the login permissions for that user.

❷ The `main()` method for this MBean allows you to register the MBean with the `JMXBookAgent` agent that you developed in chapter 3. You should recognize this code: it's identical to code used other times you've needed to register MBeans in the agent.

14.3.3 *Writing the user login client test class*

Up to this point, you have completed the EJB and the MBean that will grant management access to it. Now you need to develop a client class so that you can simulate a login attempt from a user. The test class will need to locate the entity bean and attempt to call its `login()` method. The test class will then print the status of the login attempt to standard out. The `UserLogin` test class is shown in listing 14.6.

Listing 14.6   UserLogin.java

```java
package jmxbook.ch14;

import javax.naming.*;
import java.util.Hashtable;
import javax.rmi.PortableRemoteObject;

public class UserLogin{

public static void main(String[] args)
{
  System.setProperty("java.naming.factory.initial",
                "org.jnp.interfaces.NamingContextFactory");
  System.setProperty("java.naming.provider.url", "localhost:1099");

  try{
    // Get a naming context
     InitialContext jndiContext = new InitialContext();
    System.out.println("Got context");

    // Get a reference to the UserInfo Bean
    Object ref  = jndiContext.lookup("jmxbook/ch14/UserInfo");
    System.out.println("Got reference");

    // Get a reference from this to the Bean's Home interface
    UserInfoHome home = (UserInfoHome)
    PortableRemoteObject.narrow (ref, UserInfoHome.class);

    UserInfo userInfo=home.findByPrimaryKey(args[0]);
    if(userInfo==null){
      System.out.println("No Existing userInfo Found:");
      return;
    }
    else{
      System.out.println("Existing userInfo Found:");
    }
```

```
        boolean success=userInfo.login();
        if(!success){
          System.out.println("User Login not successful: Permission "
                              + " denied");
        }
        else{
          System.out.println("User Successfully Logged in");
        }

        }
    catch(Exception e)
    {
      System.out.println(e.toString());
    }
  }

  }
```

In this class, you locate the home interface reference to the user information EJB from the Java Naming and Directory Interface (JNDI) service of the application server containing the `UserInfo` EJB. Once you have the home reference to the EJB, you can locate the actual EJB object for the particular user using the `find-ByPrimaryKey()` method. After acquiring a reference to the EJB, you can attempt a `login()` and print the status of the attempt to the standard out.

The `UserLogin` class is the last piece of code you need to write for this example. In the next section, you'll run the Login Monitor as well as this test class.

14.4 *Running the Login Monitor*

You must have the JBoss J2EE container running to provide the EJB container needed for this example. Additionally, you will need to start an instance of your `JMXBookAgent` class. After running the agent, you must register the MBean.

The following list summarizes the activities in this section:

- Deploying the EJB class files in an application server
- Starting the `JMXBookAgent` class and registering the MBean
- Running the `UserLogin` test class

14.4.1 *Deploying your entity bean in the JBoss server*

You already configured the JBoss server in chapter 13. If the server is not running, restart it. In order for the server to recognize your new EJB, you need to create a deployment descriptor. (For more about deployment descriptors, see http://www.javasoft.com.)

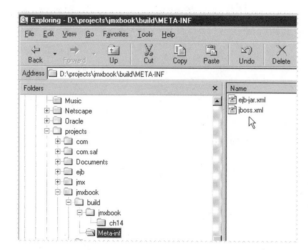

Figure 14.4
Directory structure under the
build directory for deployment
of the entity bean.

You need to create the following two XML files in a META-INF directory at the same level as the jmxbook directory containing the class files from the example:

- *ejb-jar.xml*—A standard deployment descriptor that defines the specifics of the bean. Because it is independent of the container that is deploying the EJB, it can be used with any container.

- *jboss.xml*—A JBoss-specific deployment descriptor that tells JBoss which entity to deploy and how to deploy it

Your directory structure should look like that in figure 14.4.

Writing Ejb-jar.xml

Listing 14.7 shows the ejb-jar.xml file required to describe this entity bean.

Listing 14.7   The ejb-jar.xml entity bean description

```xml
<?xml version="1.0"?>

<!DOCTYPE ejb-jar PUBLIC "-//Sun Microsystems, Inc.//DTD Enterprise
JavaBeans 1.1//EN" "http://java.sun.com/j2ee/dtds/ejb-jar_1_1.dtd">

<ejb-jar>
  <display-name>JMXBook</display-name>
  <enterprise-beans>

    <entity>
      <description>Example MBean</description>
      <ejb-name>UserInfoBean</ejb-name>
      <home>jmxbook.ch14.UserInfoHome</home>
      <remote>jmxbook.ch14.UserInfo</remote>
      <ejb-class>jmxbook.ch14.UserInfoBean</ejb-class>
```

```
      <persistence-type>Bean</persistence-type>
      <prim-key-class>java.lang.String</prim-key-class>
      <reentrant>False</reentrant>
    </entity>

  </enterprise-beans>

  <assembly-descriptor>
    <container-transaction>
      <method>
  <ejb-name>UserInfoBean</ejb-name>
        <method-name>*</method-name>
      </method>
      <trans-attribute>Required</trans-attribute>
    </container-transaction>
  </assembly-descriptor>
</ejb-jar>
```

This XML file describes the entity bean and how it is to be deployed. A display name for the bean is given along with a description and the actual name of the bean. The home, remote, and EJB class names are listed in this XML.

Writing jboss.xml

Listing 14.8 shows the jboss.xml descriptor that is specific to the container you are using.

Listing 14.8   The jboss.xml entity bean description

```
<?xml version="1.0" encoding="Cp1252"?>

<jboss>
    <secure>false</secure>
    <container-configurations />
    <resource-managers />
    <enterprise-beans>
        <entity>
      <ejb-name>UserInfoBean</ejb-name>
      <jndi-name>jmxbook/ch14/UserInfo</jndi-name>
      <configuration-name></configuration-name>
        </entity>
    </enterprise-beans>
</jboss>
```

The format and tags in this file are specific to the JBoss container and provide it with a description of the EJB to deploy. The file also contains some configuration information such as the JNDI name and security information. (You can find more information about the structure of the JBoss descriptors with the JBoss documentation.)

Creating a JAR file

Now that you have the deployment descriptors ready, it is time to create the JAR file for deployment into the container:

1 From the build directory that contains the class files and the XML files, run the command `jar -cvf ch14.jar`.

2 Copy the JAR file to the deploy directory under the JBoss main directory.

Moving the JAR file to this location should automatically deploy the bean. The output from the JBoss console should look like that in figure 14.5. The last two lines in the figure indicate that the ch14.jar file was successfully deployed.

If you connect to the JMX server in the JBoss container, you should see that your bean is deployed. Figure 14.6 should look similar to your console.

```
C:\WINNT\System32\cmd.exe - run
[INFO,MinervaSharedLocalCMFactory] Connection manager factory 'MinervaSharedLocalCMFactory bound to 'java:/MinervaSharedLocalCMFactory'
[INFO,MinervaSharedLocalCMFactory] Started
[INFO,MinervaXACMFactory] Starting
[INFO,MinervaXACMFactory] Connection manager factory 'MinervaXACMFactory bound to 'java:/MinervaXACMFactory'
[INFO,MinervaXACMFactory] Started
[INFO,MinervaDS] Starting
[INFO,MinervaDS] Started
[INFO,JmsXA] Starting
[INFO,JmsXA] Started
[INFO,AutoDeployer] Starting
[INFO,AutoDeployer] Watching directory: D:\JBoss-2.4.4\deploy
[INFO,AutoDeployer] Watching directory: D:\JBoss-2.4.4\deploy\lib
[INFO,AutoDeployer] Auto deploy of file:/D:/JBoss-2.4.4/deploy/lib/jms-ra.rar
[INFO,RARDeployer] Attempting to deploy RAR at 'file:/D:/JBoss-2.4.4/deploy/lib/jms-ra.rar'
[WARN,JmsXA] Using default value 'java:DefaultJMSProvider' for config property 'JmsProviderAdapterJNDI'
[INFO,JmsXA] FINE: Setting LogWriter: org.jboss.logging.log4j.CategoryWriter@12a848
[INFO,JmsXA] Bound connection factory for resource adapter 'JMS Adapter' to JNDI name 'java:/JmsXA'
[INFO,AutoDeployer] Auto deploy of file:/D:/JBoss-2.4.4/deploy/lib/jbosspool-jdbc.rar
[INFO,RARDeployer] Attempting to deploy RAR at 'file:/D:/JBoss-2.4.4/deploy/lib/jbosspool-jdbc.rar'
[INFO,RARMetaData] Loading Minerva Resource Adapter for JDBC 1/2 drivers
[INFO,RARMetaData] Required license terms present. See deployment descriptor.
[WARN,MinervaDS] Not setting config property 'Driver'
[WARN,MinervaDS] Not setting config property 'Password'
[WARN,MinervaDS] Not setting config property 'UserName'
[INFO,MinervaDS] Bound connection factory for resource adapter 'Minerva JDBC LocalTransaction ResourceAdapter' to JNDI name 'java:/MinervaDS'
[INFO,AutoDeployer] Started
[INFO,JMXAdaptorService] Starting
[INFO,JMXAdaptorService] Started
[INFO,RMIConnectorService] Starting
[INFO,RMIConnectorService] Started
[INFO,MailService] Starting
[INFO,MailService] Mail Service 'Mail' bound to java:/Mail
[INFO,MailService] Started
[INFO,ServiceControl] Started 47 services
[INFO,Default] JBoss-2.4.4 Started in 0m:5s.8
[INFO,AutoDeployer] Auto deploy of file:/D:/JBoss-2.4.4/deploy/ch14.jar
[INFO,J2eeDeployer] Deploy J2EE application: file:/D:/JBoss-2.4.4/deploy/ch14.jar
[INFO,J2eeDeployer] Create application ch14.jar
[INFO,J2eeDeployer] install EJB module ch14.jar
[INFO,ContainerFactory] Deploying:file:/D:/JBoss-2.4.4/tmp/deploy/Default/ch14.jar
[INFO,ContainerFactory] Deploying UserInfoBean
[INFO,EnterpriseContextCachePolicy$Scheduler] Cache policy scheduler started
[INFO,UserInfoBean] Initializing
[INFO,UserInfoBean] Initialized
[INFO,UserInfoBean] Starting
[INFO,UserInfoBean] Started
[INFO,ContainerFactory] Deployed application: file:/D:/JBoss-2.4.4/tmp/deploy/Default/ch14.jar
[INFO,J2eeDeployer] J2EE application: file:/D:/JBoss-2.4.4/deploy/ch14.jar is deployed.
```

Figure 14.5 Console output from the JBoss deployment step

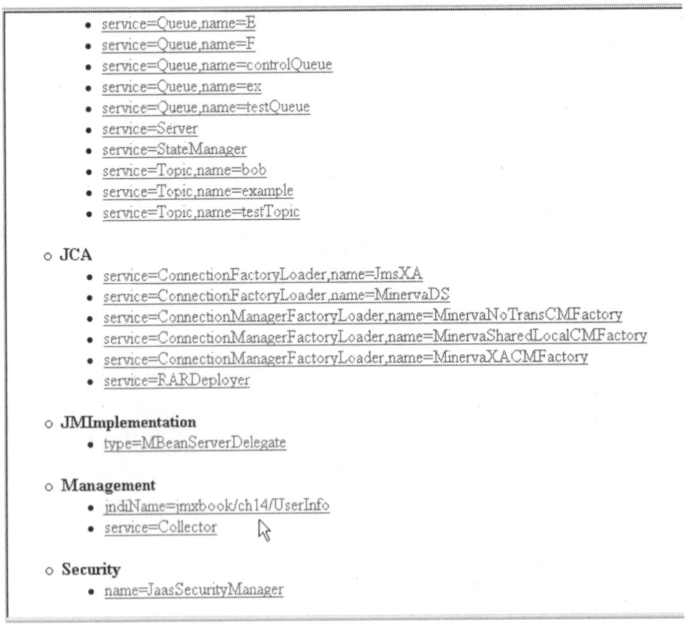

- service=Queue,name=E
- service=Queue,name=F
- service=Queue,name=controlQueue
- service=Queue,name=ex
- service=Queue,name=testQueue
- service=Server
- service=StateManager
- service=Topic,name=bob
- service=Topic,name=example
- service=Topic,name=testTopic

o JCA
- service=ConnectionFactoryLoader,name=JmsXA
- service=ConnectionFactoryLoader,name=MinervaDS
- service=ConnectionManagerFactoryLoader,name=MinervaNoTransCMFactory
- service=ConnectionManagerFactoryLoader,name=MinervaSharedLocalCMFactory
- service=ConnectionManagerFactoryLoader,name=MinervaXACMFactory
- service=RARDeployer

o **JMIImplementation**
- type=MBeanServerDelegate

o **Management**
- jndiName=jmxbook/ch14/UserInfo
- service=Collector

o **Security**
- name=JaasSecurityManager

Figure 14.6
JBoss JMX console with entity bean deployed

Notice under the Management portion of the console the presence of your `User-Info` entity bean. The management console will let you destroy, stop, start, or initialize the entity bean. At this point you can experiment with the bean, if you like.

14.4.2 *Registering with the agent*

Now that the entity bean is deployed and running, you will start your agent from chapter 3 and register the MBean that manages the entity bean data. Refer back to chapter 3 if you need to refresh yourself about starting the `JMXBookAgent`. Recall that the MBean contains a `main()` method that registers an instance of the MBean with the agent. Executing this class from a command line will register the MBean in the agent:

```
java jmxbook.ch14.UserInfoMgr
```

After registering the MBean, connect to the `JMXBookAgent`'s HTML adapter using your web browser (http://localhost:9092). You should be able to see the exposed methods of the MBean. Figure 14.7 shows the console output with the methods for the MBean.

You should see the two methods of your MBean as indicated in the figure. The first method, `allowLogin()`, takes a `String` username and a `boolean` parameter. This method allows or denies the user login capabilities. The second

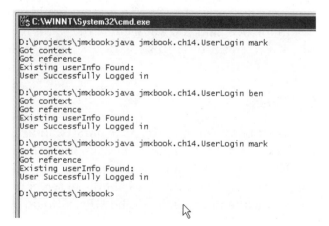

MBean description:

Information on the management interface of the MBean

List of MBean attributes:

No Attributes

List of MBean operations:

Description of allowLogin

void [allowLogin] (java.lang.String)param0 [   ]

(boolean)param1   ⦿ True ○ False

Description of getQueryCount

int [getQueryCount] (java.lang.String)param0 [   ]

Figure 14.7
Output from the agent
when the `UserInfoMgr`
MBean is registered

method, `getQueryCount()`, retrieves the number of logins for the user specified by the username parameter.

14.4.3 *Counting user login attempts*

At this point, you are ready for your first test. To simulate an attempted user login, you need to execute the `UserLogin` class. Every time you execute the class, another attempt will be performed. The first login attempt for a user will create the entity bean if it does not exist, and the login permissions will be set to `true`. The number of logins will be set to 1 during the creation call. Figure 14.8 shows the command line and output from the first execution of the `UserLogin` program.

```
C:\WINNT\System32\cmd.exe

D:\projects\jmxbook>java jmxbook.ch14.UserLogin mark
Got context
Got reference
Existing userInfo Found:
User Successfully Logged in

D:\projects\jmxbook>java jmxbook.ch14.UserLogin ben
Got context
Got reference
Existing userInfo Found:
User Successfully Logged in

D:\projects\jmxbook>java jmxbook.ch14.UserLogin mark
Got context
Got reference
Existing userInfo Found:
User Successfully Logged in

D:\projects\jmxbook>
```

Figure 14.8
Console from the
`UserLogin` attempt

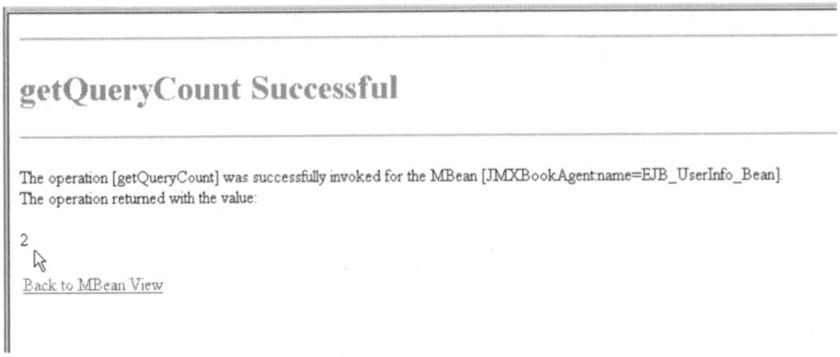

getQueryCount Successful

The operation [getQueryCount] was successfully invoked for the MBean [JMXBookAgent:name=EJB_UserInfo_Bean].
The operation returned with the value:

2

Back to MBean View

**Figure 14.9
Output from the
MBean query for
the login count**

When we tested this example, we ran several sample logins. We logged in using the name "mark" and then logged in using the name "ben". Finally, we logged in a second time using the name "mark". We assumed that if all went well, the login count for Ben would be 1 and the login count for Mark would be 2.

Figure 14.9 shows the output from the JMX console when querying the MBean for the login count for user mark. You can see that Mark has logged in successfully twice.

You can see that the number of logins for user Mark is as expected. Now that you have seen that you can track the number of logins per user, you will turn off the login capabilities of user Ben.

14.4.4 *Removing login privileges*

Let's assume that Ben has exceeded his allowed logins for the week, and you wish to turn off his account for a while. Using the JMX management console, you can deactivate his account by invoking the `allowLogin()` method and passing in a `boolean` value of `false`. Figure 14.10 illustrates this process.

When you click the allowLogins button, you should see a success status page. Now you can try to log in using the user name "ben", and you should be denied. Run the command to log in for Ben, and you will see that the status returned is `false`. Also, if you look at the count of logins for Ben, you will see that it remains at 1.

14.5 *Example: managing EJBs*

In the previous example, we showed you how to create an MBean to contact a specific EJB to perform a specific task. To complete the example, you had to take specific steps to create and register the MBean in a JMX agent. Now consider an EJB that, when created, registers an MBean with a local MBean server contained in the application server hosting the EJB container. The MBean would be specif-

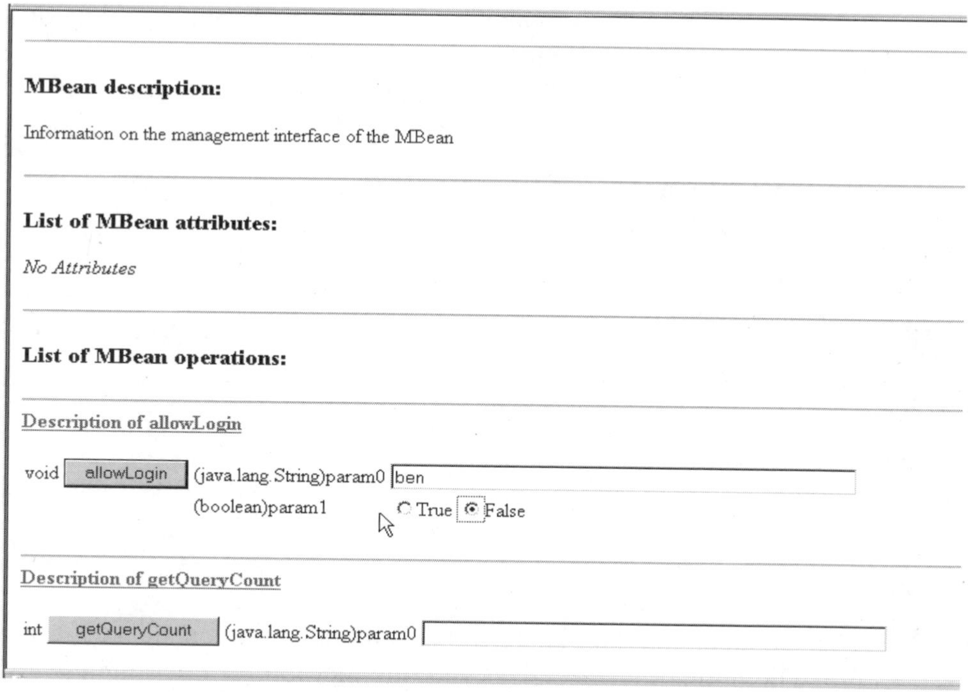

MBean description:

Information on the management interface of the MBean

List of MBean attributes:

No Attributes

List of MBean operations:

Description of allowLogin

void [allowLogin] (java.lang.String)param0 [ben   ]

(boolean)param1   ○ True ⊙ False

Description of getQueryCount

int [getQueryCount] (java.lang.String)param0 [   ]

Figure 14.10 Disabling login capabilities for user Ben

ically designed to manage this EJB type and would contain all the information it needs to find and interact with it.

When a situation arises where you need to access an attribute on the EJB, you can look up its corresponding MBean. In addition, if each EJB type creates its own type of MBean, you will have an accurate count of the number of EJBs being used. You want your MBean to exist only as long as the EJB exists. So, the EJB will create and register its MBean upon creation. When the EJB is removed, it will also remove its MBean. You can implement this feature by adding the appropriate code to the `ejbLoad()` and `ejbDestroy()` methods of the EJB.

14.5.1 *Constructing the workflow entity bean*

This example creates an entity bean like the one described in the previous section. Recall that an entity bean is an EJB that is persistent and represents specific data in a database. Imagine an application that provides business processes for users. A business process in this case is a workflow that a user goes through to accomplish a task. The following example creates a workflow EJB that acts as a specific user's current state in a workflow.

This entity bean represents a row in a relational database table with two columns: clientid and state. The EJB consists of its home interface, its remote interface, and the main bean class, which are named WorkflowHome, Workflow, and WorkflowBean, respectively.

The home interface

The following is Workflow EJB's home interface:

```
package jmxbook.ch14;

import javax.ejb.*;
import java.rmi.*;
import java.util.*;

public interface WorkflowHome extends EJBHome
{
    public Workflow create( String clientID ) throws CreateException,
                                        RemoteException;
    public Workflow findByPrimaryKey( String clientID )
                                        throws FinderException,
                                        RemoteException;

}
```

The EJB home interface enables clients to look up or create a WorkflowBean for use. The home interface gives you one method for creating a WorkflowBean instance and one method for looking up an existing instance. Both methods take a String clientID as an argument. In our scenario, this parameter represents a unique user ID for this particular workflow process.

The MBean that manages this EJB will always use the lookup method rather than the create method, because the EJB has to exist in order to create the MBean.

The remote interface

The following is the remote interface for the EJB:

```
package jmxbook.ch14;

import java.rmi.*;
import javax.ejb.*;

public interface Workflow extends EJBObject
{
    public void advanceState() throws RemoteException;
    public String getState() throws RemoteException;
    public void setState( String state ) throws RemoteException;
}
```

The EJB remote interface declares the methods that EJB uses to interact with the bean. The advanceState() method tells the Workflow EJB to move the workflow to the next step in the overall process, the getState() method returns the current state of the workflow, and the `setState()` method tells the workflow bean to jump ahead to a certain state. Notice that the state value is represented by a `String`. The MBean that the EJB creates will expose these methods as its management interface.

The WorkflowBean class

Listing 14.9 contains the code for the `WorkflowBean` class. It implements methods that correspond to both the home and remote interfaces (although it doesn't implement these interfaces). After discussing the code for the EJB, we will begin examining the code for the MBean of this EJB.

Listing 14.9   WorkflowBean.java

```java
package jmxbook.ch14;

import java.io.*;
import java.sql.*;
import java.util.*;
import javax.ejb.*;
import javax.naming.*;
import javax.sql.*;
import javax.management.*;

public class WorkflowBean implements EntityBean
{
  private DataSource ds = null;
  private EntityContext ctx = null;
  private String clientID = null;
  private int     state     = -1;

  public void advanceState()
  {
    state++;
  }

  public String getState()
  {
    return state + "";
  }

  public void setState( String state )
  {
    this.state = Integer.parseInt( state );
  }

  public void ejbLoad()
  {
    Connection conn = null;
    PreparedStatement ps = null;
    clientID = ( String ) ctx.getPrimaryKey();

    try
```

❶ Implement business methods

❷ Load EJB

```
        {
          conn = getConnection();
          ps  = conn.prepareStatement( "select state from workflows " +
                  " where clientid = ?" );
          ps.setString( 1, clientID );
          ps.executeQuery();

          ResultSet rs = ps.getResultSet();
          if( rs.next() )
          {
            state = rs.getInt( 1 );

            installEJBMBean();
          }
          else
          {
            throw new NoSuchEntityException( "Could not find data");     }
        }
        catch ( Exception e )
        {
          throw new EJBException( e );
        }
        finally
        {
          cleanup( conn, ps );
        }
    }
    public void ejbStore()
    {
      Connection conn = null;
      PreparedStatement ps = null;
      try
      {
        conn = getConnection();
        ps =
         conn.prepareStatement( "update workflows set state = ? " +
                                    " where clientID = ?" );
        ps.setInt( 1, state );
        ps.setString( 2, clientID );
        ps.executeUpdate();
      }
      catch( Exception e )
      {
        throw new EJBException ( e );
      }
      finally
      {
        cleanup( conn, ps );
      }
    }
```

```java
public String ejbCreate( String clientID ) throws CreateException
{
  this.clientID = clientID;
  Connection conn = null;
  PreparedStatement ps = null;

  try
  {
    conn = getConnection();
    ps = conn.prepareStatement( "insert into workflows " +
                   " ( clientID, state ) values ( ?, ? )" );
    ps.setString( 1, clientID );
    ps.setInt( 2, 0 );
    ps.executeUpdate();

    return clientID;
  }
  catch ( Exception e )
  {
    e.printStackTrace();
    throw new CreateException( "Error, possible duplicate Key" );
  }
  finally
  {
    cleanup( conn, ps );
  }
}

public void ejbPostCreate( String clientID)
{
  System.out.println( "Post create called" );
}

public void ejbRemove()          ❸  Remove EJB
{
  Connection conn = null;
  PreparedStatement ps = null;

  try
  {
    removeEJBMBean();

    conn = getConnection();
    clientID = ( String ) ctx.getPrimaryKey();

    ps = conn.prepareStatement( "delete from workflows where " +
                    "clientID = ?" );
    ps.setString( 1, clientID );
    ps.executeUpdate();
  }
  catch ( Exception e )
  {
    throw new EJBException ( e );
  }
```

```
        finally
        {
          cleanup( conn, ps );
        }
    }

    public String ejbFindByPrimaryKey( String clientID )
                                      throws ObjectNotFoundException
    {
      Connection conn = null;
      PreparedStatement ps = null;

      try
      {
        conn = getConnection();
        ps  = conn.prepareStatement( "select state from workflows " +
                                " where clientid = ?" );
        ps.setString( 1, clientID );
        ps.executeQuery();
        ResultSet rs = ps.getResultSet();

        if( rs.next() )
        {
          state = rs.getInt( 1 );
        }
        else
        {
          throw new ObjectNotFoundException( "No EJB Found" );
        }
      }
      catch( Exception e )
      {
        throw new EJBException ( e );
      }
      finally
      {

        cleanup( conn, ps );
      }

      return clientID;
    }

    public void setEntityContext( EntityContext ctx )
    {
      this.ctx = ctx;
    }

    public void unsetEntityContext()
    {
      this.ctx = null;
    }

    public void ejbActivate()
```

```
{
  System.out.println( "Activate called" );
}

public void ejbPassivate()
{
  System.out.println( "Passivate called" );
}

private Connection getConnection() throws Exception
{
  InitialContext newCTX = null;

  try
  {
    if( ds != null )
      return ds.getConnection();

    newCTX = new InitialContext();
    ds = ( javax.sql.DataSource )
          newCTX.lookup( "exampleDataSource" );

    return ds.getConnection();

  }
  catch( Exception e )
  {
    throw new EJBException( e );
  }

}

private void installEJBMBean ()        4  Register
{                                         MBean
  try
  {
    MBeanServer mbs = getMBeanServer();
    WorkflowManager wm = new WorkflowManager( clientID,
        "workflowBean " );

    ObjectName obn = new ObjectName( mbs.getDefaultDomain(),
                                "clientID", clientID );
    mbs.registerMBean( wm , obn );
  }
  catch( Exception e )
  {
    e.printStackTrace();
  }
}

private void removeEJBMBean ()         5  Remove
{                                         MBean
  try
  {
    MBeanServer mbs = getMBeanServer();
```

```
        ObjectName obn = new ObjectName( mbs.getDefaultDomain(),
                                 "clientID", clientID );
        mbs.unregisterMBean( obn );
    }
    catch( Exception e )
    {
      e.printStackTrace();
    }
  }

  private MBeanServer getMBeanServer()
  {

    //  Stubbed out code for locating MBeanServer

    return null;
  }

  private void cleanup( Connection dbconn , Statement stmt )
  {
    try
    {
      stmt.close();
      dbconn.close();
    }
    catch( Exception e )
    {
      e.printStackTrace();
    }
  }

}//class
```

❶ The first three methods you see when examining the EJB code are declared in the EJB's remote interface. The advanceState(), getState(), and setState() methods are implemented here and will be exposed by the MBean the EJB creates later. The three methods do nothing more than manage the state of the workflow, represented by the int class member state.

❷ The ejbLoad() method is found in every entity EJB. It is invoked when it is time for the bean instance to be initialized with the data set it represents. Notice that this EJB is managing its own persistence and therefore must interact with a database to acquire its information. The ejbLoad() method acquires the clientID that an EJB client has associated with it, and selects the state from a database using a connection acquired from a DataSource object. After the EJB has initialized itself, it is time to initialize its MBean. You haven't seen the code for the MBean yet, but the class is called WorkflowManager. The EJB invokes the installEJBMBean() method, which it implements to create a WorkflowManager MBean instance.

❸ At some point, an EJB client will complete this workflow or abort it and must remove the EJB from existence. It does so by calling the `ejbRemove()` method. This method does two things. First, it invokes the `removeEJBMBean()` method, which unregisters the MBean that was exposing the EJB for management. This way, even if the remaining operations of this method fail, the MBean will not exist. The second task for `ejbRemove()` is to delete its persistent state from the database.

❹ These next few methods are the reason you wrote this Enterprise JavaBean. The `installEJBMBean()` EJB method creates and initializes a `WorkflowManager` MBean to expose the remote interface methods from this EJB. To do this, the EJB must create an instance of the MBean. It does so by calling the constructor that takes two arguments: a `String` value acting as the `clientid` value that initialized the EJB, and a `String` value that represents the JNDI name used to look up the home interface of this EJB. Once the `WorkflowManager` MBean looks up the home interface, it can use the `clientid` value to find the appropriate `WorkflowBean` EJB to expose for management.

After creating a `WorkflowManager` MBean instance, the EJB must register it on a MBean server. How to acquire an MBean server depends on the application server containing your application. To encapsulate the MBean server discovery, the EJB provides a `getMBeanServer()` method, which stubs out the code necessary to acquire the MBean server.

After acquiring an `MBeanServer` instance, the EJB must register its new `WorkflowManager` MBean. Recall that the `ObjectName` class is a JMX class that acts as a key on the MBean server to a particular MBean instance. It contains a domain name and a property list that makes it unique across the `MBeanServer` instance. To create an instance of the `ObjectName` class, you use the constructor that accepts a domain name and a single key and value argument. Now that you have an MBean instance, an `MBeanServer` instance, and an `ObjectName` instance, you can register the MBean by invoking the MBean server's `registerMBean()` method.

❺ The `ejbRemove()` method invokes the `removeEJBMBean()` method before it deletes its state from the database. The `removeEJBMBean()` method looks up an instance of the `MBeanServer` (just like the install method) by invoking the `getMBeanServer()` method. It also creates an instance of `ObjectName` that represents the EJB's MBean, and calls the `unregisterMBean()` method to remove it.

14.5.2 *Constructing the WorkflowManager MBean*

Let's recap what you have accomplished. You have created an entity bean that represents a client's state as it moves through a business workflow. The `Workflow` EJB, when initialized, creates a `WorkflowManager` MBean to expose the EJB's remote interface for management. In addition, when the EJB is removed, it removes its associated MBean.

At this point, all you have left to do is to create the `WorkflowManager` class. The `WorkflowManager` class implements the Dynamic MBean for workflow management. Because the EJB's remote interface declares the exposed operations, it would be simple to turn that interface into the MBean interface of a Standard MBean.

However, if you changed the remote interface, you would invalidate all the interfaces to the MBean as well. In addition, what if you are creating MBeans for previously created EJBs? The Standard MBean does not provide a good way to "upgrade" if its management interface needs to change.

WorkflowManager code

The code in listing 14.10 is the implementation of the `WorkflowManager` Dynamic MBean. This MBean will expose the methods that were declared in the EJB's remote interface. Specifically, it exposes the `advanceState()` operation and the `State` attribute.

Listing 14.10 WorkflowManager.java

```java
package jmxbook.ch14;

import javax.management.*;
import javax.naming.*;
import java.rmi.*;
import java.lang.reflect.*;

public class WorkflowManager implements DynamicMBean
{
    private String clientID = null;              Construct  ❶
    private Workflow ejb    = null;                 MBean

    public WorkflowManager( String clientID, String JNDIName )
                                            throws Exception
    {
        this.clientID = clientID;
        WorkflowHome home = lookUpHome();
        ejb = ( Workflow ) home.findByPrimaryKey( clientID );
    }

    public MBeanInfo getMBeanInfo()     ❷  Create
    {                                       management
      try                                   interface
      {
        MBeanAttributeInfo[] atts = new MBeanAttributeInfo[ 1 ];
        atts[0] =
```

```
            new MBeanAttributeInfo( "State", "java.lang.String",
                    "Workflow state of client " + clientID,
                            true, true, false );

      MBeanOperationInfo[] ops = new MBeanOperationInfo[ 1 ];
      MBeanParameterInfo[] sig = new MBeanParameterInfo[ 0 ];
      ops[0] = new MBeanOperationInfo( "advanceState",
                            "Advance the workflow", sig,
                            "void", MBeanOperationInfo.ACTION  );

      Class consig[] = { Class.forName( "java.lang.String" ),
                    Class.forName( "java.lang.String" ) };
      Constructor construct =
        this.getClass().getConstructor( consig );

      MBeanConstructorInfo cons[] = new MBeanConstructorInfo[ 1 ];
      cons[0] =
        new MBeanConstructorInfo( "Constructor", construct );

      MBeanInfo mbi = new MBeanInfo( this.getClass().getName(),
                            "Manages Workflow Entity EJB",
                            atts, cons, ops, null );

      return mbi;
    }
    catch( Exception e )
    {
      e.printStackTrace();
    }

    return null;
  }

public void setAttribute( Attribute att )
                throws AttributeNotFoundException,
                    MBeanException,
                    ReflectionException,
                    InvalidAttributeValueException
  {
      if( att.getName().equals( "State" ) )
      {
        try
        {
          ejb.setState( ( String ) att.getValue() );
        }catch( RemoteException re )
        {
          throw new MBeanException( re );
        }
      }
  }

public AttributeList setAttributes( AttributeList list )
  {
    AttributeList rvalue = new AttributeList();
```

```
      try
      {
        Attribute[] values = ( Attribute[] ) list.toArray();

        for( int i = 0; i< values.length; i++ )
        {
          setAttribute( values[ i ] );
          rvalue.add( values[ i ] );
        }//for
      }
      catch( Exception e )
      {
        e.printStackTrace();
      }

      return rvalue;
  }
  public Object getAttribute( String name )
                      throws AttributeNotFoundException,
                      MBeanException,
                      ReflectionException
  {
      try
      {
        if( name.equals( "State" ) )
        {
          Object temp = ejb.getState();
          return temp;
        }
        else
          throw new AttributeNotFoundException( name );
      }
      catch( Exception e )
      {
        throw new MBeanException( e );
      }
  }
  public AttributeList getAttributes( String[] names )
  {
      AttributeList rvalue = new AttributeList();
      try
      {
        String[] list = names;

        for( int i = 0; i< list.length; i++ )
        {
          String attName = list[i];
          rvalue.add( new Attribute( attName,
                  getAttribute( attName ) ) );
```

```
      }//for

    }
    catch( Exception e )
    {
      e.printStackTrace();
    }

    return rvalue;
  }

  private WorkflowHome lookUpHome() throws Exception
  {
    Context ctx = new InitialContext();
    return ( WorkflowHome ) ctx.lookup( "workflow" );
  }
  public Object invoke( String actionName, Object[] args,
                        String[] sig )
                    throws MBeanException, ReflectionException
  {
    try
    {

      String methodName = actionName;
      Class types[] = new Class[ sig.length ];

      for( int i = 0; i < types.length; i++ )
        types[ i ] = Class.forName( sig[ i ] );

      Method m = ejb.getClass().getMethod( methodName, types );
      Object temp = m.invoke( ejb, args );
      return temp;
    }
    catch( Exception e )
    {
      throw new MBeanException( e );
    }
  }

}
```

❸ Look up EJB

❹ Implement invoke() method

❶ The single constructor for this MBean accepts a `String` object that is the `clientid` of the entity EJB, and a JNDI name used to look up the home interface of the EJB that created the MBean. After storing the `clientid` in a class member variable, the constructor invokes the `lookUpHome()` method to find the EJB home interface. Once it has a reference to the home interface, the constructor can invoke the `findByPrimaryKey()` method it provides. The `findByPrimaryKey()` method accepts the `clientid` and returns a reference to the EJB remote interface. The MBean now has a handle on the resource it exposes for management.

❷ The getMBeanInfo() method, declared by the DynamicMBean interface, defines the management interface for this MBean. Your WorkflowManager MBean creates its MBeanInfo object around the methods in the Workflow EJB's remote interface. This MBeanInfo object exposes one operation, advanceState(), and one read/write attribute, State. (We describe the MBeanInfo object and how to use the metadata classes in chapter 4.)

❸ The MBean's constructor called the lookUpHome() method in order to get a reference to the EJB's home interface. Because the MBean was provided with a JNDI name for the home interface, it simply makes a call to the JNDI lookup mechanism to find the home object reference.

❹ This MBean implements the methods declared by the DynamicMBean interface specifically for its EJB. For example, the getAttribute() method compares the incoming attribute name to see if it is State (the setAttribute() method does the same). The implementations of both setAttributes() and getAttributes() can be reused because they just operate over a collection and call the getAttribute() or setAttribute() method. In addition, the invoke() method is implemented in a resource-generic manner.

The invoke() method uses its incoming parameter values to acquire a java.lang.reflect.Method object from the EJB reference. After acquiring the Method instance, the invoke() method invokes it and returns its return value. It's important to note what is left out of this method: invoke() blindly attempts to find a method from the EJB that matches the parameters passed to it. However, what if a management tools passes in a method name and description that is not part of the MBean's MBeanInfo object, but is in fact implemented by the EJB? The invoke() implementation would allow MBean users to invoke methods not described by the MBeanInfo object value (even if there is only a small chance of that happening).

Each method implemented from the DynamicMBean interface should check requests against the MBean's management interface (described by the return value of the getMBeanInfo() method). That is, each method should make sure the requested operation or attribute is exposed in the manner in which the incoming request wishes to use it. Dynamic MBeans must guarantee that their implementation matches the management interface returned by their getMBeanInfo() method.

14.5.3 *Running the workflow manager*

To test this example, you need to deploy the EJB as you did in the previous example. In addition, before this EJB is created in memory, you must have a JMX agent already running for the EJB to register its MBean. You can rewrite the EJB code to look for an instance of the JMXBookAgent class, or you can have it use the MBean server in JBoss.

14.5.4 *Generating EJB managers*

When creating MBeans for managing EJBs, you usually expose the methods from the EJB's remote interface. If this will typically be the case for your own JMX development, consider writing a utility class that can generate MBeans from an EJB remote interface. A utility class could generate Java source for MBeans, or it could generate ModelMBeanInfo to place in Model MBeans of a JMX agent.

Listing 14.11 shows a class that generates MBean source files based on the remote interface from an EJB. The generated MBeans are Dynamic MBeans that extend the DynamicMBeanSupport class you developed in chapter 4. We won't spend time discussing this class, but rather we will leave it as an exercise for you to do with as you please.

> **Listing 14.11   EJBMBeanGenerator.java**

```
package jmxbook.ch14;

import java.io.*;
import java.util.*;
import java.lang.reflect.*;

public class EJBMBeanGenerator
{
  private String remoteInterface = null;
  private String remoteInterfaceClass = null;
  private Hashtable atts = null;
  private Hashtable attTypes = null;
  private Hashtable opsArgTypes = null;
  private Hashtable opsReturns = null;
  private Vector ops      = null;
  private Vector opNames  = null;
  private PrintWriter out = null;

  public EJBMBeanGenerator( String remoteInterfaceClassName )   ◁───┐
  {
    remoteInterfaceClass = remoteInterfaceClassName;
    remoteInterface = remoteInterfaceClassName.substring(
  remoteInterfaceClassName.lastIndexOf( "." ) + 1 );
  }

  public void buildMBean( String location )
  {
    try
    {
      Class remote = Class.forName( remoteInterfaceClass );

      buildAttributesAndOperations( remote );
```

Init generator with EJB interface

```
            out = new PrintWriter( new FileOutputStream( location +
             "/" + remoteInterface + "Manager.java" ) );

            writeClassTop();
            writeConstructor();
            writeLookupEJB();
            writeClassEnd();

            out.flush();
            out.close();
      }
      catch( Exception e )
      {
            e.printStackTrace();
      }//catch
  }

  private void writeClassTop()
  {
        out.println( "import javax.management.*;" );
        out.println( "import java.rmi.*;" );
        out.println( "import " + remoteInterfaceClass + ";" );
        out.println( "import javax.naming.*; " );
        out.println( "import java.lang.reflect.*; " );

        out.println();
        out.println( "public class " + remoteInterface +
        "Manager extends jmxbook.ch5.DynamicMBeanSupport " );
        out.println( "{");
        out.println();
        out.println( "   private String jndiName = null;" );
        out.println( "   private Object pk    = null;" );
        out.println( "   private " + remoteInterface +
        " remoteInterface = null;" );
        out.println();
  }

  private void writeClassEnd()
  {
        out.println( "} //class" );
  }

  private void writeConstructor()
  {
        out.println();
        out.println( "   public " + remoteInterface +
        "Manager( Object pk, String lookupName )
        throws Exception " );
        out.println( "   {" );
        out.println( "     jndiName = lookupName; " );
        out.println( "      " + remoteInterfaceClass
        + "Home home = ( " + remoteInterfaceClass + "Home )
        lookupEJB(); " );
```

```
out.println( "      remoteInterface = ( "
+ remoteInterfaceClass + " )
home.findByPrimaryKey( ( String ) pk ); " );
out.println( "  " );
out.println();
Enumeration enum = atts.keys();
int index = 0;
while( enum.hasMoreElements() )
{
  String attName = ( String ) enum.nextElement();
  String rw      = ( String ) atts.get( attName );
  String desc    = "MBean attribute";
  String type    = ( String ) attTypes.get( attName );
  boolean readable  =
      ( rw.indexOf( "r" ) == -1 ) ? false:true;
  boolean writeable =
      ( rw.indexOf( "w" ) == -1 ) ? false:true;

  out.println( "      addMBeanAttribute( \"" + attName
  + "\",\"" + type + "\", " + readable + ","
  + writeable + ", false ,\"" + desc + "\");" );
  index++;
}//while

enum = ops.elements();
index = 0;
out.println( "      String[] types    = null;");
out.println( "      String[] argNames = null;");
out.println( "      String[] argDescs = null;");

while( enum.hasMoreElements() )
{
  String opName = ( String ) enum.nextElement();
  String rType  = ( String ) opsReturns.get( opName );
  String desc   = "MBean operation";
  String[] types    = ( String[] ) opsArgTypes.get( opName );
  String[] argNames = new String[ types.length ];
  String[] argDescs = new String[ types.length ];
  for( int j=0; j < types.length; j++ )
  {
     argNames[ j ] = "arg" + j;
     argDescs[ j ] = "Description";
  }

  out.println( "      types    = new String[ "
  + types.length + " ];");
  out.println( "      argNames = new String[ "
  + types.length + " ];");
  out.println( "      argDescs = new String[ "
  + types.length + " ];");

  for( int k = 0;  k < types.length; k++ )
  {
```

```
                out.println( "        types[ " + k + " ] = "
                + types[ k ] + ";");
                out.println( "        argNames[ " + k + " ] = "
                + argNames[ k ] + ";");
                out.println( "        argDescs[ " + k + " ] = "
                + argDescs[ k ] + ";");
            }

            out.println( "        addMBeanOperation( \""
            + opName + "\", types , argNames, argDescs, \""
            + desc + "\", \"" + rType + "\" , "
            + MBeanOperationInfo.UNKNOWN );" );
            index++;
        }//while

        out.println( "    }");
        out.println();
    }

    private void writeLookupEJB()
    {
        out.println();
        out.println( "private Object lookupEJB() throws Exception" );
        out.println( "    {" );
        out.println( "        Context ctx = new InitialContext();" );
        out.println( "  return ( " + remoteInterface +" )
          ctx.lookup( jndiName );" );
        out.println( "    }" );
        out.println();
    }

    private void buildAttributesAndOperations( Class c )
    {
        Method[] methods = c.getMethods();

        atts       = new Hashtable();
        attTypes   = new Hashtable();
        ops        = new Vector();
        opsReturns = new Hashtable();
        opsArgTypes= new Hashtable();

        for( int i = 0; i < methods.length; i++ )
        {
          Method m = methods[i];
          String name = m.getName();

          boolean attributeSet = false;
          boolean attributeGet = false;

          if( name.startsWith( "set" ) )
          {
              atts.put( name.substring( 3 ), "w" );
              attributeSet = true;
          }
```

Build exposed
management
interface

```
            else if( name.startsWith( "get" ) )
            {
                if ( atts.containsKey( name.substring( 3 ) ) )
                  atts.put( name.substring( 3 ), "rw" );
                else
                  atts.put( name.substring( 3 ), "r" );

                attributeGet = true;
            }
            else
            {
                ops.addElement( name );
                if( m.getReturnType() != null )
                  opsReturns.put( name, m.getReturnType().getName() );
                Class[] sig = m.getParameterTypes();
                String[] params = new String[ sig.length ];
                for( int k = 0; k < sig.length; k++ )
                  params[k] = sig[k].getName();

                opsArgTypes.put( name, params );
            }

            if( attributeSet )
              attTypes.put( name.substring( 3 ),
               m.getReturnType().getName() );
            else if( attributeGet )
              attTypes.put( name.substring( 3 ), "java.lang.String" );
        }//for
    }

    public static void main( String args[] )
    {
      String classname = args[0];
      String location = args[1];

      EJBMBeanGenerator emg = new EJBMBeanGenerator( classname );
      emg.buildMBean( location );
    }

}//class
```

14.6 *Summary*

This chapter presented the idea of combining JMX MBeans with your Enterprise JavaBeans applications. EJBs deliver access and manipulation of enterprise data and are the foundation for robust enterprise applications. However, EJBs do not provide capabilities for managing EJB configurations or for EJB monitoring. By integrating an MBean into each EJB, JMX can provide a window into an EJB application and allow for back-end configuration and monitoring.

MBeans can be combined with EJBs two ways. First, the MBean exposes the business methods of an EJB as its management interface. JMX users can now invoke these methods without going directly through the EJB application. In addition, operations that serve analysis or management purposes can be shown exclusively through the MBean to separate the management capabilities from the business application. Second, EJBs can use MBeans' notification capability to inform other processes of application errors, events, or information.

This chapter showed you how to integrate an MBean into an EJB application without the EJB having any knowledge of the JMX environment accessing it. In addition, we explained how to create an EJB that instantiates its own MBean and registers it on a local MBean server for management. Both of these integration methods have their advantages, and you should be able to use them in your future EJB development to provide management and monitoring capabilities in enterprise applications.

Open MBeans

If you have some knowledge of JMX or have read the JMX specification, you might have wondered where the Open MBean was among the chapters covering the other MBean types. At the time we're writing this book, the Open MBean is an optional, and not completely defined, part of the JMX specification. Without complete knowledge of the Open MBean, we couldn't devote a complete chapter to it.

However, we can write a pretty fair appendix about what is covered in the JMX specification describing the Open MBean. This appendix contains the material found in the spec, but does not include any working examples. Be aware that the information presented in this appendix may change, and perhaps has already.

A.1 What is an Open MBean?

Open MBeans are designed to be the most flexible and most richly self-descriptive MBeans. They are built around a small set of basic data types that are used for all parameters, return types, and attributes. Open MBeans are intended to provide very meaningful descriptions of all their attributes and operations. These descriptions should be of such detail that they might include possible values for MBean attributes.

An Open MBean implements the `DynamicMBean` interface. What sets Open MBeans apart from Dynamic MBeans is the quality of their metadata. The Open MBean metadata is a rich description of its predefined data types. All Open MBeans behave identically to Dynamic MBeans, except for their sole use of the Open MBean basic data types (described shortly). It is the developer's responsibility to ensure that the Open MBean uses only the set of basic data types for every operation parameter, return type, and attribute of the MBean. Finally, an Open MBean is identifiable by its use of the `OpenMBeanInfo` object as a return type from the `getMBeanInfo()` method of the `DynamicMBean` interface.

Open MBeans would be useful in a management environment because users would know ahead of time all the possible object types needed to interact with the MBean. With Open MBeans, there would be no need for recompiling or additional class loading.

A.2 Basic data types

The following list shows the set of objects that makes up the basic data types for the Open MBean. The basic data type set includes the Java wrapper classes for primitive types, plus some additional object types:

- `java.lang.Void`
- `java.lang.Boolean`
- `java.lang.Byte`
- `java.lang.Character`
- `java.lang.String`
- `java.lang.Short`
- `java.lang.Integer`
- `java.lang.Long`
- `java.lang.Float`
- `java.lang.Double`
- `javax.management.ObjectName`
- `javax.management.openmbean.CompositeData`
- `javax.management.openmbean.TabularData`

You could expect all these classes to be present in a management environment. All the primitive wrapper classes are present in all Java virtual machines. And, the `ObjectName` class and `openmbean` package would be present in all JMX-compliant environments.

The three new data types need some explanation. The `CompositeData` and `TabularData` types are both Java interfaces used to define more complex data structures. Objects that implement these interfaces create aggregates of the other basic data types. These values can also be used in arrays. The next section discusses the `CompositeData` and `TabularData` interfaces in more detail.

A.3 *Creating more complex data structures*

MBeans that could only operate using primitive data types would quickly run out of options when trying to model and manage complex resources. To help remedy this problem and maintain an open, flexible MBean, the Open MBean uses the `CompositeData` and `TabularData` interfaces to compose more complex data structures. Objects of these types create aggregate structures made up of the other basic data types, including themselves. This means that management applications can interact with data sets of any structure from Open MBeans. In addition, both `CompositeData` and `TabularData` types are created with descriptors that contain detailed information about the data they contain.

A.3.1 *The CompositeData interface*

You can think of a `CompositeData` object as a hashtable-like object that stores key-value pairs. `CompositeData` values contain a `String` key that corresponds to an object value of one of the basic data types of the Open MBean. In addition, a `CompositeData` instance is immutable: once it's created, you cannot add more pairs or change the values of others that it already contains.

The `CompositeData` class contains methods to return values based on a specific key or to enumerate all the values.

A.3.2 *The TabularData interface*

`TabularData` objects contain sets of `CompositeData` values as rows. Each `CompositeData` object represents a single row in a `TabularData` instance. Unlike `CompositeData` objects, `TabularData` objects are not immutable—you can add and remove rows at any time. However, every row in the `TabularData` structure must have the same description as all the others. Descriptions are important in the Open MBean world, and each `CompositeData` instance contains a descriptive object explaining the meaning and purpose of the data it contains. This means that an instance of the `TabularData` type contains rows of the same `CompositeData` description.

`TabularData` objects also support methods for adding, removing, finding, and enumerating the rows they contain.

A.4 *Describing Open MBean data types*

In order for a management user (or management code) to be able to get the maximum meaning from primitive types, and to be able to understand the more complex types such as `CompositeData` and `TabularData`, Open MBeans use description classes to describe the basic data types.

These description classes are known as the *open types*, and they describe the basic data types used by all Open MBeans. Every open type class is a subclass of the `OpenType` class. There is an `OpenType` subclass for each category of classes for the basic data types (primitive, composite, tabular, and arrays). The `OpenType` class defines methods that provide a data type name, description, and actual classname. The following are the `OpenType` subclasses:

- `SimpleType`—Describes the primitive data types and the `ObjectName` class
- `ArrayType`—Describes arrays of the basic data types
- `CompositeType`—Describes the `CompositeData` class data type
- `TabularType`—Describes the `TabularData` class data type

The `SimpleType` class provides static instances of the `SimpleType` class that give the name, description, and classname of each of the primitive and `ObjectName` data types. The `ArrayType` includes the description of the type it contains as well as its number of elements.

The `CompositeType` and `TabularType` classes are recursive descriptions composed of the other open type descriptive classes. The name and description inherited from the `OpenType` super class describe the overall structure. Using the `CompositeType` class, you can acquire the open type class for each of its members. Likewise, the `TabularType` open type class allows you to describe each `Composite-Type` member it contains.

Using the open type classes, a developer or manager can name and richly describe all the attributes, operation arguments, and operation return types of an Open MBean.

A.5 *Open MBean metadata*

Because an Open MBean implements the `DynamicMBean` interface, it needs to be able to build its management interface at runtime. (For more information about this requirement, go back to chapter 5, which discusses the Dynamic MBean.)

Open MBeans provide their management interface by using subclasses of the MBean metadata objects used by Dynamic MBeans. In fact, Open MBeans are identifiable by their use of the `OpenMBeanInfo` class as a return value from the `getMBeanInfo()` method of the `DynamicMBean` interface.

Table A.1 lists the metadata interfaces used by the Open MBean.

Table A.1 The metadata interfaces and the parts of a management interface they represent. These classes are contained in the `OpenMBeanInfo` object that is the return value for the `getMBeanInfo()` method of the `DynamicMBean` interface.

Metadata interface	Description
OpenMBeanParameterInfo	Describes arguments passed to methods and constructors
OpenMBeanConstructorInfo	Describes any exposed constructors
OpenMBeanAttributeInfo	Describes readable and writable attributes
OpenMBeanOperationInfo	Describes exposed MBean operations

The table does not list any interface for notifications, because Open MBeans use the `MBeanNotificationInfo` class. This is the one metadata class that does not have an Open MBean subclass; Open MBeans still use the `MBeanNotification-Info` class to describe their notifications.

All metadata classes inherit the `getDescription()` method, which they must implement to return a non-null value. This requirement forces every meta object to provide some measure of assistance to management users. The description should provide meaningful information such as the possible values of an attribute or the effect of an operation.

The following sections provide more detail about each of the support classes that implement the interfaces listed in table A.1.

A.5.1 *The OpenMBeanInfoSupport class*

The `OpenMBeanInfoSupport` class implements the `OpenMBeanInfo` interface and extends the `MBeanInfo` class. Toward this end, it inherits the name and description methods used to describe the overall MBean.

The support class overrides the methods that return arrays of metadata objects for attributes, operations, and constructors. It does so in order to return the appropriate Open MBean metadata objects instead of the usual metadata. Open MBeans use the normal `MBeanNotificationInfo` object to describe notifications, so no new implementation is provided in the support class.

A.5.2 *The OpenMBeanOperationSupport and OpenMBeanConstructorSupport classes*

These two subclasses represent operations and constructors, respectively. Both classes override the `getSignature()` method in order to provide the correct Open MBean metadata return type.

The `OpenMBeanOperationSupport` class adds an additional method, `getReturnOpenType()`, which returns the open type descriptor object that describes the object being returned from an operation. In addition, the `getImpact()` method of the `OpenMBeanOperationSupport` class must return anything except UNKNOWN (see the `MBeanOperationInfo` class in chapter 5 for more details).

A.5.3 *The OpenMBeanAttributeSupport and OpenMBeanParameterSupport classes*

Like the `OpenMBeanOperationSupport` class, both the `OpenMBeanAttributeSupport` and `OpenMBeanParameterSupport` classes provide a new method, `getOpenType()`, which is used to describe the type of parameter or attribute they represent. The return type of the `getOpenType()` method is one of the four open-type classes previously described.

In addition, both classes implement the `getDefaultValue()` and `getLegalValues()` methods. The `getDefaultValue()` method returns a value that is applicable to the type returned by the `getType()` method of each class. The `getLegalValues()` method returns an array of objects that must be compatible with the type returned by the `getType()` method. Legal value lists can indicate the possible values for parameters or the expected values of an attribute.

A.6 *Summary*

The Open MBean is being designed to be the most flexible and richly self-describing MBean in a JMX environment. Open MBeans provide developers with enough classes to adequately describe an MBean's attributes and operations so that any management platform can make sense of them. At the time we're writing this book, the Open MBean is an optional part of the JMX specification and is incomplete.

Using Ant

When we wrote the examples for this book, we used Ant from the Jakarta implementation provided by Apache Organization to provide build capabilities. Ant is an open source tool for automating build processes.

This appendix is not a discussion of the advantages of Ant; it is a no-nonsense guide to configuring and using it to build the book's examples. For more information about Ant—its usefulness, complete capabilities, and so forth—please read *Java Development with Ant* by Erik Hatcher and Steve Loughran (you can find it at http://www.manning.com/hatcher).

B.1 Downloading and installing Ant

This book uses Ant version 1.4.1, downloadable from the Apache Organization web site, under the Jakarta project area. From this web site, you can download the documentation and installation executables. You can find out more about Ant at http://jakarta.apacke.org/ant/index.html.

Download the executables from the http://www.jakarta.org/builds/jakarta-ant/ v1.4.1/bin directory. Choose the packaging you require for either the Unix or Windows distribution. We developed the examples on Windows, so we chose the Windows distribution—specifically, the http://www.jakarta.org/builds/jakarta-ant/ v1.4.1/bin/jakarta-ant-1.4.1-bin.zip file.

Extract the zip file to a location of your choice and add its bin directory to your PATH. For example, in Windows, edit the system properties from the Control Panel and add the bin directory to the PATH environment variable.

You also need to add a system environment variable called JAVA_HOME and set its value to the location of your Java bin directory containing your Java compiler and runtime (on Windows, you can do this from the system properties under the Control Panel). For example, if you installed your Java compiler under the c:\jdk1-3 directory, you would set JAVA_HOME to c:\jdk1-3. The PATH and JAVA_HOME variables tell the Ant system where to find the Java tools it needs to run.

B.2 Setting up the build file

Ant uses an XML file to describe the build commands for an environment. Ant provides a rich set of commands in which to build a flexible and powerful build environment. In this appendix, we focus only on the commands we used for building our examples. The Manning book referenced at the beginning of this appendix is an excellent source of information on additional Ant commands.

You want to be able to compile your Java source files and clean the build directories. You will set up a simple build.xml file to describe these tasks, as shown in listing B.1. Place this file in the location in which you will run Ant.

Listing B.1   build.xml

```
<project name="JMXBook" default="compile" basedir=".">
  <!-- set global properties for this build -->
  <property name="src" value="."/>
  <property name="build" value="build"/>

  <target name="init">
    <!-- Create the time stamp -->
    <tstamp/>
    <!-- Create the build directory structure used by compile -->
    <mkdir dir="${build}"/>
  </target>

  <!-- ============[ Compile the Build ]============== -->
  <target name="compile" depends="init">
    <!-- Compile the java code from ${src} into ${build} -->
    <javac srcdir="${src}" destdir="${build}" />
  </target>
  <!-- ============[ Compile the Build ]============== -->

  <!-- ============[ Clean the Installation ]============== -->
  <target name="clean">
    <!-- Delete the ${build} directory trees -->
    <delete dir="${build}"/>
  </target>
  <!-- ============[ Clean the Build ]============== -->
</project>
```

When invoked, Ant will examine this XML file to perform the tasks being asked of it. The next two sections will walk you through the important parts of the XML file so you can tailor it to your specific environment.

B.2.1   Compiling

The first element of the XML file, <project>, describes the project related to this XML file. In this case, you define the project as the JMXBook project. This element also lets you indicate that Ant should run the compile directive by default. So, you can just type **Ant** at the command line, and the compile section of the XML will be executed.

Looking at the compile section (the `<target>` element with `name="compile"`), notice that it depends on the `init` directive. Before Ant can execute the compile commands, it must first execute the dependencies in the `init` target section.

The `init` section is at the beginning of the XML file, and the first thing it directs is a timestamp to be generated. The timestamp will keep track of files that are out of date and will help Ant synchronize them during the compile stage. The `init` section also creates a build directory for all the compiled classes and prevents clutter in the source directories by keeping out class files.

After Ant completes the `init` target section, it can continue processing the compile section. It calls the `javac` compiler against the source files from the src directory. The class files are placed in the directory specified by the `build` property. Both `src` and `build` property values are defined near the top of the XML file using the `<property>` element.

B.2.2 Cleaning

The `clean` target section simply deletes the directory defined by the `build` property. Use the following command from the prompt to clean up your build environment:

```
ant clean
```

index